THE ONE YEAR® BOOK OF SAINTS

Rev. Clifford Stevens

Our Sunday Visitor Publishing Division
Our Sunday Visitor, Inc.
Huntington, Indiana 46750

Write:
Our Sunday Visitor Publishing Division
Our Sunday Visitor, Inc.
200 Noll Plaza
Huntington, Indiana 46750

ISBN: 0-87973-417-5
LCCCN: 89-60528

PRINTED IN THE UNITED STATES OF AMERICA

Cover design by Monica Watts

417

To Linnie, Jimmie, Joey, Carrie,
and John Stephen;
to Mendie Jo, Patrick, and Nicholas;
and to all the little saints I have known.

ACKNOWLEDGMENTS

The author and publisher are grateful for the use of Scripture verses taken from *The Living Bible* © 1971 owned by assignment by Illinois Regional Bank N.A. (as trustee). All rights reserved. Used by permission. Verse selections are taken from *The Catholic One Year Bible* © 1987 by Tyndale House Publishers, Inc. All rights reserved. Used by permission. *The One Year®* is a registered trademark of Tyndale House Publishers, Inc., Wheaton, Ill. Used by permission.

Other sources used in preparing material for this work include *A Concise Guide to the Catholic Church II*, by Felician A. Foy, O.F.M., and Rose M. Avato, © 1986 by Our Sunday Visitor, Huntington, Ind.; *Butler's Lives of the Saints*, by Herbert Thurston, S.J., and Donald Attwater, © 1956 by P.J. Kenedy & Sons, New York, N.Y.; *The Saints of Ireland*, by Mary Ryan D'Arcy, © 1974 by the Irish American Cultural Institute, St. Paul, Minn.; *The New Catholic Encyclopedia*, © 1967 by McGraw-Hill Book Co., New York, N.Y.; and *Handbook of Christian Feasts and Customs*, by Francis X. Weiser, © 1952 by Harcourt, Brace & Co., New York, N.Y. If any copyrighted materials have been inadvertently used in this book without proper credit being given, please notify Our Sunday Visitor in writing so that future printings of this work may be corrected accordingly.

CONTENTS

INTRODUCTION

Saints have a perpetual fascination. Whether it is the cult of the miraculous in the Middle Ages, or the interest in the psychology and personality of saints in modern times, there is a never-ending curiosity about the remarkable people we call "saints." Styles and fashions change, as does the popularity of the saints themselves, but every age has observed them, written about them, probed their lives, explored their history, catalogued, collated, and critiqued the facts about them, and each generation sees new names and new personalities added to the catalogue of the saints.

Harvey Egan has recently written that the lives of the saints are sources of theology, and that to neglect the saints is to miss some of the excitement of knowing God. An interest in sanctity and therefore of saints is at the very heart of Catholic spirituality.

But the impression can be given that, because the saint is exceptional, he or she is therefore the exception, and this is most certainly to misunderstand completely the Catholic cult of the saints and the very meaning of the canonization process. The saint, in Catholic spirituality and theology, is considered the *norm*, not the exception, and if we understand the phrase "heroic virtue" to mean those who are larger than life, we misunderstand the meaning of "heroic" and of "virtue" in the Catholic tradition of spirituality. It is to combat this view that some of the saints themselves have written long and lengthy treatises.

The "saints" are those in whom the Christian and Catholic vision has found full growth, who followed the implications of their faith to the fullest degree, and refused to let their lives or their personalities be stunted by the circumstances of the world around them or by the slings and arrows of outrageous fortune. They did this in an amazing variety of circumstances, against human and historical backgrounds of fantastic diversity, and they did it with style, a verve, and an inimitable uniqueness so that each one remains a rich embodiment of what the Christian life is all about. No saint is ever the duplicate of another.

They are exceptional in that each is unique, but they are not the exception, since sanctity is the vocation of all. Pope Pius XII indicated this diversity and this richness:

> *One of the merits of Christianity and an indication of its inexhaustible vitality is the fact that the goal which God has set down for everyone, sanctity, can be reached by many different ways. The Spirit breathes how and where He wills, and so we see an immense variety of saints that shine like stars in the firmament of the Church and show the richness of the divine gifts.*

What fascinates is the mystery of holiness. How does a human being, while living on earth, reach out to the heavens and grasp something of God? There are as many expressions of holiness as there are individuals, and each individual captures something of the Christian vision in a different way.

No book can do justice to the variety of saints, and this book is not meant to be picked up and read each day of the calendar year, although this is one way of reading it. It is rather an "occasional book," something to open once in a while to get a glimpse of something beautiful. The saints, at first, can be merely curiosities, but they soon become dear and precious friends, and familiarity with them can open vistas to our own life with God we had never dreamed of. The saints encourage and they inspire, and the qualities and courage they showed in their own lives, under the most difficult and trying circumstances, can give courage to our own pursuit of God and throw a bright light on our own way.

The saints were Christian heroes; they were God's intimates, and in their endless diversity they have something to say to everyone. A saint is not a figure in stained glass; he lives and breathes and feels like other human beings, but there is a depth to his living and breathing and feeling that is not ordinary, as if he possessed a giant secret he could share with no one. Sanctity is not something the saints possess; it is something that possesses them. It is bigger than they are. They have found themselves in God, and in finding themselves in God, they have found completion.

To trace their footsteps is one of the great adventures of life, and many of those whose footsteps are traced here are my dearest friends, scattered throughout the calendar year. It is my hope that many will become your friends, too, and that you will come back to this book often to renew their acquaintance. "These are those who drank the chalice of the Lord and became the friends of God." With such friends, we begin to taste the wonder of God, and once that wonder has taken hold, it is something that never wears off.

Father Clifford Stevens

THE SAINTS OF JANUARY

St. Odilo of Cluny *(JANUARY 1)*

The abbey of Cluny in France had the second largest church in Christendom, and after its founding in 909, under a succession of holy abbots, became a dominant influence for clerical reform and monastic renewal. At the height of its expansion, Cluny had over two thousand dependencies, scattered over the whole of Europe, and was the head of a great monastic empire.

The first six abbots were all saints, and today's saint, Odilo, was the fifth in the line. He was scarcely thirty years of age when he succeeded another saint, Majolus, as abbot of Cluny; in fact, he had been trained for the position by St. Majolus himself, who saw in Odilo remarkable qualities of leadership. Odilo became abbot of Cluny around the year 999 and ruled that great abbey for fifty years, putting the stamp of his personality and his spirituality upon the monastic life of this great abbey.

He was known for his gentleness and tenderness and his deep love of the poor. During a famine in 1006, he melted down the sacred vessels of the monastery to help feed the poor. He was so shocked by the brutal violence of the petty wars of the period that, through his influence, the "truce of God" was established, with battles ceasing from Wednesday to Monday of each week, and churches set aside as sanctuaries for those fleeing to them. His compassion was a byword throughout the whole of Europe.

It was St. Odilo of Cluny who established the celebration of All Souls Day, and this observance was later extended to the whole Church on November 2.

Before he died at the age of eighty-seven, he left instructions that upon his death he was to be taken to the monastery church and laid on sackcloth and ashes. After receiving Viaticum, he died on January 1, 1049, and was canonized in 1063.

Thought for the Day: Saints were always known for their compassion, especially to the poor, the suffering, and, in St. Odilo's case, even to the souls of the dead. Saints are never so wrapped up in themselves and God that they forget others. Their very love of God makes them kind and compassionate, and even sweet and gentle. Odilo was a great abbot and one of the most powerful prelates of Christendom, but he never lost his sweet simplicity and his tenderness toward others.

From 'The Catholic One Year Bible': The time came when the Lord God formed man's body from the dust of the ground and breathed into it the breath of life. And man became a living person. — Genesis 2:7

SS. Basil the Great and Gregory Nazianzen *(JANUARY 2)*

This feast day is really the story of two friends who studied together, became monks together, became bishops together, and eventually joined the ranks of the great Fathers of the Eastern Church.

Both were born in Cappadocia, the eastern part of what is now Turkey, at the time a rich Christian center and the fertile soil of saints. St. Basil's father and mother are both saints as well as his grandmother and his brother, St. Gregory of Nyssa. The parents of St. Gregory Nazianzen are likewise saints, as is his brother, St. Caesarius.

Basil and Gregory studied at Constantinople together, and later at Athens, the center of education in that part of the world. After his education in Athens, Basil became a teacher of rhetoric at Caesarea, where he had been born, and through the influence of his sister, Macrina, was drawn to a life of solitude; after visiting monasteries in Egypt, Palestine, and Syria, he began a monastic life on one of his family estates. He became the founder of Greek monasticism and is ranked with St. Benedict as one of the founders of the monastic way of life.

Basil became bishop of Caesarea during the very difficult times of the Arian crisis and Gregory became bishop of the small town of Sasimis, not far from Caesarea. Both were brilliant theologians and fierceless pastors, Basil wearing himself out with amazing pastoral works and extending the influence of monasticism. After Basil's death in 378, Gregory became patriarch of Constantinople, but his election was contested and he returned to Nazianzus where he died in the year 390.

Together with St. John Chrysostom and St. Gregory of Nyssa, SS. Basil and Gregory are Fathers of the Eastern Church, and with Basil's brother, Gregory of Nyssa, are known as the Three Cappadocians.

Thought for the Day: There are times in the history of the Church when it seems the faith will be destroyed by its enemies. That is when God raises up luminous and fearless pastors to stabilize the faith and lead their people to holiness. SS. Basil and Gregory were absolutely fearless in the face of opposition and even threats of death. Let us pray for the courage to profess our faith as fearlessly.

From 'The Catholic One Year Bible': After the astrologers were gone, an angel of the Lord appeared to Joseph in a dream. "Get up and flee to Egypt with the baby and his mother," the angel said, "and stay there until I tell you to return, . . ." — Matthew 2:13

St. Genevieve *(JANUARY 3)*

Genevieve is the patroness of France, and like another maiden a thousand years later, Joan of Arc, she inspired the people of France during dark and dangerous days.

St. Genevieve was born on the outskirts of Paris in 422 and at the age of seven heard a sermon by St. Germanus of Auxerre and was inspired to dedicate her life to God. When she was fifteen, she joined the ranks of consecrated virgins and went to live with her godmother in Paris.

Following the conquest of Paris by Childeric, the people were close to starvation after a blockade of the city. Genevieve stirred up the countryside and brought boats of provisions from the surrounding cities. So magnetic was her personality that King Childeric, who was a pagan, respected her highly and spared the lives of prisoners at her request.

In 451, when Attila with his Huns besieged Paris, Genevieve urged the Parisians to fast and pray and promised them deliverance. Soon Attila and his hordes laid siege to Orléans where they were defeated by the Romans and Franks. She gave her people an example of prayer and holiness of life in very difficult and dangerous times, encouraged the building of churches and shrines to the saints, and made pilgrimages with them to the tomb of St. Martin at Tours and St. Dionysius in Paris.

In her old age, Genevieve was revered by Clovis, who had just become a Christian, and when she died in the year 500, she was buried in a church built by Clovis in honor of SS. Peter and Paul. Ever since those early days, she has been revered by the people of France, who still call upon her in times of political crisis and personal danger.

Thought for the Day: Saints like Genevieve believed in the power of prayer and in a kind and loving Providence watching over human affairs. By their own faith, they inspired others to this same kind of trust in God — that they were not alone in the human struggle and that God does marvelous things in answer to prayer. Prayer is and always has been a powerful means of accomplishing wonders.

From 'The Catholic One Year Bible': After his baptism, as soon as Jesus came up out of the water, the heavens were opened to him and he saw the Spirit . . . coming down in the form of a dove. And a voice from heaven said, "This is my beloved Son, and I am wonderfully pleased with him." — Matthew 3:16-17

St. Elizabeth Ann Seton *(JANUARY 4)*

This first American-born saint accomplished more in twelve years than most people do in a whole lifetime. From 1809 to 1821, the year she died, she laid the foundation for the Catholic parochial system in the United States, founded her Sisters of Charity, and ran her school and lived with her community at her headquarters in Emmitsburg, Maryland.

Elizabeth Ann Bayley was the daughter of a distinguished colonial family in New York City, her father a physician and professor at what later became Columbia University. Her grandfather was rector of St. Andrew's Episcopal Church on Staten Island.

Born in 1774 she married William Magee Seton, a wealthy young businessman, in 1794. They had five children. Mr. Seton had reversals in business and lost his fortune, and a sea voyage was recommended to recover his health. The couple, along with their eldest daughter, embarked for Italy in 1803 and were given hospitality by the Filicchi family of Leghorn. William Seton died in Pisa less than three months later.

Influenced by her stay in Italy, St. Elizabeth Ann Seton became a Catholic upon her return to the United States, against the opposition of her family. In August 1807, she was invited by the superior of the Baltimore Sulpicians to found a school for girls near the Sulpician seminary in Baltimore. With the help of Archbishop Carroll, she organized a group of young women to assist her in her work, received a religious rule and habit from him, and took the vows of religion.

In 1809, she moved her headquarters to Emmitsburg, adopted a modified version of the rule of St. Vincent de Paul for the French Sisters of Charity, and laid the foundation for the Catholic parochial school system in the United States. She trained her sisters for teaching, wrote textbooks for classrooms, worked among the poor, the sick, and the black people of the region, and directed the work of her congregation. In 1814, she sent her nuns to open an orphanage in Philadelphia and another in New York City in 1817.

She died at Emmitsburg on January 4, 1821, and was canonized by Pope Paul VI on September 14, 1975. Her body is enshrined at the motherhouse of the American Sisters of Charity in Emmitsburg.

Thought for the Day: Mother Seton seems almost like a neighbor down the street. But she is St. Elizabeth Seton, who found God through very difficult times. She was loving wife, devoted mother, foundress, and saint.

From 'The Catholic One Year Bible': . . . "Come along with me and I will show you how to fish for the souls of men!" And they left their nets at once and went with him. — Matthew 4:19-20

John Neumann died in 1860 and was canonized in 1977, and so his memory is fresh in the United States. He was one of the early bishops of Philadelphia, who charmed everyone by his gentleness and kindness. He was not a native-born American, however, and came to the United States to work as a missionary.

He was born in Bohemia in 1811 and as a young boy was interested in science and medicine. He had a remarkable gift for languages and in entering the seminary intended to devote his life to the missions of North America. At the end of his seminary training, before he was ordained, he left for the United States and was ordained for the diocese of New York.

After serving as a parish priest for four years, he entered the Redemptorist Order and became the first Redemptorist professed in the United States. He quickly became a leader of the Redemptorist mission in the country and a pioneer of the Catholic parochial school system. In 1852, he was appointed bishop of Philadelphia by Pope Pius IX.

In Philadelphia, St. John Neumann faced serious administrative and financial problems. During his years as bishop, over eighty new churches were built in the diocese. He organized the parochial school system and visited every parish in the diocese. He brought new orders of nuns as well as the Christian Brothers into the diocese and founded his own congregation of sisters.

He was bishop only eight years but left an indelible mark on the Catholic Church in the United States. He was revered for his holiness and loved by everyone. Before his death in 1860, he began the construction of a cathedral for his diocese and established the Forty Hours Devotion in every parish, a custom that became part of parish life in the United States.

On January 5, 1860, Bishop Neumann collapsed on the street and died soon afterward. He was only forty-eight years old. He was buried, as he wished, in the parish church of St. Peter the Apostle in Philadelphia and was the first American bishop to be canonized.

Thought for the Day: St. John Neumann was constantly facing the unexpected, and from his deep well of faith he drew the strength and courage to face new and difficult situations. He decided very young what he wanted to do and never turned back. It was his faith and trust in God that made him a great bishop and a saint. That kind of faith and trust should be ours as well.

From 'The Catholic One Year Bible': "Humble men are very fortunate! . . . for the Kingdom of Heaven is given to them. Those who mourn are fortunate! for they shall be comforted. The meek and lowly are fortunate! for the whole wide world belongs to them." — Matthew 5:3-5

Blessed André Bessette *(JANUARY 6)*

Brother André Bessette, the miracle worker of Montreal, died on January 6, 1937. His Oratory of St. Joseph in Montreal drew pilgrims from all over the world, and thousands had been cured at his word or at his touch. The oratory is still the most popular shrine in North America.

One of twelve children, Alfred Bessette was born on August 9, 1845, in the village of St.-Gregoire d'Iberville, thirty miles outside of Montreal. When he was thirteen years old, he was apprenticed to a shoemaker. In his teens, he worked at various jobs in New Hampshire and Connecticut, following other members of the family to the United States. But when he was twenty-two, he returned to Canada and in 1870 joined the Holy Cross congregation as a lay brother, where he received the name Brother André.

Because of his poor health, Brother André was assigned as porter, or doorkeeper, of Notre Dame College at Cote-des-Neiges at the foot of Mount Royal. Here, he remained a porter for forty years, acting also as the community barber. The French Holy Cross community had brought from France a deep devotion to St. Joseph and the custom of anointing the sick with the oil that burned before St. Joseph's shrine. Brother André followed this custom, and this was the beginning of his ministry of healing that became the Oratory of St. Joseph.

Soon the sick who came to Notre Dame College were disrupting the life of the community, and Brother André was given a piece of land across from the college to build a chapel where the sick could come. This was the beginning of the Oratory of St. Joseph and the work of the oratory would remain Brother André's work for the rest of his life.

The miracles at the shrine continued throughout the rest of Blessed André Bessette's life, but he remained the smiling, witty, friendly lay brother who greeted thousands at his shrine, cheerfully telling them to pray to St. Joseph, amazed that anyone would attribute any power of healing to himself.

In 1937, hearing that Pope Pius XI was ill, Brother André offered his own life that the pope might live. Brother André was dead within weeks and was revered as a saint from the moment he died. He was beatified by Pope John Paul II in 1982.

Thought for the Day: Blessed André Bessette was convinced of the goodness of God and the power of the intercession of the saints. Realizing that God was lavish in His goodness, Brother André called upon that goodness constantly. He was never disappointed. May such faith be ours.

From 'The Catholic One Year Bible': ". . . [God] gives his sunlight to both the evil and the good, and sends [his] rain on the just and the unjust, too. . . . Give to those who ask, and don't turn away from those who want to borrow. . . . You are to be perfect, even as your Father in heaven is perfect." — Matthew 5:45, 42, 48

St. Raymond of Peñafort *(JANUARY 7)*

Raymond was an old man when he died, exactly one hundred years old. He was a professor of philosophy, canonist, Dominican master-general, linguist, and co-founder of a religious order. He was born in 1175 in Catalonia, Spain, and at the age of twenty taught philosophy in Barcelona. He took no pay for his teaching, since, he said, "wisdom is not for sale." In 1222, he joined the Order of Preachers, whose founder, St. Dominic, had recently died.

During his early years as a Dominican, St. Raymond of Peñafort worked for the conversion of the Moors in Spain and, with St. Peter Nolasco, founded the Mercedarian Order, for the ransom of Christian captives of the Moors. In 1230, Pope Gregory IX called him to Rome and he served as canonist for the pope, beginning a collection of Church laws that would become the basis for the *Codex of Canon Law*. When he was appointed archbishop of Tarragona in 1235, he became so sick that the pope relieved him of this office. In 1238, he was elected master-general of the Dominicans but resigned after two years to continue his work in Spain, founding language schools for the study of Hebrew and Arabic at Barcelona and Tunis, in North Africa.

His ideas and his energies were prodigious. He badgered Dominican superiors to send young Dominicans to his language schools in Spain, encouraged St. Thomas Aquinas to write his *Summa Contra Gentiles* as a handbook for Christian missionaries in their work among the Muslims, convinced the Dominicans to have their general chapter in Barcelona in 1264, and became a legend in his order in his own lifetime.

When Raymond died in 1275, the Dominican Order was established throughout Europe, had produced the genius of St. Thomas Aquinas, and its teachers were to be found in all the great universities of Europe. King Alphonsus of Castille and King James of Aragon attended his funeral, with their royal families, and his tomb soon became the scene of countless miracles. He is one of the great lights of the Dominican Order.

Thought for the Day: Priests and apostles like St. Raymond of Peñafort realize that the future is not something merely to inhabit: it is something to create; and in this creative work, their only limitations are their own efforts. There is a certain kind of genius inspired by the faith, and this kind of genius creates great works for God. All of us, in our own way, can do great things for God.

From 'The Catholic One Year Bible': "Don't store up treasures here on earth where they can erode away or may be stolen. Store them in heaven where they will never lose their value, and are safe from thieves. If your profits are in heaven your heart will be there too." — Matthew 6:19-21

St. Pega *(JANUARY 8)*

In 664, the great abbey of Peterborough was consecrated in the English kingdom of Mercia, the gift of King Wulfhere and his brother Ethelred to the Church. The consecration was attended by kings, nobles, bishops, and clergy; among them were Wilfrid of York, one of the great monastic founders of early England, and Archbishop Deusdedit of Canterbury. Peterborough became the center of a great religious renaissance in Mercia, with monks and solitaries entering the abbey or settling near its grounds.

St. Pega belonged to one of the great noble families of Mercia, her brother being St. Guthlac, who set up his hermitage in the Peterborough Fens. He had been a member of King Ethelred's army and at the age of twenty-four laid down his arms and became a monk at Repton. Later, he retired to his isolated island in the Fens, and not far away, on the edge of the Fens, in what is now Northamptonshire, his sister, Pega, built her hermitage, in imitation of her brother.

We know little of their family. They were of the Mercian nobility and close to the king, who later laid down his crown and himself became a monk. Women solitaries were rare in those days, and St. Pega seems to have had a grant from the king for her hermitage. Later a church would be built on the spot, named after her, Peakirk (Pega's church). Still later, during Norman times, the abbey of Croyland would be built on the site of her brother's hermitage. In 714, St. Guthlac died and Pega attended his funeral, making her journey down the Welland River.

After his death, Pega went on a pilgrimage to Rome, where she died in 719. Her relics were kept in a church in Rome, but the church is not known. Along with her brother, she is remembered as one of the early saints of the Mercian kingdom and part of the religious blossoming centered in the abbey of Peterborough in eighth-century England.

Thought for the Day: The solitary life seems strange in our time, but at one time woods and islands attracted whole generations of men and women drawn to solitude. Most were gracious, friendly, and hospitable people who loved their families and their friends but felt drawn to seek God in solitude. Their passion for God drew them into places where they could be alone with Him. For all of us, solitude is a need, if not for a whole lifetime, at least from time to time, where we can be alone with God.

From 'The Catholic One Year Bible': "Do for others what you want them to do for you. This is the teaching of the laws of Moses in a nutshell." — Matthew 7:12

St. Hadrian of Canterbury *(JANUARY 9)*

In 664, the see of Canterbury in England became vacant, and the kings of Northumbria and Kent sent a priest named Wighard to Rome for consecration by the pope. Like his predecessor, Wighard died of the plague before he could be consecrated, and the pope looked around for someone else to send to England. His choice was an African, Hadrian, abbot of Nerida, not far from Naples. Hadrian declined the appointment and recommended instead a learned exile from Tarsus in Asia Minor, Theodore, offering to accompany Theodore to Canterbury and to assist in the building up of the church in the distant English island.

St. Hadrian became abbot of the monastery of SS. Peter and Paul at Canterbury and the head of a monastic school that influenced the whole of England. Greek and Latin became as familiar to the monks and students at Canterbury as their own mother tongue, and students came from all over England and Ireland to study at Hadrian's feet, one of the most notable being St. Aldhelm of Malmesbury, who in his writings praised the learning and the holiness of Hadrian and the excellence of his school.

Not only the Scriptures but also every branch of learning was studied there, including Roman law. At that time, the most notable schools of Europe were in Ireland, at the monasteries of Clonmacnoise, Movilla, Bangor, and Clonfert. Canterbury soon equaled these, and England found itself with a center of learning and knowledge that would influence the whole island. From the tradition of Canterbury came the monastic school of Wearmouth-Jarrow, where St. Bede spent his life.

Hadrian outlived Theodore by twenty years and died in 710, having spent thirty-nine years of his life in England. His body was found incorrupt in 1091.

Thought for the Day: A great teacher is a great treasure, and saints have been made from the influence of a great teacher. Most of us have reason to be grateful to those who taught us and those who molded our lives toward goodness. Knowledge joined to holiness of life has always had its own special power and attraction, as can be seen in the lives of those we call Doctors of the Church.

From 'The Catholic One Year Bible': "All who listen to my instructions and follow them are wise, like a man who builds his house on solid rock. Though the rain comes in torrents, and the floods rise and the storm winds beat against his house, it won't collapse, for it is built on rock." — Matthew 7:24-25

St. Peter Orseolo *(JANUARY 10)*

Peter Orseolo's life reads like a novel of adventure and intrigue, ending in the solitary wilds of the Pyrenees. He was a Venetian nobleman and at the age of twenty became the commander of the Venetian fleet, conducting successful campaigns against the pirates who preyed on ships in the Adriatic. He was married at eighteen and had one son. In 976, there was a popular uprising in Venice; the doge (or chief magistrate), Peter Candiani IV, was murdered, and a large part of the city was destroyed by fire. St. Peter Orseolo was chosen to replace the murdered doge and showed himself a remarkable statesman, one of the greatest to ever rule Venice.

He not only restored the city but began reconstruction of the cathedral of St. Mark, promoted peace, built hospitals, and created social programs to help widows, orphans, and pilgrims. He built a new palace for the doge and settled accounts with the murdered doge's widow, whose suit against the city threatened to destroy it financially.

With these tasks completed, on the night of September 1, 978, he secretly left Venice and took refuge in the Benedictine monastery of Cuxa, on the borders of France and Spain. For a long time, not even his wife and son knew his whereabouts. He cut himself off entirely from his former life and placed himself under the direction of the abbot of the monastery. Later, at the suggestion of St. Romuald, founder of the Camaldoli monks, whom he had met at Cuxa, he retired into even greater solitude. For all his brilliant success, Peter seems to have thought about the move for over ten years and he spent the rest of his life in total solitude with God.

His break with the world was the sensation of the age and was the talk of Venice for decades. He died in 987 and his tomb became a place of pilgrimage.

Thought for the Day: Like St. Thomas More, St. Peter Orseolo took his success very lightly and had a secret hunger in his heart for closeness to God. He was somehow touched by the wonder of God, as are all great solitaries, and that wonder drove him into the wilderness where he could be alone with God. His example said something to the people of his age, pointing the way to the reality of God and the magnitude of eternal life.

From 'The Catholic One Year Bible': When Jesus arrived in Capernaum, a Roman army captain came and pled with him to come to his home and heal his servant boy who was in bed paralyzed and racked with pain. "Yes," Jesus said, "I will come and heal him." Then the officer said, "Sir, I am not worthy to have you in my home; . . . If you will only stand here and say, 'Be healed,' my servant will get well!"
— Matthew 8:5-9

St. Theodosius the Cenobiarch *(JANUARY 11)*

In the fifth and sixth centuries, the monastic life flourished in the East, and one of the great monastic founders was St. Basil of Caesarea in Cappadocia. St. Theodosius the Cenobiarch was born in Cappadocia in 423 and after visiting St. Simeon Stylites on his pillar and asking his advice he visited Jerusalem and the holy places of the Holy Land. Putting himself under the direction of a monk named Longinus, Theodosius settled near Bethlehem and after a short time with his teacher retired to a cave at the top of a nearby mountain where disciples began to gather around him.

Soon his cave was too small for the numbers that came, and he built a large monastery not far from Bethlehem. Like St. Basil, he made his monastery the center of works of mercy and set up a hospital for the sick, the aged, and the mentally ill. He also set up a hospice for the many pilgrims who came to the Holy Land.

His monastery became something resembling a city, with sections for monks of different nationalities and four churches. The liturgy was sung in the native languages of the monks. The monks were divided into hermits and cenobites (monks living in community as opposed to hermits), with Theodosius being abbot over the cenobites.

Because of his orthodox views, Theodosius and the monastery were persecuted by the Emperor Anastasius, who ordered the monks to depart from the teaching of the Council of Chalcedon. Theodosius' famous answer was: "We follow the Four Councils as we follow the Four Gospels." He was banished by the emperor but returned to his monastery after the emperor's death.

Theodosius died in 529 after a painful illness and was buried in the cave where he first began his monastic life, called the Cave of the Magi, because many believed the Magi had stayed there during their journey to Bethlehem. Through his example the monks of Palestine retained the orthodox faith, and his monastery became the center of a great blossoming of the monastic life.

Thought for the Day: It has always been recognized that love of neighbor is part of the love of God, and the great saints have recognized this, helping the sick, the poor, and the needy without expecting any return. Monasteries were the first hospitals where the sick were cared for, free of charge, and where the goodness of God was shown in countless ways. In our own way, we can do no less.

From 'The Catholic One Year Bible': . . . "Foxes have dens and birds have nests, but I, the Messiah, have no home of my own — no place to lay my head." — Matthew 8:20

St. Benedict Biscop *(JANUARY 12)*

This English saint was the spiritual father of St. Bede the Venerable and built one of the great monasteries of the Anglo-Saxon period, the double monastery of Wearmouth-Jarrow in Northumbria. He was a young nobleman who belonged to the court of King Oswy and in 653 at the age of twenty-five went on a pilgrimage to Rome. He settled at the monastery of Lerins, off the coast of France, and after two years there made another pilgrimage to Rome and visited many of the monasteries in France and Italy to study their rules.

In 668, Pope St. Vitalian ordered St. Benedict Biscop, who was English, to accompany the new archbishop of Canterbury, Theodore of Tarsus, to England. Putting aside his own plans, Benedict went with Theodore to England and was appointed abbot of the monastery of SS. Peter and Paul in Canterbury for two years. He then made another trip to Rome, brought back many books and works of art, and with the permission of King Egfrid of Northumbria founded a monastery at the mouth of the Wear River in northern England.

In 680, he received the seven-year-old Bede as an oblate of the monastery, and a new age in English history began. In 658, he built a sister monastery at Jarrow, and Bede was sent there to study under its abbot, Ceolfrid. Concerned about the future of his monastery, Benedict made several more trips to Rome, bringing back books, stained-glass windows, artwork, and even the cantor of the Roman Church to instruct his monks in chant.

His monasteries became centers of learning and Christian culture and had a profound effect upon the history of England. After a long sickness, Benedict died in 690, his death touchingly described by Bede in his *Lives of the Abbots of Wearmouth and Jarrow*.

Thought for the Day: A love of holy learning is at the heart of any Christian culture, and saints like Benedict Biscop realized that there is more to religion than good intentions and good will. A holy environment is also necessary and holy surroundings are conducive to a holy life. Works of religious art should be part of every home, for they remind us of God and keep the thought of Him alive in our minds.

From 'The Catholic One Year Bible': ". . . People who are well don't need a doctor! It's the sick people who do! . . . Go . . . and learn the meaning of this verse of Scripture, 'It isn't your sacrifices and gifts I want — I want you to be merciful.' For I have come to urge sinners, not the self-righteous, back to God." — Matthew 9:12-13

St. Hilary of Poitiers *(JANUARY 13)*

Like St. Athanasius in the East, St. Hilary in the West was exiled because of his opposition to Arianism. As bishop of Poitiers in France, he refused to sign a decree condemning Athanasius and was sent in exile to Phrygia. He is one of the great champions of the faith in the early Church.

He was not born a Christian but of a noble pagan family of Gaul and was converted to Christianity by reading the Bible, with its elevated ideas of God, so different from his pagan readings. Married before his conversion, he was elected bishop of Poitiers in 353, much against his will.

During his exile in Phrygia, Hilary came across the monastic movement that had taken hold in the East and on returning to Gaul after his exile he encouraged another convert, St. Martin of Tours, in the establishment of a monastery at Liège. He is thus one of the founders of the monastic movement in the West.

Spurred by the spread of the Arian heresy, Hilary composed many works defending the true faith, particularly *On the Trinity*. He predated St. Augustine as the great teacher of the Latin West, and his writings were admired by both Augustine and St. Jerome. Along with St. Ambrose and Prudentius, he is the author of many Christian hymns and is considered one of the great defenders of the Council of Nicaea and one of the staunch opponents of Arianism.

Although a man of courtesy and gentleness, he firmly opposed the Arian sympathies of the Emperor Constantius and saw belief in the divinity of Christ as the very cornerstone of the Christian faith. Against the will of the emperor, he convoked a synod in Gaul to condemn the Arian heresy and encouraged others to hold fast to the true faith.

He died at Poitiers about 368 and was declared a Doctor of the Church by Pope Pius IX in 1851.

Thought for the Day: It was in reading the Bible that St. Hilary discovered the greatness of God and the sublimity of Christian teaching. The Bible is not just a revered book to be placed on our library shelves in a special place of honor; it is a book to be read, to be studied and reflected upon. It leads not only to faith and holiness of life but also to the kingdom of God itself.

From 'The Catholic One Year Bible': "The harvest is so great, and the workers are so few, . . . So pray to the one in charge of the harvesting, and ask him to recruit more workers for his harvest fields." — **Matthew 9:37-38**

St. Macrina the Elder *(JANUARY 14)*

This lady was the grandmother of saints, the most notable being the brothers Basil the Great and Gregory of Nyssa. It was Macrina and her husband who founded the faith of the family and passed it on as a splendid treasure to her children and grandchildren. That faith was born of suffering and persecution.

St. Macrina the elder was a native of Cappadocia, in what is now eastern Turkey. It was here that the great apostle of Cappadocia, St. Gregory the Wonderworker, established the faith around the year 250. When he arrived in the territory, it was said, there were only seventeen Christians in the town of Neo-Caesarea; when he died in 268, there were only seventeen pagans.

Macrina was born about the time of Gregory's death, and it was the faith of this ardent apostle that became the way of life for her family. Early in the next century, during the persecution of the Emperor Galerius, Macrina and her husband were forced to leave their home and to live in the wooded hills of Pontus for seven years, during which they suffered much. They were often without food. Later, during another persecution, their property was seized by agents of the emperor, and they lived in almost total destitution. When the persecution ended, they were honored as confessors of the faith, a much revered title among the Christians of that time.

It was at his grandmother's knee that Basil received his first instructions in the Christian faith, and it was from her that he and his family were nourished in that Christian discipline that made them saints. Macrina was known to have treasured and read the writings of Gregory the Wonderworker, and it was the fire and zeal of his writings that was passed on to Basil and his brother.

The exact date of Macrina's death is not known. She is revered as a saint in the calendars of both the Eastern and Western Churches.

Thought for the Day: Many saints have become saints because of the teaching and example of a parent or grandparent. Thus, the power of a living example. Holiness and Christian living are taught chiefly by personal influence, and it is the living instruction that flows from a holy life that leads others to holiness. As the old Latin maxim has it: *Verbum sonat; exemplum tonat* ("Words make a noise, but example thunders").

From 'The Catholic One Year Bible': "I am sending you out as sheep among wolves. Be as wary as serpents and harmless as doves." — Matthew 10:16

St. Ita *(JANUARY 15)*

Ita is one of the early saints of Ireland, and her life is woven with legend. She was the foster-mother of St. Brendan, nourished him in a life of holiness, and set him on the path to greatness. Like St. Brigid, she was revered throughout Ireland, and her influence was as great as the many holy abbots of that country.

St. Ita was born of a royal family in what is now County Waterford, and her hand was sought in marriage by a prince of another royal family. Her father favored the marriage, but Ita had other plans for herself. Fasting three days and three nights, she won the consent of her father to a life of consecrated virginity and set up her convent at Killeedy in County Limerick. There she gathered other young women around her, and her convent became a center of religious life in Ireland.

She conducted a school for small boys, and Brendan was entrusted to her by Bishop Erc, who had chosen Brendan to be a future priest Brendan once asked her to tell him the three things that God especially loved. "True faith in God with a pure heart," she answered, "a simple life with a religious spirit, and generosity, inspired by love." When he asked her the three things that God abhorred, she told him: "A face that scowls at everyone, obstinacy in wrongdoing, and an overweening confidence in the power of money." Brendan learned these lessons well, spending five years at Ita's convent.

A beautiful poem, *Jesukin*, is attributed to Ita, and churches and chapels were dedicated to her throughout Ireland, England, and Scotland. She died in the year 570, and her grave is venerated to this day, often decorated with flowers.

Thought for the Day: St. Ita's love for children gave her a special gift for nourishing them in a life of holiness. Spiritual greatness often begins in childhood when some great teacher is able to plant the seeds of genuine holiness of life. The early monasteries of Ireland were schools of holiness where the young were introduced to the wonder of God. From such wonder, a love of God is born, opening up unlimited horizons of holiness.

From 'The Catholic One Year Bible': . . . "Go back to John and tell him about the miracles you've seen me do — the blind people I've healed, and the lame people now walking without help, and the cured lepers, and the deaf who hear, and the dead raised to life; and tell him about my preaching the Good News to the poor. Then give him this message: 'Blessed are those who don't doubt me.' " — Matthew 11:4-6

This is the story of three young men, two brothers and a friend, who read together the life of St. Anthony of Egypt and decided to find their own desert and dedicate their lives totally to God.

St. Honoratus of Arles and his brother, Venantius, were sons of a Roman consul in Gaul and had become Christians when they were teenagers. Together with their friend Caprasius they set sail for Greece and found a small island to settle on. When Venantius died, Honoratus went to Italy, and finally back home to Gaul, where he set up a hermitage in the mountains near Frejus. Searching around for a more isolated place, he found the small island of Lerins, just off the coast and there set up his monastery, based on the rule of St. Pachomius.

The monastery attracted hundreds of monks and soon became the largest monastic center in the West, where many of the leaders of the Church in Gaul were trained. Honoratus was so persuasive that he convinced a relative of his, Hilary, to join him at Lerins, this relative later succeeding him as bishop.

The headquarters of the Roman prefecture in Gaul was Arles, and in 426 the archbishopric of Arles became vacant. Honoratus was compelled to accept the archbishopric and became an outstanding leader of his flock. From his monastery at Lerins, abbots and bishops would be trained for Gaul itself, for England, Ireland, and Scotland. St. Patrick is said to have studied there, as well as St. Benedict Biscop, the patriarch of English monks.

Honoratus spent three years as archbishop of Arles. He died in 429, renowned for his holiness of life, his gentleness and kindness, and his pastoral gifts. He is buried at a church bearing his name at Aliscamps and, together with St. Martin of Tours, is considered one of the founders of monastic life in the West.

Thought for the Day: It is interesting how friendships have much to do with many of the saints: St. Basil the Great and St. Gregory of Nazianzus; St. Jerome and St. Bonosus; St. John Bosco and St. Joseph Cafasso. Without his friends, St. Honoratus might just have stayed at home in Gaul, but with his friends, he took the high road to heaven. The rest is history and a great spiritual adventure.

From 'The Catholic One Year Bible': "Everything has been entrusted to me by my Father. . . . Come to me and I will give you rest — all of you who work so hard beneath a heavy yoke. Wear my yoke — for it fits perfectly — and let me teach you; for I am gentle and humble, and you shall find rest for your souls; for I give you only light burdens." — Matthew 11:27-30

St. Anthony of Egypt *(JANUARY 17)*

Twenty years after the great persecution of the Emperor Decius was begun in 250, a young Coptic Christian named Anthony began his ascetic life outside his home village in northern Egypt. He joined the army of anchorites — those who fled into the desert to prepare for martyrdom and spent their lives in prayer and solitude — and discovered a totally new Christian way of life: the ascetic, or monastic, life. After the persecution was over, many of these anchorites remained in the desert, wrapped up in the wonder of God, living alone in the desert, hence, their name: *monachos*, or monks, "those who live alone."

St. Anthony was a Coptic peasant, schooled in the wit and folk wisdom of the Coptic people, simple and direct of speech, who became the father and model of monks, his fame based chiefly on his life written by St. Athanasius soon after his death. He lived an amazing eighty-five years in the desert, coming to Alexandria at the height of the Arian heresy, to give St. Athanasius, the patriarch of Alexandria, the support of the monastic communities, which by that time filled the deserts of Egypt.

Athanasius embroidered Anthony's life with fantastic tales that appealed to the Christian audience for which he wrote; but from Anthony's own letters, it is clear that he was a man of simple tastes, who had discovered God in solitude, filled with the wonder and marvel of God. This explains his great love of solitude, as he went farther into the desert where he could be alone with God.

Later in life, he instructed a few disciples in this new form of life, and St. Pachomius would gather these scattered monks into community. But Anthony was the forerunner and the patriarch, and it is Anthony who is considered the Father of Monks and the originator of this form of life.

Anthony died in the year 356 at the age of one hundred five years. In 561, his remains were transferred to Alexandria, then to Constantinople, and finally, during the crusades, to Vienne, France.

Thought for the Day: Solitude has always had its attraction for Christians, and it is from the love of solitude that the monastic life was born. It is in solitude that the wonder of God is tasted and that the marvel of His love becomes the main occupation of the monk. In this, St. Anthony is the great model.

From 'The Catholic One Year Bible': ". . . If you had known the meaning of this Scripture verse, 'I want you to be merciful more than I want your offerings,' you would not have condemned those who are not guilty! For I, the Messiah, am master even of the Sabbath." — Matthew 12:7-8

St. Volusian *(JANUARY 18)*

Volusian was bishop of Tours, in France, the see made famous by St. Martin two centuries earlier. He lived at a time before clerical celibacy had been enforced in the West and was married to a woman famous for her violent temper, which was a great trial to the bishop. He also lived in a time when the barbarian invasions had begun and the fear of the Goths was everywhere.

In writing to a friend of his, a certain Bishop Ruricius, of nearby Limoges, St. Volusian expressed his fear of the Goths who were beginning to terrorize his diocese. Ruricius humorously replied that someone who lived with terror inside his house, meaning his wife, should have no fear of terrors from the outside.

Volusian was of senatorial rank, very wealthy, a relative of the bishop who preceded him, St. Perpetuus, and he lived in the days when Clovis was king of the Franks, the avowed enemy of the Goths.

As the Goths began to overrun Volusian's diocese, they suspected him of sympathies with Clovis and of wanting to subject them to the Franks, so Volusian was driven from his see and sent into exile.

He held the office of bishop in a very difficult time, when the whole of Western Europe was in turmoil, in the wake of the barbarian invasions from the East. Cities were sacked, government disrupted, and bishops were the only agents of stability as civil government collapsed. Gregory of Tours, who succeeded Volusian as bishop of Tours a century later, describes the turmoil of the times, and it is from his writings that we get our knowledge of Volusian.

We have no further information about Volusian's wife or his family, and we are not sure whether he died in southern France or in Spain. It is simply known that he was driven from his see, went into exile, and died after ruling as bishop for seven years.

Thought for the Day: Most of us live in very stable times, and it is difficult to imagine what it would be like if our country were invaded and national and state government ceased to exist. Our dependence on Divine Providence would be more obvious then, and our faith would have to give us strength in very different ways. The saints kept faith in the most difficult of times and leaned on God in every crisis.

From 'The Catholic One Year Bible': "A tree is identified by its fruit. A tree from a select variety produces good fruit; poor varieties, don't. . . . A good man's speech reveals the rich treasures within him. An evil-hearted man is filled with venom, and his speech reveals it." —Matthew 12:33, 35

St. Canute *(JANUARY 19)*

In 791, Vikings from the North invaded England, and for the next several years, until the Norman invasion in 1066, there was Viking rule in England. At one time, a king of Denmark, Canute, the uncle of our saint, ruled both Denmark and England, with Danish kings often laying claim to the English throne.

St. Canute, the son of King Sweyn Estrithson, was the brother of Harold, king of Denmark. Before succeeding his brother to the throne, he tried to gain the English throne for himself by an invasion of Northumbria but failed. He succeeded his brother in the year 1080.

He was an energetic king and opposed the conquest of England by William the Conqueror. In Denmark, he founded abbeys and churches, and donated the cathedral of Lund to the Church. From England, he brought in the English Benedictines to found an abbey at Odense. It was one of these monks, Aelnoth, who would be his biographer.

In 1085, Canute prepared for an invasion of England to take the throne from the Normans. Before he could sail for England, a revolt broke out among his nobles, headed by his brother Olaf, and the king fled for refuge to the abbey-church he had founded at Odense. The rebels attacked the church, broke into the sanctuary where the king had just confessed his sins and received Holy Communion, and killed the king before the altar. His brother Benedict and seventeen others died with him.

He was buried in the abbey, and miracles began to multiply at his tomb. King Erik Evergood, who succeeded him as king, requested canonization and Canute was canonized by Pope Paschal II in 1099. He is the patron saint of Denmark and his relics are still preserved in the church at Odense, named after him, Sankt-Knud, and they are still revered in the twelfth-century reliquary in the church.

Canute's holiness influenced his son, Blessed Charles the Good, who became the count of Flanders.

Thought for the Day: A king's throne is not the best place to become a saint, since power and privilege can turn the head of even the holiest of men. But sanctity can flourish anywhere, and those kings who have been saints — for example, Canute, Louis of France, and Edward the Confessor — are proof of this. Nobility of birth can become nobility of soul, and so even kings are enrolled in the calendar of the saints.

From 'The Catholic One Year Bible': "The good ground represents the heart of a man who listens to the message and understands it and goes out and brings thirty, sixty, or even a hundred others into the Kingdom." — Matthew 13:23

St. Sebastian *(JANUARY 20)*

Sebastian is one of the great heroes of the early Church and has been venerated since his death during the Great Persecution of the Emperor Diocletian. According to St. Ambrose, he was born in Narbonne, in France, but was brought up in Milan, Italy, where his parents were from. The persecution begun under the Emperor Decius was continued by Diocletian, and the days were difficult for Christians. This was the last attempt of the Roman authority to stamp out Christianity, and it failed. The courage and endurance of St. Sebastian indicate why.

Little is known with certainty about his life, except his association with the city of Milan, the fact that he was a soldier in the Roman army, and some of the details of his martyrdom. Legend has him encouraging other martyrs to endure suffering and death, converting the jailers of Christian prisoners, and openly defying the Emperor Diocletian himself for his cruelty and barbarism toward the Christians. The legends are not trustworthy, but they do indicate the great esteem in which he was held from the time of his death and his great courage in the face of a terrible martyrdom.

An early account of his martyrdom has him shot through with arrows by his fellow soldiers and then bludgeoned to death when he recovered from the arrow wounds. His death and his courage made a deep impression on his fellow Christians and he was buried on the Appian Way, close to one of the catacombs, close to what is now the basilica of St. Sebastian.

An ancient window in the cathedral of Strasbourg shows him as a knight with a sword and shield, and he has long been invoked as a patron against the plague. Because of the legend of his being pierced with arrows, he is the patron of archers, and, with St. Martin of Tours, the patron of soldiers. His name has always been linked with that of St. Fabian, a pope and martyr who died at the beginning of the Decian persecution in the year 250.

Thought for the Day: Many saints, like St. Sebastian, are merely names in history, and little is known of their life and their death. But something of their example remained aglow in the memories of their contemporaries who passed on their memory to future Christians. They were remembered for their heroic witness to Christ, and that memory was treasured and their name made immortal.

From 'The Catholic One Year Bible': ". . . The Kingdom of Heaven is like a pearl merchant on the lookout for choice pearls. He discovered a real bargain — a pearl of great value — and sold everything he owned to purchase it!" — Matthew 13:45

St. Agnes *(JANUARY 21)*

In St. Agnes, we have a youthful model of consecrated virginity, whose example inspired early Christians and whose martyrdom became quickly embroidered into legend. Agnes has always had a special charm and she remains one of the loveliest figures of the early Church.

Like St. Sebastian, she suffered in the persecution of Diocletian, just before the Peace of Constantine. Her story became one of the great Christian legends, and she is one of the great Christian heroines.

She was only thirteen at the time of her death, a beautiful young Roman girl who very early had consecrated herself to Christ. She was sought in marriage by young men of the great Roman families, but she refused all of them. There may be some historical basis for her being betrayed to the Roman authorities by a youth who had hoped to have her as his wife, and that she was accused by him of being a Christian.

Like the other Christians of Rome, she was ordered to offer sacrifice to the Roman gods. She refused, and she was condemned to death, some say by being beheaded, others by stabbing in the throat. Her calmness and her courage in the face of death were the marvel of those who watched. She was buried by her fellow Christians beside the Via Nomentana in a cemetery that was later named after her.

Her feast is recorded in the *Depositio Martyrum* in the year 354 and is mentioned by St. Ambrose in his treatises *De Virginibus* and in a hymn composed by him. Usually portrayed with a lamb in her arms, she is the patron of young Christian womanhood and her relics are kept in the church of St. Agnes on the Piazza Navona in Rome. Her popularity is shown by the many Catholic women named Agnes and by the great number of churches named in her honor.

Thought for the Day: Young saints have a special appeal, and the patron saints of youth have always had a special place in the devotion of Catholics. St. Aloysius, St. Dominic Savio, St. Maria Goretti, and St. Agnes are proof of this, and their lives are always read eagerly by the young. Heroes are needed at every age, but the young especially need heroes and examples of Christian courage and devotion to Christ. St. Agnes is one of the earliest.

From 'The Catholic One Year Bible': . . . "A prophet is honored everywhere except in his own country, and among his own people!" — Matthew 13:57

St. Vincent Pallotti *(JANUARY 22)*

A contemporary of Cardinal Newman's and the Curé of Ars', St. Vincent Pallotti was a very modern saint who organized so many remarkable pastoral programs that he is considered the forerunner of Catholic Action. He was a man of great ideas and great vision and was able to inspire others to tackle great things. He is the founder of the Pallottine Fathers and the Pallottine Missionary Sisters; however, this was but the tip of the iceberg of his accomplishments. He left behind schools, guilds, and institutes that carried the Catholic mission into the very heart of contemporary society.

He was born in Rome in 1795 and began studies for the priesthood very early. Although he was very bright, he was not attracted by studies, even though he was ordained a priest at twenty-three and earned a doctorate in theology soon afterward. He was given an assistant professorship at the Sapienza University but resigned it soon after to devote himself to pastoral work.

Before long, his zeal was known all over Rome. He organized schools for shoemakers, tailors, coachmen, carpenters, and gardeners so that they could better work at their trade, as well as evening classes for young farmers and unskilled workers. He soon became known as a "second St. Philip Neri." He gave away his books, his possessions, and even his clothes to the poor, and once dressed up as an old woman to hear the confession of a man who threatened "to kill the first priest who came through the door."

In 1835, he founded his two congregations and was instrumental in the founding of a missionary order in England and several colleges for the training of missionaries.

He died at the age of fifty-five and his body lies incorrupt in the church of San Salvatore in Rome. He was canonized by Pope John XXIII in 1963.

Thought for the Day: There is a certain genius that comes from the faith and we see it in our day in Mother Teresa of Calcutta. The saints tackled great and difficult things and accomplished wonders because they did not depend upon their own strength and effort. They knew that all things are possible with God and they took God at His word in asking for miracles and near-miracles. They were never disappointed.

From 'The Catholic One Year Bible': . . . Peter went over the side of the boat and walked on the water toward Jesus. But when he looked around at the high waves, he was terrified and began to sink. "Save me, Lord!" he shouted. Instantly Jesus reached out his hand and rescued him. "O man of little faith," Jesus said. "Why did you doubt me?" — Matthew 14:29-31

St. John the Almsgiver *(JANUARY 23)*

This saint's life reads like one of the tales of the *Arabian Nights*, with a uniquely Christian flavor. He was born of a wealthy family of Cyprus, married, and raised a large family. After the death of all his children, he devoted his wealth to helping the poor and was noted for his personal holiness. So great was his reputation that he was chosen patriarch of Alexandria during the difficult days of the Monophysite controversy.

On arriving in Alexandria, he asked that a list of his "masters" be drawn up; when he was asked who they were, he said they were the poor. There were seventy-five hundred poor in Alexandria, and he became known as the Father of the Poor. One of his first actions as patriarch was to distribute eighty thousand pieces of gold, which he found in the church's treasury, to the hospitals and monasteries of the city.

He devoted to the poor the great revenues of his patriarchal see, which was then one of the richest in Christendom. When Jerusalem was sacked by the Persians, St. John the Almsgiver gave refuge to those who fled the Holy City; moreover, he sent to Jerusalem large sums of money, food, supplies, and even workmen to rebuild the churches. He helped everyone: bankrupt businessmen, struggling doctors, indigent people of every kind. He had an unlimited confidence in Divine Providence, and his resources never failed him.

When the governor passed a law that burdened the poor with taxes, the patriarch spoke up in defense of the poor, which angered the governor, Nicetas. John sent him a message: "The sun is going down," he wrote. "Let not the sun go down on your anger." The governor apologized.

The patriarch himself lived in the greatest austerity, gave away his blankets, his rug, and would gently beg gifts from the wealthy for the poor.

On a trip with the governor to visit the emperor in Constantinople, John the Almsgiver fell ill on the island of Rhodes. "You invite me to the emperor of the earth," he told Nicetas, "but the King of Heaven calls me to himself." He sailed back to his native Cyprus and died there around the year 620. His body is enshrined in Bratislava, in Hungary.

Thought for the Day: An unbounded trust in Divine Providence is characteristic of the saints, and so they were generous with everything they had and gave lavishly to others. Love of the poor is a mark of the Christian.

From 'The Catholic One Year Bible': "I am God . . . the God of your father. Don't be afraid to go down to Egypt, for I will see to it that you will become a great nation there." — **Genesis 46:3**

St. Francis de Sales *(JANUARY 24)*

This remarkable saint, one of the most lovable men who ever lived, was born in Savoy in 1567 and began his education at the age of eight. When he was fourteen, he went to Paris — which, with its fifty-four colleges, was the intellectual center of Europe — and insisted on studying at a college run by the Jesuits.

To satisfy his father, who wanted Francis to study law, he became a gentleman-scholar and took lessons in riding, fencing, and dancing. But behind it all was a deep devotion to God and the intention to dedicate himself to God's service.

He was a doctor of law by twenty-four, was offered a seat in the senate of Savoy, and was the most eligible bachelor among the young nobility. His father planned a distinguished marriage for him, but Francis declined. Against his father's wishes, but with his consent, he was ordained a priest . . . and the rest is history.

St. Francis de Sales plunged into the work of the priesthood with a zeal that surprised everyone and even offered to do missionary work in a region strongly dominated by hostile Calvinists. His father was shocked, thinking that his son was going to his death. It was a difficult and dangerous mission, but Francis managed to strengthen the faith of the Catholics in the region and even to convert a number of Calvinists. He was attacked by hostile crowds and beaten; on one occasion he was surrounded by wolves and had to spend the night in a tree.

On the death of the bishop of Geneva in 1602, Francis was appointed bishop and began the work of organizing his diocese. In 1604, he met Jane Frances de Chantal, a prominent widow who (with Francis as her spiritual director) founded the Order of Visitation in 1610. Out of conversations with people of his diocese asking for spiritual direction grew the *Introduction to a Devout Life*, a great spiritual classic; his *Treatise on the Love of God* made him famous throughout Europe. His teaching on holiness for the layman was so novel that his books were banned from many pulpits.

He died in 1622, only fifty-five years of age, and was canonized forty years later. He is the patron of the Catholic press.

Thought for the Day: Holiness, St. Francis de Sales taught, is for everyone: from housewife to queen, from soldier to pope. He was one of the first to open the gates of holiness to everyone. We all can be saints.

From 'The Catholic One Year Bible': . . . "You are good at reading the weather signs of the skies — red sky tonight means fair weather tomorrow; red sky in the morning means foul weather all day — but you can't read the obvious signs of the times!" — **Matthew 16:2-3**

Conversion of St. Paul *(JANUARY 25)*

St. Paul's life is perhaps the best known in the annals of the saints, and his conversion was one of the most earth-shaking events of the early Church.

He was born in Tarsus, in what is now southeast Turkey, where a large Jewish population lived, and was given the name Saul. Brought up a strict Pharisee, young Saul was sent to Jerusalem to study under the most famous rabbi of the time, Gamaliel of Jerusalem. It was there that he encountered the early Christian movement and became the avowed enemy of those he considered heretics and apostates.

He hunted down these "heretics" and stood and watched the stoning of St. Stephen, approving of what he saw. Then he was given authorization by the high priest to go to Damascus, where many Christians had fled, and to arrest the Christians in that city.

It was just outside the city of Damascus that his conversion took place. He was suddenly surrounded by a bright light, was knocked to the ground, and heard a voice that said: "Saul, Saul, why are you persecuting me?" When he asked who spoke, he was told: "I am Jesus, whom you are persecuting."

He was told to go into the city and await further instructions; upon getting up from the ground, he discovered that he was blind. His companions, puzzled by what had happened, led him into the city where Saul lived in a bewildered state for several days. A Christian disciple named Ananias then baptized him, and Saul recovered his sight.

Shortly after that, Saul began proclaiming the Gospel, and the Jews started plotting to kill him. Discovering their plot, Saul escaped. Eventually Paul the Apostle, as he was now known, would bring the Gospel from one end of the Mediterranean Sea to the other and be looked upon almost as the second founder of Christianity. He was beheaded in Rome during the persecution of Nero, around the year 64, and was buried on the spot that later became the basilica of St. Paul Outside-the-Walls.

Thought for the Day: Not all of us can be knocked off our feet by a vision of Jesus Christ, but we can live our faith with the same intensity as that of St. Paul. After his conversion, Paul spent his life spreading the news of Jesus everywhere and died as his final witness to the faith. It is this Christian heroism that planted the Christian faith, and it is still needed today.

From 'The Catholic One Year Bible': "You are Peter, a stone; and upon this rock I will build my church; and all the powers of hell shall not prevail against it." — Matthew 16:18

SS. Timothy and Titus

These two saints are the best known disciples of St. Paul, and so it is fitting that their feast should follow his in this "calendar of the saints."

St. Titus, an early disciple of St. Paul, went with him to the Council of Jerusalem about the year 50 and became his companion and associate on his missionary journeys. When trouble arose in the Church of Corinth, it was Titus whom Paul sent to look into the matter and it was Titus who seems to have brought about peace in that Church.

One of Paul's "pastoral letters" is addressed to Titus, and in it Titus is left in charge of the organization of the Church on the island of Crete; legend moreover has him as the first bishop there. Paul tells us: "As for Titus, he is my fellow worker in your service." It is not known when Titus died or where he is buried.

St. Timothy became Paul's disciple on the latter's second missionary journey and was circumcised by Paul because his mother was Jewish. He, too, became the associate and collaborator in the spreading of the Gospel and was sent on several important missions by the apostle. Two of the "pastoral epistles" are addressed to Timothy and show the close bond of affection between Paul and his disciple. He is mentioned as well in several other Epistles, and in the Second Letter to Timothy he is instructed to "bring the cloak I left with Carpus in Troas, and the scrolls, especially the parchment ones."

It is to Timothy that the moving passage on his life was written in which Paul describes his labors and his suffering: "As for me, my life is already being poured out like a libation, and the time has come for me to be gone. I have fought the good fight to the end; I have run the race to the finish; I have kept the faith." And his advice to his disciple in his pastoral work is still the finest description of what a pastor should be.

Timothy is considered the first bishop of Ephesus, and his relics were believed to have been transferred to Constantinople in the year 356. He is thought to be a martyr like his master, Paul.

Thought for the Day: St. Paul urged both his disciples to "hold fast to sound teaching" and to nourish their minds on the Scriptures, from which they would draw their model of holiness. They followed his advice and became saints. The advice he gave them is good for us as well.

From 'The Catholic One Year Bible': ". . . If you had faith even as small as a tiny mustard seed you could say to this mountain, 'Move!' and it would go far away. Nothing would be impossible." — Matthew 17:20

St. Angela Merici *(JANUARY 27)*

Angela Merici was a pioneer in Catholic education and the real originator of the concept of a "secular institute": consecrated persons living in the world and carrying on a ministry of teaching, mercy, or simple Christian witness. Her Ursulines were a novel concept at the time, but they were soon forced to conform to the lifestyle of other religious communities.

St. Angela was born in the Republic of Venice in Italy in 1474; after her parents' death, she and a brother and sister lived with an uncle in Salo.

After her uncle's death, Angela returned to her hometown of Densenzano and, appalled at the ignorance of religion in the area, organized a number of local girls to help her in the teaching of religion. In 1531, she moved her work to Brescia and, through the help of the Patengolo family whom she had befriended, she organized a group of young women into the Company of St. Ursula.

From the beginning, they had no convent or monastery but remained in their own homes, bearing Christian witness in their family and giving instruction to the children of the neighborhood. They took no formal vows but dedicated themselves to the living of the evangelical counsels. Although she was elected their first superior, they were organized merely as an association of women dedicated to teaching and other good works. Her advice to them on the future of their association was simple, wise, and direct: "If according to times and needs you should be obliged to make fresh rules, do it with prudence and good advice."

St. Charles Borromeo organized the Ursulines into a formal religious congregation of women and it was given papal approval in 1544. In January of 1540, Angela Merici became ill and died on January 27, revered as a saint by the people of Brescia. She was beatified by Pope Clement XIII in 1768 and canonized by Pope Pius VII in 1807.

Thought for the Day: Sometimes the "tried and true" ways are no longer adequate and new ways have to be found to bring the Gospel to the world. Saints like Angela Merici had to find new ways to do the old tasks, and innovation has always been a part of genuine sanctity. New wineskins are often needed for the eternally new wine of the Gospel, and the saints were not only holy people, they were often creative geniuses as well.

From 'The Catholic One Year Bible': "Beware that you don't look down upon a single one of these little children. For I tell you that in heaven their angels have constant access to my Father." — Matthew 18:10

St. Thomas Aquinas *(JANUARY 28)*

Thomas Aquinas was born of a noble family of middle Italy and as a young boy of five was sent to the abbey of Monte Cassino to be educated. Later, after the soldiers of Emperor Frederick II had sacked the abbey, Thomas, at the age of fourteen, was sent to the university at Naples to continue his studies. There he met the newly founded Dominicans, and at eighteen, without the knowledge of his family, he became a Dominican.

Knowing the opposition that his family would give, the Dominicans were hurrying him out of Italy to Paris, when his brothers and a troop of soldiers met them just north of Rome, took Thomas forcefully, and imprisoned him in his father's castle of San Giovanni, near Naples. There Thomas stayed for over a year while the Dominicans and his family fought a battle before pope and emperor over his fate. Finally, with the help of his sisters, he escaped and was sent to Paris, far from the reach of his family.

It was in Paris that St. Thomas Aquinas met St. Albert the Great, the greatest teacher of the age, and it was under Albert that he was trained to be the superb theologian that made him the marvel of the age. At the age of twenty-seven, Thomas was a teacher at Paris, and four years later, in 1256, he received his doctorate from the University of Paris. Three years after that, in 1259, he became theologian to the papal court.

The world he lived in was exploding with knowledge: knowledge of philosophy from the world of ancient Greece and knowledge of the sciences from the Islamic world. It was his task to use the new knowledge for the support of the faith, and the works that came forth from his pen show him to be one of the greatest intellects of all time. His mind was open to all things true and good, and he exemplified in his life that love and wisdom are the two wings by which the Christian goes to God.

He died on March 7, 1274, en route to the Council of Lyons, at the abbey of Fossa Nuova in Italy. On his deathbed, about to receive the Eucharist, he proclaimed: "For You alone have I labored, for You alone have I studied and preached and taught." He is the patron saint of students and scholars.

Thought for the Day: For St. Thomas Aquinas, the goodness of God can be seen in everything, and the whole of creation is a mighty love song of God. He learned more at the foot of the crucifix, he said, than in all his books. He showed that learning and holiness are good companions.

From 'The Catholic One Year Bible': ". . . 'I forgave you all that tremendous debt, just because you asked me to — shouldn't you have mercy on others, just as I had mercy on you?' " — **Matthew 18:32-33**

In the year 410, the Roman legions left Britain to do battle with the barbarian invaders on the mainland, and this withdrawal of Roman troops was the beginning of the Anglo-Saxon invasion of England. First, the Anglo-Saxons came as protectors, at the request of the Britons themselves, to help in the defense of England against the Irish and Picts who invaded the island from the west and north. But soon, they saw other opportunities for themselves and during the next century and a half the invading Anglo-Saxons began pushing the native Britons farther to the west and established their own kingdoms on British soil. Most of the native Britons were Christian; the Anglo-Saxons were pagans.

The history of Christianity in Britain from the year 410 when the Roman legions withdrew is a sad and terrifying tale, as the Britons fought for their very existence and the Anglo-Saxon kingdoms were established. The one chronicler of these terrible years was a British monk named Gildas who wrote probably around the year 540, telling the story of those terrible days and the gradual extinction of Christianity in the greater part of the island of Britain. The native Britons soon were crowded into the extreme western part of the island and would eventually become the Welsh.

St. Gildas the Wise was apparently a monk of the monastery of Llanilltud, visited Ireland, and was noted for his learning and his holiness. Conditions in Britain apparently became so unbearable that he followed many of his fellow countrymen to Britanny, in France, where he lived as a hermit on an island in Morbihan Bay. He gathered a few followers around him and carried on the monastic tradition of St. Illtud and St. Samson, two of the early founders of British monasticism.

Gildas died in Britanny about 570 and his work, *On the Ruin of Britain*, is one of the early written sources of English history. As one writer has stated, "He is the only direct witness of the tragic days when Roman Britain, mauled by her last and triumphant enemies, lay dying." In his lament, he has been compared to the Old Testament prophets chronicling the ruin of their nation and people.

Thought for the Day: St. Gildas the Wise lived in difficult times, when the light of Christianity seemed to be dying and a whole nation was lost to the faith. Yet he himself kept the faith and managed to live a holy life in the midst of ruin. The man of faith walks not only in the light but sometimes also in the darkness.

From 'The Catholic One Year Bible': . . ."If you want to be perfect, go sell everything you have and give the money to the poor, and you will have treasure in heaven; and come, follow me." — **Matthew 19:21**

St. Bathildis *(JANUARY 30)*

This is a Cinderella story of an English girl, strong in her faith, who was sold as a slave in France and became the wife and mother of kings.

Bathildis was kidnapped in England and carried over to France, where she was sold as a slave into the household of the mayor of the palace, under King Clovis II. She was so efficient and apparently so attractive that she came to the notice of the king, who eventually married her and made her his queen. She gave him three sons, all of whom became kings themselves.

When the oldest son, Clotaire, was only five years old, the king died, and Bathildis became regent of the country, ruling it in the name of her son. She endowed many monasteries, did all in her power for the furtherance of religion, and redeemed many of her own people from captivity who, like herself, had been carried away from their own country. She founded the great abbey of Corbie and the royal nunnery at Chelles.

In 665, she herself retired to Chelles, where she lived in great simplicity. In the fierce politics of the time, she managed to keep her faith alive and her life unblemished, even though she was accused by some of being implicated in the assassination of a bishop, Aunemund of Lyons. In this, she seems to have been confused with the notorious Queen Brunhilda who died many years before and was involved in the plotting and intrigues of the Merovingian court.

St. Bathildis died at Chelles on January 30, 680, her death preceded by a very painful illness. She was known for her great love of the poor, to whom she distributed much of her royal jewelry and for the redemption of Christian captives, particularly of the English nation. Her memory is honored because of her opposition to slavery, simony, and oppressive taxation.

Thought for the Day: Holy women have often tamed the heart and the behavior of kings and princes, and St. Bathildis is remarkable for rising from slave to queen. Her Christian upbringing must have been outstanding, and she influenced her own sons in the tenor of their kingship. Not only slaves but even queens may be saints, and Bathildis was both.

From 'The Catholic One Year Bible': . . . "Among the heathens, kings are tyrants and each minor official lords it over those beneath him. . . . Anyone wanting to be leader among you must be your servant. And if you want to be right at the top, you must serve like a slave." — Matthew 20:25-27

John Bosco was the Father Flanagan of the nineteenth century, the founder of one of the largest religious orders in the Church, and one of the kindest, loveliest personalities, a priest who endeared himself to everyone.

He was born very poor, lost his father at the age of two, and was brought up by his saintly mother who worked hard to keep the family together. As a young boy, he had a gift for influencing children and became something of a juggler and acrobat to lure the children of the neighborhood to church.

At a very young age he dreamed of becoming a priest. He was so poor that when he went off to the seminary at the age of sixteen, all of his clothes were provided by charity.

During his seminary days at Turin, he worked with the boys of the streets and dreamed someday of being a missionary. The rector of a priest's institute in Turin, St. Joseph Cafasso, convinced him that his mission was in Turin and told him to go home and unpack his trunk, for his work was with boys.

After his ordination, he was appointed chaplain to a refuge for girls established by a wealthy marchesa who looked upon him as her private chaplain. When she told Don Bosco (as he was called) that he must choose between his boys and her patronage, he chose his boys and found himself out in the street with no place to go, no resources, and no money for his work. In desperation, he cried out to God: "Tell me what to do!"

Money began to come in, miraculously some said, and the work was begun: first, a school for boys, and then, after many years, a full-fledged order dedicated to youth. In 1863, the Salesians, as Don Bosco named them, numbered thirty-nine; when he died, there were over seven hundred. He also founded an order of nuns to help with his work as well as groups called Salesian Cooperators from all walks of life.

Among his boys, many became priests, and one of them, Dominic Savio, was declared a saint in 1954. St. John Bosco died on January 31, 1888, worn out and exhausted, and was canonized by Pope Pius XI in 1934.

Thought for the Day: In the beginning, Don Bosco's work was disappointing and seemingly impossible. He had little money, no collaborators, and hundreds of boys to take care of. But he persisted, overcame all obstacles, and saw one of his boys become a saint. He cried to God in his anguish, and God did not disappoint him.

From 'The Catholic One Year Bible': . . . "Truly, if you have faith, and don't doubt . . . you can . . . say to this Mount of Olives, 'Move over into the ocean,' and it will. You can get anything — *anything* you ask for in prayer — if you believe." — Matthew 21:21-22

THE SAINTS OF FEBRUARY

St. Brigid of Kildare *(FEBRUARY 1)*

She is the loveliest of Irish saints, the "Mary of the Gael," the "Queen of the South," the "Prophetess of Christ." Her fame spread all over Europe, and even beyond. There is a "Bride's Peak" in the Himalayan Mountains and a "Bride's Island" off the shores of Japan. She was the patroness of the Knights of Chivalry, and it is said that their custom of calling the girls they married their "brides" gave the word "bride" to the English language. As "St. Bride," she is the subject of many songs and much poetry.

She was born about the middle of the fifth century at Faughart, near Dundalk, in County Louth. Her father was a pagan nobleman of Leinster; her mother, Brocessa, was a Christian. Her father selected a husband for her, a poet, but Brigid had other plans. With seven other young maidens, all clad in the white homespun that became the garb of the nuns of Ireland, she went and made her vows before the bishop and founded the first community of nuns in Ireland. Her monastery of Kildare on the Liffey Plain became one of the great religious centers of Ireland, a double monastery of monks and nuns, and the residence of a bishop. It was also a school and a missionary center from which Brigid often went forth in her chariot to carry on works of charity throughout Ireland.

An ancient ancestor of the Book of Kells called the "Kildare Gospels" was produced at Kildare, and the monastery was noted for its scribes. St. Brigid was the friend of bishops, tribal chieftains, and common folk, who still invoke her in all kinds of trouble. She died in 525 and was buried in a great jeweled casket at the right side of the altar. Along with St. Patrick and St. Columba, she is one of the three great saints of Ireland. She is considered the protectress of travelers, the patron of the printing press, and the guardian of those who sail on the sea.

The Irish call on her in every need, for, as the ancient legends run, "everything that Brigid asked of the Lord was granted her at once. For this was her desire: to satisfy the poor, to expel every hardship, to spare every miserable man." She still carries on that mission today.

Thought for the Day: St. Brigid of Kildare took the whole of humanity into her heart and is still remembered, almost fifteen hundred years after her death. The power of goodness reaches down through the centuries. There was no limit to her charity and her power of doing good. There should be no limit to ours.

From 'The Catholic One Year Bible': . . . I will sing to the Lord, for he has triumphed gloriously; / He has thrown both horse and rider into the sea. / The Lord is my strength, my song, and my salvation. —
Exodus 15:1-2

St. Adalbald of Ostrevant *(FEBRUARY 2)*

Adalbald was honored as a martyr, even though he was killed by his wife's relatives, who had disapproved of her marriage to a foreigner. He was a saintly man from a saintly family, and it was his saintly life, it seems, that was responsible for his veneration. In those days, the violent death of a holy person was considered martyrdom, and the fact that he was killed for family reasons did not seem to make much difference. If holiness was attacked, that was an attack upon God.

Sanctity ran in Adalbald's family. His grandmother was St. Gertrude, who founded the monastery of Hamage. Adalbald himself was a young nobleman of the court of King Dagobert I and embodied in himself all the qualities of Christian nobility. On a military expedition to Gascony, he fell in love with the daughter of a certain Enold and asked for the daughter's hand in marriage. The Gascons were in rebellion at that time against the king and did not take kindly to the marriage.

St. Adalbald of Ostrevant and his wife were noted for their works of charity, and their four children were venerated as saints. It was a remarkable family and apparently drew the envy of relatives. On a journey to Gascony, Adalbald was attacked by his wife's family and killed. His wife was heartbroken but managed to get possession of his body and give it a proper burial. Miracles began to be worked at his tomb, and veneration soon spread throughout the area. In those days, when paganism was still alive in France, Christian example was treasured, and this devout father and husband was given the honors of sainthood.

It is possible that his murderers were pagans who resented his Christian life, and this would also account for his esteem as a saint. Both husband and wife are honored as saints as well as their son, St. Mauront, and they are usually represented together. His wife, St. Rictrude, is associated with the abbey of Marchiennes, which she founded after her husband's death.

Thought for the Day: Christian living does not always bring honor; rather, it sometimes excites the hatred of others. From all outward appearances, St. Adalbald was an ordinary loving husband and father, but his roots ran very deep. His example fathered saints, which shows the power of holiness. Holiness can be found anywhere, and the man down the street could be a saint.

From 'The Catholic One Year Bible': . . . [Jesus] asked them, ". . . Whose name is this. . . ?" "Caesar's," they replied. "Well, then," he said, "give it to Caesar if it is his, and give God everything that belongs to God." — Matthew 22:20-21

Blaise is one of those ancient saints whose lives are lost in legend but who have become important in Christian memory and ritual. That he was a bishop seems clear and that he was a martyr also seems clear. Other facts about his life are not so certain.

According to legend, he was a bishop in Armenia during the persecution of the Emperor Licinius, just before the Peace of Constantine. With the coming of the persecution, St. Blaise was driven to hiding in caves in the mountains where he lived with the wild animals, which he tamed by his blessing.

He was captured by hunters who led him away to the authorities, and it is an incident that happened on his way to prison that became the basis for his veneration. On the way, he met a woman whose son had swallowed a fishbone and was choking to death. By his blessing, the saint dissolved the bone and the boy's life was saved. Because of this, he has always been invoked for ailments of the throat.

He is perhaps remembered because he was one of the last martyrs of the great persecutions unleashed by the Emperors Decius and Diocletian; with the coming of Constantine, such martyrdoms ceased. Blaise was imprisoned, tortured, and beheaded, and his memory was kept alive by the Christians of Armenia.

With the crusades, his fame as a healer was brought to the West, and the custom of blessing throats on his feast day arose. In Germany, he is one of the "fourteen holy helpers," or *nothhelfer*. He is also the patron of wool combers and of wild animals and of all who suffer ailments of the throat. Most Catholics go to church on this day to have their throats blessed and to invoke his intercession.

Thought for the Day: Saints are remembered for many things, and their deeds of kindness especially are fondly remembered. St. Blaise spent his life doing good to others, and that is how he is remembered. The saints help us not only by their holy lives but also by their prayers and intercession.

From 'The Catholic One Year Bible': . . . " 'Love the Lord your God with all your heart, soul, and mind.' This is the first and greatest commandment. The second most important is similar: 'Love your neighbor as much as you love yourself.' All the other commandments and all the demands of the prophets stem from these two laws. . . ." — Matthew 22:37-40

Blessed Rabanus Maurus *(FEBRUARY 4)*

Rabanus Maurus was a young boy who loved to study and became a disciple of the great Englishmen who brought learning and holiness to the kingdom of Charlemagne. He was born in 784, when the Carolingian renaissance was at its height, and his parents sent him to be educated at St. Boniface's great monastery of Fulda, which had a famous school. So remarkable was he as a student that the abbot of Fulda sent him to study under Charlemagne's own schoolmaster, Alcuin, at Tours, and it was under this teacher that he received the name Maurus, after St. Benedict's favorite disciple. On returning to Fulda, he was first a teacher, then head of the school there, which became famous all over Europe.

He continued the tradition of sacred learning begun by St. Boniface and Alcuin. He wrote homilies, scientific treatises, poetry, hymns, and commentaries on most of the books of the Bible. Like St. Bede, he was the marvel of his time for his learning and was unequaled in his time for his scriptural and patristic learning.

In 822, Blessed Rabanus Maurus was elected abbot of Fulda, and the monastery flourished under his guidance. He increased the library, built new buildings, and fostered learning of every kind. In 842, he retired, planning to live a life of prayer in solitude for the rest of his life.

In 847, he was chosen to be archbishop of Mainz, at the age of sixty-three, and the last years of his life were spent directing the affairs of his diocese, holding provincial synods, and directing a multitude of charitable works. During a famine, he fed three hundred poor people at his own house. He became bedridden shortly before his death and from the moment of his death was regarded as a saint.

He was buried at the monastery of St. Alban's in Mainz, but later his relics were transferred to Halle.

Thought for the Day: Learning, joined to holiness of life, has always been a powerful force for good. Knowledge is a gift of God, and the cultivation of the mind an important Christian duty. Those who teach are especially the ones who should be endowed with proper knowledge. Knowledge and understanding are gifts of the Holy Spirit and important tools of holiness.

From 'The Catholic One Year Bible': "O Jerusalem, Jerusalem, the city that kills the prophets, and stones all those God sends to her! How often I have wanted to gather your children together as a hen gathers her chicks beneath her wings, but you wouldn't let me." — Matthew 23:37

St. Agatha *(FEBRUARY 5)*

Agatha is one of the great martyr-saints of the early Church whose story has become the stuff of legends and high religious drama. Little is known for sure about her life, except that she was martyred during one of the great persecutions, and the "acts" of her martyrdom appeared very early in Latin and in Greek. She is the patroness of Catania, in Sicily, and here she is supposed to have been martyred in the Decian persecution, about the year 250, one of the fiercest persecutions of Christians.

St. Agatha had consecrated herself to God, and one version of her life has her sent to a house of prostitution to break her Christian determination, where she was tortured cruelly, St. Peter appearing to her to heal her wounds. She was subjected to other tortures and died of her sufferings in prison.

Her constancy and her courage were a spur to other persecuted Christians, and the name of Agatha was soon famous throughout the Christian world. Her cult spread very quickly, and she is even mentioned in the Roman Canon of the Mass. Pope Symmachus built a church in her honor on the Via Aurelia and Pope St. Gregory the Great reconsecrated an Arian church to her. Her relics were later taken to Constantinople after the Peace of Constantine.

She is invoked to ward off the danger of fire, and in certain parts of Europe, bread, candles, and fruit are blessed in her honor. Her feast day is the occasion of much merrymaking in Sicily, where she is the patroness of foundrymen and miners. In Germany, she is also the patroness of Alpine guides and nurses.

Thought for the Day: Women saints were numerous in the early Church, and the cruelties these saints suffered for their faith encouraged many others to go to their martyrdom. These early witnesses (martyrs) to the faith became the great Christian heroes and heroines, and their example did much to establish the Christian faith. Many, like St. Agatha, suffered centuries ago, but their memory is kept fresh, as if they had died yesterday.

From 'The Catholic One Year Bible': "For as the lightning flashes across the sky from east to west, so shall my coming be, when I, the Messiah, return. And wherever the carcass is, there the vultures will gather." — Matthew 24:27-28

St. Paul Miki *(FEBRUARY 6)*

High on a hill in the middle of Nagasaki, not too far from the epicenter of the atomic bomb explosion of 1945, stands an unusual chapel with its double odd-looking spire dominating the landscape. This is the chapel of San Felipe, and the spot commemorates the martyrdom of twenty-six martyrs (mostly Japanese) in the year 1597, when Catholicism was scarcely fifty years old in the Japanese isles.

The martyrdom was triggered by the wreck of the Spanish ship *San Felipe* on the shores of the island of Shikoku. The Japanese shogun Hideyoshi seized the ship, and the captain of the ship appealed to the Spanish Franciscans of Kyoto to plead their case. The Franciscan told the shogun that if the ship were seized, the Spaniards would come to invade Japan. Hideyoshi responded by a fierce persecution of Christians, whose presence in Japan he had merely tolerated up to that time.

Among those arrested was St. Paul Miki, a Jesuit scholastic, and twenty-five others, ranging in ages from twelve to sixty-four. With their ears cut off, they were loaded in oxcarts and driven through the streets of cities as a warning to other Christians. Their execution was to take place at Nagasaki, the foreign "port" of Japan and the center of Christianity in Japan. There, on a hill called Nichizaka overlooking Nagasaki Bay, they were bound to crosses, pierced through the abdomen and heart and left to die. For the next two centuries and a half, Japanese Christianity went underground, to emerge in the middle of the nineteenth century, when Japan again opened its doors to the world.

Paul Miki was young, one of the first fruits of the work of St. Francis Xavier on the island, and his martyrdom with his companions, among them a Mexican Franciscan, St. Philip of Jesus, brought about conversions by the thousands, even though the faith was practiced secretly. The example of the martyrs was a powerful example, and when Japan opened its doors to the world under the Emperor Meiji, there were over two hundred thousand Christians in the underground Church. The blood of martyrs was indeed the seed of Christians.

Thought for the Day: These martyrs died a horrendous and agonizing death in witness to their faith in Jesus Christ. We may not be asked to make this sacrifice, but we are all called upon to bear witness to our faith, sometimes in ways that are difficult. The fortitude of the martyrs can give us strength for our own witness.

From 'The Catholic One Year Bible': ". . . Learn a lesson from the fig tree. When her branch is tender and the leaves begin to sprout, you know that summer is almost here. . . . So be prepared, for you don't know what day your Lord is coming." — Matthew 24:32, 42

Blessed Thomas Sherwood *(FEBRUARY 7)*

The days of Elizabeth I were difficult days for the Catholics of England. This was the day of the martyrs, Catholics following in the footsteps of St. Thomas More and St. John Fisher, who died for their faith. Most of the martyrs of this era were priests, educated and ordained abroad, sent back to England to minister to the Catholics there, declared outlaws and criminals by the government.

Thomas Sherwood was not a priest and he was not a religious. He had planned to study for the priesthood but had not yet carried out his plan when he was arrested.

He was by profession a wool draper and was associated with other Catholic families, in particular the family of Lady Tregonwell. The son of Lady Tregonwell turned him in to the authorities, who sent him to the Tower of London. There he was tortured in order to discover where he heard Mass, who the priest was who celebrated the Mass, and the names of other Catholics with whom he was associated.

St. Thomas More's son-in-law, William Roper, tried to send him money for medicine and food, but the officer at the Tower would not permit money to be spent on anything but clean straw for him to sleep on. Blessed Thomas Sherwood was twenty-seven years old at the time of his arrest, and his brother wrote an account of his sufferings and martyrdom. We also possess the directions given to the lieutenant of the Tower from the privy council, ordering him to obtain information from Thomas Sherwood on the rack. After his execution, his mother was arrested and put in prison, where she died fourteen years later.

During his terrible sufferings, all that he said was: "Lord Jesus, I am not worthy to suffer for thee, much less to receive those rewards which thou hast promised to those who confess thee." Three weeks after his death, his death was recorded in the daybook of Douay College, where he had been expected: "On the first of March, Mr. Lowe returned to us from England bringing news that a youth, by name Thomas Sherwood, had suffered for his confession of the Catholic Faith, not only by imprisonment, but by death itself."

Thought for the Day: Perhaps we wonder how we could possibly endure the sufferings that the martyrs suffered, such terrible and prolonged sufferings, and where we would find strength and endurance to suffer for our faith. The martyrs did not endure by their own strength, and they were well aware of this. If that time should ever come for us, the strength would be given us by God.

From 'The Catholic One Year Bible': ". . . The man who uses well what he is given shall be given more, and he shall have abundance. But from the man who is unfaithful, even what little responsibility he has shall be taken from him." — Matthew 25:29

St. John of Matha *(FEBRUARY 8)*

John of Matha, the founder of the Trinitarian Order, was born at Faucon, on the borders of Provence, in France. He was trained as a young noble in horsemanship and the use of arms, decided to study for the priesthood, and was ordained in Paris. After some years in solitude, he conceived the idea of founding an order to ransom Christian captives from the Muslims and went to Rome to obtain the blessing of Pope Innocent III.

Houses of the order were established at Cerfroid and Rome and in Spain. He was very successful in the work of ransoming captives and his order spread. Very little is known for certain about his life, and in the fifteenth and sixteenth centuries, to bolster his reputation, certain members of his order fabricated stories about him, filled his life with miracles and amazing adventures, and connected the beginnings of his order with St. Felix of Valois.

The Trinitarian Order had not preserved any archives of their order and had little knowledge of the life of their founder. Another order, the Order of Mercy, was founded for the same reason as their own, and they compiled a fictitious record of the beginnings of their order. This takes nothing away from the achievements of St. John of Matha, but it does obscure the true story of his life and work.

We do know that he received approval of his order from Pope Innocent III in 1198 and that he died in Rome in 1213. His relics were taken to Madrid in 1655, and he was recognized as a saint in 1694. At his death, there were thirty-five houses of the order throughout Europe. The Trinitarians were one of the first religious orders to combine monastic discipline with pastoral work and one of the first to become international in its work. The order flourishes today in several countries and in 1906 made a foundation in the United States.

Thought for the Day: Like Mother Teresa of Calcutta, St. John of Matha saw a critical need for the Church at the time and set about doing something about it. He devoted all of his time, his efforts, and his resources to ransom his fellow Christians from slavery, and his work continued into modern times, until slavery was abolished. Like him, we should look around us and see what good has to be done and then courageously put our hand to the task.

From 'The Catholic One Year Bible': ". . . I was hungry and you fed me; I was thirsty and you gave me water; I was a stranger and you invited me into your homes; naked and you clothed me; sick and in prison, and you visited me." — Matthew 25:35-36

Marianus Scotus was one of those rare Irish monks who migrated to the continent and influenced the spread of a Christian culture throughout Europe. He was a scribe and calligrapher of great skill. He became a monk at a very early age and in 1067 he set out with a few companions on a pilgrimage to Rome. En route, they stopped in Germany, and were invited by the bishop of Regensburg to settle there.

Marianus and his companions had brought with them that marvelous love of learning and beauty so distinctive of Irish monasticism, and their monastery became a center for the creation of beautiful manuscripts and commentaries on the Scriptures, done with consummate skill and artistry. The fame of their monastery, named St. Peter's, soon spread throughout the whole of Europe. Like Bobbio in Italy and St.-Gall in Switzerland, their monastery became a center of Christian learning and culture.

St. Peter's and a companion monastery dedicated to St. James became the headquarters of a renaissance of Irish monasticism on the continent. In time, their congregation numbered twelve monasteries, and the monks were highly regarded for their holiness, their devotion to learning, and for the beautiful manuscripts that came forth from their hands. In their scriptoria, they carried on the tradition of the Book of Kells and the Book of Durrow. For almost four centuries, all of the monks were recruits from Ireland, and Ireland continued to supply monks, funds, and other resources for the growth of the abbey and its foundations.

The significance of the work of Marianus Scotus is indicated in *The Study of History* by Arnold Toynbee: "The period of Irish cultural superiority over the continent and over Britain may be conveniently dated from the foundation of the monastic university of Clonmacnoise in Ireland A.D. 548 to the foundation of the Irish Monastery of St. James at Ratisbon, circa A.D. 1090. Throughout those five and a half centuries, it was the Irish who imparted culture and the English and the continentals who received it."

Blessed Marianus Scotus died on February 9, 1098.

Thought for the Day: Holiness and learning go hand in hand, and the cultivation of learning is at the very heart of a Christian culture. The Irish monks shared their learning with the world and became the schoolmasters of Europe. They took seriously the words of Jesus: "You are the light of the world."

From 'The Catholic One Year Bible': ". . . My soul is crushed with horror and sadness to the point of death . . . stay here . . . stay awake with me." — Matthew 26:38

Sanctity sometimes runs in the family. Almost the whole family of St. Basil of Caesarea are saints, and the family of St. Bernard followed him on the path of holiness. Among Jesus' followers were a number of siblings, including the brothers Peter and Andrew, and James and John. But perhaps the most famous brother-sister saints are St. Benedict and St. Scholastica, made famous by the *Dialogues* of St. Gregory the Great, who immortalized them in his writings.

According to one version, St. Scholastica was St. Benedict's twin and, like her brother, dedicated herself to God at a very early age. Nothing is known of her early life, but after St. Benedict's founding of Monte Cassino, she is known to have been abbess of a monastery at Plombariola, about five miles to the south. Since St. Benedict founded monasteries of nuns as well as monks, it is possible that he founded the monastery and put his sister in charge. Their two lives are linked to the origins of Benedictine monasticism, and she seems to have been a willing and wise collaborator in his work.

The most famous incident in their lives is told by St. Gregory in a touching tale about a yearly meeting between brother and sister. Since she could not enter the monastic cloister, Scholastica would meet her brother once a year at a house not far from Monte Cassino. One year, when they were both very old and both realized that they would probably not see each other again, she begged her brother to remain through the night to continue their talk. Knowing that this was against his monastic rule, Benedict refused and prepared to leave. His sister asked for God's help in detaining her brother, and a violent storm arose, preventing Benedict from returning to the monastery. The next morning, they parted, and three days later, Scholastica died.

She was buried at Monte Cassino, in a grave especially prepared for her by St. Benedict, but her relics were later moved to France and are believed to be in Le Mans.

Thought for the Day: Example is a powerful influence, and that is especially true if the example comes from the members of our own family. We sometimes forget the obligation we have to our own family to give good example. Older brothers and sisters have a marvelous opportunity to fashion the character of the younger members of their family.

From 'The Catholic One Year Bible': ". . . In the future you will see me, the Messiah, sitting at the right hand of God and returning on the clouds of heaven." — Matthew 26:64

In St. Caedmon, poetry and song have become canonized, and the art of the minstrel and bard became part of Christian holiness. His story is beautifully told by St. Bede in his *History of the English Church and People* and has become a classic of hagiography.

Caedmon was a herdsman attached to the abbey of Whitby in England, during the abbacy of St. Hilda, the foundress of the monastery. He was poor, unlettered, and keenly aware of his lack of human gifts. During the great festivals of the monastery, the harp would be passed from hand to hand and each one of the monastery workers would compose a song and sing it for the others. When the harp was passed around, Caedmon would sneak away to the stables, ashamed of his own lack of talent.

One evening, as he lay down to sleep in the stable, he heard a voice that said to him: "Caedmon, sing!" "I cannot sing," Caedmon answered. "I left the hall because I could not sing." "Sing to me," the voice repeated. "What shall I sing?" Caedmon asked. "Sing about creation," the voice answered. Caedmon began to sing and Bede recorded his verses in the Anglo-Saxon tongue, which was the only language that Caedmon knew.

Now must we praise heaven's keeper,
the might of the ruler and his heart's thought,
the work of the glory-father of every wonder,
he made the beginning, everlasting Lord.
He first shaped for the children of men,
the skies for a roof, Holy Maker;
then afterwards mankind's keeper
made the earth, the soil for man,
Almighty Ruler, and endless Lord.

When the other herdsmen found that Caedmon could sing and compose religious ballads, they took him to the Abbess Hilda, who listened to his story and made him the bard, or poet-singer, of the monastery. He is considered the first English poet, and he spent the rest of his life in the monastery, composing and singing religious songs for the monastery.

He died in the monastery of Whitby after a long life. Except for the short poem recorded by Bede, his other works are lost.

Thought for the Day: Gifts are to be shared. The gifts we have are not our own but have been given by God for the joy and happiness of others. St. Caedmon was given a very special gift and he used it for the glory of God and the enrichment of others. Gratitude for a gift is shown by using it well.

From 'The Catholic One Year Bible': . . . "I will make my goodness pass before you, and I will announce to you the meaning of my name Jehovah, the Lord. I show kindness and mercy to anyone I want to." — Exodus 33:19

St. Ethelwald *(FEBRUARY 12)*

In the British Library, guarded as one of its most cherished treasures, is the Lindisfarne Gospels, a masterpiece of calligraphy and manuscript painting, which originated on Lindisfarne Island (also known as Holy Island) soon after the death of its illustrious bishop, St. Cuthbert. It was created to honor the saint by those who cherished his memory on the island, and the man who bound the book and provided for its ornamentation was today's saint, St. Ethelwald.

He had known Cuthbert himself, and succeeded him as prior of Melrose on the mainland where both had become monks. He then became abbot of that monastery and, finally, bishop of Lindisfarne itself, where Cuthbert had been bishop.

Cuthbert died in 687, and Ethelwald in 740, so he must have been a very young man at the time of Cuthbert's death. As a novice, he was assigned to look after Cuthbert, went with him on many of his missionary journeys, and was a witness to several of his miracles of healing. Bede mentions him in his *Life of Cuthbert* and in his *History of the English Church and People.*

In those days, it was customary for young boys to be placed in monasteries to be educated, and many of them remained there for the rest of their lives. At Melrose and Lindisfarne, the education was broad and extensive and included training in the Scriptures, Latin letters, psalmody, calligraphy, and manuscript illumination. St. Ethelwald entered at Melrose, as had St. Cuthbert himself.

Ethelwald was alive in 731 when Bede completed his history and died at Lindisfarne in 740. It was into Ethelwald's hands that the Lindisfarne Gospels were placed after their composition, and it was he who assured the honored place they would hold in the life of the Lindisfarne community. Later, when the Vikings destroyed Lindisfarne and the monks had to flee with the body of Cuthbert, they took Ethelwald's relics with them as well as the copy of the Gospels associated with his name.

Thought for the Day: The young have always looked to the old for wisdom, counsel, and guidance, recognizing that wisdom comes with years and that a well-lived life has many lessons to teach. St. Ethelwald sat at the feet of St. Cuthbert and eventually became a saint. Holiness breeds holiness.

From 'The Catholic One Year Bible': "Work six days only; the seventh day is a day of solemn rest, a holy day to be used to worship Jehovah; . . ." — Exodus 35:2

St. Catherine De' Ricci *(FEBRUARY 13)*

Catherine De' Ricci was the finest flower of the Savonarola reform and was born in Florence, Savonarola's city, almost twenty-five years after Savonarola's tragic death. She was from a noble family and educated by her aunt, a Benedictine abbess. She entered the Dominican convent of San Vincenzio at Prato, undoubtedly due to the influence of Savonarola, who was a Dominican.

Her life is full of the extraordinary: visions, ecstasy, rapture, and other unusual manifestations. These so disturbed the community in which she lived that the nuns of her convent, at her request, prayed that these supernatural occurrences would cease, which they did, in 1554. St. Catherine De' Ricci was favored with the stigmata and the wounds resulting from the crown of thorns.

These unusual happenings, however, did not detract from her wisdom, her humor, or her down-to-earth practicality. She advised bishops, cardinals, generals of religious orders, and even popes; she corresponded with a wide variety of disciples and associates, in letters of great charm. She cared for the poor and found time to advise a widening circle of friends and associates. In 1560, she became prioress of her convent and administered its affairs with wisdom and energy.

For twelve years, from 1542 to 1554, she relived the Passion of Christ from Thursday noon to Friday evening, and she was known to have visited St. Philip Neri and St. Mary Magdalen de Pazzi, probably by means of bilocation, as she never left her convent. She wrote a poem in honor of Savonarola and a canticle of the Passion, which became part of the Dominican liturgy. Before it was popular, she encouraged frequent confession and Holy Communion and recommended a spiritual life joined to energetic action. Her portrait by Naldini shows her with a book in her hand and a winsome, forceful look on her face.

She died after a long illness at the age of sixty-eight on February 2, 1590. She was canonized in 1747.

Thought for the Day: Some saints, like Teresa of Ávila and Catherine De' Ricci, are noted for their extraordinary mystical experiences, but they themselves placed little value on these. Both were noted for their good sense, balanced personality, and wide circle of friends. Both were also dearly loved by all who knew them.

From 'The Catholic One Year Bible': . . . The whole earth was covered with darkness for three hours, from noon until three o'clock. About three o'clock, Jesus shouted: "Eli, Eli, lama sabacthani?" which means, "My God, my God, why have you forsaken me?" — Matthew 27:45-46

SS. Cyril and Methodius *(FEBRUARY 14)*

These two saints were brothers, born to a Byzantine military officer who commanded the forces of the army at Thessalonica. As young boys, both spoke the Slavic language, which helped them in their future missionary labors among the Slavic peoples. Both were educated at Constantinople, and both became monks. Cyril was a professor for a time, and Methodius an abbot of a monastery.

In 862, they were entrusted with a remarkable mission. The duke of Greater Moravia, wishing political and ecclesiastical independence from the kingdom of the Franks, requested of the Byzantine emperor a bishop for his newly converted people, a bishop who would not be subject to the Franks and who could instruct his people in their own tongue. Cyril was chosen, with his brother as his co-worker, to create an alphabet for the Slavonic peoples and to translate the Gospels into that language. They also composed Slavonic liturgical books and went to Moravia, becoming the first missionaries who taught the people in their own tongue.

SS. Cyril and Methodius also accomplished one other significant task: they celebrated the liturgy in the Slavonic language, something that angered the missionaries from the West who had worked among the Slavonic peoples. Training disciples in their methods, the brothers realized that little could be accomplished unless they received the approbation of Rome, which had ecclesiastical jurisdiction over Moravia. At the church of St. Mary Major in Rome, the pope solemnly approved of the Slavonic liturgy and ordained several young men who had come with the brothers, including Methodius who was not yet ordained. Then the liturgy was celebrated in Slavonic at St. Peter's.

Cyril died in Rome in 869, and Methodius returned to Moravia to continue their work. The pope took Moravia immediately under his jurisdiction, which so angered the Bavarian clergy that Methodius was imprisoned. With amazing energy, Methodius evangelized the Slavic peoples, translated sacred books into their language, and composed treatises of canon law for his people. He died in his cathedral in 884; he and his brother are called "The Apostles of the Slavic Peoples."

Thought for the Day: SS. Cyril and Methodius were thrust into a totally unexpected task, requiring astonishing energy, flexibility, and challenges. They evangelized a whole people and brought them the treasures of the Christian faith. Faith is prepared for the unexpected and adapts itself to new and changing circumstances.

From 'The Catholic One Year Bible': ". . . Go quickly and tell his disciples that he has risen from the dead, and that he is going to Galilee to meet them there. That is my message to them." — Matthew 28:7

Claude de la Colombiére is best known for his association with St. Margaret Mary Alacoque and the devotion of the Sacred Heart, but his life has its own drama. He was sent to England after his spiritual direction of St. Margaret Mary was over and became embroiled in the Titus Oates "Popish Plot," was imprisoned, then banished from England. His story is part of the history of the seventeenth century.

He was born near Lyons in 1641 and entered the Society of Jesus at Avignon. After his novitiate, he taught grammar and the humanities. Even before his ordination to the priesthood, he gained a reputation as a preacher. After completing his studies in Paris, he became tutor to the sons of Colbert, the financial minister of Louis XIV, but was dismissed from his post and returned to Avignon.

In 1675, after his solemn profession as a Jesuit, he was appointed superior at Paray-le-Monial, in which the convent of St. Margaret Mary was located. Here he became her spiritual director, encouraged her in the spread of the devotion to the Sacred Heart, and was described by our Lord as His "faithful and perfect friend."

Because of his remarkable gifts and judgment, he was sent to England, to be court preacher to the duchess of York, wife of the future James II, and took up residence in London. His radiant personality and splendid gifts were noted by everyone. When the alleged "Popish Plot" to assassinate King Charles II shook the country, Blessed Claude was accused of complicity in the plot and imprisoned. Through the intervention of Louis XIV of France, he was released, then banished from the country. He spent his last years at Paray-le-Monial, his health broken.

He died on February 15, 1682, an apostle of the devotion to the Sacred Heart, and was beatified in 1929.

Thought for the Day: Blessed Claude was an amazingly gifted man, and he recognized that his gifts should be put at the service of others. He spent himself in the service of Christ and was chosen to direct someone with an important mission to the Church. Let us emulate Claude and place our gifts at the service of others.

From 'The Catholic One Year Bible': . . . "Come, follow me! And I will make you fishermen for the souls of men!" At once they left their nets and went along with him. — Mark 1:17-18

Gilbert of Sempringham was the son of a Norman knight who had settled in Lincolnshire less than twenty years after the Norman conquest. He studied at Paris and, since his father was lord of the area, he was given benefices at Sempringham and Tirington. Although he had an ample income from his benefices, he gave most of it to the poor and set up a school for the youth of the area. He also drew up a rule for seven young women who wanted to live a monastic life, which was the beginning of the Gilbertine Order, the only monastic order originating in England.

To assist his nuns, he organized a community of lay brothers, and then a community of priests to take care of their spiritual needs. In 1147, he went to Citeaux to ask the Cistercian Order to take over the government of his monasteries, but since they were unwilling, he was encouraged by Pope Eugene III to continue the work himself.

In 1165, Gilbert was accused by officials of King Henry II of giving support to Archbishop Thomas Becket in exile, but he refused to answer the charges and said he was perfectly willing to give such support had the opportunity presented itself.

His order continued to spread in his lifetime, and one house was even established in Scotland. At the time of his death in 1189, there were thirteen houses of the order in the country and the Gilbertines were known as one of the strictest and most regular religious in England. He died at the advanced age of one hundred six, and his order continued to grow, with two houses being founded in Westmeath, in Ireland. It was suppressed by Henry VIII in 1538 and its properties turned over to the king. St. Gilbert was canonized in 1202.

Thought for the Day: St. Gilbert could have lived a life of ease from the income of his benefices, but he chose to give all to the poor and to dedicate his life to teaching. Accidentally, he stumbled upon his life's work and brought many to God. We never know how God is going to use us, and by our devotion and fidelity we have to remain open to whatever task He sets before us. "I come, Lord, to do Your will."

From 'The Catholic One Year Bible': Once a leper came and knelt in front of him and begged to be healed. "If you want to, you can make me well again," he pled. And Jesus, moved with pity, touched him and said, "I want to! Be healed!" Immediately the leprosy was gone — the man was healed! — Mark 1:40-42

This is the story of seven young men, caught up in the blood feuds of medieval Florence, who set out into the wilderness to live a holy life. They were from prominent families in Florence; two were married, two were widowers, and they all belonged to a religious fraternity called the Laudesi. The chaplain of the Laudesi was a priest, James Poggibonsi, who later joined them in their wilderness retreat.

After settling their personal affairs and making provision for the families of those who were married, they began to live a life of prayer and penance, part of the group going to Carfaggio, just outside the city, and the others retiring to Mount Senario, deeper in the wilderness. At the suggestion of the Dominican preacher St. Peter Martyr, they decided to found a community. Taking the rule of St. Augustine and a version of the Dominican habit from St. Peter, they took the name Servants of Mary, the name of a confraternity founded by Peter Martyr. The bishop of Florence approved the community and they were taken under the protection of the Holy See in 1249.

They are known as the Seven Holy Founders of the Servite Order, and so their individual names are not familiar ones: Bonfilius, John Bonagiunta, Gerard Sostegni, Bartholomew Amidei, Benedict dell'Antella, Ricoverus Ugguccione, and Alexis Falconieri. They were canonized as a group by Pope Leo XIII in 1888.

In 1253, St. Philip Benizi entered the order, and during his term of office the order spread throughout Italy and other parts of Europe. At the suggestion of the bishop of Florence, they modified their strict monastic form of life and took on the character of mendicant friars. They are best known in the United States from their American motherhouse, the basilica of Our Lady of Sorrows in Chicago, which during the 1930s and '40s drew huge crowds to its novena to the Sorrowful Mother. The Servites now have houses on every continent, including missions in Africa and South America.

Thought for the Day: Since criminals and people with evil purposes often band together for their common interests, good people often have to do the same. Faced with the immorality and blood feuds of thirteenth-century Florence, the Seven Holy Founders banded together for their own spiritual good and succeeded in founding a whole new religious order. Good companions are one of the most powerful helps toward a holy life.

From 'The Catholic One Year Bible': "You know better than to put new wine into old wineskins. They would burst. The wine would be spilled out and the wineskins ruined. New wine needs fresh wineskins." — Mark 2:22

Colman was a loser, but he took his loss graciously, remained loyal to his deepest convictions, and started his work all over again when it seemed that everything was lost.

He was bishop of Lindisfarne in northern England, at a time when certain Irish traditions were being questioned in the England of the seventh century. Lindisfarne had been founded by an Anglo-Saxon king, St. Oswald, who had brought Irish monks from St. Columba's monastery of Iona, just off the coast of western Scotland. The Irish had brought their customs with them, evangelized all of northern England and parts of south England as well, and had founded convents and monasteries all over the country.

What was in question were the traditions of Columba (who had founded Iona), particularly the celebration of Easter. The Irish followed a custom that had come to them from Rome, through St. Patrick. In 467, Rome and Constantinople decided on a common method of determining Easter, but the Irish were far from Rome and continued in their own tradition. In England, Oswy, king of Northumbria — who had been educated by the Irish but whose wife followed the new date — decided to bring unity to his kingdom in the matter of Easter and called a *witan*, or national assembly, at Whitby to decide the matter. Since the Irish were the only people in Europe following the old date, the continental custom was accepted and the Irish monasteries of northern England ordered to comply. To St. Colman, this was a rejection of the authority of Columba, to whom Colman owed his first loyalty.

Making sure that his monastery and diocese would not be disturbed in their other traditions, Colman took a large group of Irish and English monks who agreed with him and returned to Iona. Later, he established two monasteries for his monks in Ireland: one at Inisbofin and one for the English monks at Mayo.

He died at Inisbofin in the late seventh century, and his memory was revered by his own monks and the people of Northumbria whose bishop he had been.

Thought for the Day: Sometimes our plans are upset by all kinds of unforseeable circumstances, something beyond our control and beyond our own wishes, and we have to begin all over again. "We have not here a lasting city," said St. Paul. St. Colman pulled up his roots and went elsewhere. Sometimes we have to do the same.

From 'The Catholic One Year Bible': He instructed his disciples to bring around a boat and to have it standing ready to rescue him in case he was crowded off the beach. For there had been many healings that day and as a result great numbers of sick people were crowding around him, trying to touch him. — Mark 3:9-10

St. Conrad of Piacenza *(FEBRUARY 19)*

This saint was a wealthy nobleman from Piacenza in Italy, happily married to a wife he loved very much, and the owner of a large estate. One day, while hunting, he ordered his servants to start a fire to drive the hunted animals out of the woods. A wind blew the fire into nearby cornfields and soon whole villages were aflame, with hundreds of people homeless. When Conrad saw what had happened, he returned home secretly and pledged his servants to silence.

A poor villager who had lost his home and was picking up sticks near the fire, was accused of arson and sentenced to death. Conrad came forward, took the blame for the fire, and was ordered to make good the damage. In doing so, he lost all of his own property, his possessions, and was reduced to poverty himself. As he and his wife pondered over what had happened, they saw the hand of God, and they both decided to make a radical change in their way of life. His wife entered a monastery of Poor Clares, and St. Conrad of Piacenza joined a group of hermits who lived under the rule of St. Francis.

His change of life brought him notoriety as old friends began to visit him. To avoid the growing publicity, he took a boat to Sicily, where he worked with the sick at the Hospital of St. Martin and lived with another nobleman, who had become a hermit, near the village of Noto. He was gracious and hospitable and had a delightful sense of humor.

He died in 1351 and was buried in the church of St. Nicholas in Noto, his tomb becoming a favorite place of pilgrimage.

Thought for the Day: Disaster does not always have to be the ruin of everything, and very terrible blows of bad fortune can lead to blessings. St. Conrad's bad fortune made him reflect on his own way of life and the terrifying truth of his own cowardice. A man was almost executed through his neglect and he realized that God deserved better of him. The rest is the story of a man who found his joy in God and became a delightful friend to everyone. It is a lesson to be pondered.

From 'The Catholic One Year Bible': ". . . The good soil represents the hearts of those who truly accept God's message and produce a plentiful harvest for God — thirty, sixty, or even a hundred times as much as was planted in their hearts." . . . "If you have ears, listen!" — Mark 4:20, 23

St. Eucherius *(FEBRUARY 20)*

Eucherius was a young man who was given great responsibilities at a very young age, never let his position go to his head, and even opposed the wishes of the man who had put him in his place of honor. He kept his head and his humor in the most trying of circumstances and was the joy of all who knew him.

He was the son of a prominent Merovingian family of Orléans, whose members were very close to the Frankish kings and the family of Clovis. He entered the abbey of Jumieges, near Rouen, at a very young age. When his uncle, who was bishop of Orléans, died, the senate and the people of the city (influenced no doubt by his prominent family) urged Charles Martel, the powerful mayor of the palace and real head of the Frankish kingdom, to appoint Eucherius bishop of Orléans. Eucherius protested but was made bishop anyway, against his wishes and in spite of his youth.

He became a popular and beloved bishop, but he opposed the taxation policies of Charles Martel, who confiscated church lands for his many wars and heavily taxed the churches of the kingdom. Returning from a war with the Saracens in 737, Charles took Orléans, then arrested Eucherius and exiled him to Cologne. His family was deeply involved in the politics of the time and opposed the growing power of Charles who was gradually usurping the power of the Frankish king.

The bishop's popularity followed him, and Charles, fearing that he would become the center of an opposition party, sent Eucherius to Liège and placed him under the watchful eye of the governor, who was a supporter of Charles.

St. Eucherius charmed even the governor and was allowed to help the poor and then to retire to the monastery of St.-Trond near Maestricht, where he again became a monk and lived out his days. Charles Martel died in 741, and a legend (fabricated no doubt by the enemies of Charles) has Eucherius seeing him burning in hell, a sentiment quite contrary to his own gentle ways. Eucherius has been venerated as a saint since the ninth century.

Thought for the Day: A life of holiness can bring astonishing maturity at a very young age and gives balance and depth to the human personality. When God becomes important, other things fade into the background, and loyalty to Him becomes the only thing that matters. We all need that kind of maturity.

From 'The Catholic One Year Bible': . . . "How can I describe the Kingdom of God? What story shall I use to illustrate it? It is like a tiny mustard seed! Though this is one of the smallest of seeds, yet it grows to become one of the largest of plants, with long branches where birds can build their nests and be sheltered." — Mark 4:30-32

St. Peter Damian

Peter Damian was one of the most dynamic figures of the eleventh century, during a time when abuses were rampant in the Church and popes were trying to bring unity and spiritual health to a very disturbed Christendom. It was also the age of new monastic orders, and Peter himself was both monk and reformer.

He was born at Ravenna in Italy, educated by an older brother at Ravenna, Parma, Modena, and Faenza. He spent some time teaching, was ordained to the priesthood, and then decided to enter the monastic life of the Camaldoli, at Fonte Avelana in 1035. Eight years later, in 1043, he was elected prior of the monastery, and it was he who put the group's rule in order, strengthened it with new statutes, and gave it a definite organization.

In 1057, Pope Stephen IX called St. Peter Damian out of solitude and made him cardinal-bishop of Ostia, much against his own wishes. During the next twenty-five years, he was active in Church synods, diplomatic missions for the pope, and writing. He settled conflicts between bishops and people, defended the rights of the pontiff, brought peace between bishops and religious orders, and fought simony and concubinage among the clergy.

After a difficult mission to the court of Emperor Henry IV to persuade him not to divorce his wife, Bertha, in which he was successful, Peter retired to Fonte Avelana, where he again lived the life of a simple monk. Called by the pope to bring peace to the diocese of Ravenna where the archbishop was guilty of serious crimes, Peter arrived there after the archbishop's death but still brought peace to the disturbed diocese. En route to Rome to report to the pope, he became sick and died on February 22, 1072. He was buried in the cathedral at Faenza and was declared a Doctor of the Church in 1828.

Thought for the Day: St. Peter Damian reformed his own life before he tried to reform others. Example is still the most powerful influence in changing others, and preaching is useless if it is not joined to a holy life. Before we can change others, we have to change ourselves.

From 'The Catholic One Year Bible': Taking her by the hand, Jesus said to her, "Get up, little girl!" . . . And she jumped up and walked around! Her parents just couldn't get over it. Jesus instructed them very earnestly not to tell what had happened, and told them to give her something to eat. — Mark 5:41-43

St. Margaret of Cortona *(FEBRUARY 22)*

Margaret of Cortona, after an unhappy family life, became the mistress of a young nobleman of Montepulciano named Arsenio, lived with him for nine years with the promise of marriage, bore him a son, and lived the life of a grand lady on his great estate. One evening he did not come home, and following his dog who had returned home, she found her lover's body buried in the earth, murdered by those who hated him.

This shocked her into a complete change of life. She gave all of her lover's possessions to his relatives, took her young son by the hand, and returned to her own family, where her father would not even speak to her. In near despair, she turned to the Franciscans, who became her spiritual directors, helped her to provide for her son, and directed her in her life of penitence.

She worked among the poor, attended the sick in hospitals, spent long hours in prayer, and became a member of the Third Order of St. Francis. She sent her son to a school at Arezzo and he later became a Franciscan. In 1286, she founded a hospital in Cortona and a community of Third Order women to staff it as well as a confraternity to support it.

Toward the end of her life, St. Margaret of Cortona was accused of insincerity, and all kinds of malicious rumors were spread about her. Some even thought her crazy. Even some of her beloved Franciscans turned against her, but she continued in her life of prayer and penance in spite of everything.

The effects of her life of penance were remarkable: lapsed Catholics returned to the faith, miracles were multiplied by her prayers, blood feuds were healed, and hardened sinners converted. When she died at the age of fifty, she had spent twenty-nine years in a life of penance, and crowds flocked to her funeral. She was scarcely in the grave when the citizens of Cortona began to build a church in her honor.

She was canonized in 1728, and her incorrupt body is venerated in her church at Cortona.

Thought for the Day: Forgiveness is an act of love, and the love of God pursues us, like the hound of heaven, until we turn to God in love. Sin is forgiven and forgotten, and God asks only our heart. Sometimes it takes a shock to turn us back to God, as in St. Margaret's case. God reaches us in astonishing ways and asks only that we love Him in return.

From 'The Catholic One Year Bible': . . . "A prophet is honored everywhere except in his hometown and among his relatives and by his own family." And because of their unbelief, he couldn't do any mighty miracles among them except to place his hands on a few people and heal them. — Mark 6:4-5

St. Polycarp *(FEBRUARY 23)*

Polycarp is the grand old man of the age of martyrs, a gentle, kindly bishop, loved by his people, admired even by those who put him to death, who went to his death gladly for the love of Christ.

He was bishop of Smyrna, in what is now western Turkey, and as a young man was a disciple of St. John the Evangelist, most probably at Ephesus. In the early part of the second century, he was visited by St. Ignatius of Antioch on his way to martyrdom in Rome. Ignatius also addressed one of his letters to Polycarp as well as one to the Church at Smyrna. He was the teacher of St. Irenaeus, who later migrated to Gaul and became bishop of Lyons. Another of his disciples was Papias, who has given us the most ancient listing of the books of the New Testament.

In mid-century, St. Polycarp went to Rome to consult with Pope Anicetus on the question of the date for the celebration of Easter. No more is heard of him until his martyrdom during the reign of the Emperor Marcus Aurelius.

While the great persecution raged all around him, Polycarp kept out of sight, not from cowardice but from the conviction that no one should expose himself to martyrdom, that one should wait until he was actually arrested. Since Polycarp was well known and even admired by the people of the area, he was finally arrested by Proconsul Statius Quadratus and urged to offer incense to the emperor and thus save his life. When he was asked by the proconsul to deny Christ, he said: "For eighty-six years have I served Him and He has done me no wrong. How can I blaspheme my King and Savior?" "I have wild beasts," said the proconsul. "Call them," Polycarp answered. "I can have you burned to death," said Quadratus. "Do what you please," Polycarp told him.

He was taken to the place of execution, tied to a stake, and burned to death. After his death, his followers came and took away his bones. His memory lingered during the days of persecution that followed and his example gave strength to others who suffered persecution. His *Acts* became one of the early Christian classics and his brave words at death were repeated by Christians everywhere.

Thought for the Day: We may not be required to give our lives for our faith, but we all have to suffer something for our religion and for our fidelity. It is when things are difficult that faith is really faith. A faith that is good only in good times is scarcely faith at all. We are all called to witness to our faith in some way.

From 'The Catholic One Year Bible': He took the five loaves and two fish and looking up to heaven, gave thanks for the food. Breaking the loaves into pieces, he gave some of the bread and fish to each disciple to place before the people. And the crowd ate until they could hold no more! — Mark 6:41-42

St. Praetextus *(FEBRUARY 24)*

The age of the Merovingian kings of France, the descendants of Clovis, was a bloody and violent one. Assassinations were common, brutal dynastic wars were numerous, and bishops and priests often found themselves caught in the web of intrigue and violence that marked the period.

St. Praetextus was bishop of Rouen in the latter half of the sixth century and ruled that see for thirty-five years. The war at the time was between the two grandsons of Clovis, Chilperic and Sigebert, who had divided the Frankish kingdom between them, as well as the deadly feud between Chilperic's mistress, Fredegund, and Sigebert's wife, Brunhilda. Sigebert was murdered through the plotting of Fredegund, and Brunhilda was thrown into prison. Brunhilda appealed to Chilperic's son, Merovech, who took up arms against his father, freed Brunhilda, and married her. The prelate who married them was Praetextus, and he was brought before the king at an assembly of bishops in Paris and accused of treason and plotting the downfall of the king.

Praetextus denied this but was convicted and sent into exile to the island of Coutances where he remained until the death of Chilperic and was restored to his see by order of the king of Burgundy. He had earned the undying hatred of Fredegund by his friendship to her rival Brunhilda. Moreover, Fredegund resided at Rouen and made no secret of her hatred for the bishop. She threatened him constantly and plotted to send him into exile once again.

What she could not control, the queen destroyed. (She had offered Gregory of Tours huge sums if he sided with her against Praetextus, but he indignantly refused.) On Easter of 586, she hired an assassin to stab the bishop while he was at the altar. Dying on his feet, the bishop finished the service, his hands dripping with blood. After Mass, he was carried to his bed, and the queen even had the audacity to come to him and offer the services of her best physicians. "God has decreed that I must leave this world," he told her with his dying breath, "but my blood is upon your head." He was buried at Rouen.

Thought for the Day: Some saints lived in very difficult and violent times but managed to live holy lives in the midst of terror and death. The times sometimes tests the mettle of even the strongest, and their fidelity is tested again and again. With the help of God, they came through, and so can we, whatever the problems we have to face.

From 'The Catholic One Year Bible': . . . "All of you listen," he said, "and try to understand. Your souls aren't harmed by what you eat, but by what you think and say!" . . . "Can't you see that what you eat won't harm your soul?" — **Mark 7:14-16, 18**

St. Walburga *(FEBRUARY 25)*

Walburga was English, the sister of two associates of St. Boniface in the work of evangelizing Germany and the Lowlands. She was educated at the monastery of Wimborne in Dorset, which she afterward entered. Like many of the English nuns of her time, she was well educated, greatly talented, and an advocate of education for women.

In response to a letter from St. Lioba of the same monastery to St. Boniface, Boniface requested the abbess of the monastery to send nuns to the continent to help in the founding of monasteries for women. Thirty nuns were sent, one of whom was Walburga. For two years, she stayed with Lioba at Bischofsheim, where the first monastery was founded; but when her brother Winebald founded a double monastery at Heidenheim, she was sent there to rule over the monastery of nuns.

At the death of her brother, she was appointed abbess over both monks and nuns, studied and practiced medicine, and was a vital force in the establishment of a Christian culture in those missionary lands. From these great monasteries founded by the English missionaries — Bischofsheim, Fulda, Heidenheim — Christian culture spread to the surrounding areas and laid the foundations for the Carolingian renaissance that took place under Alcuin, another Englishman. St. Walburga, St. Lioba, and the other English nuns collaborated with the missionaries, and the great achievements of Anglo-Saxon Christianity blossomed on the continent.

Walburga, who was present for the transfer of her brother's body to Eichstatt, died at Heidenheim in 779. She is popular throughout Germany and the Lowlands and is buried with her brother in the church of the Holy Cross in Eichstatt. *Walpurgisnacht*, a festival named after her, is celebrated on May 1, and oil from her tomb is used to anoint the sick. Besides Germany and the Lowlands, her feast day is celebrated in the diocese of Plymouth in England.

Thought for the Day: In these days of "women's liberation," it is good to know that women like St. Walburga worked side by side with their male brothers in great works of evangelization. They are remembered for their independence, their splendid gifts, and their devotion to the work of Christ. Their example is still an inspiration today when the harvest indeed is great but the laborers are few.

From 'The Catholic One Year Bible': Jesus led [the deaf man] away from the crowd and put his fingers into the man's ears, then spat and touched the man's tongue with the spittle. Then, looking up to heaven, he sighed and commanded, "Open!" Instantly the man could hear perfectly and speak plainly! — Mark 7:33-35

Blessed Isabelle of France *(FEBRUARY 26)*

Isabelle was a princess, the sister of St. Louis IX, king of France, and daughter of Louis VIII and Blanche of Castille. She was an independent and strong-willed young girl and resisted all attempts to marry her off for political and dynastic reasons (even the strong suggestions of the pope that such a marriage would be beneficial to the Church).

To please her mother, Blessed Isabelle dressed in the fine clothes of royalty and appeared in public with all the marks of her royal station, but privately she prayed much, looked after the poor, fasted, studied Latin, and took part in the public offices of the Church. Two of the princes asking for her hand in marriage were Austria's Count Hugo and Conrad, king of Jerusalem. She outfitted ten knights for the crusade, paid for all their expenses, since she could not go on the crusade herself, and received the sad news that her brother, St. Louis, had been captured by the Muslims.

During the lifetime of her mother, Blanche of Castille, Isabelle could do little to carry out her plan to live some kind of a religious life, but after her mother's death, she founded a monastery of Poor Clares, drafted a rule for them, and had St. Bonaventure himself, minister general of the Franciscans, work on the constitutions.

Blessed Isabelle of France, however, was a wise and shrewd virgin, and she knew that because of her royal status, she would most certainly be elected abbess, which she simply did not want. She lived in the convent, dressed like a religious but refused to take vows, and even kept some of her property so that she could continue to help the monastery. In her determination to live for God, she put everything else aside, something that won her the admiration of even the pope himself, who praised her for her single-mindedness.

She died in 1270, a few months before her brother, who embarked on another crusade that year and died at Tunis.

Thought for the Day: Some are given the gift very young to see through the shallowness of honor and position and strike out on an independent course to God and holiness. Most people envy royalty, not realizing the dangers and distractions of such a high position. Blessed Isabelle made sure that nothing would keep her from God and walked a very singular pathway to Him. Something of her determination should be part of our own quest for holiness.

From 'The Catholic One Year Bible': . . . "If anyone of you wants to be my follower," he told them, "you must put aside your own pleasures and shoulder your cross, and follow me closely. If you insist on saving your life, you will lose it. Only those who throw away their lives for my sake and for the sake of the Good News will ever know what it means to really live." — Mark 8:34-35

St. Gabriel Possenti *(FEBRUARY 27)*

On a summer day a little over a hundred years ago, a slim figure in a black cassock stood facing a gang of mercenaries in a small town in Piedmont, Italy. He had just disarmed one of the soldiers who was attacking a young girl, had faced the rest of the band fearlessly, then drove them all out of the village at the point of a gun. The young man was Francesco Possenti, whose father was lawyer for the Papal States and who had recently joined the Passionist Order, taking the name of Brother Gabriel.

Francesco Possenti had been the fanciest dresser in town as well as the best dancer. He was a superb horseman and an excellent marksman. Engaged to two girls at the same time and a great partygoer, he had shocked his family by announcing after his graduation that he was going to become a Passionist monk. No one believed him and expected him back within a few weeks. He stayed, and when Garibaldi's mercenaries swept down through Italy ravaging villages, Brother Gabriel showed the kind of man he was by confronting them, astonishing them with his marksmanship, and saving the small village where his monastery was located.

He had become very sick during his school years and had promised that if he got better, he would dedicate his life to God. St. Gabriel Possenti got better and forgot about it. He got sick again and made the same promise, but again got well and forgot his promise. Once, during a church procession in which a great banner of Our Lady, Help of Christians, was being carried, the eyes of Our Lady looked straight at him and he heard the words: "Keep your promise." Shaken, he remembered his promise, changed his life completely, and entered the Passionists.

He hoped to be sent to the missions after his ordination to the priesthood, but at the young age of twenty-four, he died. Canonized in 1920, he is, along with St. Aloysius, one of the patrons of youth. He was very fond of his family and is particularly remembered as a remarkable young man who, at the age of twenty, threw all aside for God, determined to become a saint.

Thought for the Day: By his courage, St. Gabriel showed that holiness is in no way opposed to the best qualities of manhood. He showed courage in very dangerous circumstances, where he could have very well been killed. We may not have to face such dangers, but we do need that kind of courage to witness to our faith on a daily basis.

From 'The Catholic One Year Bible': . . . Suddenly his face began to shine with glory, and his clothing became dazzling white, . . . a cloud covered them, blotting out the sun, and a voice from the cloud said, "*This* is my beloved Son. Listen to *him*." — Mark 9:2-3, 7

Like her contemporary St. Margaret of Cortona, Blessed Angela of Foligno made a bad beginning. Until she was forty, she thought little of God, and her personal life left much to be desired. She was married to a very rich man and had several sons, and according to her own admission she wanted only to have a good time. She does not seem to have lived an openly sinful life, just a very careless one.

Then, when she was about forty years of age, something happened. She was never quite able to explain what it was. She changed her life completely, became a Franciscan tertiary, and simply wanted to throw everything aside to live for God. This she could not do, since her husband and her sons were still alive, as was her mother, to whom she was deeply attached. Within a short space of time, her mother, her husband, and her sons died, and she found herself free to devote herself entirely to God.

Like St. Catherine of Siena and St. Catherine of Genoa, mystical graces were poured upon her, overturning completely her way of thinking and her interior life. She tried to write down what had happened to her, and this became her *Book of Visions and Instruction*, recorded by her spiritual director, a Franciscan friar. She gathered around her a number of followers; deeply rooted in the Franciscan tradition of poverty and love of the Passion of Christ, they took care of the poor, tended to the sick in hospitals, and looked after lepers. Her mystical experiences were remarkable, a constant feature of her life, and she showed profound theological knowledge, even though she was not well educated.

Her conversion, however, was not sudden. By her own admission, she had to climb "eighteen steps" in her spiritual ascent, and only after reaching the eighteenth step did she sell the castle she had lived in and which she loved very much.

At the end of 1308, she knew that her end was near. With her spiritual family around her and giving each one of them her final words of encouragement, she died peacefully on January 4, 1309, and was beatified in 1693. Her writings have received the praise of popes and theologians, and she is considered one of the most authoritative exponents of the mystical life.

Thought for the Day: In spite of her amazing graces, it took Blessed Angela of Foligno a long time to give up her castle. That should be encouraging to us who have to walk more humble ways. Holiness does not come all in one leap, and we have to be patient with ourselves and our weaknesses.

From 'The Catholic One Year Bible': "Good salt is worthless if it loses its saltiness; it can't season anything. So don't lose your flavor! Live in peace with each other." — Mark 9:50

THE SAINTS OF MARCH

St. David *(MARCH 1)*

David, the patron of Wales, lived in the sixth century, the golden age of Welsh monasticism.

Monasticism had come to Roman Britain from France, inspired by the monasteries of St. Martin of Tours and the island monastery of Lerins. It was a new and exciting way of life, and dozens of monasteries were soon founded in the British Isles, many of them in what is now known as Wales. Wales at that time was part of Roman Britain and only took on its distinctive Welsh character after the invasion of Britain by the Anglo-Saxons around the time when St. David lived.

David was the son of a princely family. He was educated at a nearby monastery; hearing of a holy man named Paulinus, who lived on an island, he went to study under him, following his ordination to the priesthood. After his studies with St. Paulinus, he himself founded several monasteries, the most famous of which is Glastonbury, the legendary site of the King Arthur saga. His most famous abbey was Mynyw, where he settled. The members of his monastic community lived a very austere life, kept absolute silence, tilled the ground to support themselves, and drank little else besides water. For this reason, David was called *aquaticus*, the water drinker.

David attended several synods, and at one of these he was elected primate of the Cambrian Church. He accepted the position on condition that the seat of his diocese be at his monastery of Mynyw.

He seems to have traveled to Jerusalem to be consecrated, perhaps also to visit the monasteries that flourished in the Holy Land at that time. He ruled his diocese until he was a very old man, loved and revered by everyone. His last advice to his monks was: "Be joyful and keep the faith. Do those little things you have seen and heard from me."

Thought for the Day: Like many monks before and after him, St. David was noted for his gentleness and simplicity. Sometimes, from a sense of our own importance, we try to make others seem small, wrapped up in a sense of our own superiority. Nothing of this nature is found in the saints. It is something to imitate.

From 'The Catholic One Year Bible': . . . "You lack only one thing," [Jesus said to the young man seeking the kingdom of God]; "go and sell all you have and give the money to the poor — and you shall have treasure in heaven — and come, follow me." — Mark 10:21

Blessed Agnes of Bohemia *(MARCH 2)*

The life of Agnes of Bohemia sounds almost like a fairy tale. As a three-year-old princess, she is promised to a Prince Charming; when her Prince Charming dies, she is promised to another Prince Charming. This second Prince Charming ends up marrying someone else, and Agnes, tired of the whole business, decides to consecrate herself to God.

Blessed Agnes of Bohemia had "Good King Wenceslaus" as her ancestor, was a relative of St. Elizabeth of Hungary, and became a close associate of St. Clare of Assisi.

At the age of three, she was betrothed to the son of the duke of Silesia and sent off to a monastery to be educated. When she was six, the duke's son died and three years later she was betrothed again, this time to the son of Emperor Frederick II. She was sent to the Austrian court to await her marriage, but the duke of Austria had other plans and married his own daughter to the prince. By this time, Agnes had decided to consecrate herself to God but found that the emperor himself wanted her for his wife; when she was twenty-eight, her brother made arrangements for her to go to the imperial court.

Under pressure from all sides, she wrote to the pope and told him of her desire to be free from these earthly ties, prompting the pope to send his legate to her brother's court. Her brother explained her wishes to the emperor, who said: "If she had left me for a mortal man, I would seek revenge; but I cannot take offense if she prefers the King of Heaven to myself." The princess was free.

She contacted St. Clare and built a monastery for Poor Clares in her brother's kingdom. When it was completed, Clare sent five sisters to start the foundation. Agnes entered the convent, and hundreds of girls from the nobility followed her. She was later elected abbess. She lived to the age of seventy-seven and died on March 2, 1282.

Thought for the Day: Sometimes we have to break out of the mold into which others have placed us and hew our own unique pathway to God. A princess is expected to be a princess, but Blessed Agnes saw something more valuable and more important and refused the throne of an empress. She knew what she wanted and would let nothing stand in her way. When God calls, we leave all else behind.

From 'The Catholic One Year Bible': ". . . I, the Messiah, will be arrested and taken before the chief priests and the Jewish leaders, who will sentence me to die and hand me over to the Romans to be killed. They will mock me and spit on me and flog me with their whips and kill me; but after three days I will come back to life again." — Mark 10:33-34

Blessed Katharine Drexel *(MARCH 3)*

Mother Katharine Drexel died in 1955, within the memory of many of us, and so she is very close to us in time. In 1988, she became Blessed Katharine Drexel and is fondly remembered by many people who are still alive.

She was born in Philadelphia in 1858. When her father, who was the founder of a Philadelphia banking house, died in 1885, she inherited a large fortune. With the help of Pope Leo XIII, she decided to dedicate her life to God and to devote her fortune to the American Indian and black American missions of the United States.

In 1889, she made her novitiate with the Sisters of Mercy in Pittsburgh; in 1891, she founded the Sisters of the Blessed Sacrament for Indians and Colored People. Her first convent was the old Drexel summer home at Torresdale, Pennsylvania.

The need for her work was very great, and requests for sisters soon came from the South and Southwest. She built and maintained missions and schools and sent her nuns to staff them. In 1915, she founded Xavier University in New Orleans and continued to expand the facilities of the university. By 1935, she had made forty-nine foundations throughout the country, mostly in the South and Southwest. She kept up continual correspondence with her missions and schools and in each letter usually included a generous check for the missionary work her sisters were doing.

She suffered a heart attack in 1935 but continued to travel to her missions, taking an active interest in the work of each one. She celebrated the golden jubilee of her congregation in 1941, and Pope Pius XII described her work as "a glorious page in the annals of the Church."

During the last years of her life, Mother Katharine Drexel was an invalid, spending much time in prayer, an example of love and devotion to her nuns. At her death in 1955, at the age of ninety-six, she had spent twelve million dollars of her inheritance for the American Indian and black American missions. She was beatified by Pope John Paul II on November 20, 1988.

Thought for the Day: At first Blessed Katharine was going to give only her fortune to the work of the missions but instead, at the suggestion of the pope, gave herself. Her long life was spent bringing the faith to others and inspiring others to join her. God wants more than our generosity — He wants us. Perhaps we should look around and see how we might serve Him.

From 'The Catholic One Year Bible': . . . "If only you have faith in God — this is the absolute truth — you can say to this Mount of Olives, 'Rise up and fall into the Mediterranean,' and your command will be obeyed." — Mark 11:22-23

Casimir died at the age of twenty-three, a remarkable young man who spent his life in palaces and courts. He was a prince of the royal house of Poland, the third of thirteen children; his father was King Casimir IV.

He was given an outstanding education, as was fitting for a prince; his tutor was Jan Dlugosz, the noted historian. When St. Casimir was thirteen, the Hungarians, unhappy with their king, requested King Casimir to replace him, and Prince Casimir was sent to take over the throne, at the head of a large army. Hearing that the incumbent king was preparing for battle, coupled with the fact that Casimir's own soldiers were deserting on every side, the prince returned to Cracow, convinced that his mission was unjust.

This angered his father, who sent him from the capital to a castle at Dobzki. Sickened by the injustice of the dynastic battles of his time, Casimir refused to ever again lead an army, even though his father commissioned him several times and the Hungarians again requested Prince Casimir for their throne. For a time, he was regent of the Polish kingdom when his father was in Lithuania. Later, his father wanted to arrange a marriage for him with the daughter of Emperor Frederick III, but Casimir had vowed himself to a life of celibacy and declined the marriage.

The young prince was also grand duke of Lithuania and died en route to that country, most probably of tuberculosis, at the age of twenty-three. He was buried in the cathedral at Vilna and is the patron saint of both Poland and Lithuania. He was canonized in 1521.

Thought for the Day: The calendar of the saints is studded with young saints: Agnes, Aloysius, Dominic Savio, Maria Goretti . . . and Casimir. They chose to be different, independent, and very bold, and they had to walk a very singular path to sanctity. Casimir and Aloysius were princes and chose devotion to God at a very early age. Youth, too, needs its saints.

From 'The Catholic One Year Bible': ". . . Tell us, is it right to pay taxes to Rome, or not?" [Jesus' answer was:] "Show me a coin and I'll tell you." When they handed it to him, he asked, "Whose picture and title is this on the coin?" They replied, "The emperor's." "All right," he said, "if it is his, give it to him. But everything that belongs to God must be given to God!" — Mark 12:14-17

St. Eusebius of Cremona *(MARCH 5)*

Cremona is famous for the violin makers who lived there in the seventeenth century, but it was also the birthplace of Eusebius, who was born there in the fourth century. On a visit to Rome, he made the acquaintance of St. Jerome, then secretary to the pope and spiritual director of a wide circle of people. When Jerome left for Antioch and Bethlehem with St. Paula and St. Eustochium, Eusebius went along, and became the friend, associate, and confidante of the great biblical scholar.

Planning to set up a hostel for the many pilgrims coming to Bethlehem, Jerome sent Eusebius to Dalmatia (Jerome's birthplace) and Italy to collect funds, selling property that Jerome had in Dalmatia and property that Eusebius had in Cremona. Spending some time in Rome, Eusebius lived near Rufinus, an old friend of Jerome's, but one with whom, at the time, he was not on the best of terms. Noticing that Rufinus was translating the writings of Origen, St. Eusebius of Cremona, who was an anti-Origenist, secretly took the copy and sent it to Jerome, causing a serious rift between Rufinus and Jerome and causing as well a number of Jerome's most explosive letters.

Eusebius returned to Bethlehem to be near his friend but later returned to Italy and died there. He is mentioned in letters of Jerome, and Jerome dedicated several of his biblical commentaries to him.

As a loyal friend of Jerome's, Eusebius became involved in Jerome's disputes over Origen, and he seems to have been responsible for Pope Anastasius' condemnation of Origen's writings. Eusebius died in 423 and was said to have been buried beside Jerome in Bethlehem, but this is doubtful. There is an altar in the crypt of the Nativity dedicated to him. Most of the information about him is gleaned from Jerome's writings.

Thought for the Day: Even saints sometimes do disgraceful things, and St. Eusebius's theft of Rufinus's manuscript was the thoughtless act of an overzealous friend embroiled in the controversies of the day. It is good to know that even saints have faults and that such faults detract nothing from their holiness. A saint is a sinner who kept on trying.

From 'The Catholic One Year Bible': . . . "Of all the commandments, which is the most important?" Jesus replied, "The one that says, 'Hear, O Israel! The Lord our God is the one and only God. And you must love him with all your heart and soul and mind and strength.' The second is: 'You must love others as much as yourself.' No other commandments are greater than these." — Mark 12:28-31

St. Colette

Nicolette was her baptismal name, but everyone called her Colette. Her father was a carpenter at the abbey of Corbie in France, and after the death of her parents, when she was seventeen, the abbot of Corbie took her under his wing. She gave all her inheritance to the poor, entered the Third Order of St. Francis, and lived in a small hermitage beside the abbey church.

She was providentially called to restore the primitive observance of the Poor Clares, and St. Francis himself appeared to her giving her a mandate to do this. She consulted her confessor and eventually went on foot to Nice to obtain permission of the antipope Benedict XIII, who was recognized by the French as pope. He gave her his mandate to reform the convents and made her superior of all the convents she might reform.

It was a huge task, and discouragements were many and great. Her persistence, however, broke down opposition, and, one by one, Poor Clare monasteries accepted her rule. St. Colette became the friend of dukes and duchesses, kings and princes — and people from all walks of life sought her advice and her prayers. She charmed everyone she met, and miracles multiplied by her prayers.

These were the days of Joan of Arc and the occupation of France by England, and there is even a legend that Colette met the Maid of Orléans, leading her army to battle. In the midst of severe political upheavals, Colette founded seventeen convents, reformed others, and a number of Franciscan friars accepted her rule.

Like St. Francis she loved animals and was very fond of children. Her life of prayer was unceasing and she prayed for the whole world. At the age of sixty-seven, while visiting her convents in Ghent, Belgium, she became very sick and died there. She was canonized in 1807.

Thought for the Day: Like St. Joan of Arc, St. Colette had a mission from the Lord, and, when she was sure of that mission, gave her whole life to it. In her day, holiness had declined even among religious and she was determined to recover a life of holiness for the daughters of St. Clare. No obstacles turned her back, for God was on her side. With her God, she could accomplish all things.

From 'The Catholic One Year Bible': . . . "Don't let anyone mislead you," he said, "for many will come declaring themselves to be your Messiah, and will lead many astray. . . . And everyone will hate you because you are mine. But all who endure to the end without renouncing me will be saved." — Mark 13:5-6, 13

SS. Perpetua and Felicity *(MARCH 7)*

The *Passio Perpetuae et Felicitatis* (Latin for *The Suffering of Perpetua and Felicity*) is one of the most ancient Christian documents and was so highly regarded in the early Church that St. Augustine had to warn against its being revered as Holy Scripture.

The martyrdom of SS. Perpetua and Felicity took place during the persecution of Septimius Severus in the year 202, in Carthage, where many Christians refused to deny their faith. Perpetua was a young wife and mother, twenty-two years of age, and Felicity was a slave who was expecting a child. At first, they were confined to their homes, and Perpetua's father, who was not a Christian, urged her to apostatize to save her life. A few days later, the two women, along with several others, were in prison.

Much of the *Passio* is written by Perpetua herself, and she tells of her sufferings and visions in down-to-earth graphic language.

Her father again tried to dissuade her and pleaded with her, even when she stood before the Roman court. "He departed full of grief," she wrote.

At first Felicity was not with them, since it was unlawful to execute a woman with child. Three days before the execution, Felicity gave birth to her child and she joined the others in their prison. They were flogged, led into the amphitheater of Carthage, and beheaded. Four others died with Perpetua and Felicity, and one of them, Saturus, who authored the rest of the account during their imprisonment, was killed by a wild leopard.

The martyrdom took place before crowds of people who enjoyed the spectacle of Christians dying by violence, although some were converted by the courage of the martyrs.

In 1907, a French priest, excavating in the ruins of Carthage, found an ancient inscription where these martyrs were buried. The inscription read: "Here are the martyrs Saturus, Saturninus, Revocatus, Secundulus, Felicity and Perpetua who suffered on the nones of March." It is hard to believe that it happened almost eighteen hundred years ago.

Thought for the Day: SS. Perpetua and Felicity were ordinary wives and mothers, who were swept up in the madness of persecution, who loved their families and their children, and certainly were not eager to die. But heroism can be found everywhere, and their example has inspired Christians who have had to suffer for their faith. Their example should inspire us to bear witness to our faith openly.

From 'The Catholic One Year Bible': "Keep a sharp lookout! For you do not know when I will come, at evening, at midnight, early dawn or late daybreak. Don't let me find you sleeping. *Watch for my return!"* — Mark 13:35-37

St. John of God

Everyone thought he was crazy, this former soldier who ran around town begging for mercy, dressed in outlandish clothes, and had tried to run off to Africa to become a martyr. He had lived the wild life of a soldier in the army of Charles V and had outdone his companions in evil living. Now, he wanted to change his life, but he didn't know how. A great preacher, John of Ávila, had touched his soul and everyone thought he was a lunatic. For a while, St. John of God was committed to an insane asylum.

The preacher found him and convinced him to care for the sick poor of the city, who had no one to take care of them. This was the beginning of John of God. He was no youngster; he was over forty years old, and what he was to do in the next few years was astonishing. He became the marvel of the city, others joined him in his work, and the archbishop of Granada gave his blessing to the work. Another bishop gave him a habit and a rule, but this was incidental. All he wanted were co-workers, and the work grew beyond his wildest imaginings.

When he had to raise money for his sick, he went about the streets rattling a tin can, saying: "Do yourselves a good turn, ladies and gentlemen, do yourselves a good turn."

He died in a very strange way. There was no limit to the good he would do for others. He passed by a river one day and saw a man drowning. He jumped in the river and saved him, but he caught a severe cold and came home shivering with a high fever. He lay down upon a bed in his hospital and could not get up. The bishop ordered him to get better care, and he was removed to a private home. He asked if he could be alone for a little while, and everyone left. When they returned, he was on his knees before a crucifix, dead. It was the eighth of March, a little after midnight in the year 1550. He was fifty-five years of age.

Thought for the Day: It is possible to do much good for others, if we only put our minds to it and don't count the cost and don't worry about who gets the credit. For all his pains, many thought St. John of God a lunatic, but it didn't bother him. He gave back good for ill treatment and never stopped doing good to others.

From 'The Catholic One Year Bible': . . ."Why pick on me, to give me the burden of a people like this? Are these *my* children? Am I their father?. . . . Where am I supposed to get meat for all these people? . . . I can't carry this nation by myself! The load is far too heavy! If you are going to treat me like this, please kill me right now, . . ." — Numbers 11:11-15

St. Frances of Rome *(MARCH 9)*

This was a sane, practical woman, who married young (she was barely thirteen), became a devoted wife and mother, banded together with her friends to look after the poor and unfortunate, and made the whole city of Rome her special mission.

It was a troubled time for Rome, what with political upheavals of every kind, terror and death stalking the streets, a time when Rome was the battleground between pope and antipope. Frances with her little band spread out through the city as disaster struck, helping the poor, getting the sick to hospitals, her own family, the Ponziani, taking over the administration of a hospital. During one assault upon the city by the troops of the antipope, the Ponziani home was devastated, family possessions were destroyed, homes were pillaged, and the sick and dying were everywhere. Lorenzo (Frances' husband), who was one of the leaders loyal to the legitimate pope, had to go into hiding, leaving his family behind.

Frances was holed up with the rest of her family in a corner of their ruined home. One of her sons died of the pestilence and Frances turned the home itself into a hospital. She was adored by her husband, who was amazed at her astonishing achievements, at the same time never neglecting her household. "It is good for a married woman to be devout," she once said, "but she must never forget she is a housewife."

The family had lost its possessions and its fortunes, and after the Council of Constance, which brought an end to the violence, they again recovered their lands. Her husband, a broken man, told her he would release her from her marriage vows if she would only live under the same roof with him, and here the marvel of St. Frances of Rome began. She founded a group of women to work with the poor, gave them a place to stay, and established them as Benedictine Oblates. When her husband died, she joined them as a simple novice, refusing to be called their foundress. She still cared for her children and spent much time in prayer.

She died in her son's house, tired and sick, but watched over by an angel whom she had seen beside her since the death of her daughter. "He beckons me to follow him," were her last words.

Thought for the Day: What an amazing lady! St. Frances of Rome was an ordinary wife and mother whose love for God and others knew no bounds and who trusted in God to give her guidance. There was nothing she felt she could not do and she let nothing stop her. We need something of that love and that trust and that energy. We, too, can accomplish wonders.

From 'The Catholic One Year Bible': "Father, Father," he said, "everything is possible for you. Take away this cup from me. Yet I want your will, not mine." — Mark 14:36

St. Dominic Savio *(MARCH 10)*

Here is a boy-saint who died at the age of fifteen, was one of the great hopes of St. John Bosco for the future of his congregation, and was canonized in 1954.

He was one of ten children of Carlo and Birgitta Savio. Carlo was a blacksmith and Birgitta was a seamstress. When Don Bosco was looking for young men to train as priests for his Salesian Order, his parish priest suggested Dominic Savio. Dominic became more than a credit to Don Bosco's school — he single-handedly organized those who were to be the nucleus of Don Bosco's order.

St. Dominic Savio was twelve when he met Don Bosco and organized a group of boys into the Company of the Immaculate Conception. Besides its religious purpose, the boys swept and took care of the school and looked after the boys that no one seemed to pay any attention to. When, in 1859, Don Bosco chose the young men to be the first members of his congregation, all of them had been members of Dominic's Company.

For all that, Dominic was a normal, high-spirited boy who sometimes got into trouble with his teachers because he would often break out laughing. However, he was generally well disciplined and gradually gained the respect of the tougher boys in Don Bosco's school.

In other circumstances, Dominic might have become a little self-righteous snob, but Don Bosco showed him the heroism of the ordinary and the sanctity of common sense. "Religion must be about us as the air we breathe," Don Bosco would say, and Dominic Savio wore holiness like the clothes on his back.

He called his long hours of prayer "his distractions." In 1857, at the age of fifteen, he caught tuberculosis and was sent home to recover. On the evening of March 9, he asked his father to say the prayers for the dying. His face lit up with an intense joy and he said to his father: "I am seeing most wonderful things!" These were his last words.

Thought for the Day: "I can't do big things," St. Dominic Savio once said, "but I want everything to be for the glory of God." His was the way of the ordinary: cheerfulness, fidelity in little things, helping others, playing games, obeying his superiors. This heroism in little things is the stuff of holiness.

From 'The Catholic One Year Bible': . . . The High Priest tore at his clothes and said: "What more do we need? Why wait for witnesses? You have heard his blasphemy. What is your verdict?" And the vote for the death sentence was unanimous. — **Mark 14:63-64**

This holy man lived in a very difficult time and, as patriarch of Jerusalem in 638, he saw the Holy City taken over by the Muslims and himself an exile. It was the bitter crown of a very dedicated life.

He was born in Damascus, Syria, and as a young man was a brilliant student. He became a monk, lived at St. Sabas in Jerusalem with a friend, the famous John Moschus, and then made a tour of the monastic settlements in Egypt. The patriarch of Alexandria at the time was St. John the Almsgiver, who invited the two friends to stay for a time in Alexandria.

Later, the two friends made a trip to Rome where John Moschus died. Sophronius returned to the Holy Land and was elected patriarch of Jerusalem. At this time, both East and West were disturbed by the Monothelite controversy, which denied a human will in Christ, and Sophronius became the defender of orthodox teaching. He wrote, traveled to Alexandria and Constantinople, and furthered the calling of a council to condemn the heresy. This was done by the Council of the Lateran in 649, which brought about the imprisonment and death of the reigning pope who had called the council, Pope St. Martin I.

Earlier, in 636, Sophronius's home city was taken by the Saracens and in 638 they surrounded Jerusalem. Sophronius strengthened his people by his words and example, but the city fell and Sophronius fled to Alexandria where he died soon afterward of a broken heart. In Jerusalem, the remains of the great Temple were destroyed, replaced by the Dome of the Rock by Caliph Omar.

We have in Latin one of the many sermons of St. Sophronius, which he gave at Christmas of 634, when Bethlehem had been captured by the Muslims and the usual Christmas pilgrimage to the place of Jesus' birth could not be made. The loss of his patriarchal city, the holiest in all Christendom, undoubtedly hastened his death.

Thought for the Day: Good bishops and pastors carry on the work of Christ in our midst, and we should always be grateful for the shepherds that God gives to His Church. "I send you as a sheep among wolves," Jesus told His disciples, and being shepherd of the flock of Christ is not easy. We should pray for the shepherds God has given us.

From 'The Catholic One Year Bible': And they brought Jesus to a place called Golgotha (Golgotha means skull). Wine drugged with bitter herbs was offered to him there, but he refused it. And then they crucified him — and threw dice for his clothes. — Mark 15:22-24

She was a little girl, very pretty, born into a very poor family, whose father died when she was very young. As a little girl she learned to sew and spin, spending most of her time at home.

After her father's death, she was struck with a strange and paralyzing illness. She became misshapen and ugly, in constant pain, unable to get out of bed or even to move. Her mother took care of her but had to leave her for hours at a time to attend to her work. Seraphina's only consolation was the crucifix, and she realized that she was called to imitate the suffering Christ.

Yet she never complained. She managed to remain serene, and something beautiful shone out of her face. Then she was struck another blow. Her mother died, and she was left completely destitute, her neighbors repelled by her appearance and her sickness, her only friend a girl named Beldia who visited her and brought her food.

In her reading, St. Seraphina had heard of the great sufferings of Pope St.Gregory the Great and he became her special saint. She prayed to him, drew strength from the sufferings that he had to endure, and prayed that he would obtain for her the patience she needed to bear her own sufferings. She was now so weak and helpless that it was clear to everyone she could not live very long.

Eight days before her death, alone and almost completely forsaken, St. Gregory appeared to her and told her: "Dear child, on my feast day, God will give you rest" (in those days his feastday was celebrated on March 12). On that day, she died. The whole city attended her funeral and from that moment everyone began to pray to her. On the place where she had lain, her neighbors found white violets growing, and even today in the village of San Gcminiano where she lived, the white violets that bloom in March are called Santa Fina flowers. She died on March 12, 1253, at the age of fifteen.

Thought for the Day: Sufferings and pain are difficult for anyone to bear, and in St. Seraphina's case they were a true martyrdom. Seraphina had to make sense out of it, young as she was. She drew strength from the sufferings of Jesus and found her happiness in God, in spite of her terrible afflictions. We have little reason to complain about ours.

From 'The Catholic One Year Bible': . . . "Don't be so surprised. Aren't you looking for Jesus, the Nazarene who was crucified? He isn't here! He has come back to life! Look, that's where his body was lying. Now go and give this message to his disciples including Peter: 'Jesus is going ahead of you to Galilee. You will see him there, just as he told you before he died!' " — Mark 16:6-7

St. Euphrasia *(MARCH 13)*

The story of this saint could well have been written by Hans Christian Andersen as a fairy tale. She was a close relative of the Emperor Theodosius, and her father, who was a senator, died soon after she was born. The emperor took Euphrasia and her mother under his special protection and, when Euphrasia was five years old, betrothed her to the son of another senator, the marriage to take place when she was of age.

Euphrasia's mother had many suitors as well at the court in Constantinople, and to avoid all this attention, determined to remain unmarried, she took her little daughter to Egypt and settled near a convent of nuns. The little girl was fascinated with the nuns and asked to live with them, and her mother let her do so for a short while, thinking the little girl wanted to play at being a nun. The mother found that her little seven-year-old thrived on the life, and the sisters persuaded her to let Euphrasia stay.

Young as she was, St. Euphrasia was clothed with the habit of a nun, considered herself betrothed to Christ, and was the delight of the other nuns. Sometime later, her mother died and she was left in the care of the mother abbess.

Meanwhile, in Constantinople, the young man she had been betrothed to came of age and asked for his bride. A letter was dispatched by the emperor for Euphrasia to come to the imperial court to be married. Euphrasia wrote to him, begging to be allowed to remain in the life she had chosen, placing her property and inheritance in the hands of the emperor. He allowed her to remain, and she began to devote herself to the tiniest duties in the convent, afraid that the thought of what she might have been would start distracting her.

Some of the nuns thought she had hopes of becoming the abbess of the monastery, a position of great importance, and that was why she turned down the offer of marriage. They told her so to her face, and her only response was to fall at their feet and beg them to pray for her. She remained a simple nun for the rest of her short life, dying at the age of thirty in the year 420. She is honored in the Greek, Russian, and Roman calendars.

Thought for the Day: Some, like St. Euphrasia, find their vocation very early, and it becomes a treasure that enriches their whole life; others come to their vocation late. What is important is not when the call comes; what is important is living the faith, and that is something that is done day by day, hour by hour, and minute by minute. There is no short cut.

From 'The Catholic One Year Bible': . . . "Don't be afraid, Zacharias! For I come to tell you that God has heard your prayer, and your wife Elizabeth will bear you a son! And you are to name him John." — Luke 1:13

St. Matilda *(MARCH 14)*

Matilda, the daughter of the count of Westphalia, came from a long line of independent-minded Saxons who had fought against Charlemagne in his hunger for territory. She was sent to the convent at Erfurt to be educated, where her grandmother was abbess. She was a remarkable beauty, it was said, deeply religious, and one of the most learned women of her time. She married Henry the Fowler, at that time heir to the dukedom of Saxony, later to succeed to the German throne.

They had five children: two became kings, two became queens, and one became archbishop of Cologne. St. Matilda, while eminently queenly, was kind and gracious to everyone, gave liberally to the poor, loved her husband and children, and was the joy of her husband who trusted her in all things, supporting the great liberality for which she was noted.

After twenty-three years of marriage, her husband died and her son Otto succeeded him. Otto's younger brother, Henry, rebelled, wanting the throne for himself, but Matilda brought peace to the two brothers. When she gave away all of her jewelry and began living a simple life, she was accused by Otto of squandering the royal treasures. He sent spies to watch her every move; Henry, now duke of Bavaria, joined the campaign against their mother. Matilda's only remark, showing her subtle sense of humor, was: "At least they are united in something. It's better than seeing them fighting."

To get rid of their suspicions, she resigned her inheritance and went back to her childhood home. At her leaving, disaster fell upon the kingdom, and the sons asked their mother's forgiveness, persuading her to return to court. Henry again revolted against his brother, and there was war between them. On Henry's death, Otto went to Rome to be crowned by the pope, and Matilda was made regent in his absence.

In 965, she retired to her monastic foundation at Nordhausen and died soon afterward. She was buried beside her husband and was venerated as a saint from the moment of her death.

Thought for the Day: St. Matilda had to be many things: wife, mother, queen, grandmother, even regent of the kingdom. She never had a false sense of her own importance and was simply good to everyone. Her position enabled her to do a lot of good and she did not shirk from the effort. Our greatest opportunity for good is to those we live with and to the people around us.

From 'The Catholic One Year Bible': . . . "The Holy Spirit shall come upon you, and the power of God shall overshadow you; so the baby born to you will be utterly holy — the Son of God." — **Luke 1:35**

Clement Hofbauer was a baker's son who was too poor to study for the priesthood and became a baker himself for a time. He decided to live as a hermit, but the Emperor Joseph's decree against religious hermits sent him into the mountains of Tivoli, where the bishop gave him permission to live in his diocese. There he realized that his vocation was elsewhere and returned to Vienna.

After Mass one day, he offered to hail down a carriage for two ladies at Mass, and when they discovered that he was too poor to study for the priesthood, they paid for his education at the University of Vienna. He and his friend Thaddeus Hubl visited Rome, met St. Alphonsus de Liguori, and joined the Redemptorists.

The friends were ordained and returned to Vienna, but because of the hostility of the government against religious orders, they went to Warsaw where the papal nuncio gave them a church, and their work began among the German-speaking Catholics in the city. There St. Clement's amazing apostolate began. He founded schools and orphanages, begged in taverns to support his work, set up religious associations, and established Redemptorist houses in southern Germany and Switzerland.

Then, it seemed that everything that he had worked for would be destroyed. Napoleon suppressed all religious orders in 1808, and Clement and his Redemptorists were arrested and imprisoned. After their release, they spread out through Europe and Clement of Hofbauer returned to Vienna.

He was appointed chaplain to the Ursuline nuns, became the most popular preacher and confessor in Vienna, and made friends with writers, philosophers, and scientists as well as among the poor of the city. His influence was universal, and he worked with the prince of Bavaria to defeat the Congress of Vienna, which wanted to create a German national church.

He was indefatigable. He visited the sick in all the hospitals of the city, never refused a sick call, and was even accused of being a spy because of his many contacts. Single-handedly he restored Catholicism to Austria and firmly planted the Redemptorists on German soil. He died on March 15, 1820, and the whole of Vienna crowded into the cathedral for his funeral. He was canonized in 1909.

Thought for the Day: There is no limit to the good we can do and the lives we can reach. Each one of us is called to be an apostle of Jesus Christ and a bearer of good tidings. We all have a mission from Jesus Christ and the opportunity is all around us.

From 'The Catholic One Year Bible': ". . . You, my little son, shall be called the prophet of the glorious God, for you will prepare the way for the Messiah. You will tell his people how to find salvation through forgiveness of their sins." — Luke 1:76-77

St. Heribert of Cologne *(MARCH 16)*

Heribert found his life ambition thwarted by his father, but he made the best of it and found another pathway to holiness. He was born at Worms in the latter part of the tenth century and wanted to become a Benedictine monk, after studying as a youth at the abbey of Gorze. But his father disapproved and called him home; upon his return, he was made a canon of the cathedral and was ordained. He became the chancellor of Emperor Otto III and in 998 became archbishop of Cologne.

Since he could not become a monk, St. Heribert of Cologne cultivated an intense spiritual life, at the same time serving his people and his diocese tirelessly. He accompanied the emperor on a trip to Italy, where the emperor caught smallpox and died. It was Heribert who accompanied the body back to Aachen for burial, carrying with him the imperial insignia for the next emperor, St. Henry II. His relations with the new emperor were not the best, but Heribert served the new ruler loyally.

As time went on, the new emperor learned to appreciate the qualities of his chancellor and toward the end of their lives the two saints were very close. All the money he could spare from his own personal income, Heribert gave to the poor, sent money to priests throughout his diocese to help the destitute, and even went to hospitals and private homes to help the poor and the sick. During a great drought in the city, he led a procession through the streets of the city to the church of St. Severinus, and when he rose from his knees at the altar, a torrential rain came down and the year's harvest was saved. People in that part of Germany still pray to him for rain.

While on a pastoral visitation of his diocese, Heribert became ill with fever and had himself brought back to Cologne. He died a few days later and was buried at the monastery of Deutz, which he had founded with the help of Emperor Otto III. He was revered as a kindly bishop who gave himself intensely to prayer and poured the riches of his own spiritual life on his people. The confidante of emperors, he never lost touch with the God he served or the people to whom he was father and shepherd. He died in the year 1021.

Thought for the Day: Sometimes we can be put in what seems an impossible situation, with duties and obligations that seem to contradict each other. Politics and religion do not mix very well, but some are called to have one foot in both. What is important is that God should come first; then everything else falls into place.

From 'The Catholic One Year Bible': . . . "Don't be afraid!" he said. "I bring you the most joyful news ever announced, and it is for everyone! The Savior — yes, the Messiah, the Lord — has been born tonight in Bethlehem! How will you recognize him? You will find a baby wrapped in a blanket, lying in a manger!" — Luke 2:10-12

In the year 410, the Roman legions left Roman Britain for the last time, never to return. With their going, Irish pirates began to raid and pillage the western coast of Britain, burning villages and carrying off Britons into slavery in Ireland. On one of these raids, one of those taken was a sixteen-year-old named Patrick, whose life and history would be forever bound up in the Ireland of his captivity.

After six years, St. Patrick escaped and was taken to France; he returned home but had the memory of pagan Ireland burning in his mind. He went back to France, became a priest and eventually a bishop, then returned to Ireland. He came to be known as the prince of Irish saints and the Apostle of Ireland.

Whether the story of the great fire on the hill of Tara is true or not, it is symbolic of what happened. Patrick brought the light of the Catholic faith to the Irish, converted kings, founded churches, and set up his headquarters at Armagh. There he held a synod and consolidated his work, reading, according to one account, a papal letter, probably from Pope St. Leo the Great.

His life was often threatened. He faced the hardships of bad weather, friends who betrayed him, clergy in his home country who criticized him, and saw no reason to labor among the "barbarians." He was belittled by other bishops because of his lack of formal learning and was threatened with death many times. His spirit is caught in the *Deer Cry*, that lovely story of his escape from danger, and by his *Breastplate*, which expresses his deep faith in Christ.

Toward the end of his life, the legend runs, "St. Patrick went forth to the top of Mt. Aigli, and remained there for 40 days and 40 nights. . . . From this hill, Patrick blessed all the people of Ireland. . . . God told all the saints of Erin, past, present and future to come to the top of that mountain . . . to bless the tribes of Erin, so that Patrick might see the fruit of his labors, . . . for the choir of the saints of Erin came to visit him who was the father of them all."

That tells it all, as it tells the place he has had in the hearts of the Irish ever since.

Thought for the Day: The amazing influence of one man! St. Patrick converted a whole island and a whole nation, which shows the power of one good person. We have no way of knowing the fruit of our own lives or how many people our lives may touch. That is the power of holiness: it endures forever.

From 'The Catholic One Year Bible': . . . The child became a strong, robust lad, and was known for wisdom beyond his years; and God poured out his blessing on him. — Luke 2:40

St. Cyril of Jerusalem *(MARCH 18)*

Cyril was a man caught in the doctrinal and ecclesiastical battles of the third century in the wake of the Arian heresy, which caused a crisis through the whole Christian world. Bishops fought bishops, patriarchs fought patriarchs, emperor fought pope, and sees changed hands as one party gained the upper hand.

St. Cyril of Jerusalem was born perhaps at Caesarea by the sea, Herod's great maritime city, and was ordained a priest by Maximus, bishop of Jerusalem. Jerusalem at that time was a suffragan see under Caesarea. The bishop of Caesarea was Arian in his sympathies, and Maximus and a number of other bishops declared him deposed at a synod held at Sardica. This caused something resembling a religious civil war in the Holy Land. The bishop of Caesarea, Acacius, in turn deposed Maximus.

When Maximus died in 348, Cyril succeeded him, favored by Acacius. The battle between Arian and orthodox continued all through Cyril's life, and his part in the drama is not fully clear. He is known, however, for other achievements.

We have in hand his catechetical instructions, which are a clear commentary on the Creed of Jerusalem, and in these he shows himself to be a superb teacher and a brilliant theologian, and we get a glimpse as well of the way in which new Christians were received into the Church. It is an unusual view of early Christian catechesis and the formation that was given those desiring baptism.

In the battle with Arianism, Cyril was three times banished from his see by order of the emperor; but with the accession of Theodosius to the imperial throne, Cyril was returned to Jerusalem and governed his see unhindered. He attended the Council of Constantinople in 381, and for the first time Jerusalem was recognized as a patriarchal see, along with Rome, Alexandria, Antioch, and Constantinople.

Cyril died about 386, a pillar of orthodoxy, one of the great teachers of the first Christian century. He was declared a Doctor of the Church in 1882.

Thought for the Day: In times of great turmoil and controversy, it is difficult sometimes to know what is true and what is right, and sometimes we have to grope our way along. We have to follow the truth as we see it and give it our full loyalty, at whatever cost. Sometimes that will mean that we are a majority of one. That is what truth demands of us.

From 'The Catholic One Year Bible': . . . "I baptize only with water; but someone is coming soon who has far higher authority than mine; in fact, I am not even worthy to be his slave. He will baptize you with fire — with the Holy Spirit." — Luke 3:16

St. Joseph *(MARCH 19)*

Little is known of St. Joseph's true history, and it is often forgotten that the Joseph who moves through the first pages of the Gospel was a very young man, possibly in his teens.

He was perhaps eighteen or twenty, Jewish to the core, a man who lived from a very young age perpetually on the threshold of mystery. He was also caught up in a political turmoil that split his nation right down the middle, and, for a young man, he was called upon to make some rather pressing and painful decisions.

The scenes in the Infancy Narratives of the Gospels are like scenes in an old icon, with very little revealed; but what is revealed is painted in rich, striking colors. The Son of God will be born into what appears to be a normal human famly, a normal Jewish family, and Jesus will be known to his neighbors as the "son of the carpenter."

The mysteries Joseph had to ponder and be a part of are bound up with the very salvation of the world: the trip to Bethlehem and the birth of Jesus; Herod's hatred and the Holy Family's flight in the night across the desert; the return to Nazareth and the years of Jesus' boyhood. Joseph did not live to see the fulfillment of Jesus' mission but must have glimpsed something of the wonder and marvel of it all, and perhaps something of the terror and tragedy. Like Mary, he must have kept all these things in his heart, pondering them.

In spite of his obscurity, or perhaps because of it, Joseph is the most popular of saints, the saint for all times and all peoples, the provider and the refuge, the patron of work and family, and the protector of the universal Church.

On the spur of the moment, he followed the divine call into the darkness, ready to face whatever challenges history would thrust upon him. He was uniquely the man of silence and the man always in readiness, ready to do God's will when he knew it, and ready to sacrifice everything for the mission thrust upon him. He is a fitting patron, not only for the universal Church, but for every one of us in the carrying out of our own mission.

Thought for the Day: St. Joseph was not spared the difficulties and hardships of normal living, and his closeness to the mystery of Jesus did not spare him problems and labor. He had to use his wits and his judgment and sometimes grope in the darkness. We should not be surprised if we, too, have to grope our way.

From 'The Catholic One Year Bible': The evil man gets rich for a moment, but the good man's reward lasts forever. The good man finds life, the evil man, death. — Proverbs 11:18-19

St. Cuthbert *(MARCH 20)*

In Durham Cathedral, in northern England, the body of St. Cuthbert rests under a stone slab, where it has rested for over a thousand years. Among the people of northern England, his memory is as fresh as if he had been buried yesterday.

He was a shepherd boy in the hills above the River Leader, and it was while tending sheep, late one night, that he saw in the sky an army of angels descending to escort a bright soul into heaven, and he marveled at what he had seen. The next day he was told that St. Aidan, bishop of Lindisfarne, had died at Bamburgh.

Not far from where he lived was another monastery, founded by the same Irish monks that lived at Lindisfarne, Melrose, and it was there that Cuthbert entered when he was scarcely sixteen and began that life that would make him the luminous contemplative that he became. After he was ordained, he would go on missionary journeys into the hill country, living in the hovels of the poor and cheering them in their many sufferings. Later, he was called by the bishop of Lindisfarne to lead the monastic community on that island monastery, since the bishop had to travel around his great diocese.

After a few years, Cuthbert received permission to live as a hermit seven miles out in the sea, but even there, people came from miles around to ask for his prayers and seek his advice. He lived alone on his island for almost ten years when the king, the bishops, and the people asked him to be bishop. He refused, but the king himself came to the island and begged him to take on the burden. Seeing the will of God, Cuthbert left his island solitude reluctantly.

He was bishop for less than two years, when he sensed that his life was nearing its end. He went back to his island home, wrapped up in God and the desire of heaven, slowly getting weaker. When he died, the few monks with him lit a great torch to signal to the monks on Lindisfarne that their holy father was dead. They carried him back to Lindisfarne and buried him. It was March 20, 687.

Eleven years later, his tomb was opened and they found his body, wrapped in his bishop's robes, totally incorrupt. Later, when the Vikings destroyed Lindisfarne, they carried his body all over northern England and finally brought it to rest at Durham where they built a beautiful cathedral over his body. His body is still there.

Thought for the Day: O God, who made St. Cuthbert a shining example of holiness and a lovely and luminous contemplative, help us, like him, to be homesick for eternity and to love You with a strong and powerful devotion.

From 'The Catholic One Year Bible': . . . "It is written in the Scriptures, 'Other things in life are much more important than bread!' " — Luke 4:4

Enda was a young Irish warrior, intent upon war and the slaughter of his enemies; he had a remarkable sister by the name of Fanchea, the abbess of a convent who would eventually be canonized. His father was Conall Derg of Oriel, and when his father died, he succeeded him as king and went off to fight his enemies.

Coming back from a bloody battle, St. Enda stopped by his sister's convent, the victory cries of his soldiers disturbing the convent and distressing his sister. Fanchea faced her brother and told him his hands were dripping with blood and that he should turn his mind to things spiritual. He promised to amend his ways if she would give him one of the young girls in the convent to marry, and Fanchea pretended to agree to his stipulation. Soon after, however, the "promised" bride-to-be died, and Fanchea brought her brother to look upon the corpse.

Faced with the reality of death, and by his sister's persuasion, Enda decided to study for the priesthood, and Fanchea sent him to Candida Casa in Roman Britain, a great center of monasticism in England. There he took monastic vows and was ordained.

Enda returned to Ireland and received a grant of land in the Aran Islands from Oengus, king of Cashel, his brother-in-law. There he founded a monastery, one of the first in Ireland, and he is considered the patriarch of Irish monks.

Most of the great Irish saints had some connection with Aran: St. Brendan was blessed for his voyage there; Jarlath of Tuam, Finnian of Clonard, and St. Columba called it the "Sun of the West." Aran became a miniature Mount Athos, with a dozen monasteries scattered over the island, the most famous, Killeany, where Enda himself lived. There that great tradition of austerity, holiness, and learning was begun that was to enrich Europe for the next thousand years.

Enda died in his little rock cell by the sea around the year 530, a very old man, and the *Martyrdom of Oengus* says that "it will never be known until the day of judgment the number of saints whose bodies lie in the soil of Aran."

Thought for the Day: The shortness of life strikes most people only on their deathbeds, and they never really reflect on how fleeting life is. Those who do think about it seriously, like St. Enda, usually end up doing something about it and investing their time in something really worthwhile. From such thinking, saints are born.

From 'The Catholic One Year Bible': As the sun went down that evening, all the villagers who had any sick people in their homes, no matter what their diseases were, brought them to Jesus; and the touch of his hands healed every one! — Luke 4:40

In his old age, St. Nicholas of Flüe was known as Bruder Klaus and holds a unique place in the history of Switzerland. In a way, he is something of a national symbol and a rallying point for the Swiss spirit. But he was not always Bruder Klaus.

He had been a soldier, a loving husband and devoted father of ten children, a judge and magistrate, deeply involved in the politics of his country. Deep down, he had always longed for a solitary life, and when he was about fifty years old, three months after the birth of his youngest child, with the consent of his wife, he began a solitary life in the valley of Ranft. Here he remained for the rest of his life, and his little hermitage became a mecca for pilgrims of all kinds who came to ask his advice.

His hermitage was above a lovely waterfall. Those who had known Nicholas when he was judge and magistrate came to him for political advice — and friends, neighbors, and strangers came seeking all kinds of advice. He would spend the night in prayer and during the day devote himself to those who came to him. Once a year, he took part in the great procession at Lucerne and occasionally visited the abbey at Einsiedeln.

These were the days when the Swiss Confederation was forming and the cantons were almost at war with one another over who should be admitted to the federation. A war almost broke out, when someone suggested that they ask Nicholas to arbitrate the matter. The result was the Edict of Stans, a charter that some think was drawn up in the hermitage of Bruder Klaus. Although Nicholas could not read, he had a rare wisdom and has become something of a Swiss hero, considered almost the "father of his country."

Nicholas was tall, brown, and wrinkled, with long locks and a short beard. He was eminently the peacemaker, urging all to work and labor for peace. Six years after the Edict of Stans, he fell ill, suffered intensely for eight days, and died on his seventieth birthday on March 21, 1487. He is honored in Switzerland as a patriot and patron saint and was canonized in 1947. His body lies in a black marble altar in the church at Sachseln.

Thought for the Day: St. Nicholas of Flüe is proof that holiness can be found anywhere. He did spend the last twenty years of his life as a hermit, but this was because of a youthful desire. He could just as well remained the father of his family and devoted husband, and his holiness would have been no less. We, too, can be saints.

From 'The Catholic One Year Bible': . . . As Jesus left the town, he saw a tax collector — with the usual reputation for cheating — sitting at a tax collection booth. The man's name was Levi. Jesus said to him, "Come and be one of my disciples!" So Levi left everything, sprang up and went with him. — **Luke 5:27-28**

St. Turibius de Mogrovejo *(MARCH 23)*

This archbishop of Lima, Peru, is noted for his saying: "Christ said, 'I am the truth'; he did not say, 'I am the custom.' " Since he had to root out a lot of evil customs in the Lima of his day, people heard it often.

He was a young and brilliant law student at the University of Salamanca in Spain, and later became an even more brilliant professor. Philip II chose him to head the ecclesiastical court at Granada, even though he was not a priest. So great was his reputation for courage and fairness that when the archbishopric of Lima in the New World became vacant, he was appointed, even though he protested that it was against Church law for a layman to be promoted to Church office. He was consecrated anyway, against his objections, and sent to the most distant and difficult post in the Spanish empire.

First of all, his diocese was huge, and the Spanish colonists in Peru were there only to make their fortunes. Religion as well as morals was lax, and the lot of the native Indian was wretched; the Indians were abused and exploited without feeling by the Spanish conquistadors. Violence and immorality were the order of the day, and it was in this explosive environment that St. Turibius de Mogrovejo set out to work.

His most serious problem was the clergy, whose lives were little better than the colonists'. He made a visitation of his diocese, corrected abuses, confronted authorities with their cruelty and exploitation, and brought the hatred of the Spanish officials down upon his head. He fought injustice and vice, protected the poor and the oppressed, and succeeded in rooting out the most flagrant abuses. He founded churches, religious houses, and hospitals and established the first seminary in the New World.

He even studied the Indian dialects so that he could preach to the Indians in their own language. His influence was effective, and among those he influenced and confirmed were St. Rose of Lima, Blessed John Massias, and St. Martin de Porres.

He died on March 23, 1606, while on a journey into the Andes, at the age of sixty-eight, worn out with his labors. He was canonized in 1726.

Thought for the Day: A true man or woman of God is a symbol of hope to every life he or she touches. Evil is not inevitable, and injustice must be fought. Faith gives courage that is willing to face any danger. The firm foundation of any reform is a truly holy life.

From 'The Catholic One Year Bible': . . . "It is the sick who need a doctor, not those in good health. My purpose is to invite sinners to turn from their sins, not to spend my time with those who think themselves already good enough." — Luke 5:31-32

Her mother was St. Bridget of Sweden and, like her mother, she married young. After the death of her own husband, Ulf, Bridget went to live in Rome, and Catherine followed her, with the consent of her husband. Her mother begged her to stay with her, and Catherine reluctantly agreed. While in Rome, Catherine's husband died. She stayed on with her mother, accompanied her on several journeys, one to the Holy Land, refusing every offer to remarry.

At the death of Bridget, Catherine returned to Sweden with her mother's body, which was buried at her great monastery of Vadstena. Bridget founded her order there, but it had not been fully established and approved. Catherine took on the mammoth task of forming the community in the rule her mother had written and directing the Order of the Holy Savior, or Bridgettines, as they were called. After some years, she returned to Rome to work for her mother's canonization.

She stayed there five years and returned to Sweden before her mother was canonized but obtained from Pope Urban VI the ratification of the Bridgettine rule. While in Italy, she formed a close friendship with St. Catherine of Siena and almost accompanied her on a trip to the court of Joanna of Naples, a notoriously immoral queen. Joanna had brought about the moral disgrace of Bridget's son, Charles, and St. Catherine of Vadstena could not bring herself to face the woman who had endangered her brother's soul. She returned to Sweden at the outbreak of the Great Western Schism.

Sometime after her return, Catherine's health began to fail, and she died peacefully at Vadstena after a painful illness. She was never formally canonized, but her name was added to the *Roman Martyrology* and her feast is observed in Sweden and in the Bridgettine Order. A chapel in the Piazza Farnese in Rome is dedicated to her.

Thought for the Day: Bridget was a saint and influenced her daughter, St. Catherine of Vadstena, greatly in her own search for holiness. Parents can have a profound effect upon their children, but something is required of the children as well. Consider Catherine's brother, Charles, who did not follow in his mother's footsteps. Living with a saint does not necessarily make one holy.

From 'The Catholic One Year Bible': "Love your *enemies*! Be good to *them*! Lend to *them*! And don't be concerned about the fact that they won't repay. Then your reward from heaven will be very great, and you will truly be acting as sons of God: for he is kind to the *unthankful* and to those who are *very wicked*." — Luke 6:35

St. Margaret Clitherow *(MARCH 25)*

Margaret Clitherow, born in Yorkshire, England, was the wife of John Clitherow, whose family was Catholic, although he had taken on the state religion of England long before he married. Two or three years after her marriage, Margaret became a Catholic. Her home became a stopping-off place for priests, and Mass was offered secretly there.

Her husband went along with her interests, even when she sent their oldest son to Douai, in France, to be educated. Not only was she devout, she was also a zealous promoter of the faith, converting others and bringing back backsliders to the practice of their religion. Meanwhile, the laws against the Catholic faith became more harsh, and the government was determined that Catholicism should be stamped out in Yorkshire where it was especially strong.

Everyone loved St. Margaret Clitherow, and even her servants knew that she hid fugitive priests, but no one betrayed her. She was a good housewife, capable in business, dearly loved by her husband, whose only regret was that she would not attend church with him. Her husband was summoned by the authorities to explain why his oldest son had gone abroad, and the Clitherow house was searched. A Flemish boy, from fear, revealed the hiding place of the priests where chalices and vestments were kept. Margaret was arrested along with a neighboring housewife who had attended Mass at the Clitherow home. Margaret's only concern was that her family was safe.

She was brought to trial and would not plead, her only statement being, "Having made no offense, I need no trial." If she had been tried, her family would have been called as witnesses against her, and she was determined that this would not happen. Reluctantly, the judge sentenced her to be "pressed to death," a bizarre death sentence in which the condemned was placed under a door (or similar object) and rocks piled on the door until the person was crushed to death.

Margaret died on March 25, 1586, her last words being, "Jesu, Jesu, Jesu, have mercy on me!" She was only thirty years old and was canonized in 1970.

Thought for the Day: Through everyday fidelity we are given the strength to face the great crisis. St. Margaret Clitherow did not expect to die a martyr, but she was faithful in the everyday practice of her religion. When the great crisis came, she was ready.

From 'The Catholic One Year Bible': "A tree from good stock doesn't produce scrub fruit nor do trees from poor stock produce choice fruit. . . . A good man produces good deeds from a good heart. And an evil man produces evil deeds from his hidden wickedness." — Luke 6:43-45

St. Ludger

(MARCH 26)

Ludger was one of the finest fruits of St. Boniface's missionary work in what is now Belgium and Holland. He had met Boniface once, as a very young boy, and had been sent to the school that Boniface had set up at Utrecht. From here he was sent to York in England to study under Alcuin, who was the head of the school there. When he returned to the continent, an ordained deacon, he was sent on missionary assignments to Friesland. Ordained to the priesthood at Cologne, he was then sent to Ostergau, where he built a church over the spot where Boniface had been martyred.

St. Ludger's work was prospering when the whole country was overrun by Saxons, who drove out the Christian missionaries, destroyed the churches, and abolished the Christian religion. Ludger made a pilgrimage to Rome, and then spent three years at Monte Cassino, hoping to build a monastery in his own country when he returned.

Meanwhile, Alcuin had been called to the court of Charlemagne to become the schoolmaster of the Franks, and Ludger was sent by the emperor to work in Friesland and Westphalia. He set up his headquarters at what is now Münster, built a monastery, and was consecrated bishop of the territory. He tried to evangelize the Danes and Norwegians, but old age prevented him from continuing. He was courageous enough to face up to Charlemagne when he had been falsely accused of being too generous with the poor, and he was known for his fidelity to prayer and the chanting of the canonical hours.

The day that Ludger died found him preaching at two different churches in his diocese, then he went home and peacefully died. Like Boniface, he had labored in a very difficult mission where paganism and violence were rampant, but he built up the Church in that part of Germany, leaving a memory and a legacy that would be remembered for ages. He died on Passion Sunday, in the year 809, and was buried at Werden, where his relics still remain.

Thought for the Day: Some people are given the mission to start from scratch, to begin working where no one has worked before. We owe much to the great missionaries who brought our ancestors the Christian faith and left us a legacy of faith and devotion. It is something to thank God for, and we should find ways to pass on the faith to others.

From 'The Catholic One Year Bible': "Who is this man you went out into the Judean wilderness to see?" [Jesus] asked. "Did you find him weak as grass, moved by every breath of wind? Did you find him dressed in expensive clothes? No! Men who live in luxury are found in palaces, not out in the wilderness. But did you find him a prophet? Yes! And more than a prophet." — Luke 7:24-26

In 1169, the English pope, Adrian IV, by the bull *Laudabiliter*, granted sovereignty over Ireland to King Henry II of England, who wreaked havoc in the Irish Church by pillaging monasteries and replacing Irish bishops with Norman bishops. The archbishop of Armagh at the time was St. Gelasius, who tried desperately to undo the damage done by the Normans and work for the upbuilding of the Irish Church.

Before the Norman takeover, Ireland was undergoing something of a religious renaissance: literary, artistic, and architectural activity flourished throughout Ireland; the art of illumination was recovered; monastic centers, like Clonmacnoise, were flourishing; Clonfert was rebuilt; Mellifont had been founded; and Irish monks were staffing the remarkable monastery founded by Marianus Scotus in Regensburg.

No one really knows the reason for Adrian IV's "donation of Ireland" to Henry II, but it spelled the end of a uniquely Irish Church.

Gelasius had been abbot of Derry, St. Columba's famous monastery. His father was a bard, an honored profession among the Irish and most probably a teacher at Derry, where Gelasius was educated.

Gelasius called a synod at Armagh in 1170 to try to deal with the Anglo-Norman takeover, but a synod at Cashel in the following year called by the papal legate who supported the Normans made any effort of the Irish useless. Norman usages and customs were imposed on the Irish, many Irish princes submitted to Henry II, and the English king's religious decrees became the law of the land. In 1172, Pope Alexander II confirmed Adrian's "donation" to Henry, with Gelasius trying to undo the harm until his death in 1174. It was a sad time in the history of the Irish Church, and Gelasius died a broken man with a broken heart.

Gerald of Wales thus describes what happened in the time of Gelasius: "The clergy of Ireland are reduced to beggary, the cathedral churches have been stripped of their possessions." It would take almost seven hundred years for Ireland to recover.

Thought for the Day: Sometimes we have to face complete failure, and there is often a mystery of Divine Providence in the work of the Church. God does not always ask us to succeed, only to give our best. When that best is not enough, we have to leave the rest in His hands.

From 'The Catholic One Year Bible': "You must obey all the commandments I give you today. If you do, you will not only live, you will multiply and go in and take over the land promised to your fathers by the Lord. . . . Obey the laws of your God. Walk in his ways and fear him." — Deuteronomy 8:1, 6

St. Tutilo *(MARCH 28)*

When St. Gall, the companion of St. Columbanus, died in Switzerland in 640, a monastery was built over the place of his burial. This became the famous monastery of St.-Gall, one of the most influential monasteries of the Middle Ages and the center of music, art, and learning throughout that period.

About the middle of the ninth century, returning from a visit to Rome, an Irishman named Moengul stopped off at the abbey and decided to stay, along with a number of Irish companions, among them Tuathal, or Tutilo. Moengul was given charge of the abbey schools and he became the teacher of Tutilo, Notker, and Radpert, who were distinguished for their learning and their artistic skills. Tutilo, in particular, was a universal genius: musician, poet, painter, sculptor, builder, goldsmith, head of the monastic school, and composer.

He was part of the abbey at its greatest, and the influence of Gall spread throughout Europe. The Gregorian chant manuscripts from the monastery of St.-Gall, many of them undoubtedly the work of St. Tutilo, are considered among the most authentic and were studied carefully when the monks of Solesmes were restoring the tradition of Gregorian chant to the Catholic Church. The scribes of St.-Gall supplied most of the monasteries of Europe with manuscript books of Gregorian chant, all of them priceless works of the art of illumination. Proof of the Irish influence at St.-Gall is a large collection of Irish manuscripts at the abbey dating from the seventh, eighth, and ninth centuries.

Tutilo was known to be handsome, eloquent, and quick-witted, who brought something of the Irish love of learning and the arts to St.-Gall. He died in 915 at the height of the abbey's influence, remembered as a great teacher, a dedicated monk, and a competent scholar.

Thought for the Day: Beauty is one of the names of God, and we often forget that the cultivation of beauty can give glory to God. "O Lord, I have loved the beauty of Your house and the place where Your glory dwells." St. Tutilo loved God deeply and expressed it in a thousand beautiful ways, leading many people to God. Beautiful things can lift our minds to God.

From 'The Catholic One Year Bible': ". . . The good soil represents honest, good-hearted people. They listen to God's words and cling to them and steadily spread them to others who also soon believe." — **Luke 8:15**

St. Berthold **(MARCH 29)**

Berthold seems to have had a connection with the beginnings of the Carmelite Order. He was a relative of Aymeric, the Latin patriarch of Antioch who was installed in Antioch during the crusades. At the time, there were a number of hermits from the West scattered throughout Palestine, and Berthold gathered them together, founded a community of priests who settled on Mount Carmel, and became their first superior.

There is a legend that he was born at Limoges in France, studied in Paris, and was ordained a priest there. According to the legend, he accompanied Aymeric on the crusades and found himself in Antioch when it was being besieged by the Saracens. Through his urgings, the Christians in Antioch turned to prayer and penance, and the city was delivered.

What is known for certain is that St. Berthold directed the building of a monastery and church on Mount Carmel and dedicated the church in honor of the prophet Elias, who had defeated the priests of Baal there and seen the vision of the cloud out over the sea. This is confirmed in a letter of Peter Emilianus to King Edward I of England in 1282.

Berthold lived out his days on Mount Carmel, ruling the community he had founded for forty-five years until his death about 1195. His example and way of life stamped the beginnings of the Carmelite Order, leading to the drawing up of the order's rule by St. Albert, Latin patriarch of Jerusalem, about 1210. That rule was approved by Pope Honorius III in 1226 and it is this primitive rule that is considered the foundation of the Order of Mount Carmel.

But it seems to have been Berthold who first organized the monastic life of the hermits on Mount Carmel and governed them until his death. St. Brocard, who apparently was his successor, petitioned Albert to compose a rule for them, undoubtedly codifying and completing the work begun by Berthold.

Thought for the Day: St. Berthold became aware of something that had to be done, and he put his hand firmly to the task before him, unknowingly laying the foundation of a great religious order. We have no way of knowing what fruit will grow from the seed we plant. What is important is that we plant well.

From 'The Catholic One Year Bible': . . . A fierce storm developed that threatened to swamp them, and they were in real danger. They rushed over and woke him up. "Master, master, we are sinking!" they screamed. So he spoke to the storm: "Quiet down," he said, and the wind and waves subsided and all was calm! Then he asked them, "Where is your faith?" — **Luke 8:23-25**

St. John Climacus *(MARCH 30)*

John Climacus was the abbot of the Byzantine monastery of St. Catherine in the Sinai, founded by the Emperor Justinian in the sixth century and still flourishing today at the foot of Mount Sinai. Born in Palestine, he settled on Mount Sinai when he was sixteen. He was professed at the age of twenty and for the next fifteen years lived under the spiritual guidance of a monk named Martyrius.

After Martyrius's death, St. John Climacus became a complete solitary at Thole, coming to the monastery on Saturdays and Sundays for the celebration of the Divine Liturgy. He spent forty years as a solitary, was a student of Scripture and of the Fathers, and buried himself in a life of prayer and asceticism. He was widely sought out as a spiritual director, by monks and by others. It was said of him that "he went up into the mountain of contemplation, talked to God face to face, and then came down to his fellows bearing the table of God's law, his Ladder of Perfection."

The *Ladder of Perfection* (*Klimax* — "the ladder" — is where he gets his name from), which he wrote at the request of the abbot of a monastery, shows the steps by which the monk goes to God, and the innocence of life he must cultivate to reach the heights of perfection. "It treats first of the vices and then of the virtues in the form of aphorisms or sentences illustrated by curious anecdotes of monastic life."

When he was seventy years old, the abbot of St. Catherine's died and John Climacus was chosen to succeed him. Once, by his prayers, rain fell at a time of great drought, and Pope St. Gregory the Great wrote to him asking for his prayers and sending beds and money for the pilgrims who came to Mount Sinai.

After ruling as abbot for four years, John laid down his charge and died soon afterward, in the hermitage that had been so dear to him.

His *Ladder of Perfection* was one of the most widely copied writings in the Eastern Church and was translated into Latin, Syriac, Arabic, Armenian, and church Slavonic. It is one of the most widely used treatises on the spiritual life and is still a classic to be read and appreciated.

Thought for the Day: Each one of us has to begin our spiritual journey somewhere and begin to climb, step by step, to closeness to God. It is fortunate that we have masters like St. John Climacus to guide us, who can show us the hazards of the journey and the streams of living water from which we can drink on the way.

From 'The Catholic One Year Bible': A good man's mind is filled with honest thoughts; an evil man's mind is crammed with lies. — Proverbs 12:4

St. Acacius *(MARCH 31)*

All that is known for certain about St. Acacius is that he lived in Antioch during the persecution of the Emperor Decius in the third century, that he was a sharp and witty controversialist, and that he was hauled before the authorities and imprisoned for the faith.

He is sometimes listed as a martyr and a bishop, but it is not known for certain that he was either.

He was arrested and brought before a Roman official named Martian and, when questioned, boldly replied that Christians were loyal subjects of the emperor, prayed for him, but refused to worship the emperor as a god.

Martian, it appears, was something of a philosopher and he and Acacius discussed Greek and Roman mythology, the nature of angels, the Incarnation, morality, the nature of God, and Eastern religions.

When Martian ordered St. Acacius to accompany a Roman officer to the Temple of Jupiter and Juno to sacrifice, Acacius replied: "I cannot sacrifice to someone buried on the isle of Crete, or has he come to life again?" He continued: "You make your own gods and are afraid of them. When there are no masons, or the masons have no stone, you have no gods."

When Martian accused the Christians of inventing a religion, Acacius told him: "We stand in awe of our God — but we did not make Him, He made us; for He is Lord. He loves us, for He is Father, and in His goodness He has snatched us from everlasting death."

When Acacius was told to reveal the names of other Christians, he replied: "You want names? All right, I am called Acacius. Do what you like." He was then returned to prison. An account of his questioning was sent to the emperor who was humored by Acacius' wit and pardoned him.

His answers did not stop the persecutions of Christians, but the Roman officials realized that Christians were neither superstitious nor enemies of the state and that they were scarcely a threat to the Roman empire.

Thought for the Day: We should always be able to "give a reason for the hope that is in us." To be uninformed about our faith and unable to defend it, is to give the impression that our religion has no solid foundation. We should be able to give a good answer to those who make inquiries about our faith.

From 'The Catholic One Year Bible': . . . "Anyone who wants to follow me must put aside his own desires and conveniences and carry his cross with him every day and *keep close to me*! Whoever loses his life for my sake will save it, but whoever insists on keeping his life will lose it." — Luke 9:23-24

THE SAINTS OF APRIL

St. Hugh of Grenoble *(APRIL 1)*

When St. Bruno decided to set off into the wilderness to lay the foundations of the Carthusian Order, the man he consulted about his plans was St. Hugh of Grenoble, bishop of that see and himself a lover of solitude and silence. He directed the Carthusians to a deserted section of his diocese called Chartreuse, and it is from this place that the order received its name.

Hugh had a remarkable father, Odilo, who himself became a Carthusian monk. The young Hugh was given an outstanding education and appointed to a canonry in the cathedral of Valence. He was taken into the household of St. Hugh of Die and at a council at Avignon, the younger Hugh was appointed to the diocese of Grenoble, which was noted for its laxity of morals and serious abuses among the clergy. Although he had not been ordained, Hugh was given holy orders and consecrated bishop by Pope Gregory VII.

In Grenoble, he worked tirelessly for two years, bringing about remarkable changes but was deeply discouraged by the conditions under which he had to work. He left his diocese and became a monk at the Benedictine abbey of Chaise-Dieu. Ordered by the pope to return to his diocese and continue his work of reform, Hugh obeyed, and it was at this time that Bruno and his companions came to him with their desire for solitude. Hugh would often join them in their solitude and was looked upon as almost a second founder of the order.

He hoped to join the monks in their solitude and asked several times to be released from his pastoral duties, but each time the pope refused him. He was generous with the poor, even selling sacred vessels to help them. He was often sick and toward the end of his life was struck with a long and painful illness. He was loved by everyone and left his diocese a living example of what a bishop should be like. He died on April 1, 1132, almost eighty years of age, having been a bishop for fifty-two years. Two years later, he was canonized by Pope Innocent II.

Thought for the Day: St. Hugh of Grenoble would have preferred to live in solitude, but God had other plans for him. Sometimes we have to be satisfied with what we think is "second best," and that turns out to be "first best" after all. We cannot determine all the details and circumstances of our lives, but we can mold those circumstances to the will of God.

From 'The Catholic One Year Bible': . . . [Jesus] stood a little child beside him and said to them: "Anyone who takes care of a little child like this is caring for me! And whoever is caring for me is caring for God who sent me." — Luke 9:47-48

St. Francis of Paola *(APRIL 2)*

Francis of Paola lived at the end of the fifteenth century, when the Church was in turmoil, and he became something of a wonder in his native Italy and in France, where he spent the last twenty-five years of his life.

Around the age of twelve, he was sent to the Franciscans for his education; at fifteen he received his parents' permission to live a solitary life near Paola. He moved into a cave and was discovered by some hunters who spread news of him all over the region. When he was nineteen, others joined him, and the peasants of the region helped to build the first church and monastery of the community. He was a defender of the poor and oppressed and did not hesitate to face rulers responsible for oppressing the poor.

After thirty years in Italy, with his order spreading, at the command of the pope he set out for France where King Louis XI lay dying and had requested him to come, since he was near death and hoped the saint's prayers would save him. St. Francis of Paola went, prepared the king for death, and remained in France, restoring peace between France and Britanny, advising the royal family, and preventing war between France and Spain over territories.

King Charles VIII revered the saint highly and consulted him on matters of state. He built a monastery for the Minims, as St. Francis' order was called, at Plessis and Amboise, as well as one in Rome on the Pincian Hill.

On Palm Sunday, 1507, Francis fell ill, and on Holy Thursday, he gathered his friars around him, encouraging them in their way of life. He died on Good Friday, at the age of ninety-one, and was canonized in 1519 by Pope Leo X.

He was remembered for centuries in France and inspired paintings by Murillo, Goya, and Velásquez. Franz Liszt composed a sonata in his honor: "St. Francis of Paola Walking on the Waters."

Thought for the Day: Saints sometimes become the counselors of kings, and a holy life has an influence even in the palaces of kings. When the Church is in trouble, as it was in St. Francis' day, God raises up saints to bear witness to Him, when leadership in the Church is not what it should be. Thus the tradition of holiness is carried on.

From 'The Catholic One Year Bible': . . . "Remember, I don't even own a place to lay my head. Foxes have dens to live in, and birds have nests, but I, the Messiah, have no earthly home at all." — Luke 9:58

It is to this saint that we owe the prayer "Lord Jesus, Savior, Friend and Brother: grant that I may know You more clearly, love You more dearly, and follow You more nearly."

St. Richard of Chichester was born in Worcester, England, about 1198, and his parents died when he was very young. His guardian squandered his parents' estate, and when Richard realized what had happened, he worked day and night as a common laborer to restore the family's fortune. When his grateful brother made over to him the deeds to their property and chose for him a wealthy bride, Richard, who had other plans for himself, turned over everything to his brother and went to Oxford to study. From Oxford, he studied at Paris and Bologna, then returned to England and was appointed chancellor of Oxford.

St. Edmund Rich, archbishop of Canterbury, invited him to become his chancellor, and in Edmund's struggles with King Henry III, Richard followed his archbishop into exile in France. After Edmund's death, Richard studied at Orléans, planned to join the Dominicans, and was ordained to the priesthood.

He returned to England to accept a parish given him by Edmund, and when the bishopric of Chichester fell vacant, he was consecrated by Innocent IV at Lyons in 1245. King Henry refused to recognize him. He returned to England, but the king had given orders for no one to receive him and confiscated the revenues of his diocese. Without residence and without funds, he became a missionary bishop. Finally, under threat of excommunication, the king recognized Richard.

Richard's generosity with the poor was legendary and, once, when his steward told him there was nothing left to give, he replied: "Sell the furniture and the dishes, and sell my horse, too." Returning to England after preaching the crusade, he was taken ill at Dover and he died at a hostel for the poor, surrounded by devoted friends. He was fifty-five years old and was canonized nine years later.

Thought for the Day: With singularity of purpose, St. Richard chose his own pathway to God and refused to let circumstances get in his way. Loaded with honors, he let none of these go to his head; instead, he remained gentle, simple, and generous, always witty and gracious. Character is not something we inherit — it is something we carefully fashion ourselves by means of our deeds.

From 'The Catholic One Year Bible': ". . . What does a man need to do to live forever in heaven? . . . You must love the Lord your God with all your heart, and with all your soul, and with all your strength, and with all your mind. And you must love your neighbor just as you love yourself. . . . *Do* this and you shall live." — Luke 10:25, 27-28

St. Isidore of Seville *(APRIL 4)*

Isidore is chiefly responsible for converting the Visigoths of Spain from Arianism to Catholicism and for originating Church councils noted for their democratic methods and parliamentary procedure. He was born in Spain about 560, was the brother of St. Leander and St. Fulgentius, and was educated by his older brother, Leander, archbishop of Seville, whom he succeeded.

As archbishop, St. Isidore of Seville founded monasteries and convents, decreeing that in monasteries there was to be no distinction between freemen and slaves — all were equal in the sight of God. He worked under six Visigothic kings and succeeded in converting the Visigoths to Christianity. He established seminaries and cathedral schools for the education of the clergy, and his educational system embraced every known branch of knowledge. Not only did his future priests study the liberal arts, medicine, and law, but Hebrew and Greek as well, together with philosophy and theology.

Through his efforts, Spain became a center of culture, and his writings influenced education in Europe into the sixteenth century. He wrote voluminously, covering every known science and discipline, including histories of the Goths, rules for monks, commentaries on the Bible, dictionaries, books on geography, astronomy, and biographies of illustrious men. He is also responsible for the creation of the Mozarbic Rite in Spain, one of the many variations of the Latin liturgy.

Like St. Bede, a century later, he was considered the most learned man of his age, loved by the poor to whom he was very generous and by his priests and bishops to whom he was an outstanding father and leader. He was almost eighty years of age when he died, clad in sackcloth and ashes, asking for the prayers of those who attended him. He was the driving inspiration of the Fourth Council of Toledo, which brought about a religious renaissance in Spain, decreed the democratic election of kings, and made provision for an educated clergy. The results of Isidore's work in Spain endured for centuries.

Thought for the Day: It is amazing what one person can accomplish, and St. Isidore is a good example of this. We all find ourselves in some position of leadership or in some circle of influence, and the good we can do by our labor and example is measureless. We should look around us and see the lives we can touch and become a genuine influence for good.

From 'The Catholic One Year Bible': ". . . Keep on asking and you will keep on getting; keep on looking and you will keep on finding; knock and the door will be opened. Everyone who asks, receives; all who seek, find; and the door is opened to everyone who knocks." — Luke 11:9-10

St. Vincent Ferrer *(APRIL 5)*

Vincent Ferrer was a man caught in the crossfire between pope and antipope, who took the wrong side in the battle but stayed on the right side of God, and became a saint.

He was born in Valencia, Spain, about 1350, entered the Dominican Order at the age of fifteen, became a brilliant philosopher and then the most outstanding preacher in Europe. He was ordained to the priesthood in 1379 by Cardinal Pedro de Luna, the future antipope Benedict XIII. These were the days of the Black Death and the Great Western Schism, when every country of Europe was devastated by the plague, and Christendom was divided into two loyalties: one to the pope in Rome, Urban VI; the other to the pope in Avignon, Clement VII. St. Vincent Ferrer took the side of the Avignon pope, convinced that the Roman election had been invalid. (Naturally he did not know that history would see Clement as the antipope.)

Upon the death of the Avignon pope, Vincent's friend Pedro de Luna was elected to succeed him, taking the name Benedict XIII. Vincent became the antipope's preacher and confessor, but their relations became strained as Benedict refused to come to terms with his rival in Rome. Vincent tried to persuade him, but Benedict stubbornly refused. Tired of papal politics, Vincent set out on a grueling preaching mission, taking him all over Europe, accompanied by crowds of penitents and converting thousands.

Concerned about the unity of the Church, Vincent again urged Benedict to resign, but the antipope refused. Convinced finally that Benedict's obstinacy was harming the Church, Vincent mounted the pulpit in the antipope's presence and denounced him thunderously before a huge assembly. Benedict fled, abandoned by all his followers. At the Council of Constance in 1414, the three contenders for the papal throne were deposed, and unity was restored. "But for you," the French statesman and writer Gerson told Vincent, "this union could never have been achieved."

Worn out by his labors, after a great crusade of preaching, Vincent died at Vannes in Britanny in 1419. He was seventy years old. Thirty-six years later, he was canonized.

Thought for the Day: St. Vincent Ferrer was obviously on the wrong side, but he followed his convictions and everything came out right in the end. Sometimes it is difficult to see the truth and to know what to do. We have to follow the truth as we see it, whatever the consequences. Even if we are wrong, as in Vincent's case, we can become saints.

From 'The Catholic One Year Bible': "No one lights a lamp and hides it! Instead, he puts it on a lampstand to give light to all who enter the room. Your eyes light up your inward being. A pure eye lets sunshine into your soul." — Luke 11:33-34

Blessed Notker Balbulus

He was a young man who stuttered, and his name means literally Notker "the Stutterer." As a young boy, he had a speech defect that stayed with him all his life, but this did not prevent him from becoming a great musician, a great teacher, a superb scholar, and a saint. He is one of the glories of the great monastery of St.-Gall in Switzerland and one of the pioneers of Gregorian chant.

He entered the monastery school very young and was taught by Moengel the Irishman, with his fellow students Tutilo and Radpert. He became a teacher in the monastery school, was appointed librarian, and was also guestmaster of the monastery. St.-Gall was at the height of its influence at this time, founding a school of chant that rivaled that in Rome, and Blessed Notker was one of the most eminent chantmasters.

He was not only beloved by his fellow monks, but his advice was sought by the Emperor Charles the Fat. He was the monk of St.-Gall, mentioned in several manuscripts, who developed the "sequence" in the liturgy of the Mass, basing his work on a manuscript from the sacked monastery of Jumièges. He also is thought to have composed the *Gesta Caroli Magni*, folk tales and legends of Charlemagne, written in colloquial Latin prose and very popular in the Middle Ages. He composed hymns and long metrical compositions, and his letters reveal him to be a man of liveliness and wit.

His biographer Ekkehard describes him as "weakly in body, but not in mind, stammering of tongue but not of intellect, pressing forward boldly in things divine, a vessel filled with the Holy Spirit, without equal in his time."

After his death in 912, his fellow monks could not speak of him without tears in their eyes. His vibrant, lively spirit breathes through his writing, and his style is highly personal and a delight to read. There is a vast literature on his literary and musical influence, and some consider him the greatest Latin poet of the Middle Ages.

Thought for the Day: A gracious lovable personality does more than anything else to draw others to holiness. Some preach by words and some by their whole person. Blessed Notker Balbulus was one of the latter. The fact that he was dearly loved by those with whom he lived is the finest witness to his holiness.

From 'The Catholic One Year Bible': "What is the price of five sparrows? A couple of pennies? Not much more than that. Yet God does not forget a single one of them. And he knows the number of hairs on your head! Never fear, you are more valuable to him than a whole flock of sparrows." — Luke 12:6-7

St. John Baptist de la Salle *(APRIL 7)*

Generations of schoolboys have been taught by the Christian Brothers, and their founder, St. John Baptist de la Salle, is familiar in their prayers and devotions. "Brothers Boys" are scattered all over the world and all of them have fond memories of their "De la Salle" days.

John Baptist de la Salle was born at Rheims in 1651, became a member of the cathedral chapter at Rheims when he was sixteen, and was ordained a priest in 1678. Soon after ordination he was put in charge of a girls' school, and in 1679 he met Adrian Nyel, a layman who wanted to open a school for boys. Two schools were started, and Canon de la Salle became interested in the work of education. He took an interest in the teachers, eventually invited them to live in his own house, and tried to train them in the educational system that was forming in his mind. This first group ultimately left, unable to grasp what the saint had in mind; others, however, joined him, and the beginnings of the Brothers of the Christian Schools were begun.

Seeing a unique opportunity for good, Canon de la Salle resigned his canonry, gave his inheritance to the poor, and began to organize his teachers into a religious congregation. Soon, boys from his schools began to ask for admission to the Brothers, and the founder set up a juniorate to prepare them for their life as religious teachers. At the request of many pastors, he also set up a training school for teachers, first at Rheims, then at Paris, and finally at St.-Denis. Realizing that he was breaking entirely new ground in the education of the young, John Baptist de la Salle wrote books on his system of education, opened schools for tradesmen, and even founded a school for the nobility, at the request of King James of England.

The congregation had a tumultuous history, and the setbacks that the founder had to face were many; but the work was begun, and he guided it with rare wisdom. In Lent of 1719, he grew weak, met with a serious accident, and died on Good Friday. He was canonized by Pope Leo XIII in 1900, and Pope Pius XII proclaimed him patron of schoolteachers.

Thought for the Day: St. John Baptist de la Salle stumbled on his life's work, quite by accident, and had to draw upon all of his inner strength to accomplish the mission given to him. He was faced with something entirely new and had to find new ways to do his work. Discouragement dogged his every step, but he carried on boldly. Faith and boldness go together, and we have need of both.

From 'The Catholic One Year Bible': "Look at the ravens — they don't plant or harvest or have barns to store away their food, and yet they get along all right — for God feeds them. And you are far more valuable to him than many birds!" — **Luke 12:24**

St. Julia Billiart (APRIL 8)

Julia Billiart was born in Picardy, France, in 1751. As a very young girl, her father lost his business and the family was impoverished. Shocked at the attempted murder of her father in her own presence, she became paralyzed and lost her voice. In her sickness, she helped find hiding places for fugitive priests during the French Revolution, and several times her life was in danger. A friendly family in Amiens took her in, and she recovered her speech, becoming the center of a group of young women who spent their time and money helping the poor.

So remarkable was her influence on the young that a priest, Father Joseph Varin, recognizing Julia's capabilities, encouraged her to devote herself to the spiritual care of children and to the training of religious teachers. Thus was the foundation laid for the Institute of Notre Dame of Namur.

On a visit of a certain Father Enfantin to Amiens, at the close of a great parish mission conducted by him, and after five days of intense prayer, he said to her: "If you have any faith, take one step in honor of the Sacred Heart of Jesus." Mother Julia got up, completely cured.

With her recovery, St. Julia Billiart became a veritable dynamo of activity. She consolidated and extended her institute, opened convents in Namur, Ghent, and Tournai, and the future seemed bright. Suddenly, from the ill will of a priest who tried to take over leadership of her institute, she found herself banned from Amiens and had to move her headquarters to Namur. She faced the difficulties courageously and began again.

She journeyed often, establishing convents, training teachers for the young, and expanding her work. "She can do more in a few years," one bishop said of her, "than others can in a century."

In 1816, it was clear to her nuns that she was failing fast. With her sisters around her, chanting the *Magnificat*, she passed to her reward on April 8. She was beatified in 1906 and canonized in 1969.

Thought for the Day: Overcoming obstacles seems to be part of the business of holiness. St. Julia Billiart was crippled — paralyzed, with complete loss of speech — but she managed to lead and inspire others in spite of her infirmities. Nothing is too difficult for those who trust in God, and she accomplished remarkable things. We can do the same.

From 'The Catholic One Year Bible': "Be prepared — all dressed and ready — for your Lord's return from the wedding feast. . . . There will be great joy for those who are ready and waiting for his return. . . . Whenever he comes there will be joy for his servants who are ready!" — Luke 12:35-38

Blessed Thomas of Tolentino *(APRIL 9)*

From the earliest Christian times, there was a fascination with the land of the East: Persia, India, and China, especially after Marco Polo's account of his journeys in the thirteenth century. The first Christian missionaries to reach China were Franciscans, and one of them, John of Monte Corvino, became archbishop of Peking. The man responsible for the Franciscans' going to China was Blessed Thomas of Tolentino, martyred on an island near Bombay, India, in 1321.

He joined the Franciscans in Italy a few years after Marco Polo's story aroused the imagination of Europe and was sent to Armenia at the request of the ruler of that country, along with four other Franciscans. At that time, Armenia was being threatened by the Saracens, and Thomas returned to Europe to beg the help of the kings of England and France in turning back the Saracen armies.

On his return to Armenia, he started moving to the East, reaching Persia. After some years there, he returned to Italy to report to Pope Clement V and to ask permission to advance into China. Much to his surprise, the pope appointed an archbishop for China, together with seven bishops, and sent them with Archbishop John of Monte Corvino as papal legate for the East. It is known that these did reach China, made many converts, and carried on a fruitful mission in the Chinese capital.

Thomas on his return to the East took a ship for Ceylon and China. His ship was blown off course, landing on Salsette Island, near Bombay, a stronghold of the Saracens. He and his companions were arrested and thrown into prison and, after being scouraged and exposed to the scorching rays of the sun, were beheaded. His body was later recovered and sent to Xaitou. His memory is venerated in India, and he is one of the pioneer missionaries in the evangelization of the Far East.

Thought for the Day: Some are called to be pioneers and to open whole new territories for the Christian faith. The obstacles are numerous, the difficulties almost insurmountable, and the dangers many. We all have to labor and suffer for our faith in some way and, although this may not lead to martyrdom, we can share somewhat in the reward of the martyrs.

From 'The Catholic One Year Bible': . . . "What is the Kingdom of God like? . . . How can I illustrate it? It is like a tiny mustard seed planted in a garden; soon it grows into a tall bush and the birds live among its branches." — Luke 13:18-19

St. Fulbert of Chartres *(APRIL 10)*

In 1020, the cathedral at Chartres burned to the ground, one of the many times in its history. It was St. Fulbert of Chartres who rebuilt it, not the great cathedral that we know today, but a great church nevertheless. Fulbert is one of the glories of Chartres.

He was born in Italy and later studied at Rheims under the celebrated teacher Gerbert, who later became Pope Sylvester II. Called to Rome by the pope, Fulbert stayed there until the death of Sylvester, then returned to France to become a canon at Chartres. He was made director of the cathedral school and he made it the educational center of France, attracting students from all over Europe.

He also became the counselor and spiritual adviser of kings, abbots, and bishops. In 1006, he became bishop of Chartres and worked toward the rooting out of clerical abuses, which were widespread in the Church, particularly simony and clerical marriage. In this, he predated the work of Pope Gregory VII later in the century.

He was an ardent promoter of devotion to the Blessed Virgin, and Chartres Cathedral became a center of devotion and pilgrimage to the Mother of God. It is undoubtedly due to Fulbert's inspiration that Chartres later became the center of an intense devotion to Mary and that the cathedral itself with its superb stained-glass windows and sculptures became a magnificent shrine and a monument to the Mother of God.

After serving as bishop for twenty-two years, Fulbert died on April 10, 1029, leaving behind a legacy of writings, sermons, letters, and hymns that were greatly admired. He is one of the founders of the "School of Chartres" that became during the twelfth century one of the theological lights of Europe, attracting scholars from everywhere, leading finally to the construction of the Queen of Cathedrals and the highest monument to Christian art and culture.

Although Fulbert has long been venerated as a saint, it was only in the mid-1800s that his cult was officially sanctioned for the dioceses of Chartres and Poitiers.

Thought for the Day: Chartres Cathedral has been called a "sermon in stone and stained glass," and it demonstrates what can happen when faith bursts into culture. St. Fulbert of Chartres recognized that unless faith influences culture, its voice remains very weak. It is not enough to believe — we have to make the Christian faith part of our lives and part of the world we live in.

From 'The Catholic One Year Bible': "The door to heaven is narrow. Work hard to get in, for the truth is that many will try to enter but when the head of the house has locked the door, it will be too late." — Luke 13:24-25

St. Stanislaus of Cracow *(APRIL 11)*

Stanislaus was born in 1030 and was educated at Gnesen and at Paris. After his ordination to the priesthood he was made a canon of the cathedral at Cracow as well as archdeacon and preacher. Upon the death of the bishop of Cracow, he was nominated bishop of the diocese by Pope Alexander II.

The king at the time, Boleslaus II, trying to strengthen his own power, led an expedition against the grand duchy of Kiev, making himself very unpopular with the nobles of the country, who opposed his policies. St. Stanislaus of Cracow sided with the nobles, led by the king's brother, Ladislaus, and this brought him into conflict with the king.

Stanislaus had opposed the king before for his tyrannical ways and once confronted him boldly for his immoral behavior when Boleslaus had abducted the wife of a Polish nobleman and carried her off to his castle. No one seemed willing to face the king from a fear of his rage, but Stanislaus boldly went to the king and threatened excommunication if he did not change his ways. Furious, the king promised revenge on the bishop. Later, Stanislaus sided with the nobles in their opposition to the king's political policies, and the king accused him of being a traitor and condemned him to death.

At first the king commanded his soldiers to kill the bishop when he was celebrating Mass at St. Michael's chapel in Cracow, but the soldiers refused, fearing to bring down upon themselves the wrath of God. Undeterred, the king himself entered the church, drew his sword, and killed the bishop, ordering his soldiers to dismember the body.

Pope Gregory VII placed the country under interdict and Boleslaus fell from power, fleeing to Hungary, where he entered the monastery of Osiak to do penance for his crime. Stanislaus, canonized by Pope Innocent IV in 1253, is one of the patron saints of Poland.

Thought for the Day: Sometimes evil has to be confronted boldly, whatever the consequences. Brave men like St. Stanislaus of Cracow risked death in facing evil; there is little chance that we will ever be in that danger, but we do have to take a stand at times, and it should be very clear, in the face of genuine evil, where we stand. Christ our Lord can expect no less from us.

From 'The Catholic One Year Bible': "What good is salt that has lost its saltiness? Flavorless salt is fit for nothing — not even for fertilizer. It is worthless and must be thrown out. Listen well, if you would understand my meaning." — Luke 14:34-35

Blessed Angelo of Chivasso *(APRIL 12)*

Angelo of Chivasso lived in very difficult times, when self-serving popes occupied the see of Peter and the Papal States were in disarray. He was a doctor of civil and canon law, educated at Bologna, and after his studies was made a senator of his native region of Piedmont. He took care of his aging mother, took a special interest in the poor, and showed promise of a distinguished career in government.

At the age of thirty, after the death of his mother, he surprised everyone by entering the Franciscans of the Cismontane Observance, showing the same talent for leadership that he had shown as a senator. He was four times chosen vicar general of his order and continued his special interest in the poor, particularly by promoting the "Montes Pietatis," the credit organizations (similar to pawn shops) that provided low interest rates to the poor, who were often exploited by usurers.

Blessed Angelo of Chivasso was given the difficult mission of preaching the crusade against the Turkish invaders of Otranto; he was also given the delicate mission of working against the spread of Waldensians in Savoy and Piedmont. He was known for his competency as a moralist, and his *Summa Angelica* was a favorite of confessors. He had a keen pastoral sense, joined to vast knowledge and wide experience, reflected in both his work and his writings. In 1491, when he was eighty years old, he was commissioned to work for the evangelization of the Waldensians, and his astuteness and clarity of mind did not diminish with age. Pope Innocent VIII wanted to make him a bishop, but he refused.

His last two years were spent in the monastery of Cuneo, where he had gone to prepare himself for death. His simplicity and love of the poor remained with him to the end. He died in 1495 at the age of eighty-four.

Thought for the Day: Talented people like Blessed Angelo of Chivasso see the stupidity of most personal ambition that seeks to lord it over others; rather, talents and gifts should be for the service of others, for enriching and benefiting their lives. We all tend to put down others or to make ourselves look good at another's expense. It has to be recognized that this is thoroughly un-Christian.

From 'The Catholic One Year Bible': . . . "If you had a hundred sheep and one of them strayed away and was lost in the wilderness, wouldn't you leave the ninety-nine others to go and search for the lost one until you found it? . . . In the same way, heaven will be happier over one lost sinner who returns to God than over ninety-nine others who haven't strayed away!" —Luke 15:3-4, 7

Martin was pope at a turbulent period in Church history: the time of the Monothelite heresy, in which the Byzantine emperors involved themselves. The details of the heresy are not important; what is important is that the emperor considered it his duty to settle theological questions and ecclesiastical disputes and he ordered the pope to submit to his will. In political matters, the pontiff was quite willing to submit but not in matters that had to do with doctrine.

St. Martin I was elected pope in 649 and immediately called a council at the Lateran to face the Monothelite question. The Emperor Constans had issued two decrees favorable to the heresy and ordered silence on the matter throughout the whole empire. The decrees of the Lateran Council criticized the imperial edicts. The emperor was furious and ordered that the pope be brought to Constantinople for trial, after an unsuccessful attempt on the Holy Father's life.

The pope was taken prisoner in the Lateran Basilica and began the long journey to Constantinople, already a sick man. He arrived at Constantinople in 654, was tried on the charge of treason for ignoring the imperial edicts, and was at first condemned to death, following long periods of imprisonment. He was even accused of being responsible for the loss of Sicily to the Muslims. There was no one to plead his case, no one had been allowed to accompany him, and he was sent into exile to the island of Kherson in the Crimea. The emperor tried to force the Romans to elect a pontiff approved by him, but instead a successor for Martin was chosen, Pope St. Eugene I, who carried on in the same courageous spirit. He was elected and began his pontificate during Martin's lifetime, but Martin approved of the choice and died knowing that the papal office would be in good hands.

Lonely and friendless, Martin I died in exile in September of 655. He is the last pope venerated as a martyr.

Thought for the Day: Jesus taught that His followers would "suffer persecution for the sake of justice," and that is often the lot of the followers of Christ. If we follow our Christian convictions and live them, we will sometimes be opposed and criticized. That is part of the price of being a Christian, and we should accept such opposition as part of our loyalty to Christ.

From 'The Catholic One Year Bible': ". . . Neither you nor anyone else can serve two masters. You will hate one and show loyalty to the other, or else the other way around — you will be enthusiastic about one and despise the other. You cannot serve both God and money." — Luke 16:13

St. Benezet

Some saints are noted for their austerities, others for their pastoral genius, and still others for their mystical life; but St. Benezet is known for one thing only: he built a bridge over the Rhone River. He originated the idea for the bridge, convinced others that it should be built, and directed the operations of the bridge himself, dying about four years after the bridge was completed. Why is he a saint? For the simple reason that you cannot put saints into categories.

Benezet was a shepherd boy from Savoy or Ardenne. He was a thoughtful, meditative child who was very sensitive and compassionate. During his days as a shepherd, he used to reflect on the perils of those crossing the Rhone River and, like all little dreamers, determined to do something about it. Like St. Joan of Arc, he heard voices telling him to go to Avignon and build a bridge.

In those days, ferrying people across rivers and building bridges were considered great works of charity (remember the legend of St. Christopher?), and Benezet put his hand to the most important work of charity at hand. He had no experience, influence, or money, but he was determined to build his bridge, and he looked upon the task as a call from God.

First, he convinced the bishop of the authenticity of his call, then when he had received the bishop's approval for the work, he began. The year was 1177.

He helped to draw up the plan for the bridge, arranged for the materials, and directed the construction of the bridge. For seven years, the bridge was in construction, and then, when most of the obstacles and difficulties had been overcome and the bridge was nearly finished, Benezet died, still a very young man.

He was buried upon the bridge itself, and a chapel was built to enshrine his body, a symbol of the selflessness and devotion with which he served others. In 1669, part of the bridge was washed away, and his coffin was rescued. When it was opened the following year, the body was found to be incorrupt.

Benezet inspired the founding of the Order of Bridge Brothers, who continued his work, and he is one of the patrons of the city of Avignon.

Thought for the Day: St. Benezet saw a danger and an opportunity and, however unusual it seemed, he put his hand to what he considered a most important work of mercy. He helped his neighbor in the only way he knew how and became a saint in the work he did. There is a lesson in this for all of us.

From 'The Catholic One Year Bible': "If your faith were only the size of a mustard seed, . . . it would be large enough to uproot that mulberry tree over there and send it hurrying into the sea! Your command would bring immediate results!" —Luke 17:6

St. Magnus of Orkney *(APRIL 15)*

Magnus was a Viking prince who lived in the Orkney Islands, just north of Scotland, which in the twelfth century had been conquered and settled by Norsemen. Magnus was the son of Erling, one of the minor kings of the country, and had a brother named Paul, both heirs to their father's kingdom.

The other king of the island also had a son, Haakon, but he was so belligerent that his father sent him to the court of the king of Norway to get him out of the way. In Norway, he convinced the Norwegian king to conquer other islands along the Scottish and Irish coast, and St. Magnus of Orkney joined them on the expedition. However, when they attacked the island of Anglesey, Magnus refused to fight, saying that the attack was unjust and that he would have nothing to do with that kind of conquest. The king of Norway called him a coward and imprisoned him on one of his ships. Magnus escaped, sought refuge with the king of Scotland, and began to reflect upon the moral dangers of political life.

Later, Haakon returned to the Orkneys and tried to make himself sole ruler of the islands. He killed Magnus's brother in battle, forcing Magnus to come out of his exile to fight for his throne. He secured his right to govern and he and Haakon began to rule the islands together, Haakon a constant threat. Finally, Haakon invited Magnus to the island of Egilsay to discuss a treaty of peace between them. Magnus was attacked, but he refused to fight and was killed by Haakon's men. Highly revered by his people for his gentleness and sense of justice, Magnus was buried in the cathedral at Kirkwall where his bones were found in 1919.

Although Magnus was killed more for political than religious reasons, it was his holy life and Christian spirit that bore witness to his holiness. It is said that it was through his prayers that Robert Bruce won the battle of Bannockburn, and his feast is still observed in the diocese of Aberdeen.

Thought for the Day: St. Magnus of Orkney refused to fight in a battle which he knew to be unjust, and this made him reflect upon his own conduct and the purposes of government. Sometimes it takes a great evil to shock someone into scrutinizing what life is really all about. This kind of reflection made Magnus a saint. It certainly would not do us any harm.

From 'The Catholic One Year Bible': A good man hates lies; wicked men lie constantly and come to shame. A man's goodness helps him all through life, while evil men are being destroyed by their wickedness. — Proverbs 13:5-6

St. Benedict Joseph Labre *(APRIL 16)*

In 1776, the Coliseum in Rome became the home of a French beggar who made it his life's work to go on a continual pilgrimage to the churches and shrines of Europe. At the time, he was twenty-eight years old and he would live in Rome for another seven years. He was already a familiar sight in the city, for he had made many pilgrimages there from the age of twenty-two, when he began his strange religious odyssey.

He was born at Amettes in France, the oldest child of fifteen children, his father a local shopkeeper. When he was twelve, his parents sent him to study with an uncle who was the parish priest in a nearby town. There he became fascinated with the Scriptures and with the lives of the saints and decided to dedicate his life to God.

When his uncle died in a cholera epidemic, St. Benedict Joseph Labre returned home but soon convinced his parents to let him enter the abbey of La Trappe as a lay brother. Since he was only eighteen, he was told that he was too young. Disappointed, he waited and tried again to enter both the Cistercians and the Carthusians, but his health broke and he was told that his vocation was elsewhere. When he left the abbey of Septfons at the age of twenty-two, his only remark was: "God's will be done."

It was then that his pilgrimage began. He dressed as a beggar, begged for his food, and stayed at friendly homes and hostels. He went from church to church and from shrine to shrine, often sleeping on the ground, sometimes arrested for vagrancy, sharing whatever he had with other beggars. Then, in 1776, he remained in Rome, lived in the ruins of the Coliseum and made constant visits to the churches of Rome, especially those holding the Forty Hours. The Romans nicknamed him "the saint of the Forty Hours."

Early in 1783, he caught a severe cold accompanied by a violent cough and had to let up on his pilgrimages. On Wednesday of Holy Week, at the church of Santa Maria de Monti, he fainted, and a local butcher took him to his house. Everyone saw that he was dying. He received the Last Sacraments and died peacefully that evening. He was no sooner dead than the children in the street began shouting: "The saint is dead! The saint is dead!" One hundred years later, in 1883, he was canonized by Pope Leo XIII.

Thought for the Day: St. Benedict Joseph Labre discovered his own way to holiness: it was strange and different from anyone else's, but that didn't matter. He realized that he could find God anywhere and he chose to do it in his own unique way. Whatever the circumstances of our life, we can find God. Holiness is possible anywhere.

From 'The Catholic One Year Bible': . . . "Let the little children come to me! Never send them away! For the Kingdom of God belongs to men who have hearts as trusting as these little children's." — Luke 18:16-17

Stephen Harding, the legislator of the Cistercian Order, wrote its Charter of Charity, the foundational law of the order, and guided the order in its formative years.

He was born at Dorset in England and was educated at the abbey of Sherborne. He left England as a very young man for a pilgrimage to Rome and, en route back, stopped at the abbey of Molesmes in Burgundy. Impressed by the simplicity and austerity of the monks, he became a monk of Molesmes.

These were the days of monastic reform, and St. Stephen Harding was the driving force for a stricter form of monastic life. When other monks opposed the reform movement, he left Molesmes with the abbot Robert and twenty other monks to found another monastery. With the consent of the papal legate and at the invitation of the duke of Burgundy, they settled at a place called Citeaux. This was the beginning of the Cistercian Order.

Abbot Robert was called back to Molesmes by the pope, and the prior St. Alberic headed the new community. Upon Alberic's death in 1109, Stephen was elected abbot, the monastery having dwindled in numbers by the death of the first monks. No new novices joined the monastery, and it seemed that the life would not flourish.

In 1112, St. Bernard arrived with twenty-nine others to join the new foundation, and the order began to grow with this infusion of new blood. Within five years, three new monasteries were founded, and by 1119, when the first general chapter of the order was held, the order numbered over twelve monasteries. At the great chapter of 1119, Stephen read his Charter of Charity as the law of the order, and within a dozen years there were over a hundred Cistercian monasteries throughout Europe.

In 1131, now an old man, Stephen begged to step down as abbot of Citeaux, but the other abbots urged him to remain. Finally, in 1134, he resigned his charge. A few months later he was dead, having seen his order spread to every part of the known world.

He is considered the "prince and lawgiver" of the Cistercian Order and was canonized in 1623.

Thought for the Day: St. Stephen Harding had to search long and hard for the kind of life he wished to live for God, but he persevered and God rewarded his search. He wanted to live the life of a simple monk, but God had other plans. By his fidelity to his chosen vocation, he became the father of an order, enriching the Church with his own holiness and generations of Cistercian monks.

From 'The Catholic One Year Bible': The good man's life is full of light. The sinner's road is dark and gloomy. Pride leads to arguments; be humble, take advice and become wise. — **Proverbs 13:9-10**

Barbara was the daughter of Nicholas Avrillot, a French government official, and was educated at a convent at Lonchamps where her aunt was superior. When Barbara was seventeen, she married Peter Acarie, a young lawyer with an important position in the treasury. He was known for giving much help to the English Catholics exiled in France during the reign of Elizabeth I.

Peter and Barbara had six children, whose education was deeply religious. Her three daughters became nuns, one son became a priest, and the other two sons lived lives that were a credit to their faith and to their parents.

Peter Acarie had been a supporter of the Catholic League and went heavily into debt for the Catholic cause. He was banished from Paris by King Henry IV, and his property was seized by his creditors. Barbara Acarie defended her husband before the king, made settlements with his creditors, and convinced the king to let the family return to Paris. So impressed was the royal family with Barbara that they supported her plan to bring the Carmelites to Paris. She was the prime mover in establishing the reform of St. Teresa in France. In this work, she was advised by St. Francis de Sales and Peter de Berulle, the founder of the French Oratorians. On the death of her husband in 1613, Barbara Acarie became a Carmelite herself and lived as a simple lay sister at the convent at Amiens, where her daughter was subprioress. She took the name Mary of the Incarnation.

The last four years of her life were spent in obscurity. She was known for her life of intense prayer, for deep mystical gifts, and for the kindest and gentlest of dispositions. Through some misunderstanding with Father Berulle, she was transferred to the convent at Pontoise before she died. Early in 1618, she became paralyzed and realized the end was near. At three o'clock on Easter morning, she received Viaticum and died while receiving the Last Anointing. She was beatified in 1791.

Thought for the Day: Blessed Mary of the Incarnation became a saint as a wife and mother and was a saint before she put on the habit of Carmel. She showed indomitable energy in bringing up her family, supporting her husband, and spreading good all around her. She became holy where God had placed her, and it was as a married woman that she found her way to God.

From 'The Catholic One Year Bible': . . . "This shows that salvation has come to this home today. This man [Zaccheus] was one of the lost sons of Abraham, and I, the Messiah, have come to search for and to save such souls as his." — Luke 19:9-10

St. Paul of the Cross *(APRIL 19)*

Paul of the Cross, the founder of the Passionists, was a mystic, a missionary, and an outstanding preacher. He was born in Ovada, Italy, in 1694, and his father was a cloth merchant. He was the second of sixteen children, and, although his family was of the nobility, the family was often in deep financial distress.

Because of his family's poverty, St. Paul of the Cross had to leave school; but, determined to further his education, he studied on his own. In 1717, he enlisted in the Venetian army, hoping to die for the faith in a war with the Turks. In 1720, he felt a call to found his own religious order and, after forty days in prayer, composed the rule that would become the foundation of the Passionist Order.

In 1727, together with his brother John Baptist he was ordained a priest and began a preaching and missionary career that would span almost fifty years. Slowly he gathered around him a group of followers, and in 1741 his rule was approved by Pope Benedict XIV. He also carried on a vast program of spiritual direction, sending thousands of letters to his penitents, showing himself a vibrant mystic and a master of the spiritual life.

His congregation expanded rapidly, and at the time of his death, he had founded twelve houses of his order, established two provinces, and founded as well an order of cloistered, contemplative nuns. In all of his works and writings, he showed himself the mystic of the cross, wrapped up in the Passion of Christ, and making the Passion effective in the souls of others.

In 1769, the Congregation of the Passion received final authorization from Pope Clement XIV, and Paul wanted to retire into solitude for the remainder of his life. His followers and the pope, however, begged him to remain as the head of the congregation. Old and ill, he spent his last years in Rome and died on October 18, 1775, at the age of eighty. He was canonized by Pope Pius IX in 1867.

Thought for the Day: The Passion of Christ is the cause of our salvation, and the fruits of the Passion flow through the Church like a mighty river. Devotion to the Passion of Christ is at the very heart of Christianity, and meditation on the Passion brings us closer to Jesus Christ. We should always be mindful of the price paid for our salvation.

From 'The Catholic One Year Bible': . . . The crowds spread out their robes along the road ahead of him, and as they reached the place where the road started down from the Mount of Olives, the whole procession began to shout and sing as they walked along, praising God for all the wonderful miracles Jesus had done. — Luke 19:36-37

St. Hildegund (APRIL 20)

Hildegund's story reads like one of the fantastic adventures from the *Arabian Nights*, but the story is authenticated, and many versions of it were written after 1188, the year that St. Hildegund died.

In 1188, a novice was dying in the Cistercian monastery of Schonau, a novice who had entered as a lay brother and who, before "his" death, had told the prior and the monk who attended "him," the story of "his" life. After the death of this novice, it was discovered that "he" was a woman.

Hildegund was the daughter of a knight from the town of Neuss on the Rhine River, and after his wife's death, he decided to make a pilgrimage to the Holy Land and took along with him his little girl, who was twelve years old. He dressed her as a boy and called her Joseph. On the way home, he died; but before he died, he put his daughter in the care of a man who subsequently robbed her of her money and deserted her.

Still posing as a boy, she made her way back to Europe and became the servant of an old canon in Verona. She was mistaken for a robber and when released was almost hanged by the robbers themselves. She finally reached Germany and on the advice of an old recluse decided to enter Schonau monastery as a lay brother, disguised as a man. She succeeded in deceiving everyone, led a quiet, prayerful life, and on her deathbed told her life's story to the monk who attended her but not revealing her sex.

The story became something of a sensation in Germany, and the manuscript of Hildegund's life was widely circulated. In the very year of her death, Engelhard, abbot of Ebrach, wrote an account, when the facts of the story were still fresh in the memories of the monks at Schonau. Her story was popular in the Middle Ages and is printed in the *Acta Sanctorum* of the Bollandists.

Thought for the Day: It takes all kinds to make a world, the popular saying goes, and it takes all kinds to make a saint. Fantastic as St. Hildegund's story is, there is no doubt about its truth. She had to go to God in a most unusual way, and God accepted her the way she was. That she was different there is no doubt; that she was also a saint there is also no doubt.

From 'The Catholic One Year Bible': A man with good sense is appreciated. A treacherous man must walk a rocky road. A wise man thinks ahead; a fool doesn't, and even brags about it all! — Proverbs 13:15-16

Anselm — a monk, a scholar, and a most lovable bishop — was archbishop of Canterbury during a very difficult period in English history. He was not English, however, having been born in Piedmont, Italy, about the year 1033. He wanted to enter a monastery at the age of fifteen, but his father opposed the decision. After his mother's death, the young Anselm went to France for his education and, after considering entering Cluny, finally chose the abbey of Bec, in Normandy.

When Lanfranc, the prior of the monastery, was appointed abbot of St. Stephen's in Caen, St. Anselm became prior of Bec and remained in that post for fifteen years, making Bec the most outstanding center of theology in France. It was at Bec that Anselm wrote some of his most notable works, particularly his *Monologium* and his *Proslogium*. In 1078, he was elected abbot of Bec. Meanwhile, Lanfranc had been appointed archbishop of Canterbury by William the Conqueror.

In 1093, after the death of Lanfranc, Anselm himself was appointed archbishop of Canterbury by William Rufus, and there began that conflict between king and archbishop that would last until the death of the king. The king refused to fill vacant bishoprics, demanded huge sums for his wars, and confiscated the revenues of monasteries. Finally, in 1097, Anselm left the the country to consult with the pope, the king reluctantly granting him permission to leave. In Rome, he asked to be relieved of his office, but the pope refused and wrote a stern letter to the king. In 1098, Anselm attended the Council of Bari, which condemned the king for his treatment of his archbishop.

On the death of William Rufus in 1100, the new king, Henry I, recalled Anselm to England. But he insisted on continuing the policy of royal investiture of bishops, something forbidden by the pope and by Church councils, and Anselm felt obligated to leave England again and place his case before the pope. Anselm threatened the king with excommunication, and upon his return to England, at a royal council, the king renounced his policy of investiture. Anselm's future relations with the king were amicable — Henry even sought his advice and made him regent of England during his absence.

Anselm died in 1109, surrounded by the monks of Canterbury. In 1720, he was declared a Doctor of the Church.

Thought for the Day: St. Anselm was the student and scholar who felt out of place in the archbishop's chair but courageously opposed those who trampled on the rights of the Church. He would have preferred to study and teach, but he had to do battle with the enemies of the Church. We can't always choose where or how we will serve; what is important is that we serve well.

From 'The Catholic One Year Bible': An unreliable messenger can cause a lot of trouble. Reliable communication permits progress. If you refuse criticism, you will end in poverty and disgrace; if you accept criticism, you are on the road to fame. — Proverbs 13:17-18

St. Maelrubha *(APRIL 22)*

The great monastery of Bangor in County Down in Ireland was notable not only for its rich monastic life but also for the many missionaries who went forth from its cloisters to evangelize Europe. It was from Bangor that St. Columbanus set out on his journey through France, Switzerland, and Italy, founding the monasteries of Luxeuil in France and Bobbio in Italy, and leaving at Bobbio the *Antiphonary of Bangor*, one of the most valuable manuscripts of the Middle Ages.

St. Maelrubha was also trained at Bangor and, like St. Columba, was a prince of the Niall clan. Like Columbanus, Maelrubha received the best education available, and his mother was related to the monastery's founder, St. Comgall.

Maelrubha did not follow in Columbanus's footsteps but in those of Columba. At the age of twenty-nine, he left Bangor for Iona, Columba's island monastery off the west coast of Scotland, where Columba's memory was still alive. Leaving Iona, he set up his own monastic and mission headquarters at Applecross in Ross and from there he extended his missionary work in Scotland, among the Picts. And just as in the south, in Northumbria, the whole country north of the Tyne was called St. Cuthbert's land, so in Scotland, the whole coast from Applecross to Loch Bloom was referred to as St. Maelrubha's land. His name is everywhere. Like all Irish monks, he loved islands, and his favorite in Scotland was Inis Maree, where he had a small church and a favorite spring, still known as St. Maelrubha's Well.

Later legends had him martyred by Viking pirates who ravaged the coast, but this is unlikely, since the Viking menace did not begin until much later. Maelrubha carried on his work at Applecross for fifty-one years, dying at the age of eighty. A small hill at Applecross called Cload Maree marks the spot where he was buried. His feast is observed in the diocese of Aberdeen.

Thought for the Day: Preparation for a life's work is everything. St. Maelrubha spent long years at Bangor preparing for his missionary work in Scotland, preparing his mind and his spirit for the work God had called him to. Our first mission is to ourselves, and only when we have made God's work fruitful in ourselves can we turn our efforts to others. "Look to thyself," is the first law of the spiritual life.

From 'The Catholic One Year Bible': ". . . This poor widow has given more than all the rest of them combined. For they have given a little of what they didn't need, but she, poor as she is, has given everything she has." — Luke 21:3-4

St. George *(APRIL 23)*

The patron saint of England came to be honored in England chiefly through the crusades, which brought back to the British Isles the legends of his exploits, a Christian Perseus who slayed dragons and rescued fair maidens. The origin of his fame among the English must be traced to his tomb at Lydda in the Holy Land, site of the crusades, a city near Jaffa.

The legends of the Greek hero Perseus have him slaying a sea monster near Jaffa and rescuing a maiden named Andromeda, and it seems that St. George became the Christian counterpart of Perseus. That he was a martyr seems certain, and the city where his martyrdom took place was the city of Nicomedia, in what is now northern Turkey, during the persecution under the Emperor Diocletian. The emperor had built a palace there, and when the persecution began, hundreds of Christians were martyred. George was most probably a soldier in the Roman army, martyred, like St. Sebastian, because he would not renounce his Christian faith.

His remains apparently were brought back to Lydda, his native city, and his tomb was a place of local veneration when the deacon Theodosius passed through Lydda about 530. The early church historian Eusebius mentions an unnamed Christian soldier who was martyred by Diocletian in Nicomedia in 303, and it is quite possible that this soldier was George.

The *Acts of St. George* are an early form of Christian legend, which has him doing fantastic exploits, and the legend became part of Western religious lore in the *Golden Legend* of James de Voragine in the thirteenth century. St. George's association with Cappadocia is the mistake of a compiler who linked St. George with George of Cappadocia, a notorious figure in the Arian controversy.

St. George's association with England is undoubtedly due to Richard the Lion-Heart, the English hero of the crusades, who must have seen his tomb in Lydda or came across the legend in the East.

Thought for the Day: The Christian hero is not the slayer of dragons and the knight who wields the sword. The Christian hero is the saint, although saints, like St. Joan of Arc, could wield the sword, too. St. George became lost in legends and folklore, but he was a real soldier who gave his life in witness to Christ. That is the ultimate in Christian heroism.

From 'The Catholic One Year Bible': "I solemnly declare to you that when these things happen, the end of this age has come. And though all heaven and earth shall pass away, yet my words remain forever true." — Luke 21:32-33

St. Fidelis of Sigmaringen *(APRIL 24)*

Mark Roy was a brilliant law student at the university at Freiburg in Breisgau, Germany, and during his student years he taught philosophy at the university. In 1604, he became tutor to a group of German youths who wanted to complete their studies in several cities of Europe. The trip lasted six years, and the young men grew fond of their tutor whose generosity to the poor was becoming legendary.

On returning to Germany, he obtained his law degree and began to practice law in Upper Alsace. His complete integrity of character was notable, as was his advocacy of the poor and oppressed, so much so that he was known as "the poor man's lawyer." But he found the lay profession unscrupulous and crooked, and decided to dedicate his life to something better. He was ordained to the priesthood and entered the Capuchin Order in Freiburg in 1612, taking the name of Fidelis of Sigmaringen.

He became a dynamo of priestly activities: preaching, hearing confessions, and visiting the sick. He was elected superior several times. Finally, he was sent with other Capuchins to win back to the Catholic faith sections of Germany that had been converted to Calvinism.

In Rome, the Congregation for the Propagation of the Faith had been recently founded, and St. Fidelis of Sigmaringen was made the head of the mission. He brought hundreds back to the Catholic faith, spent whole nights in prayer, and gave fiery sermons that drew crowds. He was so successful that he made enemies, and these enemies stirred up the peasants by accusing him of being an agent of the Austrian government. Fidelis was told that his life was in danger, but he continued his work. Warned that it was dangerous for him to go to a place called Seewis, he went anyway, preached boldly in the church, and had scarcely finished when he was shot at, the bullet fortunately missing him. Taking to the road again, he was attacked by armed men who killed him. He was forty-five years old.

He is considered the proto-martyr of the Congregation for the Propagation of the Faith and was canonized in 1746.

Thought for the Day: Certain saints, like Fidelis of Sigmaringen, realizing that they were wasting their lives in the midst of greed and foolish ambition, decided on another course. Their gifts were turned to doing good and in this they devoted their whole lives. Sometimes a change is demanded in our lives and we have to have the courage to make the change.

From 'The Catholic One Year Bible': "Simon, Simon, Satan has asked to have you, to sift you like wheat, but I have pleaded in prayer for you that your faith should not completely fail. So when you have repented and turned to me again, strengthen and build up the faith of your brothers." — Luke 22:31-32

St. Mark

(APRIL 25)

Mark was the son of a Jerusalem Christian named Mary, whose home was a meeting place for Christians after the Ascension of Jesus. He is the author of the shortest of the New Testament Gospels and was an associate of both Peter and Paul.

When St. Peter escaped from prison under Herod Agrippa, it was to St. Mark's mother's home that he went. Mark was a cousin of St. Barnabas who, with St. Paul, spread the Gospel in Antioch, and when Paul and Barnabas began their missionary journey to Cyprus, Barnabas took Mark along. However, before their journey had scarcely begun, Mark returned home.

After the Council of Jerusalem, Mark accompanied Paul and Barnabas back to Antioch, and Barnabas wanted to take Mark on their next missionary journey, but Paul refused and there was a "violent quarrel" between Paul and Barnabas. Paul took Silvanus and went north and west, across Asia Minor (modern-day Turkey), and Barnabas took Mark and returned to Cyprus.

Later, Mark and Paul were reconciled, and during his imprisonment, Paul in his letter to Timothy asks for Mark's help. Peter in his first letter called Mark "my son," indicating that they had worked closely together. It is thought that Mark was probably Peter's secretary and that it is this close association with Peter that gives his Gospel its special character.

Early Christian legends associate Mark with Alexandria in Egypt. Eusebius, the early Church historian, mentions that Mark evangelized Egypt and was the first bishop there. According to this legend, Mark was martyred there and his bones brought back to Venice, where for many centuries they were kept in the basilica of St. Mark. Recently, the Holy See returned them to Alexandria, to the Coptic Church, whose members revere Mark as the founder of their Church.

Thought for the Day: St. Mark was the inadvertent cause of a quarrel between St. Paul and St. Barnabas. Saints were not immune from human failings, and it is good to know that saints sometimes could not get along. We should not be discouraged by our own failings; rather, we should try to turn all things to the good.

From 'The Catholic One Year Bible': . . . "Father, if you are willing, please take away this cup of horror from me. But I want your will, not mine." Then an angel from heaven appeared and strengthened him. — Luke 22:41-43

St. Stephen of Perm *(APRIL 26)*

In the fourteenth century, the Russian Church sent missionaries into remote parts of Russia, and their efforts of evangelization carried on the tradition of SS. Cyril and Methodius who brought Christianity to the Slavic peoples. One missionary in particular brought the Christian faith to the Zyriane people, beyond the Volga River, southwest of the Ural Mountains. He was so remarkable and so successful in his missionary methods that he is compared to Matteo Ricci in China and Robert de Nobili in India. St. Stephen of Perm was this person.

Stephen was a monk of Rostov, at a time when Russian monks became missionaries, in the tradition of St. Columbanus and St. Boniface. He believed that every people should worship God in their own language, and one of his first missionary tasks was to translate the liturgy and the Scriptures into the Zyriane language. In translating, he did not use the Russian alphabet; instead, he invented one, based on the symbols and signs that the people used in their embroidery and in their carvings.

He attracted these people to the faith by the beauty and solemnity of public worship and used all of the arts to make this worship something truly impressive. He was also a champion of the poor and oppressed, and as bishop of Perm was a true father to these newly converted people. He had been born among these people; he had a special love for them and brought to them the riches of the Christian faith and culture.

It was through his sensitivity to their customs and traditions that the conversion of the Permiaks (another name for the Zyriane), Chuvashes, Mordvins, and Lapps was brought about, and it was his concern to communicate with them in their own language that made his work among them successful. Stephen began work among the Zyriane in 1370, was made bishop of Perm in 1383, and died in Moscow in 1396.

Thought for the Day: Often the old ways do not work anymore and we have to come up with something new to spread the work of Christ. We cannot reach people who do not understand us or for whom we are strange and distant. God became a human being to bring us closer to Himself. For St. Stephen, this gave him his missionary method. We all have something to learn from this.

From 'The Catholic One Year Bible': A truthful witness never lies; a false witness always lies. A mocker never finds the wisdom he claims he is looking for, yet it comes easily to the man with common sense. —
Proverbs 14:5-6

Zita was not a nun, nor was she a mystic; she was not a queen, nor was she a foundress of a religious order. She was a simple servant girl who did her job well, devoted herself to the family she worked for, and bore witness to her faith by her fidelity and good-heartedness.

Born in 1218, she came from a poor family in the village of Monte Sagrati, Italy, and at the age of twelve went to work for the Fatinelli family in nearby Lucca. The head of the family was a weaver of wool and silk. It was a large household, and in the beginning St. Zita was harshly mistreated by many of the other servants. She crept out of the house early to attend the first Mass at the local parish church, rose to pray during the night while the others were asleep, and gave most of her food to the poor.

To the other servants her diligence was looked upon as a form of snobbery aimed at themselves, and they also resented her open distaste for foul language. Once, when one of the menservants made dishonorable advances toward her, she defended herself by scratching his face but refused to report the incident to the master of the house. Gradually, her patience, kindness, and firmness of disposition won the respect of everyone, and the family realized what a treasure they had in this young girl.

Her work was part of her religion, and she often remarked that a lazy servant was lacking in a religious spirit. She was put in charge of the children of the house and in time was appointed housekeeper. But she did not limit her work to household duties. She visited prisons, the sick, and the poor, and was the only one in the house who could subdue the violent temper of the head of the household. She became a familiar figure in Lucca, making her rounds of the hospitals, prisons, and homes of the poor.

Zita died on April 17, 1278, and was buried in the church of San Frediano in Lucca. Pope Pius XII proclaimed her the patron of domestic workers in 1953.

Thought for the Day: The life of St. Zita shows that fidelity to ordinary duties is a sure way to holiness. She was simply a servant girl, but she made her work a song of praise to God and her whole life an expression of religious devotion. Her life was full of the ordinary, and this is what made her a saint. That kind of holiness is within the reach of all of us.

From 'The Catholic One Year Bible': If you are looking for advice, stay away from fools. The wise man looks ahead. The fool attempts to fool himself and won't face facts. — **Proverbs 14:7-8**

St. Peter Chanel *(APRIL 28)*

On April 18, 1841, a band of native warriors entered the hut of Father Peter Chanel on the island of Futuna in the New Hebrides islands near New Zealand. They clubbed the missionary to death and cut up his body with hatchets. Two years later, the whole island was Catholic.

St. Peter Chanel's death bears witness to the ancient axiom that "the blood of martyrs is the seed of Christians." He is the first martyr from Oceania, that part of the world spread over the south Pacific, and he came there as the fulfillment of a dream he had had as a boy.

Peter was born in 1803 in the diocese of Belley, France. At the age of seven, he was a shepherd boy, but the local parish priest, recognizing something unusual in the boy, convinced his parents to let him study in a little school the priest had started. From there Peter went on to the seminary, where it was said of him: "He had a heart of gold with the simple faith of a child, and he led the life of an angel."

He was ordained a priest and assigned to a parish at Crozet. In three years he had transformed the parish. In 1831, he joined the newly founded Society of Mary, since he had long dreamed of being a missionary; but for five years he was assigned to teach at the seminary in Belley. Finally, in 1836, his dream was realized, and he was sent with other Marists to the islands of the Pacific. He had to suffer great hardships, disappointments, frustration, and almost complete failure as well as the opposition of the local chieftain. The work seemed hopeless: only a few had been baptized, and the chieftain continued to be suspicious and hostile. Then, when the chief's son asked for baptism, the chief was so angry that he sent warriors to kill the missionary.

Peter's violent death brought about the conversion of the island, and the people of Futuna remain Catholic to this day. Peter Chanel was beatified in 1889 and canonized in 1954.

Thought for the Day: Success or failure is often not completely in our hands, and sometimes we have to face what seems almost certain failure. But success is not required of us, only fidelity. St. Peter Chanel's work ended in his own death in the face of what seemed total failure. Out of that failure, God brought about the success Peter was seeking.

From 'The Catholic One Year Bible': . . . "Why are you looking in a tomb for someone who is alive? He isn't here! He has come back to life again! Don't you remember what he told you back in Galilee . . . that he would rise again the third day?" — Luke 24:5-7

Catherine of Siena is one of the most remarkable figures of the fourteenth century and had an influence far beyond her holiness of life. She took part in the politics of both Church and State and was a beacon of light in a very difficult time. She was born in Siena in 1347, the youngest of twenty-five children. Her father, Giacomo, was a dyer; her mother, Lapa, was a remarkable woman in her own right.

The mystical experiences that were to last throughout her whole life and an intimacy with her Savior that transformed her whole existence began when St. Catherine of Siena was but six years of age. She grew up, known for cheerfulness and merriment, with no indication of the astonishing role she was to play in the work of the Church.

In 1364, she became a member of the Third Order of St. Dominic, and from this time her influence began to grow in Siena as she gathered around her a circle of followers. She began dictating letters to this wide circle of friends and to take part in public affairs. (She had never learned to write, which was not uncommon for women of that era.) In 1374, given an adviser by the Dominican Order, she began to interest herself in furthering a crusade against the Turks and in the return of the pope from Avignon to Rome. In 1376, she went to Avignon to urge Pope Gregory XI to return to Rome. With her encouragement, he did, but he died shortly thereafter. She worked also to bring peace between the city of Florence and the papacy but without much success. In 1375, while on a visit to Pisa, she received the stigmata.

Pope Gregory's successor, Urban VI, so alienated the cardinals who elected him that they decided to elect another pope. This was the beginning of the Great Western Schism in which two — and later, three — popes divided the allegiance of Christendom. Catherine was shattered by this division in the Church and went to Rome to work for the reunification of the Church.

Burdened down with sorrow, and offering herself for the unity of the Church, Catherine died in Rome on April 29, 1380. She left a huge collection of letters as well as her chief work, the *Dialogues*. Canonized in 1451, she was declared a Doctor of the Church in 1970.

Thought for the Day: By the sheer force of her personality, St. Catherine converted thousands, and the mere sight of her would convert hardened sinners. We may not have her kind of personality, but we can reach into the lives of others and influence them for good. We cannot have warmth ourselves without giving it to others.

From 'The Catholic One Year Bible': They began telling each other how their hearts had felt strangely warm as he talked with them and explained the Scriptures during the walk down the road. — Luke 24:32

In December of 1565, Pope Pius IV died, his one monumental achievement the resumption and successful conclusion of the Council of Trent. The man chosen to succeed Pius IV and upon whose shoulders rested the responsibility for carrying out the decrees of the council was Michael Ghislieri, a Dominican friar. It was the late pontiff's nephew St. Charles Borromeo who had been the driving force in the election of the new pope, for he recognized that a remarkable leader would be needed if the decrees of the council were to bear fruit.

Michael Ghislieri was a poor shepherd boy who entered the Dominicans at the age of fourteen, became a lecturer in philosophy and theology at Pavia, and very early became involved in the reform movement in the Church. His reforming labors brought him to the attention of other members of the reform movement, and he was given important positions in Como, Bergamo, and Rome. In 1556, he was consecrated bishop of Sutri and Nepi, and then to the diocese of Mondevi, lately ravaged by war. In a very short time, the diocese was flourishing and prosperous. His views on reform were often asked by the Holy Father, and he was noted for his boldness in expressing his views.

His holiness and austerity of life were notable, and he succeeded in bringing simplicity even into the papal household. He refused to wear the flowing garments of previous popes and insisted upon wearing his white Dominican habit even as head of the Church. To this day, the pope wears white, a custom begun by this Dominican pontiff.

The announced intention of St. Pius V was the carrying out of the decrees of the Council of Trent. He insisted that bishops reside in their diocese under pain of losing their revenues; he made a systematic reform of religious orders, established seminaries, held diocesan synods, and reformed the Breviary and Missal. He brought unity into divine worship, published catechisms, ordered a revision of the Latin *Vulgate* and revitalized the study of theology and canon law. During his pontificate, the Turks were definitively defeated at the battle of Lepanto, due, it was said, to the prayers of the pope.

Pius V died in 1588, at the age of sixty-eight, deeply grieved by the troubles besieging the whole Church. He was canonized by Pope Clement XI in 1712.

Thought for the Day: Pope St. Pius V shows the critical importance of leadership in the Church and the astonishing influence of one great leader. Holiness anywhere is a source of great blessing, but in a pope, the influence touches the whole Church. We should pray that God will give us holy shepherds.

From 'The Catholic One Year Bible': . . ."I am a voice from the barren wilderness, shouting as Isaiah prophesied: 'Get ready for the coming of the Lord!' " — John 1:23

THE SAINTS OF MAY

St. Sigismund *(MAY 1)*

The era of the Merovingian kings of France was brutal and barbaric, and these kings were especially noted for their savagery and cruelty. But it was also a period of high sanctity, some saints martyred and others converting or converted. St. Sigismund was the king of Burgundy, whose father had been an Arian, and he was converted to the Catholic faith by St. Avitus, bishop of Vienne. But at heart he remained a barbarian, subject to violent, uncontrollable rages, like many kings of the period. He succeeded to the throne in 516 and, in 522, in one of his fits of rage, ordered his own son to be strangled.

The shock of this barbaric act brought him to his senses and in reparation he founded the monastery of St.-Maurice in present-day Switzerland, bringing monks from Lerins, Gigny, Ile-Barbe, and St.-Claude. He arranged that the *laus perennis*, the perpetual chanting of the canonical hours, should take place there and endowed the monastery liberally.

He also asked that God punish him in this life for his barbaric behavior; soon after, the kings of France declared war upon him to avenge the death of their grandfather, Chilperic, who had been put to death by Sigismund's father. Sigismund was defeated in battle, escaped, and fled to Agaunum, where he began to live as a hermit near the monastery of St.-Maurice, which he had founded. He was later captured by King Clodomir and, even though Bishop Avitus begged for Sigismund's life to be spared, he was killed by being drowned in a well.

The dead king was revered as a martyr from the day of his death and his relics were taken to St.-Maurice. In 1354, part of his relics were brought to the cathedral in Prague, Czechoslovakia, and others were transported to Freising in Germany.

Thought for the Day: Power can intoxicate, and kings in their lust for power have often lacked a sense of decency and justice. Association with St. Avitus made St. Sigismund realize that his behavior was anything but Christian and he tried to make amends. Sigismund listened to the voice of his conscience and found that it led to martyrdom. We, too, may have to suffer for trying to live our faith. It is one of the consequences of following Christ.

From 'The Catholic One Year Bible': . . . "Do you believe all this just because I told you I had seen you under the fig tree? You will see greater proofs than this. You will even see heaven open and the angels of God coming back and forth to me, the Messiah." — **John 1:50-51**

St. Athanasius *(MAY 2)*

Athanasius was the great champion of orthodoxy during the Arian crisis, patriarch of Alexandria during this critical period, and one of the first promoters of monasticism in the East and in the West. He is not only one of the most luminous figures in the early Church, he is also one of the Greek Fathers and a Doctor of the Church.

He was born about 293 of Egyptian parents and received a classical Greek education in the intellectual center of early Christianity, Alexandria. He was ordained a deacon under Alexander, patriarch of Alexandria, and accompanied his bishop to the Council of Nicaea in 325. In 328, he succeeded to the see of Alexandria and would remain the head of that see and the stalwart champion of orthodoxy for the next forty-five years.

From the beginning, he was beset by enemies who resented his strong anti-Arian stand and was exiled in 335 to Trier. The pope defended him, but the Eastern bishops refused to accept his decision, and St. Athanasius remained in the West promoting the monastic way of life.

He returned to Alexandria in 346. Ten years later, the Emperor Constantius began his persecution of anti-Arian bishops, and in that year, 356, Athanasius was driven from his see again, seeking refuge among the monks of the Egyptian desert. On the death of Constantius in 361, Athanasius again returned to Alexandria. He was exiled again, this time during the reign of Julian the Apostate; but on the death of Julian in 363, Athanasius recovered his see. Under the Emperor Valens, he was exiled once more, but now the Alexandrians, tired of the doctrinal war, forced the emperor to let Athanasius return. He ruled his see in comparative peace, working for the unity of the Church and defending orthodoxy by his numerous writings.

Athanasius was a prolific writer and has left a remarkable legacy of theological, ascetical, historical, and polemical works. He died in Alexandria on May 2, 373, and his body was first brought to Constantinople and then transferred to Venice.

Thought for the Day: At certain periods in Church history, it is one man who saves the Church for orthodoxy, one human instrument that God uses to further His work. We should all realize how important we are to the good of others and that, without us, certain people would never hear of God or come to a knowledge of Jesus Christ. Upon our fidelity may well depend the growth in the faith of many others.

From 'The Catholic One Year Bible': ". . . Usually a host uses the best wine first, and afterwards, when everyone is full and doesn't care, then he brings out the less expensive brands. But you have kept the best for the last!" —John 2:10

SS. Philip and James *(MAY 3)*

Philip and James were Apostles, mentioned in the Gospels, although there is some uncertainty about the identity of this particular James. For some scholars, he is James, the son of Alphaeus, mentioned in the Gospel of Matthew and in the Acts of the Apostles; for others he is James, the "brother of the Lord," mentioned in Acts and Galatians. For still other scholars, both men are the same. This St. James is also called "James the Less," to distinguish him from James, the son of Zebedee.

James, the "brother of the Lord" (in reality, probably a close relative of Jesus), became leader of the Jerusalem Church after Pentecost and the Ascension of Jesus. He was a highly respected figure in the early Church and a firm follower of Jewish traditions. He is thought to be the son of Mary's sister and "Clopas," whom some consider the same person as Alphaeus.

Because of his strong devotion to Jewish law, James was held in high esteem by the Jewish community in Jerusalem but was not in favor with the high priest. During a change of governors in the year 62, the high priest Ananus brought James before the Sanhedrin, who condemned him to death. The reason for the death sentence seems to have stemmed from the Sanhedrin's fear and resentment of the great respect in which James was held, giving a certain credibility to the Christian Church. According to one account, James was thrown from the pinnacle of the Temple and then clubbed to death. Ananus himself was dismissed from office by the next Roman governor, Lucceius Albinus.

St. Philip was an early follower of St. John the Baptist and was one of the first disciples called by Jesus. It was he who brought Nathaniel to Jesus, and he is mentioned in the account of the miracle of the loaves and fishes. On Palm Sunday, he was approached by certain Greeks who wanted to see Jesus, and Jesus spoke to him in his discourse at the Last Supper.

We know nothing more about the Apostle Philip, but it is presumed that he died a martyr to the faith like most of the other Apostles. The two Apostles have been associated in the liturgy since about the sixth century.

Thought for the Day: SS. Phillip and James left all to follow Jesus, to become His heralds to the whole world. They faced only difficulties, opposition, and — finally — death. We cannot avoid the difficulties that come with professing our faith and we are all in some respects called to be apostles. We should face our task with the same courage with which the Apostles faced theirs.

From 'The Catholic One Year Bible': ". . . As Moses in the wilderness lifted up the bronze image of a serpent on a pole, even so I must be lifted up upon a pole, so that anyone who believes in me will have eternal life." — John 3:14-15

Blessed Michael Giedroyc *(MAY 4)*

During the long period of peace in Lithuania, when Casimir IV was grand duke of Lithuania and king of Poland, the nobility of Lithuania were devout Catholics who built churches and monasteries and gave sons and daughters to the Church. King Casimir IV's own son St. Casimir became grand duke of Lithuania under his father, died of tuberculosis on a trip to that country, and was buried in the cathedral at Vilna.

Blessed Michael Giedroyc was a contemporary of St. Casimir's, born at Giedroyc castle in Vilna, his parents undoubtedly influenced by the wave of religious fervor that swept the country. Because of the political unrest, most sons of noble families were trained to be soldiers, but Michael was born deformed, a dwarf and a cripple. So very early, he took to study, even though his ill health and bad teachers hampered his progress.

He learned, too, that he had a very special talent: he was skilled at metalwork and made beautiful chalices and other sacred vessels of bronze and silver. Like St. Aloysius of Gonzaga, he learned the liberating power of fasting and as a very young man showed a strong attraction for the life of a hermit. With Poland and Lithuania united under one sovereign, many Lithuanians traveled freely in Poland; in Cracow, Michael discovered a penitential order of canons regular who had founded the monastery of Our Lady of Metro. Since his ailments made it difficult for him to live in community, he was given permission to live as a hermit in a cell beside the church.

Michael Giedroyc lived to be a very old man, and it is quite possible that St. Casimir himself consulted him. He was known to live a life of great simplicity and austerity and died in his cell by the church in 1485. An account of his life is given in the *Acta Sanctorum* of the Bollandists, and a description of the canons of Our Lady of Metro is found in a book on religious orders by Helyot, published in 1849.

Thought for the Day: Some people seem to be born with only disadvantages, and the future must have looked bleak for Blessed Michael Giedroyc. But he found his way to God in spite of his handicaps and was revered as a saint. No one is at a disadvantage when it comes to God, and no handicap can keep us from finding Him, serving Him, and loving Him.

From 'The Catholic One Year Bible': . . . "God in heaven appoints each man's work. My work is to prepare the way for that man so that everyone will go to him. You yourselves know how plainly I told you that I am not the Messiah. I am here to prepare the way for him — that is all." — John 3:27-28

Hilary was a relative of St. Honoratus, one of the early monastic founders (who founded the monastery of Lerins and later became bishop of Arles). Hilary had been persuaded by Honoratus to join him in Lerins and later became his close associate at Arles. When Honoratus died in 429, Hilary was chosen to succeed him.

Like Honoratus, St. Hilary of Arles was a monk-bishop, chanted the canonical hours in his cathedral, built churches and monasteries, and presided at church councils, particularly at the Council of Orange. He also engaged in a dispute with Pope Leo I over the jurisdiction of his metropolitan see. These were the days when jurisdiction over all the Western churches had been granted to the pope by the Emperor Valentinian III and there were many controversies over whose authority dominated in a certain area. Hilary was convinced of the rightness of his position and held his ground. In consequence, his see was deprived of metropolitan status for a while.

He was very young when he was consecrated bishop, only twenty-nine years old, but he showed a remarkable maturity in his spiritual life, spent time in manual labor to earn money for the poor, and spent much of the revenues of his diocese to ransom captives. He was a stirring orator and was able to speak to people of all classes and be easily understood. He traveled everywhere on foot, wore very simple clothing, and was a living example to his priests and suffragan bishops.

He died at the age of forty-nine, worn out by his labors, and in spite of his disagreements with Pope Leo was held in great esteem by that pontiff who referred to him after his death as "Hilary of sacred memory." At the Council of Orange in 441, he presided over the discussion of the very difficult question of predestination, raised by St. Augustine, and brought that council to a successful conclusion. As one of the first monk-bishops, he established monasteries and furthered the expansion of the monastic way of life.

Thought for the Day: In the monastic life, St. Hilary of Arles was faced with something new and original, but he recognized its value and became a monk himself. It was not the popular thing to do, and with his background and education he could have been successful in anything. Sometimes we have to recognize that the old ways simply will not do and put our hands to something new and different as our way of following Christ.

From 'The Catholic One Year Bible': Jesus replied that people soon became thirsty again after drinking this water. "But the water I give them," he said, "becomes a perpetual spring within them, watering them forever with eternal life." —John 4:13-14

St. Petronax *(MAY 6)*

In 581, the abbey of Monte Cassino, birthplace of Benedictine monasticism, was destroyed by the Lombards, and the monks took refuge in Rome, where St. Gregory the Great immortalized St. Benedict in his *Dialogues*. In 717, St. Petronax on a visit to Rome was encouraged by Pope Gregory II to make a pilgrimage to the tomb of Benedict, where he found only the ruins of the great monastery. Among the ruins, he found a few solitaries who chose him to be their abbot. This brought about the rebirth of this great abbey, and Petronax is considered the second founder of Benedictine monasticism.

With great effort, helped by the generosity of Lombard noblemen who were now Catholic, and with the support of three popes, Petronax rebuilt the great abbey. Among the treasures given to him during these years was a copy of the *Rule of St. Benedict*, written by St. Benedict himself, and thus the cornerstone for a great monastic revival was laid.

Under Petronax, Monte Cassino became the mecca of Benedictine monasticism, drawing monks from all over Europe, including several kings. It is believed that Petronax died in 747, the year that Carloman, brother of King Pepin of France, retired to Monte Cassino, and Rachis, king of the Lombards, joined him there in 749. St. Sturm, future abbot of Fulda in Germany, spent some time at Monte Cassino studying the Benedictine rule, and St. Willibald of England spent ten years at Monte Cassino as Petronax's disciple, afterward becoming bishop of Eichstatt in Germany.

With the restoration of Monte Cassino by Petronax, the monastic life began to flourish in Western Europe, especially after Charlemagne's visit in 787, when he ordered that the Benedictine rule followed at Monte Cassino be made the standard text for monasteries in his kingdoms.

Thought for the Day: It is difficult to begin all over again when something has been destroyed, and it sometimes takes more courage to begin over again than to begin in the first place. St. Petronax had to rebuild a whole monastic tradition, yet he recognized the great good that would come from his labors. But for him the great Benedictine monastic tradition might have died. He had the courage to start all over.

From 'The Catholic One Year Bible': Reverence for God gives a man deep strength; his children have a place of refuge and security. Reverence for the Lord is a fountain of life; its waters keep a man from death. — Proverbs 14:26-27

St. John of Beverly *(MAY 7)*

John of Beverly was an early English bishop, a contemporary of St. Bede's, and a monk of St. Hilda's great monastery at Whitby. As a young man, he studied at the school set up by Archbishop Theodore at Canterbury and was taught by Abbot Hadrian there.

After the death of St. Eata, who had been St. Cuthbert's abbot at Melrose and later bishop of Lindisfarne, St. John of Beverly was appointed to replace him in 686. He ordained Bede to the diaconate and later to the priesthood, and Bede in his *History of the English Church and People* speaks of him with great affection.

John's love and care of the poor as well as his love of solitude and prayer became legendary. Bede tells the lovely story of John's concern and care of a young boy who had difficulty speaking and who could say little more than "Ah." The bishop patiently taught him to speak, first one-syllable words like "yes," and then longer words and sentences. It is indicative of the great charity of the man and his deep interest in the welfare of others.

In 705, on the death of St. Bosa, John of Beverly was appointed archbishop of York. This was a difficult position, since St. Wilfrid had been driven from that see by the king of Northumbria and was still alive. John of Beverly had taken little part in the controversy but found himself in a delicate position. He carried on at York with the same simplicity and devotion he had shown at Hexham, building himself a monastery at Beverly to which he would retire from time to time.

He spent a dozen years at York, beloved by all, deeply revered by his priests and people, and noted for his many miracles. In 717, a very old man, he resigned his bishopric to St. Wilfrid the Younger, retired to his monastery at Beverly, and spent the last four years of his life in prayer and contemplation. He died on May 7, 721, and his feast is kept in Hexham and the northern dioceses of England. His shrine at Beverly became a place of pilgrimage and sanctuary during the Middle Ages and his relics are still kept at the church in Beverly.

Thought for the Day: The surest sign of closeness to Christ is kindness, kindness to all, especially the poor and the unfortunate. St. John of Beverly went out of his way to be kind, and his memory lived on among the people he served. The cultivation of kindness is at the very heart of holiness, and if we are seriously interested in being holy, we have to be kind.

From 'The Catholic One Year Bible': Jesus told [the sick man], "Stand up, roll up your sleeping mat and go home!" Instantly the man was healed! He rolled up the mat and began walking! — **John 5:8-9**

St. Peter of Tarantaise *(MAY 8)*

The Cistercian abbey of Tamié in France overlooks the Alpine pass from Geneva to Savoy, and the monastery became a hospice and resting place for travelers en route through the Alps. It was here that St. Peter of Tarantaise became abbot when he was only thirty and he was to become the glory of this monastery and of the see of Tarantaise.

He came from a poor peasant family near Vienne and as a young man entered the Cistercian monastery of Bonnevaux. Later his father and two brothers joined the same monastery. When a new monastery was built at Tamié, Peter became its abbot and with the help of the Count of Savoy founded a hospice for pilgrims and paupers, taking care of these guests himself and looking after their needs.

In 1142, he was chosen to be archbishop of Tarantaise, but he refused to accept, and it took the urging of St. Bernard and of the Cistercian general chapter to make him accept. The diocese was in shambles, churches were neglected, and priests lived anything but exemplary lives. He made a visitation of the diocese, appointed worthy priests to parishes, set up schools, and restored the dignity of divine worship.

After he had been archbishop for thirteen years, he suddenly disappeared, entered a monastery in Switzerland as a simple lay brother, and lived unknown there for a whole year. When he was discovered, he returned to his see and continued his work with renewed zeal. He rebuilt the great monastery of St. Bernard, which was a refuge to travelers in the Alps, and inaugurated the tradition of May Bread to the poor at harvesttime, when food was scarce. He supported Pope Alexander III against the antipope Victor, who was backed by the notorious Frederick Barbarossa.

On a mission from the pope to reconcile the kings of France and England, Peter became ill near Besançon and died as he was being carried to the abbey of Bellevaux. He was deeply mourned and his work as a peacemaker remembered for centuries. He was canonized by Pope Celestine III in 1191.

Thought for the Day: Our Lord said, "Blessed are the peacemakers." A most difficult and dangerous task: peacemaking. This was a task that St. Peter of Tarantaise took upon himself and he saw its critical importance in the violent period in which he lived. His own heart was at peace, and so he could reconcile others. We should look around us and see where we can heal and bring peace. It is a godly work and brings us close to the heart of Christ.

From 'The Catholic One Year Bible': A relaxed attitude lengthens a man's life; jealousy rots it away. Anyone who oppresses the poor is insulting God who made them. To help the poor is to honor God. — **Proverbs 14:30-31**

St. Pachomius *(MAY 9)*

Pachomius is the father of monasticism and it is to him that we owe the founding of monasteries as we know them: communities of contemplatives dedicated to celibacy, silence, solitude, study, and divine worship. He was a contemporary of St. Anthony's, who is considered the patriarch of monks, and both began their work in Egypt, south of the city of Alexandria, in the desert wilderness that gave many of these monks their official name: the Fathers of the Desert.

St. Pachomius was born a pagan in the Upper Thebaid of Egypt about 292, during the great persecution of the Emperor Diocletian against the Christians. He was a soldier in the army of the emperor and while being transported down the Nile was impressed with the kindness of Christians who came out to help the soldiers, offering them food and helping them in many ways. Pachomius was so moved by this display of kindness that when he returned home to Chenoboskion, he enrolled among the catechumens.

Hearing of an old hermit named Palaemon, Pachomius went to him and became his disciple, receiving the monastic habit and living a life of solitude, silence, and prayer. After six years with Palaemon, he moved a short distance away to Tabennisi and there founded the first *coenobium*, the first community of monks living under a common rule and governed by an abbot. It was he who conceived this form of life, organized it, gave it structure and purpose, and gave it a firm scriptural base. He founded several monasteries that formed a closely knit congregation and ruled his vast monastic family with great discretion.

He was a strong opponent of Arianism and welcomed St. Athanasius, when that saint was in exile. He also founded a community of nuns and gathered into communities many of the Coptic hermits who peopled the region. When he died, there were over three thousand monks in his many monasteries, and it was he who laid the foundation for the future development of monastic life.

Pachomius died on May 15, 348, during an epidemic that struck that part of the country. Within a few years, monasticism spread throughout the East and had begun to take firm root in the West.

Thought for the Day: St. Pachomius was noted for his discretion. He saw a need and he answered it with unusual judgment and creativity. As Christians, we are always facing new frontiers and with great discretion we have to find new ways to do the work of Christ.

From 'The Catholic One Year Bible': . . . Jesus took the loaves and gave thanks to God and passed them out to the people. Afterwards he did the same with the fish. And everyone ate until full! — John 6:11

He wanted to join the Dominicans, but he was so small he scarcely reached above the tabletop in the office of Blessed John Dominici, the Dominican prior of Santa Maria Novella in Florence. To put him off, the prior told him to go home and memorize the *Decrees of Gratian*, a compilation of Church law. Within a year, the boy had returned, had committed the decrees to memory, and was given the habit of a Dominican.

St. Antoninus was one of the first novices at Fiesole, which Blessed John had built, and among his fellow novices was the future artist Fra Angelico. After his ordination to the priesthood, Antoninus was made prior at Rome, Gaeta, Siena, Fiesole, and finally at Florence where he founded the famous Convento di San Marco, where Fra Angelico did some of his most memorable work.

He was summoned by Pope Eugene IV to take part in the Council of Florence in 1438, and as prior of San Marco, welcomed many of the prelates and scholars to Florence for the sessions of the council that took place there. It was at this time also that the great library of San Marco was opened to the public.

In 1446, much against his will, he was appointed archbishop of Florence but continued to live as a simple Dominican friar. Then, he became a veritable dynamo of activity: he rebuilt churches, visited parishes, preached incessantly, and brought about peace between political factions and religious orders. He was in Rome at the deathbed of Pope Eugene IV and was consulted by succeeding pontiffs in the reform of the papal curia. He was a superb theologian, his writings on moral theology and economics considered pioneer works in the changing society of his times.

Shortly before the death of Antoninus, a plague hit Florence, decimating the city, with many of his friars dying, and the people starving from famine. He sold everything to help the hungry and destitute. When a violent earthquake hit Florence, he helped to rebuild the city, housing some of the victims in his own home. He died on May 2, 1459, and Pope Pius II himself came to attend his funeral. The people of Florence, who loved Antoninus, placed his statue in the Uffizi Palace, the city's hall of fame.

Thought for the Day: St. Antoninus was noted for his love of people: people of all kinds, from those in high places to the poorest of the city. To help the poor, he organized the Poor Men of St. Martin, who exist to this day. What have you done for the poor lately?

From 'The Catholic One Year Bible': . . . "I am the Bread of Life. No one coming to me will ever be hungry again. Those believing in me will never thirst. . . . The true Bread is a Person — the one sent by God from heaven, . . ." — John 6:35, 33

Carthusian Martyrs *(MAY 11)*

It is one of the saddest stories in the annals of Christendom: Carthusian monks who wanted only to be left alone to live quiet lives of contemplation, caught up in the violent politics of the England of Henry VIII.

They were monks of the London Charterhouse, and the monks there had lived their quiet lives for over three centuries. Thomas More had spent his early years in residence there and the Carthusian cloister drew many sons of England to the quiet, secluded life. In 1534, Parliament passed the Act of Succession, on orders of the king himself, aimed at legalizing his marriage to Anne Boleyn and assuring that any son born of Anne would be king and supreme head of the Church in England.

The Act of Succession looked harmless enough and in its strict legal terminology did not involve matters of faith. When the monks were asked to swear to uphold the act, Prior John Houghton refused and he and his procurator were taken into custody. He was persuaded, however, by the archbishop of York that the act was purely a legal matter and Houghton deferred to the judgment of the archbishop and took the oath demanded by the king.

But soon the intent of the Act of Succession became clear when Parliament passed the Act of Supremacy, which made it high treason not to acknowledge King Henry as supreme head of the Church in England. When the Carthusians were asked to submit to the Act of Supremacy, they refused. They consented to obey the king "insofar as the law of God might allow," but this they were not permitted to do. Their trial took place in Westminster Hall on April 28 and 29, 1535. As they left the Tower of London for Tyburn where they were to be martyred, Thomas More watched them from his own cell in the Tower, and the peace and joy on their faces gave him strength to endure his own upcoming ordeal.

They were executed in their monastic habits, the executioner hacking their bodies to pieces through the thick robes that they wore. Those who were not executed were imprisoned and died in their chains, systematically starved, God accepting their total consecration to Him in a way that demanded the last full measure of sacrifice.

Thought for the Day: We may never have to face martyrdom, certainly not the terrible martyrdom that the Carthusian monks of England suffered. But our obligation to bear witness to our faith is no less. Sometimes it is more difficult to live for the faith than to die for it. When it comes to what we believe, it should be very clear where we stand.

From 'The Catholic One Year Bible': ". . . I am the Bread of Life! When your fathers in the wilderness ate bread from the skies, they all died. But the Bread from heaven gives eternal life to everyone who eats it. I am that Living Bread that came down out of heaven." — **John 6:48-51**

SS. Nereus and Achilleus *(MAY 12)*

Nereus and Achilleus have been honored in the Church from the earliest centuries, and a church in their honor was built in the cemetery of St. Domitilla in Rome, where St. Gregory the Great gave a homily in their honor during his pontificate. "These saints," he said, "despised the world and trampled it under their feet." A new church in their honor was built by Pope Leo III in the year 800, and this church in turn was rebuilt by Cardinal Baronius in the sixteenth century.

SS. Nereus and Achilleus were soldiers of the Praetorian Guard, the elite corps of soldiers who guarded the very person of the Roman emperor. They were banished from Rome with Flavia Domitilla, the grandniece of the Emperor Domitian, when it was discovered that her family was Christian. She was banished to the island of Ponza, together with those of her household who were also Christians.

Later, during the reign of the Emperor Trajan, all three were taken to the island of Terracina. According to St. Jerome, the banishment itself was one long martyrdom. Nereus and Achilleus were beheaded and their relics were placed in the family vault, in the cemetery of Domitilla. In 1874, their empty tomb was discovered in the underground church constructed in the year 390 by Pope St. Siricius.

From the inscription in that tomb, the two martyrs had been ordered by the emperor to take the life of his niece because of her Christian faith; but moved by her example, they became Christians themselves, refused to carry out the order, and were themselves banished and finally martyred. Their martyrdom, described in the *Acta Sanctorum* of the Bollandists, contains much legendary material and much embroidery of the facts; however, the basic account of their martyrdom is trustworthy, and they have been honored from the earliest centuries. The discovery of their empty tomb in 1874 confirms the great honor in which they were held and the example of Christian witness that made them early heroes of the Church.

Thought for the Day: At one time it was a crime merely to bear the name of Christian, a crime punishable by death. In spite of this, many became Christians and many went cheerfully to their deaths. As the thought-provoking saying goes: "If you were arrested for being a Christian, would there be enough evidence to convict you?"

From 'The Catholic One Year Bible': . . . "I'm not teaching you my own thoughts, but those of God who sent me. If any of you really determines to do God's will, then you will certainly know whether my teaching is from God or is merely my own." — John 7:16-17

Blessed Julian of Norwich *(MAY 13)*

Julian of Norwich is known only from the book that she wrote, which is considered a classic of spiritual and mystical teaching and one of the finest fruits of English mysticism.

In the fifteenth century, the period in which Blessed Julian of Norwich lived, it was not uncommon for anchorites (male hermits) and anchoresses (female hermits) to live in small cells by a parish church, spending their lives in silence, prayer, and study. Often, a little window in the hermit's cell looked into the main part of the church, and the hermit could take part in the Mass and other divine services that took place there. Julian was one of these many anchoresses and she has left us a record of her spiritual life in her *Revelations of Divine Love.*

Her cell was attached to the old church of St. Julian in the city of Norwich and, even in her lifetime, she had a great reputation for sanctity. She lived to a ripe old age and recorded her *shewings* (revelations) in language as quaint as it was colorful. From these *shewings* we get some idea of her mind and her personality.

When she was about thirty years old, Julian became deathly sick and was given the Last Sacraments. All she could do was keep her eyes on the crucifix. Then, suddenly, all her pains left her. It was then that she experienced her *shewings,* which taught her that love is the meaning of everything done by God. "Thus I learned," she wrote, "that Love was Our Lord's meaning."

She shows herself an excellent theologian in her writings, manifesting a love for the common and the ordinary as well as a remarkable insight into God's intentions for herself and for all mankind. From her little cell, she taught others, even though she never left her place of solitude. She tried to communicate to others the infinite kindness of God that she herself had experienced. She quotes our Lord as saying: "I can make all things well; I will make all things well; I shall make all things well; and you will see yourself that everything will be all right."

It is not known exactly when she died, but it is known that she was no longer living in her cell in 1423. Hers is no lofty doctrine but is addressed to the "little and the simple" and she calls her revelations, or *shewings,* exactly what she intended them to be: *"Comfortable Words for Christ's Lovers."*

Thought for the Day: Blessed Julian of Norwich pondered well the mystery of Christ's redemption and tried to understand its meaning for herself. Meditation has always been considered the first step to prayer and to the love of God, and no Christian life is possible without it. Through meditation, Julian discovered the wonder of God's love.

From 'The Catholic One Year Bible': Only a fool despises his father's advice; a wise son considers each suggestion. There is a treasure in being good, but trouble dogs the wicked. Only the good can give good advice. Rebels can't. — **Proverbs 15:5-7**

St. Matthias *(MAY 14)*

Matthias is mentioned only once in the whole New Testament. After our Lord's Ascension, he is chosen by the other Apostles to take the place of Judas and thus to complete the number of the Apostles. But from the short account given of him in the Acts of the Apostles, we know something about him.

He had to be an early disciple of Jesus, since the one chosen, in the words of St. Peter, must be "someone who has been with us the whole time that the Lord Jesus was traveling around with us, someone who was with us right from the time when John was baptizing until the day he was taken up from us." Since he was to be one of the Apostles, it was necessary that he be able to bear witness to Christ's resurrection, as this was the key to apostolic preaching.

There were two disciples who qualified: St. Matthias and another disciple named Joseph Barsabbas. According to an ancient Jewish custom, the selection was made by drawing lots, which was regarded as divinely directed. "And the lot fell upon Matthias; and he was numbered with the eleven Apostles."

That is all that we know about this Apostle. There were writings and legends about him in the early Church, and Clement of Alexandria mentions that he was one of the seventy-two disciples whom Jesus sent out, two by two. Early legends have his ministry in Judea, then in Cappadocia, and then along the coast of the Caspian Sea. It is said that he was ill-treated by the people among whom he preached and that he died by crucifixion. Legend says that his body was kept for a long time in Jerusalem and then was taken to Rome by St. Helena.

Like all of the Apostles, Matthias spent his life spreading the Gospel of Jesus Christ and gave his life as his final witness to faith in Jesus. He is considered the patron saint of carpenters.

Thought for the Day: The Apostles were given the mission to bring the Good News of Jesus Christ to the world, bearing witness to His resurrection and beginning the kingdom of God upon earth. For that, they left all things. All of us share somewhat in that mission and we all have to be apostles in some way. By our very baptism, we are sent to share the Gospel with others, just as St. Matthias did.

From 'The Catholic One Year Bible': . . ."I am the Light of the world. So if you follow me, you won't be stumbling through the darkness, for living light will flood your path." — John 8:12

St. Isidore

(MAY 15)

Isidore is the patron saint of farmers and workers and was born in Madrid, Spain, in the year 1070. As soon as he was old enough to work, he entered the service of a wealthy landowner named Juan de Vergas, and he remained in his service for the rest of his life. He married María Torribia, and they had one son, who died very young.

St. Isidore was noted for his deep religious faith and his religious attitude toward work. Every day was begun with Mass, and even though he often arrived later for work than his fellow laborers he never neglected his own work. His employer began to look upon him as a source of blessing for his own family and came to revere him highly. Some of his fellow workers once complained that his devotion to religion caused him to neglect his work, but de Vergas watched him one day and saw that the accusations were groundless.

Although poor himself, Isidore was generous to the poor. The poor would often follow him home, and on one occasion he arrived at a parish supper followed by a whole crowd of beggars. When it was pointed out to him that there was not enough food for such a large crowd, he told them that Christ would provide for his poor, and there was more than enough for all.

Isidore died on May 15, 1130, and his wife, who is also honored as a saint, survived him by several years. In Spain, she is known as Santa María de la Cabeza. Four hundred years after his death, King Philip III of Spain fell sick and his doctors did not expect him to live. The relics of Isidore were brought in solemn procession to his sickroom and suddenly the fever left him and he recovered completely. The Spanish royal family promoted devotion to Isidore and worked for his canonization. In March 1622, he was canonized along with SS. Ignatius, Francis Xavier, Teresa of Ávila, and Philip Neri.

His tomb is in the church of St. Andrew in Madrid, and he is the patron in the United States of the National Catholic Rural Life.

Thought for the Day: There was nothing exceptional about St. Isidore's life except his obvious holiness. He was a husband, father, and common laborer who did all things exceptionally well and took his religious duties seriously. His life teaches that holiness is within the reach of everyone and that the life of the ordinary man can be a pathway to God.

From 'The Catholic One Year Bible': . . . "You come to me with a sword and a spear, but I come to you in the name of the Lord of the armies of heaven and of Israel. . . . And Israel will learn that the Lord does not depend on weapons to fulfill his plans. . . ." —1 Samuel 17:45, 47

St. Brendan *(MAY 16)*

In Brendan we have one of the most colorful figures in the annals of the saints, on whose life a mass of legends has been built. He early became the Christian Sinbad the Sailor. His travels and exploits equaled his Asian counterpart and earned him the title of St. Brendan the Navigator.

Brendan was descended from the Irish king named Fergus MacRoy, himself a figure in Irish mythology, and he was sent away at a very early age to be educated by Bishop Erc. He was placed in the care of St. Ita, who had set up a school for the education of the young at her monastery at Killeedy, and when he was young he was sent around to the great Irish abbots to be taught, including Jarlath of Tuam, Finian of Clonard, and Enda of Aran. Erc ordained Brendan at Tralee, and Brendan became the founder of many monasteries, the most famous that of Clonfert, which became one of Ireland's great monastic schools. One of his monks was the first to build a cell on Skellig Michael, that lonely monastic outpost off the coast of Ireland.

But Brendan's claim to fame rests on the *Navigatio Brendani*, the fantastic tale of his voyages and adventures in search of the legendary Isle of the Blessed, somewhere in the Western ocean. In spite of its fantastic form, scholars see some historic basis for the legends, and it is thought that Brendan and his companions may have touched the shores of Iceland, Greenland, and North America.

But to his contemporaries, Brendan was a spiritual father and monastic founder, some three thousand monks looking to him as their leader. His school at Clonfert rivaled Bangor, Moville, and Clonmacnoise as a center of learning. His sister, Briga, headed a monastery for nuns that he had founded for her at Enach Duin, and it was here that Brendan died, on a visit to her about the year 583. His body was taken secretly back to Clonfert. His feast day is celebrated throughout Ireland.

Thought for the Day: St. Brendan was anything but a conventional saint, and his life is filled with the marvelous and the unusual. Saints do not come in ready-made packages, and Brendan had a flair for the bold and the different. Each one of us has to go our own way to God and, except for sin, God accepts us just the way we are. That should be an encouragement to all of us.

From 'The Catholic One Year Bible': . . . "You are truly my disciples if you live as I tell you to, and you will know the truth, and the truth will set you free." — John 8:31-32

St. Paschal Baylon *(MAY 17)*

Paschal is another shepherd boy who became a saint. Besides his strong religious spirit, what was notable in his boyhood was a keen sense of justice, and he would insist on compensating local farmers for any damage that his sheep caused by nibbling on their vines.

When he was eighteen or nineteen, he tried to enter a monastery of the Alcantarines, a strict Franciscan observance founded by St. Peter of Alcantara; but he was turned down because of his youth. He was later accepted and from the first showed a remarkable independence of spirit. He went out of his way to feed the poor and, since he was the cook of the friary, his schemes were a source of entertainment for the other friars. He used to dance while cooking and preparing meals, and he was such a delightful companion that the other friars liked to have him with them when they traveled.

He was especially noted for his deep devotion to the Eucharist, and his face would practically glow when he knelt in the presence of his God. He liked to write prayers for himself or record his thoughts on odd scraps of paper, and some of these survived him.

Knowing his cheerfulness and complete lack of fear, St. Paschal Baylon was sent by his superiors into France with important papers for the minister general of their religious order, who lived in Britanny. He spoke no French, was accosted, beaten, and stoned by Huguenots and ridiculed for his religious habit; but he escaped harm and returned, his own cheerful self.

He was fifty-two years old when he died in 1592, on Pentecost, the very day he was born. Such a deluge of miracles followed his death that he was beatified even before Peter of Alcantara himself, the founder of the Franciscan reform to which Paschal belonged.

Paschal was canonized in 1690 by Pope Alexander VIII, and Pope Leo XIII proclaimed him the patron of eucharistic congresses in 1897. He is also known as the patron saint of the kitchen.

Thought for the Day: St. Paschal had a delightful sense of humor and a playful spirit that endeared him to everyone. Gloom seemed to depart whenever he was around. This kind of cheerfulness, however, is something not easily won and it has to be worked at. He simply refused to be a wet blanket to others and was remembered for making everyone's burden lighter.

From 'The Catholic One Year Bible': ". . . All of us must quickly carry out the tasks assigned us by the one who sent me, for there is little time left before the night falls and all work comes to an end. But while I am still here in the world, I give it my light." — **John 9:3-5**

John the Tuscan became pope in a very difficult time, in the year 523, when Theodoric the Ostrogoth was king of Italy and Justin I was emperor of Constantinople. Although Theodoric was an Arian, he had a policy of religious freedom in Italy and showed immense respect for the see of Peter. When the emperor, with the ending of the Acacian schism that divided Rome and Constantinople, inaugurated a policy of reunification for the whole empire, the policy included the closing of the Arian churches in Rome and throughout the empire.

This angered Theodoric, who expected the same tolerance for Arians that he showed toward Catholics, and he sent Pope St. John I on a mission of conciliation to Constantinople, meanwhile suspending his own policy of toleration toward Catholics. Suspecting Catholics in the West of conspiring with the emperor against him, Theodoric arrested and executed the philosopher Boethius and his father-in-law, the senator Symmachus.

Pope John made the long and difficult trip to Constantinople and was received with great honor by the emperor; he crowned the emperor as part of the festivities in his honor. He successfully negotiated the return of the Arian churches but was not able to reverse the policy of reunification of the empire and its policy of intolerance toward the Arians. On his return to Italy, Pope John was imprisoned by Theodoric, who looked upon the emperor's policy as undermining his own rule in Italy. Imprisoned in Ravenna, and cruelly mistreated, John died of starvation on May 18, 526. He was considered a martyr from the time of his death, and his bones were interred in St. Peter's.

Besides many gifts from the emperor, which were distributed to the basilicas of Rome, Pope John brought about the adoption of the Paschal cycle of the Alexandrian church, which had been adopted throughout the East. From this time also, the custom began of dating years from the birth of Christ, rather than by the years of the reigning emperor. This custom was later popularized and made universal by St. Bede in his *History of the English Church and People*.

Thought for the Day: St. John I tried to bring peace between king and emperor but succeeded only in endangering his own life. Such seems to be the lot of peacemakers. However, he was willing to take the risk and so should we in trying to reconcile others. Sometimes we succeed, but sometimes both sides turn against us. That is the risk, but that is also the challenge of being a Christian.

From 'The Catholic One Year Bible': "I am the Good Shepherd. The Good Shepherd lays down his life for the sheep. A hired man will run when he sees a wolf coming and will leave the sheep, for they aren't his, and he isn't their shepherd. . . . I lay down my life for my sheep."
—John 10:11-12, 15

St. Celestine V *(MAY 19)*

Celestine V is one of the few popes who resigned from office, and his life has a humor and a tragedy about it that illuminate the kind of man he was and his own particular brand of sanctity. It is significant that Dante placed him in hell in his *Divine Comedy*, because Dante looked upon him as betraying the cause of the Church by resigning.

Peter de Morone was the eleventh of twelve children, born of peasant parents in 1210 near Abruzzi, Italy. When he was twenty, he became a hermit on a solitary mountain. After a few years, he went to Rome to be ordained, took the Benedictine habit, then resumed his solitary life. When woodcutters invaded his forest solitude, he fled to another mountain, but at the request of his followers, he consented to head their community of hermits. His community received the approbation of Pope Gregory X, and they were called Celestines. For the rest of his life, until he was eighty-four years old, he lived the life of a solitary, revered for his holiness.

Then, unwittingly, this old hermit became involved in the politics of the time, when the see of Peter had been vacant for over two years after the death of Pope Nicholas IV. Two parties were deadlocked over the election of a new pope. A fiery letter from Peter de Morone told them to get on with the election, and the two sides decided to elect him as a compromise candidate. Peter protested that he was too old, but Charles of Anjou himself, the king of Naples, went to urge Peter to accept. It was said that two hundred thousand people greeted him on the way to his coronation.

Peter took the name Celestine V, and his pontificate was a disaster. He was manipulated by Charles of Anjou for his own political purposes, was forced to reside in Naples where Charles resided, and even appointed Charles's own son as archbishop of Lyons. He signed papers and decrees with no reason or logic, and the whole papal chancery was in disorder. Finally, after five months in office, St. Celestine V signed a decree authorizing his own abdication and resigned.

His successor was Boniface VIII, who, fearing that the former pope would be manipulated by his enemies, ordered Celestine to Rome. Celestine fled into the hills but was captured and kept in a papal castle near Anagni. "I wanted nothing but a cell," he said, "and a cell they gave me." He died on May 19, 1296, and was canonized in 1313.

Thought for the Day: St. Celestine V tasted bitterly his own failure, but this did not prevent him from being a saint. When he realized he was in the wrong place, he quickly did something about it, whatever the consequences. To admit failure takes a rare kind of courage, and that kind of courage is the stuff that saints are made of.

From 'The Catholic One Year Bible': "My sheep recognize my voice, and I know them, and they follow me. I give them eternal life and they shall never perish." — **John 10:27-28**

St. Bernardine of Siena *(MAY 20)*

Bernardine of Siena, whose father was the governor of the Tuscan town of Massa Marittima, was left an orphan. He was raised by his aunt, who sent him to school in Siena, where he grew up a happy lad who was the life of the party and something of a playful wit. In 1400, Siena was hit with a plague, and Bernardine organized a group of young men to take care of the sick, help families in need, and bury the dead. He himself became sick and was laid up several months.

When his aunt took ill, he cared for her until she died. He then entered the Franciscans and was ordained a priest in 1404. For twelve years, he lived a life of obscurity, then in 1417 he was assigned to preach at Milan, and soon his preaching was the talk of Lombardy, in northern Italy. He traveled on foot preaching everywhere, the churches not big enough to hold the crowds who came to hear him. Blood feuds were common in those days, and he reconciled enemies and healed deadly feuds. He stirred up the jealousy of other preachers and for a time was silenced by the pope.

He was offered the archbishopric of Siena but refused the appointment, and then in 1430 he was elected vicar general of the Friars Minor of the Observance (a group within the Franciscans) and had to give up preaching for a while. He brought the whole Franciscan Order back to a stricter observance and is considered the second founder of the order. Aware of the danger of ignorance, he was a strong advocate of learning and scholarship, and he himself was fluent in Latin and in Greek.

In 1441, St. Bernardine of Siena resigned his office and went back to preaching. Now his health was failing, and it was said that he looked like a skeleton. In the last year of his life, he preached for fifty consecutive days in Lent in his hometown of Massa Marittima, then tearfully told the townspeople farewell, begging them to keep peace with each other.

Returning to Naples, he collapsed on the way there and died at Aquila on the eve of the Ascension, May 20, 1444. He was sixty-four years of age. So numerous were the miracles at his tomb that he was canonized six years after his death.

Thought for the Day: In St. Bernardine's day, cursing was almost part of the common speech, and he combated it by promoting devotion to the holy name of Jesus. He even had cards printed inscribed with the holy name, and they were more popular than playing cards. He knew that you do not root out an evil merely by preaching against it; instead, you must put something good in its place. That is a piece of wisdom we can all afford to follow.

From 'The Catholic One Year Bible': . . . "I am the one who raises the dead and gives them life again. Anyone who believes in me, even though he dies like anyone else, shall live again. He is given eternal life for believing in me. . . ." — John 11:25-26

St. Godric *(MAY 21)*

Godric was a pirate, born at Walpole in Norfolk, England. He became a peddler as a young boy traveling from village to village. Soon he expanded his trade and attended the great fairs and festivals in the larger cities. On the coastal cities, a chance of greater gain beckoned him, and he became a trader on the seas. He traveled from port to port in Scotland, Flanders, and Scandinavia. He bought half shares in one ship and quarter shares in another, and also found other ways to add to his profits as he met lone vessels on the high seas.

One of his ships must have anchored at Lindisfarne, for he acquired a special veneration for St. Cuthbert. Then, with Jerusalem once again in Christian hands, he set out for the Holy Land, stopping off on the way home for a visit to the shrine of St. James at Compostela. He then became steward to a wealthy Norfolk landowner who pillaged the poor, giving some of the profits to Godric; but Godric's conscience began to bother him and he quit, setting off on a pilgrimage to Rome with his mother.

Something had happened to him on his many pilgrimages and, with the example of St. Cuthbert before him, St. Godric joined a hermit near Durham, spent two years in his company, and then took off for another pilgrimage to Jerusalem. Having made some kind of a promise to Cuthbert, he returned to England, founded his own hermitage on the River Wear, at Finchale, and spent the rest of his life there. The woods were full of animals of all kinds and, like Cuthbert, Godric had such a way with animals that they gathered around him, delighting him with their antics.

He had a special interest in ships and seemed to know when one was in danger and would break off conversation to pray for one. He foretold the day of his death, as did his patron, Cuthbert, and died on May 21, 1170, the year of the murder of St. Thomas Becket, whose martyrdom he had foretold.

He had a psalter that he treasured; he wrote and played music and left delightful memories to those who knew him, talked to him, and heard him sing his lovely songs.

Thought for the Day: As a young man, St. Godric saw great opportunities opening before him, opportunities for making money in very dangerous ways. At Lindisfarne, he glimpsed a different kind of opportunity. The thought stayed with him until he did something about it and started trading in the treasures of the kingdom of heaven.

From 'The Catholic One Year Bible': The road of the godly leads upward, leaving hell behind. The Lord destroys the possessions of the proud but cares for widows. The Lord hates the thoughts of the wicked but delights in kind words. — **Proverbs 15:24-26**

St. Rita of Cascia *(MAY 22)*

Rita of Cascia was caught up in the blood feuds of fourteenth-century Italy, married to a husband who mistreated her and was unfaithful, with sons to match his brutal and dissolute ways. The choice of the marriage was not hers; she had made other plans for herself, but in obedience to her parents' wishes she submitted.

The child of her parents' old age, she had a goodness that shone and was drawn to the life of the Augustine nuns at Cascia, a dream that never left her. Her husband was known for his violent temper even before she married him, and for eighteen years she bore with every kind of insult, cruel treatment, and harsh words. Once he begged her forgiveness for his violent ways, but shortly after that he was carried home dead, the victim of some vendetta. Her sons swore revenge for their father, and she prayed that they might die rather than be guilty of another murder.

Her prayer was answered. Both sons became very sick and, persuaded by their mother, died forgiving those who had killed their father.

Now St. Rita of Cascia was alone and looked forward to carrying out her dream of religious life. But the Augustinian sisters informed her that widows were not accepted. She tried again, begging to be received in any capacity, but she was turned down again. She would not give up, however, and applied once again; this time the rule was relaxed in her favor.

She became an exemplary nun, with special devotion to the Passion of Christ. For fifteen years before her death, this mystic of the Cross bore Christ's bloody thorn in her forehead. Because of this, she had to live as a recluse for the rest of her life.

Her last years were spent wasted by disease, and she died on May 22, 1457. Her body has remained incorrupt since the time of her death, and she was canonized by Pope Leo XIII in 1900. Her symbol is the rose, and she has been called "the saint of impossible and desperate cases." In 1946, a new basilica was built at Cascia to enshrine her body, and her tomb has become the site of countless pilgrimages.

Thought for the Day: St. Rita of Cascia's early life was filled with disappointment and frustration, and she seemed caught up in a web of violence she could do nothing about. Facing seemingly impossible obstacles, she became the saint of the impossible, the inspiration and advocate of those in desperate circumstances. Through her desperation, she learned to trust in God and He led her out of the maze.

From 'The Catholic One Year Bible': . . . "I must fall and die like a kernel of wheat that falls into the furrows of the earth. Unless I die I will be alone — a single seed. But my death will produce many new wheat kernels — a plentiful harvest of new lives." — **John 12:23-24**

St. Desiderius of Vienne *(MAY 23)*

In the year 602, Queen Brunhild of Austrasia in France was at the center of intrigue and conspiracy to keep her sons and grandsons on the thrones of Austrasia and Burgundy. Anyone she did not favor she conspired to kill, and anyone who opposed her will she ruthlessly destroyed. One of the churchmen who crossed this dangerous lady was Desiderius, bishop of Vienne, admired friend of Pope St. Gregory the Great and host to St. Augustine of Canterbury on his journey to the Anglo-Saxon kingdoms.

Little is known of his early life, but he was a student of the classics, was devoted to grammatical and religious studies, and had been offered several bishoprics, which he refused. In 595, he was persuaded to accept the bishopric of Vienne; he made enemies in trying to make reforms, enforcing clerical discipline, repressing simony, and objecting to the loose morals of the royal families.

Like St. Columbanus a few years later, St. Desiderius of Vienne experienced the wrath of Queen Brunhild, and she first tried to discredit him in the eyes of Pope Gregory, accusing him of paganism because of his knowledge and love of the Greek and Roman classics. Desiderius defended himself with the pontiff, and Pope Gregory accepted his explanation. The queen then had him accused of immoral behavior, and he was banished from his see by the Council of Chalon-sur-Saone. Four years later, he was recalled from exile and restored to his bishopric. He continued to reprove King Theodoric II for his disgraceful life as well as the queen herself.

This was too much for the ambitious and proud queen, and she first had the bishop arrested in his own church, then had him assassinated by henchmen of the king as he returned home from court. He was, however, a much beloved bishop and a town named after him, St.-Didier-sur-Chalaronne, grew up over his tomb.

Thought for the Day: St. Desiderius of Vienne lived in a period when power-hungry kings and queens oppressed their people, lived evil lives, and killed anyone who came in their way. Like St. John the Baptist, Desiderius boldly faced the ruthless rulers of which he was the shepherd and risked his life to remind them of their solemn duties to God. His saintly example was remembered for centuries.

From 'The Catholic One Year Bible': "How true it is that a servant is not greater than his master. Nor is the messenger more important than the one who sends him. You know these things — now do them! That is the path of blessing." — John 13:16-17

This remarkable Englishman was a writer of distinction, a composer of Latin riddles and popular Anglo-Saxon songs, and one of the most learned men of his time. His riddles have puzzled and delighted Latin scholars for centuries, and his popular religious songs were favorites of King Alfred the Great.

He was a relative of Ine, king of the West Saxons, and was a student of an old Irish monk named Maildub, for whom the abbey of Malmesbury is named. He learned all he could from Maildub, all the learning that Ireland could give, and then, in his early thirties, he went to Canterbury, the Canterbury of Theodore of Tarsus, where Abbot Hadrian was master of the monastic school. He received the monastic habit at Canterbury and then returned to Malmesbury to head the school there. About 683, he became abbot.

When the Wessex diocese was divided, he became bishop of the westernmost diocese, with his headquarters at Sherborne. He was familiar with the great men of his age and tried to brings words of peace when St. Wilfrid was driven from his see by the king of Northumbria. He corresponded with the learned King Aldfrid, when he became king of Northumbria, who had been a student at Malmesbury before going to Ireland to complete his studies. It is to Aldfrid that he wrote many of his Latin riddles and that strange Hisperic prose that so puzzled and irritated students of classical Latin.

St. Aldhelm was bishop of Sherborne for four years, "constant in preaching night as well as day, diligently journeying to the various parts of his diocese, given to fasting and good works, even as in the prime of his age." Since he remained also abbot of Malmesbury, he guided and encouraged his monks and furthered that sacred learning which had been the joy of his youth.

He died in May of 709 while visiting the church at Doulting. Knowing that his end was near, he asked to be carried to the church and there, sitting on a stone, he passed to his reward. He was carried in solemn procession back to Malmesbury and buried there.

Thought for the Day: St. Aldhelm delighted in sacred learning and searched England for the best teachers. Then, as teacher, abbot, and bishop, he drew from his storehouse treasures of wisdom for his students, his monks, and his people. For him, knowledge was the high road to God, and he followed it joyfully until the end of his life.

From 'The Catholic One Year Bible': ". . . I am giving a new commandment to you now — love each other just as much as I love you. Your strong love for each other will prove to the world that you are my disciples." — John 13:34-35

St. Bede the Venerable *(MAY 25)*

About the year 680, in the monastery of Wearmouth in northern England, a small boy stood in the sanctuary of the monastery church and, in a touching ceremony, was consecrated to God. He was about six years old, and the abbot was Benedict Biscop, founder of the monastery. The boy was Bede, or as he wrote it in Anglo-Saxon, Baeda, and he was to become the most learned man of his time and the light of Europe as it emerged from the Dark Ages.

When St. Bede the Venerable was twelve years old, an epidemic struck the country, and most of the monks at Wearmouth died. Bede and an old abbot buried the monks one by one, then took their places dutifully in choir to chant the divine praises. When he was young, another monastery was founded six miles away, the monastery of Jarrow, and there Bede would be sent and would spend the rest of his life, "learning, teaching and writing," dying in 735, in his sixty-fifth year.

At the age of nineteen he was raised to the diaconate, and at the age of thirty to the priesthood. He probably made a short visit to Lindisfarne to gather material for his *Life of Cuthbert* and may have spent a short time at York, when his friend Egbert was archbishop there. Otherwise, he never left Jarrow, set on the banks of the Tyne River, where the monks in their scriptorium created the *Codex Amatianus*, written on vellum, one of the loveliest copies of the Gospels surviving from the Middle Ages. Benedict Biscop had gathered in his two monasteries books from all over Europe, and Bede first became the student, then the teacher, and finally the writer. His *History of the English Church and People* makes him the father of English history, and his other writings throw light on a period that is all but lost in the dust of the past.

Bede died on Ascension Eve, 735, and his death is touchingly described by one of his students in a letter to a fellow monk. Bede was first buried at Jarrow, but in the eleventh century his bones were secretly carried away by a monk from Durham and now rest in the Galilee chapel of the great cathedral close to the tomb of St. Cuthbert.

Thought for the Day: St. Bede the Venerable delighted in "learning, teaching, and writing," and he realized that without holiness of life, teaching falls flat. It is the personal influence of the teacher that fashions goodness in others, not the mere passing on of information. Those of us who have to teach others should be mindful of this.

From 'The Catholic One Year Bible': "If you love me, obey me; and I will ask the Father and he will give you another Comforter, and he will never leave you. He is the Holy Spirit who leads into all truth." —
John 14:15-17

Philip Neri was one of those rare religious geniuses who leave the familiar paths of conventional religion and create something entirely new. He is the kind of saint that you simply cannot put into a category, for what he did was original, unique, and totally unprecedented. He was a Florentine, born when the memory of Savonarola was still alive in Florence, a lover of art and beauty, like all Florentines, and fired with something of the vibrant spirit of the Dominicans of the Convento di San Marco.

He was born in Florence in 1515, and from the age of seventeen lived with an uncle who wanted to set him up in business. Having other plans for himself, St. Philip Neri left for Rome where he tutored the two small sons of a fellow Florentine. He studied philosophy and theology at the Sapienza and at Sant' Agostino and then for thirteen years became the center of a group of laymen interested in living a more dedicated Christian life. He organized them into a confraternity to help poor and sick pilgrims. In 1551, while the Council of Trent was still in session, he was ordained a priest and became a popular confessor and preacher.

It was then that his concept of the Oratory began to take shape: a place for informal talks, discussions, prayers, and excursions into the country, stopping off at places of pilgrimage along the way. There were also musical performances in the evening and even picnics. This was so novel that Pope Paul IV forbade Philip to continue his activities. He suspected him of conspiracy against the papacy. His successor, however, Pius IV, permitted Philip to continue his work.

Several of Philip's followers became priests, and this was the beginning of the Oratory proper. His Oratories were beehives of activity with the most noted speakers of Rome attending and musicians like Palestrina providing the music. Pope Pius V became suspicious of all this strange activity, but St. Charles Borromeo interceded and saved the Oratory. Pope Gregory XIII formally approved the work, and the Oratory became part of the work of the Church.

Philip died in 1595 and was canonized in 1622. His body rests at the Oratorian Chiesa Nuova in Rome.

Thought for the Day: St. Philip Neri was called the "Apostle of Rome," and his work touched everyone in that bustling city. He knew how to reach everyone and made himself approachable to all. He attracted people by the sheer force of his goodness and showed them the grandeur of holiness. What do we do to attract others to goodness?

From 'The Catholic One Year Bible': "I am the true Vine, and my Father is the Gardener. He lops off every branch that doesn't produce. And he prunes those branches that bear fruit for even larger crops." — John 15:1-2

St. Augustine of Canterbury *(MAY 27)*

In the year 596, on the isle of Thanet, just off the coast of Kent in southern England, a strange procession made its way from the small church on the island to where the king of Kent sat under an oak tree, afraid that these strange messengers might be magicians to do him harm. The priest who approached him — dressed in the ceremonial vestments of a priest, with acolytes carrying a silver cross and a deacon holding high an icon of Christ the Lord — was St. Augustine of Canterbury, a monk of St. Andrews on the Coelian Hill in Rome.

Accompanied by thirty monks, Augustine had come at the express command of Pope Gregory the Great to evangelize the Anglo-Saxon kingdoms of Britain and to restore the ancient Roman discipline to the island, based on the provincial structure of Roman Britain. Before coming to England on what was considered a most dangerous mission, since the Anglo-Saxons were looked upon as little more than savages, Augustine probably consulted the *Notitia Dignitatum*, the official record of Roman government in Britain. But that record would be of little value to him in the evangelization of the Anglo-Saxon kingdoms.

He had been ordered to set up his see in London, but the headquarters of the king of Kent was Canterbury, and so Canterbury became the primatial see of England and remains so to this day. Within the year, Augustine had converted the king of Kent, whose wife was a Christian princess from Gaul, and very painfully and slowly began the work of restoring Christianity to Britain. There were bishops there already, successors to the Celtic bishops of Roman Britain, but the Anglo-Saxons were their hated enemies who had conquered their country and driven them from their homes and cities. Augustine's task was beset with discouragement and almost insurmountable obstacles, and he lasted less than ten years in his difficult mission.

Soon after his arrival, Augustine went to Arles, the prefectural headquarters, to be consecrated bishop and came back and consecrated bishops for London and Rochester, capitals of two kingdoms closely allied with Kent. He died in 605 and was buried in the monastery of SS. Peter and Paul in Canterbury.

Thought for the Day: St. Augustine of Canterbury was given a mission that seemed almost impossible, and he almost turned back and gave up. But he returned and tackled his mission one step at a time and saw a small beginning to his work. He had to leave the greater part to others, but he laid the foundations well. Sometimes that is all that is asked of us.

From 'The Catholic One Year Bible': "In just a little while I will be gone, and you will see me no more; but just a little while after that, and you will see me again!" — **John 16:16**

Blessed Margaret Pole *(MAY 28)*

Among the victims of King Henry VIII's purge of English Catholics was a widow whom Henry VIII at one time had called "the saintliest woman in England." She was of the house of the Plantagenet, the niece of Edward IV and Richard III, and the mother of Cardinal Reginald Pole. Her father, the duke of Clarence, had been put to death in the Tower of London in the confused politics that brought Richard III to the throne. She saw other relatives ruthlessly murdered as Henry VII took over the throne, including her brother, Edward.

She married Sir Richard Pole and was made countess of Salisbury by Henry VIII, partly to atone for her brother's murder under Henry VII's rule. At the birth of Princess Mary, the future Queen Mary Tudor, Margaret Pole became her governess and was very close to Henry's queen, Catherine of Aragon. With Henry's announced divorce and marriage to Anne Boleyn, Margaret Pole retired from the court. Then an action of her own son spelled her doom.

In 1536, Reginald Pole, soon to be made a cardinal, wrote a treatise attacking King Henry's divorce and his claim to be supreme head of the Church in England. Reginald Pole was in Rome, but his family was still in England, and Henry declared at that time that he intended to get rid of the whole family.

One son, Henry Pole, was arrested and executed. After the ill-fated Pilgrimage of Grace — a Catholic uprising in the north, which Henry quickly suppressed — Blessed Margaret Pole and her family were accused of conspiracy in the plot. Under questioning, she completely exonerated herself, but she was arrested anyway and eventually imprisoned in the Tower of London. The sole evidence against her was a banner of the Five Wounds of Christ, which had been the emblem of the Pilgrimage of Grace.

She was never brought to trial, for she was so beloved and obviously so completely innocent that no jury would have convicted her. Instead, Parliament passed an act of attainder against her and her family that effectively deprived them of their rights. After two years of extreme neglect and suffering, on May 28, 1541, Margaret Pole was led out of the Tower and beheaded. She was beatified by Pope Leo XIII in 1886.

Thought for the Day: Blessed Margaret Pole was caught in the politics of the time when evil men were determined to stamp out every vestige of goodness and honesty. She remained honest and good in spite of everything, faithful to her God to the last. Honesty and goodness were rare then and they are just as rare today.

From 'The Catholic One Year Bible': "As you sent me into the world, I am sending them into the world, and I consecrate myself to meet their need for growth in truth and holiness." — **John 17:18-19**

In the days of Charlemagne, before the stories of King Arthur and his Knights of the Round Table became popular, there were several *chanson de geste*, tales of noble knights, which, like the *Song of Roland*, sang of the heroism and bravery of the soldiers of Charlemagne. One of the knights so sung about was today's saint, St. William of Gellone, great general of Charlemagne, count of Toulouse, duke of Aquitaine, who led the armies of the Frankish emperor against Basques and Muslims, and brought about the surrender of Barcelona.

He married, had a son equal to himself in nobility and courage, and suddenly in 806 decided to take steps to dedicate his life to God. At Gellone, not far from the great abbey of Aniane, made famous by St. Benedict of Aniane, he found a site and built a monastery, taking monks from nearby monasteries to found it. He himself remained for a while at the court of Charlemagne, respected and loved by the king, who depended upon him for leading his armies. His sisters decided to become nuns, and he built a convent for them, not far from his monastery at Gellone.

Charlemagne himself had begun his great reforming program of monasteries that would be carried on by his son, Louis the Pious, and Benedict of Aniane would be the man commissioned to carry out this work. With some difficulty, and no doubt through the influence of Benedict of Aniane, William obtained permission from Charlemagne to dedicate his life to God. True knight that he was, he rode to the church of St. Julian in the Auvergne, hung up his sword, lance, shield, and armor in the sanctuary of the church, kept a long vigil before the altar, and entered the monastery at Gellone, which he had founded. St. Benedict of Aniane was there to receive him, and William took the saint as his director and spiritual guide.

William's example said much to the men of his own time, and many followed him into the cloister. He died on May 28, 812, and was buried in his monastery at Gellone. It was afterward renamed St. William in the Wilderness.

Thought for the Day: During these violent days, the Church made knighthood something resembling a religious order, with the knight consecrated to purity, justice, and devotion to Christ the Lord. These very ideals led many to the further step of consecrating their lives totally to God in monastic life. The appeal is as great today as it was then.

From 'The Catholic One Year Bible': A little, gained honestly, is better than great wealth gotten by dishonest means. We should make plans — counting on God to direct us. — Proverbs 16:8-9

St. Joan of Arc *(MAY 30)*

The Maid of Orléans is one of the most striking figures in the history of Western Christendom and has no parallels in secular or sacred history. She died when she was not even twenty years old and made a remarkable impression on all who knew her, even her enemies.

She was born at Domremy, a village in Champagne on the banks of the Meuse. A high-spirited, religious young girl, she was deeply distressed by the state of France, occupied by the English, her own little village of Domremy once sacked by Burgundian mercenaries, allied with the English.

The king of England had overrun France and claimed the French crown. France was caught up in a civil war, the two contending parties led by the duke of Burgundy and the duke of Orléans. When the soldiers of the dauphin, heir to the French throne, murdered the duke of Burgundy, Burgundy sided with the English.

When she was fourteen, St. Joan of Arc began to hear her "voices," urging her to save France, and finally giving her detailed instructions on what to do. They told her to go to Robert Baudricourt, who commanded the dauphin's forces at nearby Vaucouleurs. She did so and was laughed at and told to go home. At the insistence of her voices, she tried again and told Baudricourt of a French defeat that had taken place.

Impressed, Baudricourt sent her to the dauphin at Chinon, accompanied by three soldiers. At Chinon, the dauphin disguised himself, but she identified him and revealed to him a secret that convinced him of her mission.

She led the French armies to victories at Orléans and Patay, which were followed by the coronation of the dauphin at Rheims as Charles VII. An attack on Paris failed, and at a sortie at Compiègne she was captured by the Burgundians and turned over to the English.

She was imprisoned, cruelly mistreated, and brought to trial before the bishop of Cauchon, her captors doing everything to break her and convict her of heresy. After a trumped-up trial in which, under pressure, she denied her voices and then recanted, she was condemned as a witch and heretic and burned at the stake on May 29, 1431. She was canonized on May 20, 1920, and declared the patroness of France.

Thought for the Day: St. Joan of Arc was chosen for a mission that led only to disgrace and death, and she seemed aware of this from the very beginning. But this was the will of God for her, and she carried out that will, even though it destroyed her. That kind of fidelity should inspire us in our own carrying out of the will of God, no matter the cost.

From 'The Catholic One Year Bible': . . . Pilate posted a sign over him reading, "Jesus of Nazareth, the King of the Jews" . . . written in Hebrew, Latin, and Greek, . . . —John 19:19-20

Today is the Feast of the Visitation, and so we would do well to look at the other players in the drama of this feast day, SS. Zachary and Elizabeth, the parents of St. John the Baptist. It is to this event that we owe the great hymn of Mary, the *Magnificat*, and the song of Zachary, the *Benedictus*.

Zachary was a priest of the Temple in Jerusalem, and his wife was Mary's cousin. Mary's family had originally come from Jerusalem, and she still had relatives in Judea, even though she and Joseph lived in Galilee. In answer to their prayers, God enabled Elizabeth to conceive John the Baptist, and Mary had been told of this by the angel at the time of the Annunciation. When John the Baptist's future birth was announced to Zachary, he had hesitated to believe and had been struck dumb but recovered his speech after the birth of his son.

Mary came on her mission of mercy from Galilee in the north, taking the long road to Jerusalem, then to Ain Karim, south of Jerusalem. It was a long and wearying journey, much like the one she would take later for the birth of Jesus at Bethlehem.

Mary greeted Elizabeth, and Elizabeth sensed that Mary herself was to be the mother of the Savior. Mary sang her *Magnificat* to proclaim God's goodness to herself and His great plans for the redemption of His people. Later, at the birth of John the Baptist, Zachary consents to the name given him by Elizabeth, recovers his speech, and sings his own great hymn, the *Benedictus*, proclaiming his son as the herald of the Messiah.

We hear no more of Zachary and Elizabeth, but we will meet John the Baptist again when Jesus' work begins and John is baptizing in the Jordan. Mary returns to Nazareth to await the birth of Jesus. These two saints, Zachary and Elizabeth, play their part in the drama of the Gospels and disappear from the scene. They undoubtedly lived on at Ain Karim, perhaps dying before their son began his work thirty years later.

Thought for the Day: SS. Zachary and Elizabeth are living examples of the observant Jews of their day, steeped in the Scriptures and awaiting the redemption of Israel. Their admirable fidelity and devotion made them key figures in the coming of Jesus. Mary's kindness in going to help Elizabeth shows her own sensitivity to the welfare of others. It is something we should strive to imitate daily.

From 'The Catholic One Year Bible': . . . Joseph of Arimathea, who had been a secret disciple of Jesus . . . boldly asked Pilate for permission to take Jesus' body down; and Pilate told him to go ahead. So he came and took it away. — John 19:38

THE SAINTS OF JUNE

St. Justin, Martyr *(JUNE 1)*

He had studied all of the philosophies current in the Mediterranean world and had made his way from Nablus, in Samaria, just north of Jerusalem, to the city of Ephesus, listening to all the teachers, from those espousing Stoicism to those embracing Platonism. Then, an old Christian that he had met on the seashore opened to him a whole new world: the world of the Hebrew prophets and of Jesus Christ. The young Justin became a Christian. He became a teacher of Christian "philosophy," and then he left for Rome and spent the rest of his life there.

St. Justin was born near the Samaritan town of Sichem, at what is now Nablus, then called Neapolis. He was restless for truth, and when he found it on the seashore that day around the year 135, he became its great defender and "apologist." He is one of the earliest thinkers who were Christian, those who tried to explore their faith and relate it to other branches of knowledge. He was so convinced of the truth he had discovered that he wanted to share it. "It is our duty to make known our doctrine," he wrote, "lest we incur the guilt and the punishment of those who have sinned through ignorance."

He carried on dialogues with other learned men of his day and even wrote a defense of the Christian faith addressed to the Emperor Antoninus. He felt that if the truth about Christian teaching were known, many of the prejudices and persecutions of Christians would cease. In his writings, all the basic Christian truths are touched upon as well as Christian ritual and sacraments, and he gives an accurate description of the eucharistic sacrifice, as it was celebrated in his day.

After a public disputation with a Cynic philosopher named Crescens, whom he showed to be guilty of willfully misrepresenting Christians, Justin was reported to the prefect of Rome, examined on his profession of the Christian faith, and condemned to death. With several other Christians, he was scourged and beheaded. His writings were among the most popular of early Christian literature and gave the Christian faith a new respectability with those who called themselves philosophers.

Thought for the Day: When St. Justin found the truth, he studied it, tried to understand it, and strived to share it with others. He realized that it provided the solution to every human problem. But his was not just a verbal profession of faith: he died in witness to it. It was that important to him. How important is our faith to us?

From 'The Catholic One Year Bible': When they kept telling [Thomas], "We have seen the Lord," he replied, "I won't believe it unless I see the nail wounds in his hands — and put my fingers into them — and place my hand into his side." — **John 20:25**

St. Eugene I *(JUNE 2)*

When Pope St. Martin I was sent into exile by the Emperor Constans II, the emperor gave orders that a new pope should be elected who would not oppose the Monothelite heresy, which was troubling the empire and the Church at that time. For over a year, the Roman clergy refused to carry out the emperor's orders; but seeing the Holy See leaderless they elected one who they knew would oppose the wishes of the emperor.

St. Eugene I sent legates to discuss the Monothelite problem with the emperor, and the emperor wrote back demanding that the new pope recognize the newly appointed patriarch of Constantinople who was sympathetic to the emperor's views. The patriarch sent a letter to Pope Eugene that was ambiguous about the Monothelite question, and it so angered the clergy and people of Rome that they demanded that Eugene reject this intrusion by the emperor into the affairs of the Church.

Pope Eugene's reply to Constantinople so infuriated the emperor that he was determined to deal with the new pontiff the way he had dealt with Pope Martin I. But a new Arab threat on his borders prevented his acting, and Eugene was dead before the emperor could take any action. Eugene was known for his outstanding sanctity and for his gentle disposition. But he made it very clear that he was not someone to be bullied by an emperor, and Pope Martin I, from his place of exile, approved of Eugene's election. (Pope Eugene's is an unusual case of a pontiff being elected while his predecessor was still alive, but it is possible that he did not formally reign as pope until after the death of Martin I.)

Eugene died in 657 and was buried in St. Peter's.

Thought for the Day: There is an old Latin saying, *post honores, labores,* which means that there is more labor to a position of leadership than there is honor. Being elected pope is certainly a great honor, but the truly great pontiffs have labored to keep the Church free to do the work of Christ, sometimes risking their own lives to do so. Many of them, like Eugene I, have *Saint* before their name.

From 'The Catholic One Year Bible': "... Come and have some breakfast!" Jesus said; and none of us dared ask him if he really was the Lord, for we were quite sure of it. Then Jesus went around serving us bread and fish. —John 21:12-13

It is hard to believe that the brutal deaths of these young African saints took place in comparatively modern times. All of them were young, some no older than thirteen. Most of them were the pages of the tribal chieftain Mwanga, and it was well known that the loose-living Mwanga often used his pages for immoral purposes.

Mwanga had massacred a Protestant missionary and his caravan, and one of his Catholic subjects, St. Joseph Mkasa, reproached him for the massacre and for his evil habits. Joseph Mkasa was summarily beheaded.

Until the coming of Christian missionaries, Mwanga had had a free hand with his pages, and he found their sensitivity in the matter of chastity something unbearable. St. Denis Sebuggwawo who had been giving the pages religious instruction was sent for, and Mwanga ran him through with a spear. St. Charles Lwanga had baptized several of the pages and had saved several from the evil designs of the chieftain.

Angered by what he considered a revolt on the part of his pages, Mwanga called them together and told the Christians to separate themselves from the rest. Fifteen did so, including thirteen-year-old St. Kizito. When Mwanga asked them if they intended to remain Christians, they shouted: "Till death!" The king, livid with rage, ordered them put to death. They were sent to a place thirty-seven miles away to be executed, and three of them were killed on the way. At Namugongo, where they were to be executed, they were treated cruelly. A huge pyre was prepared and they were stripped of their clothing, wrapped in mats of reed, and set aflame. They all died calling on the name of Jesus.

Mwanga began a systematic murder of all Christians, including several Protestant missionaries. Along with the young pages, two older men, St. Matthias Murumba and St. Andrew Kagwa, were among Mwanga's many victims. But the example of the martyrs only encouraged more conversions. Within a year, there were over two thousand catechumens under instruction and hundreds of baptisms. The blood of martyrs was indeed the seed of Christians.

Thought for the Day: These young men went courageously to their deaths, happy in their newfound faith, something completely baffling to the African chieftain. To them, their faith was a treasure and they were willing to die for it. We may never be called upon to do that, but it should be very clear to everyone that we are Christians.

From 'The Catholic One Year Bible': During the forty days after his crucifixion he appeared to the apostles from time to time, actually alive, and proved to them in many ways that it was really he himself that they were seeing. And on these occasions he talked to them about the Kingdom of God. — **Acts 1:3**

At the age of twenty-two, Ascanio Caracciolo saw his world tumble around him when he was stricken with something resembling leprosy. He promised that if he recovered, he would dedicate his life to God. Finding himself suddenly cured, he took steps to carry out his promise, went to Naples, and was ordained to the priesthood in 1587. Then he joined the Bianchi della Giustizia, a fraternity that visited prisons and prepared condemned criminals for death.

A case of mistaken identity sent him in another direction. He had a distant relative whose name was the same as his own, dean of the church of Santa Maria Maggiore in Naples. A letter was sent to this distant relative by Giovanni Adorno, a Genoese patrician, inviting him to join in the founding of a new religious order. The letter was mistakenly delivered to Ascanio who, looking upon this as a providential act, joined Adorno in his plan.

At his profession, Ascanio took the name Francis. When Adorno died in 1591, St. Francis Caracciolo headed the new community, and a number of houses were opened in Rome and in Spain. Their work was chiefly in hospitals and prisons and they also set up hermitages for their members who wanted to spend more time in prayer and contemplation. Francis himself was in the confessional every morning and he would beg in the streets for the poor who came to him, invite them to eat with him, and even give them his clothing. He was known to cure sick people by a sign of the cross and because of his luminous preaching he was called the "Preacher of the Love of God."

In 1607, he gave up all administrative duties in his order and occupied a room under the stairs in the order's house in Naples. St. Philip Neri offered the clerks regular minor, as they were called, a house in Agnone that belonged to him, and Francis went there to open the new house. After a short illness, he died at Agnone on June 4, 1608. Considered a saint from the moment he died, he was beatified in 1769 and canonized by Pope Pius VII in 1807.

Thought for the Day: A missent letter sent St. Francis Caracciolo on his life's work. In the mistake, he saw an opportunity. He could have shrugged his shoulders and let the opportunity pass. God speaks to us in the circumstances of our lives, and we should be sensitive to His voice and His hand. Can we discern His hand in our own lives?

From 'The Catholic One Year Bible': As the believers met together [on the day of Pentecost], suddenly there was a sound like the roaring of a mighty windstorm in the skies above them and it filled the house where they were meeting. Then, what looked like flames or tongues of fire appeared and settled on their heads. And everyone present was filled with the Holy Spirit. . . . — Acts 2:1-4

St. Boniface *(JUNE 5)*

It is hard to believe that any one man could accomplish as much as St. Boniface did in his own lifetime. He planted the Catholic faith firmly in the soil of Western Europe and helped to create what became known as Christendom. His is an amazing record, and he is the glory at once of Anglo-Saxon England where he was born and trained and the Frankish and Germanic nations that he evangelized.

Boniface was born in Devonshire, in Wessex, England, and was trained by the Benedictines of Exeter, where he entered as an oblate. His English name was Winfrid, and very early he left Exeter for Nursling abbey, ruled by the holy and learned Abbot Winbert. At Nursling, after his ordination, he became director of the abbey school. He took part in local synods. Like St. Bede, he was deeply versed in Sacred Scripture and the Fathers and, like many Anglo-Saxon monks, looked longingly at the missionary fields on the continent.

When he was forty years old, Winfrid received permission of his abbot to do missionary work in Frisia, where St. Wilfrid had labored with such startling results. But Frisia was in a state of revolt, and St. Willibald who had come there years earlier had to flee the country. Winfrid returned to Nursling and was almost elected abbot of the monastery. Realizing he could accomplish little in missionary work without a commission from the pope, he went to Rome and was given missionary jurisdiction by Pope Gregory II, who also changed Winfrid's name to Boniface.

He first joined St. Willibrord in Frisia, then went on to Hesse where he baptized thousands; from there he was called to Rome and consecrated bishop. He left Rome with letters to Charles Martel who gave him a letter of safe conduct. For ten years, Boniface worked in Thuringia, then returned to Rome to be appointed archbishop. In 738, he was made papal legate to Germany, consecrated bishops throughout the new Christian territories, presided at synods, and founded his famous monastery at Fulda. From 742 to 747, he worked for the reform of the Frankish Church and saw archbishops consecrated for Rouen, Rheims, and Sens.

In 754, Boniface set out on a final mission to the Frisians and was massacred with fifty-three companions near Dokkum. His body was returned to Fulda where it still rests.

Thought for the Day: This untiring missionary did not let old age slow him down, and he began his final mission when he was almost eighty years old. What St. Boniface accomplished can only be called fantastic. So often we keep our faith to ourselves, when we should be sharing it with others.

From 'The Catholic One Year Bible': . . ."We don't have any money for you! But I'll give you something else! I command you in the name of Jesus Christ of Nazareth, *walk!*" —**Acts 3:6**

St. Norbert *(JUNE 6)*

The name of St. Norbert's order is unfamiliar to most Americans, but the Premonstratensians are an ancient order, founded in 1121. His canons regular of Premontré made a huge contribution to the religious culture of Europe and are as active today as they were when they were founded. One of its members founded and directs the "Church in Need," which works quietly in the Iron Curtain countries to assist Catholics where the faith is suppressed.

Norbert was a canon in the church of St. Victor at Xanten, with no higher ambition than to enjoy life and make a name for himself at the court of the emperor. In 1115, while riding in Westphalia, his horse was struck by lightning, and this close call with death changed his whole life. He put himself under the spiritual direction of the abbot of Siegburg, sold his estates, and gave all his money to the poor. He made a trip to Languedoc where the pope was residing, made a general confession to him, and put himself at the service of the Holy Father.

The pontiff gave Norbert a universal mission to preach, and he took on the life of a wandering preacher. He became the leader of a small band of itinerant preachers, living in poverty and simplicity. On the advice of Pope Callixtus II, Norbert established a monastery of canons regular in the isolated valley of Premontré, near Laon. His monastery grew, and he founded another, then drew up for his followers a rule based on that of St. Augustine: monastic in form but pastoral in its work. His monasteries multiplied throughout Europe and his order received the approval of Pope Honorius II. Much against his will, he was elected archbishop of Magdeburg. He entered his cathedral barefoot and was almost turned away because the porter thought he was a beggar.

He showed himself a forceful reformer of clerical life and was almost assassinated several times. During the schism that followed the death of Honorius II, Norbert supported Innocent II and with the help of St. Bernard had Innocent recognized throughout France and Germany. After this, his health declined, and he died on June 6, 1134. He was buried at the Premonstratensian church in Magdeburg. Later, his body was moved to Strahov near Prague. He was canonized by Pope Gregory XIII in 1582.

Thought for the Day: St. Norbert was thirty-three years old before he took God seriously, and during the next twenty years he made up for lost time. He did not stop to bewail his lost years but gave everything he had to God. It is never too late to begin, and God is always waiting for our service. We do not need a bolt of lightning to get started.

From 'The Catholic One Year Bible': All the believers were of one heart and mind, and no one felt that what he owned was his own; everyone was sharing. — Acts 4:32

Blessed Anne of St. Bartholomew *(JUNE 7)*

Anne of St. Bartholomew is the lay sister who was at the side of St. Teresa of Ávila when she died. She wrote a graphic description of Teresa's last journey from Medina to Alba and of Teresa's last moments. She had been Teresa's special companion on her many journeys, and Teresa valued the sound common sense of Anne and the practical gifts with which Anne was blessed.

Anne was the child of Ferdinand Garcia and Catherine Mançanas, peasants living not far from Ávila, and she had been a shepherdess as a young child. At the age of twenty, she entered the Carmelite Convent at Ávila, the first professed lay sister of St. Teresa's reform. During Teresa's lifetime, Anne refused to become a choir sister and was content to remain as she was.

Six years after Teresa's death, Marie Acarie and Cardinal Berulle invited the Discalced Carmelites to France, and Anne was part of the company that left for France, along with Teresa's successor, Anne of Jesus. Much against her will Blessed Anne of St. Bartholomew was chosen to be a choir sister; eventually she was made prioress of the convent at Pontoise, and then at Tours. She was not happy in a position of leadership, but she was told by our Lord: "It is with straws I light my fire."

When a Carmelite house was opened in the Netherlands, she went with Anne of Jesus to found the convent there and later headed a group of nuns who founded a convent at Antwerp. This monastery was soon filled. When Antwerp was besieged by the prince of Orange, it was Anne's prayers that saved the city, and she was declared the "Liberator of Antwerp." It was in Antwerp that she wrote her autobiography as well as instructions for her sisters.

When Anne died on June 7, 1626, twenty thousand people came to view her body. For many years afterward, she was honored with an annual candlelight procession to her tomb, led by all the city officials. She was beatified by Pope Benedict XV in 1917, and her memory is still honored by the Discalced Carmelites and by the city of Antwerp.

Thought for the Day: Although she wanted to remain a simple lay sister, Blessed Anne found that God had other plans for her. She had a practical common sense and a gift for guiding others that helped the expansion of St. Teresa of Ávila's reform. She chose one vocation for herself and she was given another, yet another example of how "God often writes straight with crooked lines."

From 'The Catholic One Year Bible': . . . "Men of Israel . . . leave these men alone. If what they teach and do is merely on their own, it will soon be overthrown. But if it is of God, you will not be able to stop them, lest you find yourselves fighting even against God." — Act 5:35, 38-39

St. Columba of Iona *(JUNE 8)*

This prince of Irish saints was himself a prince of the Ui Neill, of royal lineage. His first tutor was a priest-guardian whom he remembered fondly. At an early age, St. Columba of Iona was sent to St. Finnian's monastic school at Moville, then studied music and song at the bardic school at Gemman. All his life he treasured the bardic clan and even came back to Ireland to plead for the bards when an angry king would disband them.

He studied at Clonard, where he was ordained a priest, and then spent the next fifteen years preaching and founding monasteries: Derry, Durrow, and Kells, among the most notable. In 563, he went to Iona, some say in penance for a war fought in his name, but it is more likely that, like many Irish monks, he left his homeland to spread the Gospel elsewhere.

What he founded on an island off the western coast of Scotland was a headquarters for his own monastic *paruchia,* a federation of monasteries of which he was the head, which his clan would administer after his death and to which all the monasteries and all the lands he evangelized owed allegiance.

He converted kings, crowned monarchs, established churches, built monasteries, and sent his monk-missionaries far North, into the land of the Picts, into the Hebrides and Orkneys. His name is everywhere in Scotland, and the very name Scotland derives from him, for the Irish in his day were known as Scoti. With the Gospel, his monks brought culture as well: books and learning, music and poetry, sculpture and illumination. His monasteries always remained centers of learning as well as religion, and many kings of Scotland and Anglo-Saxon England were tutored by his monks.

He returned to Ireland in 475 to prevent the suppression of the bardic clan. At Iona, he was visited by kings and commoners, saints and strangers, scholars and students. When he died in 597, he had opened up a whole new field for the Christian faith, and within a few years his monks would evangelize northern England, founding Lindisfarne, which became the Iona of Northumbria.

Before he died, Columba made a trip around his beloved island, blessing every corner, then worked on a transcription of the Bible, laid down his pen, and died that night before the altar. His memory has lasted for almost fourteen centuries and gives no evidence of fading.

Thought for the Day: St. Columba of Iona could have been a king, but he chose to serve the King of Kings. Instead of an earthly kingdom, he founded a vast religious kingdom that brought the Christian faith to whole peoples. He always looked to the harvest to be gathered. His faith ignited the faith of others, and the flame he lit is still burning today.

From 'The Catholic One Year Bible': Hunger is good — if it makes you work to satisfy it! Idle hands are the devil's workshop; idle lips are his mouthpiece. — **Proverbs 16:26-27**

St. Ephrem of Syria *(JUNE 9)*

Syrian Christianity is lost in history, and its vibrant spirituality produced theologians and saints who had a profound effect upon the culture of the early Church. Ephrem is one of the glories of the Syrian Church and lived during the golden age of Syrian Christianity, the fourth century.

St. Ephrem of Syria was a teacher, orator, poet, and scriptural commentator, who possessed a deep insight into the mysteries of God. He influenced St. Basil and St. Jerome and has been called the "Harp of the Holy Spirit." He was born in Nisibis, Mesopotamia, about 306, and was baptized by James of Nisibis, whom he accompanied to the Council of Nicaea. He quickly became the most eminent teacher in the School of Nisibis and his fame spread throughout the Eastern Church.

When the Persians conquered Nisibis, Ephrem moved to Edessa, where he continued his teaching and his writing, becoming a friend and counselor to the bishop of Edessa. In 370, Ephrem made a journey to Cappadocia to meet Basil, and their meeting is mentioned by Basil's brother, St. Gregory of Nyssa. Jerome spoke of "the sublime genius of the man" and treasured his writings.

The richness of the Syriac liturgy owes much to Ephrem's musical and poetic skill, and it is to him that we owe the introduction of songs into public worship. In many ways, he can be considered the father of Christian hymnody.

In 372, there was a great famine in Syria, and Syria became the center of a great program to feed the poor and hungry and nurse the sick. This great effort was too much for Ephrem, and a few months later he returned to the little cave where he lived outside of Edessa and died there in 373. In his writings, he shows his devotion to the Eucharist, to the Blessed Virgin Mary, and to the Holy Trinity. He was declared a Doctor of the Church by Pope Benedict XV in 1920.

Thought for the Day: St. Ephrem's eloquence came from his deep knowledge and his intense love of God. His whole person radiated the depths of his faith and the intensity of his devotion. This is what he communicated in his sermons and in his writings. Something of that faith should shine in our lives and spread its glow to those we live with.

From 'The Catholic One Year Bible': An evil man sows strife; gossip separates the best of friends. Wickedness loves company — and leads others into sin. — Proverbs 16:28-29

St. Aelred

(JUNE 10)

This is one of the most lovable saints who ever lived, who wrote a classic on friendship and ruled a monastery with hundreds of monks by the sheer power of love.

St. Aelred was the son of a noble family in Hexham, in northern England, whose father was one of the last of the hereditary priests of England. Hexham was the seat of a diocese, and Aelred was educated there and at Durham, where the body of St. Cuthbert was enshrined. As a young man, he was invited to the court of King David of Scotland and formed close friendships with several young men of the court. His friends were very important to him and he found it difficult to tear himself away from them, even when he felt called to the monastic life.

He entered the Cistercian monastery of Rievaulx in Yorkshire, was later elected abbot of a daughterhouse of the abbey, and then finally elected abbot of Rievaulx itself.

There he became one of the most influential men of his time, and his influence spread all over England. He preached and wrote and was adviser to vast numbers of people, including abbots, bishops, and kings.

Because of his warm personality and the spiritual quality of his writings, he was called the "Bernard of the North," and St. Bernard himself wrote to him, urging him to write. He was widely read in Scripture, the Fathers, the great monastic writings, and the best of contemporary authors. He wrote histories, rules for anchorites, ascetical works, and his most famous work, *On Spiritual Friendship*, the only treatise of its kind in the whole history of spirituality.

He governed a huge monastery and many daughterhouses, and he traveled all over England, his advice sought by king and commoner alike. After his death, his life was written by one of his monks, Walter Daniel, who lived under him for seventeen years and left an intimate portrait of him.

Aelred died in 1167, was a contemporary of St. Thomas Becket's and Henry II's, and, like them, was deeply involved in the history of the times. His monastery of Rievaulx still survives today, one of the loveliest monastic ruins in England.

Thought for the Day: Friendship is a precious thing, one of the great gifts of God. To cultivate friendship, especially with really good people, is to do something God-like. St. Aelred cherished his friends, spent himself for them, and deeply influenced them by his own noble spirit. We should emulate Aelred and cherish our friends.

From 'The Catholic One Year Bible': Blessings on all who reverence and trust the Lord — on all who obey him! Their reward shall be prosperity and happiness. — Psalm 128:1-2

St. Barnabas *(JUNE 11)*

When St. Paul came to Jerusalem after his conversion at Damascus, it was St. Barnabas who befriended him, convinced the Apostles of Paul's change of heart, and introduced him to the Jerusalem community. The two later worked together in Antioch and on St. Paul's first missionary journey.

Barnabas was born in Cyprus, a Hellenist Jew from the Diaspora. Early on he was a member of the Jerusalem community and may have been one of Jesus' disciples. He was well-to-do, of a Levite family, and gave the proceeds of his property to the Church. His name was Joseph, but he was called *bar-nabas* (Hebrew for "son of encouragement"), apparently for his ability to encourage others.

When the Apostles first received word of the conversion of Gentile Christians in Antioch, it was Barnabas whom they sent to look into the matter. He, in turn, went to Tarsus where Paul had been sent, and brought him back to Antioch to work for the stabilizing of the Church there. It was in Antioch that Paul and Barnabas conceived the idea of evangelizing their own home territories, Cyprus and the region around Tarsus. Receiving the blessing of the Antioch Church, they set out for Cyprus, accompanied by St. Mark, a relative of Barnabas, and then northward to the region around Tarsus. When they returned after a successful mission, they were sent by the Antioch Church to Jerusalem to settle the question of what would be required of Gentile converts to Christianity.

On returning to Antioch, Paul and Barnabas planned to set out again for a wider mission, but they quarreled over taking Mark along, and parted company. With Mark, Barnabas set out for Cyprus again. According to legend, Barnabas was martyred in Cyprus. He is mentioned by Paul in his First Letter to the Corinthians. St. Luke described Barnabas as "a good man, full of the Holy Spirt and of faith." But for him, Paul may have never left Tarsus, and it was through his acceptance of Paul that opened the way for Paul to become the "Apostle of the Gentiles."

Thought for the Day: St. Barnabas recognized the great gifts that God had given to St. Paul, and he stepped aside to let his confrere begin his great work. We should be able to recognize the gifts of others and should encourage them. It is for a good reason that Barnabas was known as the "son of encouragement": he encouraged others and was glad to see their work prosper.

From 'The Catholic One Year Bible': . . . As the murderous stones came hurtling at him, Stephen prayed, "Lord Jesus, receive my spirit." And he fell on his knees, shouting, "Lord, don't charge them with this sin!" and with that, he died. —**Acts 7:59-60**

Leo is the pope who crowned Charlemagne in Rome in the year 800, thus recognizing him as emperor of the West. This was the beginning of the Holy Roman Empire.

St. Leo III was elected pope in 795, but relatives of the dead pontiff Adrian I were unhappy with Leo's election and drove him from Rome. The pope fled to the court of Charlemagne in Paderborn, and Charlemagne restored him to Rome under the protection of the Frankish kingdom.

In 800, Charlemagne himself came to Rome to hold a meeting with Roman and Frankish officials to examine Leo's conduct, and the pope was cleared of all the accusations against him. On Christmas Day, while Charlemagne was still in Rome and was attending Mass at St. Peter's, Leo solemnly crowned him "emperor of the Romans." With this momentous act, the pontiff disassociated himself from the emperor in Constantinople, and the Western Church declared its intention to "go it alone." It was from this event that the great division between East and West began, culminating in the formal schism of 1054.

Unfortunately, Charlemagne began to conduct himself as a true emperor in the West, taking religious matters and religious questions into his own hands and attempting to compel the pope to follow his decisions. The Holy Father refused to be drawn into this obvious subversion of his authority and resisted Charlemagne's interference. But Charlemagne's patronage enabled him to act freely in the Church as a whole and even to settle disputes in the Eastern Church. After Charlemagne's death in 814, the Saracens invaded Italy and there was another attempt on Leo's life. It was through Charlemagne's overlordship that the pope stabilized his dominion over the Papal States and that the patrimony of Peter became linked to the see of Peter.

Leo III died on June 12, 816, after a pontificate of twenty years. His name was added to the *Roman Martyrology* in 1673.

Thought for the Day: In the midst of the violence of the times, St. Leo kept his tranquillity of spirit, guided the Church through difficult times, and gave it a totally new direction in the West. That he was a great pope is clear from history; that he was a saint is demonstrated by his deep devotion to Christ and his determination to put first things first.

From 'The Catholic One Year Bible': . . . When they came up out of the water, the Spirit of the Lord caught away Philip, and the eunuch never saw him again, but went on his way rejoicing. Meanwhile, Philip found himself at Azotus! He preached the Good News there and in every city along the way, as he traveled to Caesarea. — **Acts 8:39-40**

St. Anthony of Padua *(JUNE 13)*

In Anthony of Padua we have perhaps one of the most popular saints in the Catholic Church, the one that Catholics pray to more than any other saint, and the patron of lost things and a hundred other causes. In Brazil, he is considered a general of the army; he is the special patron of the poor and has been recognized as a wonder-worker from the moment of his death.

He was born in Portugal and entered the Augustinian monastery of São Vicente in Lisbon when he was fifteen. When news of the Franciscan martyrs in Morocco reached him, he joined the Franciscans at Coimbra. At his own request, he was sent as a missionary to Morocco, but he became ill, and on his return journey his boat was driven off course and he landed in Sicily. He took part in St. Francis' famous Chapter of Mats in 1221 and was assigned to the Franciscan province of Romagna.

He became a preacher by accident. When a scheduled preacher did not show up for an ordination ceremony at Forli, the Franciscan superior told Anthony to go into the pulpit. His eloquence stirred everyone, and he was assigned to preach throughout northern Italy. Because of his success in converting heretics, he was called the "Hammer of Heretics" and because of his learning, St. Francis himself appointed him a teacher of theology. St. Anthony of Padua was such a forceful preacher that shops closed when he came to town, and people stayed all night in church to be present for his sermons. He became associated with Padua because he made this city his residence and the center of his great preaching mission.

After a series of Lenten sermons in 1231, Anthony's strength gave out and he went into seclusion at Camposanpiero but soon had to be carried back to Padua. He did not reach the city but was taken to the Poor Clare convent at Arcella, where he died. He was thirty-six years old, and the whole city of Padua turned out in mourning for his passing.

He was canonized within a year of his death and was declared a Doctor of the Church by Pope Pius XII in 1946.

Thought for the Day: St. Anthony of Padua was a tireless preacher and brought others back to God by his words and example. But he first gave himself to God, and preaching was simply the overflow of his own inner life. For all of us, God comes first and the cultivation of intimacy with Him. Everything else flows from this as water flows from its source.

From 'The Catholic One Year Bible': As [Paul] was nearing Damascus . . . suddenly a brilliant light from heaven spotted down upon him! He fell to the ground and heard a voice saying to him, "Paul, Paul! Why are you persecuting me?" — **Acts 9:3-4**

St. Methodius of Constantinople *(JUNE 14)*

As a young man, Methodius went from his native Sicily to the emperor's court at Constantinople, hoping to obtain a position at court but instead decided to become a monk and built himself a monastery on the island of Chios. Called back to the imperial city by Patriach Nicephorus, he spoke out against the iconoclast policies of the emperor, in support of the patriarch. When the emperor sent the patriarch into exile for his views, Methodius went to Rome to inform the pope on the situation. He returned to Constantinople with a letter from the pontiff to a new emperor, Michael II, but the iconoclasts had Methodius imprisoned on the island of St. Andrew.

On the death of the emperor, his widow, Theodora, who opposed the iconoclast policies of previous emperors, deposed the patriarch of Constantinople and appointed Methodius in his place. St. Methodius of Constantinople immediately called a synod to endorse the decrees of the Second Council of Constantinople on the veneration of images and instituted a feast to further a sound doctrine of images. He is considered in both East and West as a key figure in the overthrow of the iconoclast heresy, and for his suffering under persecution and great endurance in suffering he is sometimes called St. Methodius the Confessor or St. Methodius the Great.

The iconoclast heresy is difficult for us to understand, but it broke out in the East as a result of the Arab conquests and a growing concern on the part of the Byzantine emperors for good relations with Muslims, some of whom were subjects of the empire. Many of the advocates of iconoclasm (which forbids the use of images) were monks, who were numerous in the Byzantine world and brought great pressure to bear upon the emperor.

As a heresy, it never took root in the West, and it was through the efforts of saints like Methodius that the heresy was eventually overthrown. At the Second Council of Constantinople in 786, the true doctrine regarding the veneration of images was proclaimed and it was the decrees of this council that Methodius enforced.

Methodius died on June 14, 847, and is venerated in both Eastern and Western churches.

Thought for the Day: St. Methodius suffered for his beliefs, enduring even imprisonment and near death. Sometimes our own fate is not under our control and we simply have to leave things in the hands of God, looking to Him for our hope and our deliverance. This is an old and unpopular doctrine, but the lives of the saints bear it out.

From 'The Catholic One Year Bible': . . . The church had peace throughout Judea, Galilee, and Samaria, and grew in strength and numbers. The believers learned how to walk in the fear of the Lord and in the comfort of the Holy Spirit. —**Acts 9:31**

St. Germaine of Pibrac *(JUNE 15)*

This is a Cinderella story about a young shepherdess who was mistreated by her stepmother and forced to live in a stable. But she became a saint, dying at the age of twenty-two.

She was the daughter of a farmer, Laurent Cousin, and was born in 1579 at Pibrac near Toulouse in France. Her mother died when she was a baby, and she was sick from the day she was born. Her father did not care for her and her stepmother developed an intense dislike for her and, because of her sickness, kept her away from the other children in the family. Eventually, she was made to live in a stable, eat what was left over from the family's meals, and take care of the sheep.

Alone in the fields, St. Germaine of Pibrac learned how to pray and opened her heart to God. The Mass was her joy and when the bell for Mass rang, she would place her shepherd's staff on the ground, commend her sheep to God, and go off to church. She loved children, and they would often gather around her in their play. She looked after beggars, fed them with what little food she had, and began to earn the love and respect of everyone, except the members of her own family.

Finally, her father and stepmother began to recognize her worth and invited her into their home, giving her a room under the stairs. But she continued to live as before, tending her sheep, going to Mass, and looking after her beggars. One morning she was found dead on her bed of straw. It was the year 1601 and she was twenty-two years old.

In 1644, when Germaine's grave was opened for another burial, her body was found incorrupt and in a state of perfect preservation. She was canonized by Pope Pius IX in 1857, and an annual pilgrimage is made to her tomb in the Pibrac church where her body now lies.

Thought for the Day: St. Germaine found God in the most trying and difficult circumstances: she was a sickly little girl, neglected by her family, and forced to live in a stable. She rose above these circumstances, however, and found God in her everyday life and even won over those who despised her. Whatever the circumstances of our own lives may be, it is possible to rise above them and cling to God.

From 'The Catholic One Year Bible': . . . Peter went up on the flat roof of his house to pray. . . . He saw the sky open, and a great canvas sheet, suspended by its four corners, settle to the ground. In the sheet were all sorts of animals, snakes, and birds. Then a voice said to him, "Go kill and eat any of them you wish." — Acts 10:9-13

St. John Francis Regis *(JUNE 16)*

John Francis Regis demonstrates the truth that missionary work is not only to be found in distant lands but that there is a mission field in one's own backyard for a whole lifetime. He was born in 1597 at Fontcouverte in Narbonne, France. At the age of fourteen, he entered the Jesuit college at Beziers, and in 1616 he entered the Society of Jesus. Although very studious, he spent the greater part of each night in prayer and even as a young student he had a powerful influence on both children and adults. He was ordained in 1631 and was assigned by his superiors to preach in the churches of the area. His simple eloquence attracted thousands, and he had a knack for helping the poor in numerous ways.

St. John Francis Regis spent every morning in the confessional and sometimes forgot his meals. He worked especially among the Protesant Huguenots, formed a committee to look after those in prison, and even brought about the conversion of women of the streets. He would go to the most out-of-the-way places and get close to people by speaking to them in their own dialect.

Civil strife had decimated France, and there were places where law and order had disappeared. Parish churches were neglected or deserted, and indifference to religion was widespread. John Francis Regis, in the less than ten years in which he labored, brought about a spiritual revival throughout France; he revitalized whole dioceses and concentrated especially on the mountain towns where priests were few and morals were lax.

He was criticized, snowbound at times, attacked by those who hated religion, and often went without food. He established social services for the poor, the sick, wayward women, and those in prison, and literally transformed the Church wherever he labored. He applied several times for the missions of North America, but his superiors, recognizing the importance of his work, refused to grant his request.

In 1640, after being exposed to the cold in an abandoned house in which he had stayed all night, he caught pleurisy. He preached continually for the next three days but fell unconscious in the confessional, was taken to the priest's house, and died five days later. His body remained at La Louvesc where he died. He was canonized in 1737.

Thought for the Day: St. John Francis Regis found his whole strength in prayer: prayer was his life, the air he breathed, the food and drink of his spirit. He found in it inspiration and insight, strength and support, and the only real comfort that he had in life. For the saints, prayer is the solution to everything, and that is a lesson that they pass on to us.

From 'The Catholic One Year Bible': . . . "I see very clearly that . . . [God favors] those who worship him and do good deeds and are acceptable to him." — Acts 10:34

St. Hervé

In ancient Britain, as in Ireland, the bard was a sacred calling and it was the bard who kept alive the traditions of the tribe and sang of the exploits of kings and warriors. When the Saxons invaded Britain, many of the native bards fled, first to Britanny and then to other parts of the continent. One of them, named Hyvarnion, came to the court of King Childebert in Paris about the year 525 and became something of a bard for the court of the king. He then went to Britanny where he married a girl named Rivanon; they had a son who was born blind, whom they named Hervé (or Harvey, as he is also known).

When Hyvarnion died, his mother put the boy in the care of an old hermit named Arthian, and he later joined the monastic school at Plouvien, headed by his uncle.

St. Hervé had a special love for animals, and it was rumored that he had even tamed a wolf to pull his plow when his donkey died. Even though blind, he had something of his father's love of music and may even have been the minstrel of the monastery. At a very young age, he was given charge of the monastery at Plouvien; a few years later he left with a group of monks to found a monastery of his own. With the permission of the bishop of Leon, he founded a monastery at Lanhouarneau, which became famous throughout the country, due undoubtedly to the blind abbot who loved animals and music and surrounded himself with monk-scholars.

He used to go around the countryside preaching, even though he was only a simple exorcist, not a priest, and was led by a child guide named Guiharan. He was beloved by the people of the region, venerated for his sanctity, and noted for his many miracles. As he died, it was said, he heard the music of the celestial choirs welcoming him to heaven.

Hervé is usually represented with a wolf and with his child guide. He is invoked for ailments of the eye and is a popular saint in Britanny, where his name is given to Breton boys more than any other name.

Thought for the Day: St. Hervé charmed everyone and never lost that childlike quality that comes from innocence of life. Even though he was blind, he delighted in God's creation and drew others to sense something of the wonder of God. It is this sense of wonder that nourishes a deep love of God, something we should try to acquire.

From 'The Catholic One Year Bible': . . . Some of the believers who went to Antioch from Cyprus and Cyrene also gave their message about the Lord to some Greeks. And the Lord honored this effort so that large numbers of these Gentiles became believers. — **Acts 11:20-21**

St. Botolph *(JUNE 18)*

It is said that Boston, in Lincolnshire, England, is named for St. Botolph (Boston being the contraction for "Botolph's stone"). There are over seventy churches dedicated to Botolph, sixteen of them in the city of Norfolk alone. Whoever he was, he made a deep impression on the people with whom he lived, and his name is immortalized forever in the city that bears his name.

According to legend, he was an Irishman whose parents sent him to Germany to be educated, together with his brother, Adulf. His brother became a regional bishop, one without a diocese in the area of Utrecht or Maestricht, in what is now the Netherlands.

Our story goes on to say that Botolph went to England where he was favorably received by Ethelmund, king of the southern Angles. The king granted him a small peninsula on which to build a monastery, and it was called Icanhoh. He began to build his monastery in 654, and followers soon joined him.

He was visited by Ceolfrid, abbot of St. Bede's monastery of Wearmouth, whose monastery was founded before his own and from whom he wanted to learn something of monastic discipline and ecclesiastical traditions. Along with St. Wilfrid and St. Benedict Biscop, he seems to have been one of those who brought the rule of St. Benedict to England, introducing a continental form of monasticism to the Anglo-Saxon kingdoms.

The church at Icanhoh was destroyed by the Danes in the ninth century, but the relics of Botolph were saved. In the reign of King Edgar, the relics were transferred to the abbey of Thorney and Ely. The feast of Botolph is kept in the dioceses of Brentwood, Northampton, and Nottingham.

Thought for the Day: Many of the towns and cities of Europe were named after saints, either because of churches they founded or because the city was built over their tomb. These saints were remembered as friends of God who went about doing good and left an indelible impression on popular memory. It is always good to remember our forebears and to acknowledge the debt that we owe them.

From 'The Catholic One Year Bible': [Elijah] replied, "I have worked very hard for the Lord God of the heavens; but the people of Israel have broken their covenant with you and torn down your altars and killed your prophets, and only I am left; and now they are trying to kill me, too." — **1 Kings 19:10**

St. Romuald *(JUNE 19)*

As a young man, St. Romuald witnessed a bloody duel between his father and a relative over a piece of property. He was so horrified by what he saw that he fled to a nearby monastery, appalled by the hatred and violence of his family. In the quiet of the place, he decided to dedicate himself to solitude and put himself under the direction of a hermit named Marinus, near Venice. He and Marinus had a hand in the retirement of St. Peter Orseolo to a monastery; moreover, they encouraged many others to enter the monastic life, even Romuald's father, Sergius.

After this small success with his family, Romuald began a campaign to found monasteries and hermitages all over Italy, and the next thirty years of his life were spent spreading the life of solitude everywhere. He wanted to be a missionary and received the pope's permission to preach in Hungary, but sickness prevented him from working there. So dynamic was his personality that members of noble families and even king's sons joined him in the monastic life.

His most famous monastery was that of Camaldoli in Tuscany, which he founded in the year 1012. Here he combined the cenobitic life of St. Benedict with that of the hermits and created a new monastic family and a new monastic tradition. The Camaldolese exist to this day and are one of the great branches of monasticism. Several of his monasteries became centers for the training of priests and missionaries, and another, Vallambrosa, became an order in its own right.

Romuald died in 1027 in his monastery at Val-di-Castro, and in 1481 his body was exhumed and found incorrupt. His relics are interred at Fabriano.

Thought for the Day: Sometimes a brush with evil or depravity can turn someone to a holy life. The custom of "vendetta" was part of the Italian culture of St. Romuald's day, and watching a violent death inspired by such a custom moved him to look for another kind of life and another kind of solution. This brought him face to face with God and his own soul, and he spent the rest of his life profiting from the lesson. Horror for evil can help one to begin to see the face of goodness.

From 'The Catholic One Year Bible': [Paul said to the sorcerer:] ". . . Will you never end your opposition to the Lord? And now God has laid his hand of punishment upon you, and you will be stricken awhile with blindness." Instantly mist and darkness fell upon [the sorcerer], . . . — Acts 13:9-11

Blessed Osanna of Mantua *(JUNE 20)*

Like St. Catherine of Siena, Blessed Osanna of Mantua was a mystic who had a profound influence upon the Italy of her times and, like St. Catherine, she was a mystic who lived in the world. She lived during the terrible times of Sixtus IV and Alexander VI, popes who used the high office of the papacy for their own personal ends, and her deep suffering over the state of the Church was part of her mysticism.

She was related to the Gonzaga family, the reigning dukes of Mantua, and was the oldest in her family. Her brothers and sisters were a constant concern of hers throughout her life. As a young child, she became deeply impressed with the wonder of God and saw this as the source of the deepest human happiness. It was a conviction that never left her.

Her father wanted her to marry, but she convinced him at the age of fourteen to let her join the Dominican Third Order; strangely enough she did not make her profession as a tertiary for another thirty-seven years, remaining a novice all that time. She was still young when her parents died, and she remained in the family home, devoting herself to the care of her brothers and sisters.

Her influence went beyond her own home. When Duke Frederick, who was a relative, went off to war, he asked her to take over his own household, and she found herself taking care of two families. She showed a genius for organization and administration, and when the duke returned he continued to consult her on family matters and even on matters of state. She, in turn, used her influence with the duke to plead for victims of injustice and mercy for prisoners. She is an example of the power of mysticism in practical affairs and of the sane, down-to-earth common sense of genuine mystics.

From the age of five, she was granted unusual mystical experiences, and her spirituality was bound up with the Passion of Christ and intense suffering for the Church. She died on June 20, 1505, at the age of fifty-six. The duke and duchess of Mantua were with her when she died, and she was given a state funeral.

Thought for the Day: The secret of sanctity is hard to explain, but it is evident to those who knew the saints. Blessed Osanna of Mantua was no different from many other women of her day, but her influence on others was profound. It was her deep dedication to God and others that attracted others and led them to understand something of the goodness of God.

From 'The Catholic One Year Bible': ". . . Barnabas and I are here to bring you this Good News — that God's promise to our ancestors has come true in our time, . . ." — Acts 13:32-33

This Renaissance prince, heir to the Gonzaga title and wealth, chose God over worldly riches and prestige and never let go of the treasure he had found.

He was a Gonzaga, the ruling family of Mantua in northern Italy, a family noted for its brutality and loose morals. His father was Ferrante Gonzaga, marquis of Castiglione and prince of the empire; his mother was Marta Tana Santena. At a very early age, St. Aloysius Gonzaga realized the moral dangers of court life and of his princely position, and he determined before he was ten years old to renounce his position. His father, however, saw his worth and was determined that Aloysius would succeed him.

He was fortunate in his tutor, Pierfrancesco del Turco, who fostered in him a nobility of soul and spirit. When Aloysius was thirteen, his father was called to the court of Philip II of Spain, and Aloysius became a page of Don Diego, the crown prince. It was in Spain that Aloysius determined to become a Jesuit and, at Don Diego's death, on a walk with his brother, Rodolfo, he sat down on the steps of the Jesuit house in Madrid, sent the servants home, and refused to leave. His father, who was sick with the gout, finally persuaded him to come home, with the promise that Aloysius could carry out his wishes after the family's return to Italy.

Back in Italy, his father did everything to persuade him to change his mind, but Aloysius was adamant and eventually broke his father's resolve. He entered the Jesuit house in Rome in 1585, renouncing his title in favor of his brother, Rodolfo. He returned home briefly to settle family affairs after the death of his father, then went back to Rome to complete his studies.

In March 1591, as a result of caring for the victims of the plague that had hit Rome, he contracted the plague himself and died three months later at the age of twenty-three. His amazing courage and determination to follow his chosen vocation caused a sensation in Italy. He was canonized in 1726 by Pope Benedict XIII and three years later he was declared the patron of youth. He is buried in the church of St. Ignatius in Rome.

Thought for the Day: St. Aloysius Gonzaga was a tough-minded young man who knew exactly what he wanted and never turned back in his resolve. In all doubt and uncertainty, he would cry to God: "Direct me!" In every peril and danger, he turned to the God he loved with all the passion of his soul and he was never disappointed.

From 'The Catholic One Year Bible': As [Elijah and Elisha] were walking along, talking, suddenly a chariot of fire, drawn by horses of fire, appeared and drove between them, separating them, and Elijah was carried by a whirlwind into heaven. —2 Kings 2:11

Who has not been moved by this *Man for All Seasons* (to use the name of the book and movie based on St. Thomas More's life), whose love of life, joy in his family, great gifts of personality, and unshakable conscience endeared him to the people of his own time? He was a friend of Erasmus, the best-known humanist of his day; he was a jurist, writer, beloved father, and lord chancellor of England.

He was born in 1477, and his father was John More, an alderman of the city of London. As a young boy, Thomas More became a page in the household of Archbishop John Morton where his affability, good manners, and fine intellect impressed the future cardinal. At the age of fourteen, he entered Canterbury College at Oxford but left two years later to study law at New Inn and Lincoln's Inn. He was admitted to the bar in 1501. His studies, however, included the best humanist education of the day: Greek, patristics, philosophy, and theology.

In 1504, he married Jane Colt and the couple had four children. When his wife died in 1511, More married a widow, Alice Middleton, whom he loved very much. His competency in law came to the attention of Henry VIII, who sent him on an embassy to Flanders in 1517 and 1518. He became a member of the king's council in 1518 and served in this position for eleven years. In 1521, he was knighted.

The affair of Henry VIII's "great matter," his divorce from Catherine of Aragon, began in 1527. More's opinion in the matter was important because of his widespread reputation, but he told the king that in conscience he could not support his case. Upon Cardinal Wolsey's death in 1529, Thomas More was made lord chancellor of England.

When King Henry married Anne Boleyn and declared himself head of the Church in England, More resigned as chancellor and, seeing what the final results of his convictions would bring, retired to prepare for the inevitable.

He was harassed at first by accusations of misuse of office and treasonable activities. Then when he was ordered to take the oath to uphold the Act of Supremacy, which effectively made Henry VIII "head of the Church of England" and required all English subjects to accept the king's claim without question, Thomas More refused and was imprisoned in the Tower of London. In 1535, he was convicted of treason and on July 6 was beheaded. Before his execution, he publicly declared that he was the "king's good servant, but God's first." He was canonized four hundred years later, in 1935, by Pope Pius XI.

Thought for the Day: To follow his conscience was the first rule of life of St. Thomas More, and he never swerved in this loyalty to his own convictions. He was asked to do something that he could not in conscience do, and he died as a martyr to conscience. His example rings down through the centuries.

From 'The Catholic One Year Bible': A cheerful heart does good like medicine, but a broken spirit makes one sick. — **Proverbs 17:22**

St. Joseph Cafasso *(JUNE 23)*

Joseph Cafasso was the friend and adviser of St. John Bosco and the one who encouraged him to work for youth. He was Don Bosco's spiritual director and was the one who told him to go home and unpack his trunk when Don Bosco was thinking of becoming a missionary.

St. Joseph Cafasso was born in Piedmont in 1811 and entered the seminary at Chieri for the archdiocese of Turin. Even as a seminarian, he had an influence on young people and after his ordination in 1833 joined a group of priests studying at an institute founded by Luigi Guala. When his own studies were completed, he became a lecturer at the same institute.

His greatest influence was on the young priests of the archdiocese of Turin, to whom he became a confidante and spiritual guide. His advice to them in their preaching was "Jesus Christ . . . used simple words that everyone could understand. Do the same." He became a popular confessor noted for his gentleness and great compassion. "We must not drive people away," was his watchword.

In 1848, Joseph became rector of the institute. He directed and guided sixty young priests, among them John Bosco, and brought about a spiritual revolution in the archdiocese of Turin. His other notable work was among convicts. Prisons were dangerous, barbarous places, where violence was common. He accompanied many of the prisoners to their execution and often spoke of his "hanged saints."

Joseph Cafasso met John Bosco in 1827 when Bosco was still a young boy, and it was Joseph who became his model of priesthood and his guide to sanctity. There was something about the gentle, smiling young priest that left an indelible impression on the young Bosco. It was Joseph's advice and encouragement that kept the Salesian founder going as he put his hand to his remarkable work for boys.

Joseph died on June 23, 1860. He had come down with pneumonia and died worn out and ill. He was canonized by Pope Pius XII in 1947.

Thought for the Day: St. Joseph Cafasso was a gentle preacher and a compassionate confessor, realizing that harshness with the weak only does harm. It was his consummate compassion that was noted by everyone, and he could face the most hardened criminals with his easy laugh and gentle manner. He realized that it is love alone that conquers.

From 'The Catholic One Year Bible': . . . When Elisha the prophet heard about the king of Israel's plight, he sent this message to him: "Why are you so upset? Send Naaman to me, and he will learn that there is a true prophet of God in Israel." —2 Kings 5:8

St. John the Baptist *(JUNE 24)*

The birthday of St. John the Baptist was celebrated throughout medieval Europe with great bonfires that were lit from Scandinavia to Spain. It fell at the time of the summer solstice and heralded the time when days became shorter and daylight began to lessen, bearing symbolic witness to St. John the Baptist's own statement: "He must increase, I must decrease."

John the Baptist's birth is recorded by St. Luke in his Gospel; the story of his parents, SS. Zachary and Elizabeth, is also recorded there. Zachary was a priest of the Temple in Jerusalem and lived with Elizabeth at Ain Karim, just south of Jerusalem. Elizabeth was a cousin of the Blessed Virgin Mary, and it was John's conception that was announced to Mary when the angel Gabriel told her that she was to be the Mother of Jesus.

Mary went on her errand of mercy to Ain Karim to be with Elizabeth while she was carrying her child and returned to Nazareth before the birth of John the Baptist. At John's birth, his father, Zachary, recovered his speech, which he had lost for doubting the angel's message to him, and it is the event of the Baptist's birth that gave us the *Benedictus*, the canticle in St. Luke's Gospel that sings the praises of God's deliverance of His people. In this canticle, John's own role in the work of salvation is indicated: "And you, O child, shall be called prophet of the Most High; for you shall go before the Lord to prepare straight paths for him."

We know nothing of John the Baptist's boyhood, but it is thought that he might have been part of the Essene community at Qumran, since it was customary for them to admit young boys and train them in a life of righteousness. We meet John again when he comes out of the Judean desert to preach "a baptism of repentance which led to the forgiveness of sins."

John the Baptist was beheaded by Herod Antipas, tetrarch of Galilee, whom John denounced for Herod's marriage to his brother's wife. Jesus said of John that "he was the lamp, set aflame and burning bright." His feast day is almost exactly six months from Christmas and so marks the halfway point in the great drama of the liturgical year.

Thought for the Day: St. John the Baptist was fearless in denouncing evil and was not even afraid of kings. By his very life, he stood for something and what he stood for was clear to the whole world. What we stand for should be so clear that no one has any doubt about it.

From 'The Catholic One Year Bible': Wisdom is the main pursuit of sensible men, but a fool's goals are at the ends of the earth! — **Proverbs 17:24**

St. Gohard

In 793, Viking raiders attacked the monastery of Lindisfarne, off the eastern coast of northern England, and for the next two centuries they brought destruction to England, Ireland, and France. Fifty years after the raid on Lindisfarne, the Vikings were at the mouth of the Loire River and began a journey up the river, sacking cities as they went and slaughtering the inhabitants. They went out of their way to attack religious houses, which were usually well provisioned and possessed sacred vessels of gold and silver.

St. Gohard was bishop of Nantes on the fateful day in 843 when the Norseman came up the river in their huge ships, led by a Frenchman named Lambert who hoped to be given a position of importance by the marauding Vikings. As the ships sailed up the river, the people fled and monks from local monasteries took up their relics and sacred vessels, crowding into the church of SS. Peter and Paul, where Bishop Gohard was celebrating the feast of St. John the Baptist.

The church was secured, hundreds of people crowding around their bishop as the Norsemen overran the area. With axes and pikes and swords, the Norsemen broke down the door, knocked out windows, forced their way into the church, and slaughtered people left and right. When they came to the altar where Gohard was celebrating Mass, they killed him and the priests who were with him. Then they set fire to the church, took the city officials as captives, and after sacking the city of Nantes moved up the Seine River and attacked Paris.

Gohard and the priests who were killed with him are honored as martyrs. This Viking menace troubled Europe for another century, but the king of France finally came to terms with the Norsemen and ceded to them a part of France that came to be called Normandy.

We know nothing of Gohard's life, except that he was bishop of Nantes and died in the midst of his people, like the Good Shepherd laying down His life for His sheep.

Thought for the Day: The only thing we know about some saints is that they died as martyrs, but although they are unknown to us, they are known to God, and that is all that really counts. What others think of us does not really matter — it is how we are in the eyes of God that is important.

From 'The Catholic One Year Bible': Around midnight, as Paul and Silas were praying and singing hymns to the Lord . . . suddenly there was a great earthquake; the prison was shaken to its foundations, all the doors flew open — and the chains of every prisoner fell off! — **Acts 16:25-26**

St. Anthelm *(JUNE 26)*

Anthelm is considered the second founder of the Carthusian Order, whose prior he became in 1139. He had entered the order at the monastery at Portes, but during his novitiate he was sent to La Grande Chartreuse, which had been almost completely destroyed by an avalanche.

It was St. Anthelm's far-seeing practical gifts that restored the physical condition of the abbey; he rebuilt the monastic buildings, constructed an aqueduct, and restored the life itself of the abbey to its primitive simplicity. He also organized the Carthusians into a unified order. Before his time, the individual Carthusian monasteries had been subject to the local bishop; Anthelm summoned the first general chapter of the order, designated La Grande Chartreuse the motherhouse of the order, and became the first superior general.

His work and reputation brought new monks into the order, including his own father and brother. After twelve years in office, he resigned but was appointed abbot of his own monastery of Portes. He found Portes in a state of great prosperity, too prosperous, he felt, for monks; so, giving away the monastery's store of grain, he brought the monastery back to the simplicity of Carthusian life.

In 1159, the Church was split into two camps, with one pope, Alexander III, considered the true pontiff, but another, Victor IV, supported by Emperor Frederick Barbarossa. Anthelm gave his support to Alexander and began to organize France, Spain, and England to support the true pope. When Pope Alexander's position was secure, Alexander appointed Anthelm to the see of Belley, much against his will. Anthelm reformed his diocese, fought the intrusion of kings into ecclesiastical affairs, and was sent to England by the pope to try to reconcile King Henry II and St. Thomas Becket.

Anthelm died at the age of seventy-two on June 26, 1178, and his tomb quickly became a popular shrine, noted for its many miracles. St. Hugh of Lincoln, an old friend of his and a fellow Carthusian, visited Anthelm's tomb on his own last trip to La Grande Chartreuse.

Thought for the Day: Those who labor for the spiritual good of others begin by taking themselves in hand, directing their own life to God, and living totally for Him. That is why their work and their example are so powerful: their own lives are a living witness of what they preach and do. That is the only sound foundation of holiness.

From 'The Catholic One Year Bible': . . . "Men of Athens, I notice that you are very religious, for as I was out walking I saw your many altars, and one of them had this inscription on it — 'To the Unknown God.' You have been worshiping him without knowing who he is, and now I wish to tell you about him." — **Acts 17:22-23**

St. Cyril of Alexandria *(JUNE 27)*

Cyril was a successor of St. Athanasius in the see of Alexandria, the great champion of the Council of Ephesus, the opponent of Nestorianism, and the defender of Mary's title of *Theotokos*, or "Mother of God." He succeeded his uncle Theophilus as patriarch of Alexandria in 412 and had a part in the condemnation of St. John Chrysostom in 403.

In spite of his great defense of orthodoxy, St. Cyril of Alexandria was a very difficult individual, used his position to attack and defeat his opponents, and may have had a hand in the murder of the woman philosopher Hypatia in Alexandria in 415. The early years of his patriarchate were marked by violence, and much of it was due, it seems, to Cyril's obstinate and high-handed tactics.

His doctrinal significance stems from his opposition to Nestorianism and the dominant role he played in the Council of Ephesus in 431. Nestorius, who was patriarch of Constantinople, objected to the title Mother of God, and preferred for her to be called Mother of Christ. Cyril wrote to Nestorius trying to correct his error, appealed to the pope in Rome for a clarification of the true doctrine, and opened the council called at Ephesus by Emperor Theodosius II. The council sessions were stormy, but Nestorius was condemned and Mary's title *Theotokos* became her official title in the Church.

The Church, however, was divided after Ephesus, even though Cyril did much to bring about unity. The problem of the "two natures and one person" in Christ did not see its final clarification until the Council of Chalcedon in 451, but by that time Cyril was dead. He died in 444, venerated by the Christian world, one of the great champions of the Mother of God.

In 1881, he was declared a Doctor of the Church by Pope Leo XIII, and in 1944, on the fifteenth centenary of Cyril's death, Pope Pius XII issued his encyclical *Orientalis Ecclesiae*, commemorating Cyril's place in the history of the Church.

Thought for the Day: *Theotokos* is the official name of Mary, and it is well to remember the great battle that was fought over this title. She is the Mother of God: the Son of God was born of her in His human nature, without ceasing to be God. The whole mystery of the Incarnation is bound up in Mary, and she is at the very heart of the work of Jesus' redemption.

From 'The Catholic One Year Bible': "I must by all means be at Jerusalem for the holiday," [Paul] said. But he promised to return to Ephesus later if God permitted; and so he set sail again." — **Acts 18:21**

St. Irenaeus *(JUNE 28)*

Irenaeus was one of the first missionaries to Western Europe and had been a disciple of St. Polycarp in Asia Minor, present-day Turkey. He became a presbyter of the Church of Lyons in Gaul during the reign of the Emperor Marcus Aurelius. He was elected bishop of Lyons and was the first important Christian theologian to face the Gnostic heresy that was shaking Christianity.

He was one of the best-educated men of his day, had a thorough knowledge of Sacred Scriptures as well as a background in Greek philosophy and literature. It is possible that he was sent as a missionary by Polycarp himself. True to his missionary purpose, St. Irenaeus spoke the native Celtic language rather than his native Greek and he himself sent out other missionaries into the surrounding regions.

He is best known for his writings in opposition to Gnosticism, which had spread even into Gaul where he was bishop of Lyons. Gnosticism looked upon the visible world as the creation of an evil God or an evil power and placed salvation, not in the grace of God, but in a secret kind of knowledge or initiation into a select cult. Since Gnosticism appealed by its secret character, Irenaeus was determined, as he said, to "strip the fox," expose it for what it really was and to show how radically it was opposed to the Christian faith and to sound doctrine. This he did in five books called *Against the Heresies*.

About 190, Pope Victor III was threatening to excommunicate the Christians of Asia Minor over the "Easter Controversy" (they celebrated Easter at a different time than the Christians of Rome). Irenaeus went to Rome to plead for the Christians of his homeland and convinced the pope not to break the unity of the Church over a mere custom.

He died about the year 202 and was buried in the crypt of the church of St. John in Lyons.

Thought for the Day: Faith sometimes needs a champion, someone who will speak out and make clear what we really believe. Such champions in history are called Doctors of the Church, and St. Irenaeus is one of the first. To combat the pessimism of Gnosticism, he wrote: "The glory of God is man fully alive, the universe and the whole of creation is His gift and His intentions for us are good."

From 'The Catholic One Year Bible': . . . God gave Paul the power to do unusual miracles, so that even when his handkerchief or parts of his clothing were placed upon sick people, they were healed, and any demons within them came out. —Acts 19:11-12

They both died at Rome — one crucified upside down as a foreign criminal, the other beheaded as befitted a Roman citizen. The exact date is not known, but it was sometime during the persecution of the Emperor Nero, the madman who blamed the fires of Rome on Christians. From the time of the deaths of SS. Peter and Paul, Rome became the center of Christianity and the seat of the Catholic Church.

They were unlikely partners: Peter, the very Orthodox Jew and Galilean who had been at Jesus' side during the whole of the public life of the One he called "the Master"; Paul, from the Diaspora, a Hellenist Jew who was open to the salvation of the Gentiles. They had had differences, had agonized over the style the faith should take in the Gentile world, had even had an open conflict at Antioch. But, in the end, they were brothers in the faith, Peter speaking of the writings of "our brother, Paul," and both dying in a wave of intense hatred toward the new religion.

Their deaths brought to an end the first era of the Church, the apostolic era, even though other Apostles like John would continue to have an influence until the end of the century. The record of the years of Peter and Paul is chronicled in the Acts of the Apostles of St. Luke and in the Letters of both Apostles, giving us a rather complete account of their labors and journeys. After Christ, they were the cornerstones of the Church and as such they are enshrined in the Church's memory. These two saints embodied in themselves everything the Christian admired in a follower of Christ: they were Apostles, martyrs, witnesses, teachers, prophets, and founders of Christian communities.

By their life and labors, Peter and Paul established the faith, and by their deaths they bore witness to its power and truth. They are part of the Church's own confession of faith; they were the architects of that faith and have left their mark indelibly upon Christian history and belief.

Thought for the Day: The two great basilicas in Rome are dedicated to St. Peter and St. Paul: St. Peter's is the largest church in Christendom, and St. Paul Outside the Walls is the site of St. Paul's martyrdom. We owe our faith to these two great Apostles and should hold them in hallowed memory. Like Jesus Himself, their death was our life.

From 'The Catholic One Year Bible': Afterwards, Paul felt impelled by the Holy Spirit to go across to Greece before returning to Jerusalem. "And after that," he said, "I must go on to Rome!" He sent his two assistants, Timothy and Erastus, on ahead to Greece while he stayed awhile longer in Turkey. — Acts 19:21-22

Martyrs of Rome *(JUNE 30)*

SS. Peter and Paul did not die alone in the great martyrdom under Nero in the year 64. There were other victims of his savagery, and their deaths are linked with those of Peter and Paul in history and in the calendar of the Church.

In July of 64, a great fire devastated Rome. It began near the Great Circus, one of the great shopping districts of Rome, spreading quickly and raging for six days. Many buildings were demolished to contain it, but the inferno eventually burst out again in the garden of the prefect of the Praetorian Guard. When it finally died down, two thirds of Rome was a mass of smoldering ruins.

There was a rumor that the emperor himself had set the city aflame, and, as the rumor grew, Nero grew fearful that the rumor might be believed. He accused Christians of setting the fire. They were the most despised group in the city and were considered revolutionaries by many Romans. No one really believed the accusation, but Christians were rounded up and Nero took particular delight in finding barbaric ways to put them to death. Some were sewn up in the hides of animals and thrown to hungry dogs; some were covered with wax or pitch and burned like huge torches; others were crucified, and the emperor made their deaths part of a huge party that he gave in his own gardens.

The Roman historian Tacitus wrote: "Nero provided his garden for the spectacle, and exhibited displays in the Circus, at which he mingled with the crowd. . . . Despite their guilt as Christians . . . the victims were pitied. For it was felt that they were being sacrificed to one man's brutality rather than to the national interest."

It was the first great Roman persecution of Christians, and such persecutions would continue, with varying forms of ferocity, for the next two hundred fifty years, ending with the Peace of Constantine in 312. But like all such martyrdoms, the "blood of martyrs was the seed of Christians." These first are remembered as "the first fruits of Rome" and are linked most especially with the names of Peter and Paul.

Thought for the Day: At one time, it was a crime to be a Christian, as it still is in certain parts of the world. In places less distant from us than a day's plane ride, Christians are outlawed and imprisoned. How would we respond to those who ask: "Are you willing to give up everything for the sake of Christ?"

From 'The Catholic One Year Bible': ". . . I am going to Jerusalem, drawn there irresistibly by the Holy Spirit, not knowing what awaits me, except that the Holy Spirit has told me in city after city that jail and suffering lie ahead." — Acts 20:22-23

THE SAINTS OF JULY

St. Shenoute *(JULY 1)*

Together with St. Anthony and St. Pachomius, St. Shenoute is considered one of the founders and patriarchs of monks. He was one hundred eighteen years old when he died. He is the first real monastic legislator, originated the practice of monastic vows, and ruled the famous "White Monastery" at Dair-al-Abiad in Egypt from the year 385 until his death in 466.

He was born around the year 348 at Shenalolet and joined his uncle's monastery in the Thebaid when he was very young. Monastic recruits at this monastery were mostly unlettered Coptic peasants. His was the task of organization, fashioning the rule of St. Pachomius into a daily schedule, creating rituals and customs to direct the practical everyday realities of monastic life, and defining more exactly the duties and obligations of the monastic state. Under Shenoute, Eastern monasticism became a definite social institution, and he himself became the first archimandrite of monks, or abbot general, ruling over twenty-two hundred monks and eighteen hundred nuns.

He was known to be a severe disciplinarian, and he undertook a number of journeys to combat heresy. In 431, he accompanied St. Cyril of Alexandria to the Council of Ephesus and he himself was regarded as a saint, with great influence in the Egyptian Church. He died around 466, a venerable old man who brought the monastic form of life from its pioneer state to a point of high development and saw it begin to take root in the West.

His monastery existed right into modern times, and in 1833 there were three Coptic monks living there. Shenoute wrote in the Coptic language, and his influence upon Coptic monasticism was the greatest for this reason. He wrote many letters and sermons, which have been preserved, dealing mostly with monastic questions. He was a driving force in the preservation and extension of the monastic ideal, and his life reaches from the death of St. Pachomius, the year he was born, to the beginnings of monastic life in Ireland.

Thought for the Day: Saints like Shenoute lived many centuries ago, but during their lifetime they were well known and powerful in their influence for good. St. Shenoute was known to be a somewhat difficult character, ruling his monks with an iron hand. Somehow he molded his disposition and became a saint in the process. It is our character, not our disposition, that makes for sanctity.

From 'The Catholic One Year Bible': . . . "Why all this weeping? You are breaking my heart! For I am ready not only to be jailed at Jerusalem, but also to die for the sake of the Lord Jesus." — Acts 21:13

St. Otto of Bamberg *(JULY 2)*

Otto of Bamberg was the chancellor of Emperor Henry IV during that emperor's difficulties with the Holy See and the rebellion of his own nobles. When the emperor set up his own antipope and brought about a schism, Otto tried to bring about Henry's submission to the pope, but he carried out the policies of the emperor wherever these did not go contrary to his conscience.

It was a difficult time, with Henry's nobles in revolt and the German hierarchy itself opposed to papal policies. In 1102, Henry appointed Otto bishop of Bamberg, but Otto refused to be consecrated until he could go to Rome and receive consecration from the hands of Pope Paschal II. When the emperor's son, Henry V, deposed his father in 1106 and received the crown himself, Otto worked to heal the breach with the Holy See, with some measure of success.

He was a dedicated and capable bishop who established monasteries while working as conciliator between the emperor and the pope. Because of his outstanding character, he was trusted by both sides in the controversy. When Henry V went to Rome to be crowned emperor by the pope, St. Otto of Bamberg accompanied him and received the pallium from the pontiff, a recognition of his efforts to bring about peace. He had a major part in the preparation for the Concordat of Worms in 1122, which ended the investiture struggle between emperor and pope, thus ending the hostilities between pontiff and emperor that had lasted for over fifty years.

In 1124, King Boleslaus of Poland asked Otto to undertake the evangelization of Pomerania, which he had recently conquered. Taking with him priests and catechists, Otto began his mission there, baptized twenty thousand people, and appointed clergy to serve them.

Otto died in 1139 and was buried in one of the monasteries he had founded, Michelsberg, near his see city. He was canonized by Clement III in 1189.

Thought for the Day: St. Otto of Bamberg was a man always in the midst of conflict and found himself a peacemaker in a time of great trouble. Through his efforts, Church and Empire found peace. The work of peace is always difficult and requires something resembling heroic sanctity. In our own way, each one of us has to be a peacemaker and, according to the Gospel, brings down blessings on those who work for peace.

From 'The Catholic One Year Bible': The second day Paul took us with him to meet James and the elders of the Jerusalem church. After greetings were exchanged, Paul recounted the many things God had accomplished among the Gentiles through his work. — **Acts 21:18-19**

St. Thomas, Apostle *(JULY 3)*

Thomas the Apostle is the famous "doubting Thomas" of the New Testament, and it is from his lips that we have the great confession of faith, "My Lord and my God," the most explicit statement of the divinity of Jesus in the Gospels. We have little information about this Apostle, and most of it is contained in the Gospel of St. John. His name is not Hebrew but Aramaic and means "the twin," the significance of which is not known.

He appears to have been a Galilean, like many of the other Apostles, and showed great courage when the other Apostles were fearful to return to Jerusalem on news that Lazarus was sick. Jesus had fled from Jerusalem with His Apostles because of threats to His life, and the others were afraid to return. Thomas's reply was: "Let us go that we may die with Him."

It was also to St. Thomas that Jesus addressed His words: "I am the Way, the Truth, and the Life," after Thomas had expressed ignorance of where Jesus was going. It was his doubt and profession of belief that drew from Jesus the words: "Blessed are those who have not seen and have believed."

Christian legend has Thomas evangelizing the lands between the Caspian Sea and the Persian Gulf and has him even going as far as India, where "the Christians of St. Thomas" along the Malabar Coast claim him as the apostolic founder of their Church. So prominent was Thomas in the early Church that an apocryphal Gospel of St. Thomas, recently discovered among the so-called Gnostic Gospels at Naj Hammadi in Egypt, is attributed to him.

Because he was thought to be a carpenter, Thomas is the patron saint of architects, masons, and stonecutters.

Thought for the Day: "Ten thousand difficulties do not make one doubt," said Cardinal Newman. St. Thomas's doubt led to a great profession of faith, and all of our difficulties with the faith can be resolved by seeking the right information and by a renewal of our own act of faith. Faith is the firm rock upon which all doubts can be shattered.

From 'The Catholic One Year Bible': . . . Paul stood on the stairs and motioned to the people to be quiet; soon a deep silence enveloped the crowd, and he addressed them in Hebrew. . . . — Acts 21:40

Elizabeth of Portugal was married young: she was only twelve years old when she became the wife of King Denis of Portugal. She was the daughter of King Peter III of Aragon and at her baptism in 1271 received the name of her great-aunt, St. Elizabeth of Hungary. Even at that early age, she had a well-disciplined character and, like her namesake, looked after the poor and pilgrims, with the consent of her husband.

She inaugurated what today we would call social works in her kingdom, set up hostels for pilgrims and travelers, provided for the poor, established dowries for poor girls, founded a hospital and a house for penitent women at Torres Novas, and built an orphanage. Her husband was notoriously unfaithful to her, but she bore all this with patience and her sweetness of disposition, her greatest asset. She even looked after his illegitimate children as if they were her own and made provision for their proper education.

She had two children of her own, Alfonso and Constance, the son later rebelling against his father. St. Elizabeth of Portugal became the peacemaker and several times reconciled the son to the father. Through her efforts, war was averted between Castile and Aragon.

In 1324, her husband became ill and she devoted all of her attention to him, never leaving his room except to go to church. His illness was long and tedious, but he sincerely repented of his disordered life and died at Santarem in 1325. After his burial, she made a pilgrimage to Compostela and decided to enter the Poor Clare convent at Coimbra. Persuaded not to do this, she became a Franciscan tertiary and lived in a house close to the convent.

Elizabeth died at Estremoz at the age of sixty-six, en route there to bring about peace between her son and her nephew, Alfonso XI, of Castile. She was canonized by Urban VIII in 1625.

Thought for the Day: Our own circle of personal influence is usually where we can do the most good. It is useless to dream of going to faraway places to accomplish great deeds, when there is much to be done in our own backyard. We can influence those around us and, like St. Elizabeth of Portugal, can accomplish wonders.

From 'The Catholic One Year Bible': . . . Paul thought of something! Part of the Council were Sadducees, and part were Pharisees! So he shouted, "Brothers, I am a Pharisee, as were all my ancestors! And I am being tried here today because I believe in the resurrection of the dead!" — Acts 23:6

St. Anthony Zaccaria *(JULY 5)*

Cremona, Italy, is known for more than violin-making. It was also the birthplace of this remarkable priest who founded one of the great religious orders of the sixteenth century. St. Anthony Zaccaria was born in 1502, and his mother, Antonietta Pescaroli, left widowed at the age of eighteen, gave all of her attention to the education of her son. He studied at Cremona and Pavia and in 1524 obtained a degree in medicine from the University of Padua.

It was while working among the sick poor that the young doctor felt called to a different vocation. He began to exercise a ministry among the sick, the poor, and the dying and in 1528 was ordained a priest. In 1530, he became chaplain to the countess of Guastalla in Milan and joined the Confraternity of Eternal Wisdom there and with two friends founded the Congregation of Clerks Regular, which eventually became popularly known as the Barnabites. He also founded an institute for religious women.

He then became something of a pastoral dynamo in Lombardy, preaching everywhere, conducting missions, and pioneering something similar to the lay apostolate. He began the custom of the Forty Hours, encouraged daily Communion, worked among the plague-stricken, and brought spiritual renovation of the whole city of Milan. In 1539, he acquired the church of St. Barnabas in Milan as the headquarters for his congregation and from this came the popular name of the congregation.

In 1539, Anthony took on the mission of restoring peace to Guastalla, which had been placed under a papal interdict, and after two months of fatiguing labor became seriously ill and was carried to his mother's house at Cremona where he died at the age of thirty-seven. His body still rests in the crypt of the church of St. Barnabas in Milan. He was canonized by Pope Leo XIII in 1897.

Thought for the Day: Compassion for the sick and poor often leads to a special vocation. St. Anthony Zaccaria saw beyond the sick bodies of his patients and recognized the need for a different kind of healing. He saw a need that he could fill and dedicated his whole life to it. It was not something he had planned; sometimes God steps in and gives us a whole new set of plans.

From 'The Catholic One Year Bible': That night the Lord stood beside Paul and said, "Don't worry, Paul; just as you have told the people about me here in Jerusalem, so you must also in Rome." — **Acts 23:11**

Maria Goretti was murdered by a young man, angry that she would not submit to his advances; she was only twelve years old at the time. When Maria was six, her father, a poor farmer named Luigi Goretti, caught malaria and died, and the mother, Assunta Carlini, was faced with the task of supporting Maria and her five brothers and sisters.

While her mother worked in the fields, Maria took care of the house. In July 1902, while she was sitting at the top of the stairs in her home mending a shirt, Alessandro Serenelli, the nineteen-year-old son of a neighbor, drove up in a cart, ran up the stairs, and motioned Maria into one of the bedrooms. He had tried this before and each time Maria had angrily refused. This time, he took hold of her, pulled her in the room, and closed the door.

Maria struggled and called for help, but Alessandro was strangling her, and her feeble cries went unheard. He ripped her dress from her body and began to stab her with a long dagger. She fell to the floor, where Alessandro stabbed her in the back with the dagger before fleeing the house.

St. Maria Goretti was taken to the hospital and in her last hours forgave her murderer and told her mother that she had been afraid of Allesandro for a long time but was afraid to say anything for fear it would cause trouble to the family. She died after lingering on for twenty-four hours, her mother beside her as well as the parish priest of Nettuno.

Alessandro was sentenced to thirty years in prison and for a long time was unrepentant. Then one night in a dream he saw the girl he had murdered promising she would pray for him. This brought about a sudden conversion and at the end of twenty-seven years he was released. His first act was to visit Maria Goretti's mother and beg her forgiveness.

Maria was canonized by Pope Pius XII in 1950, in a ceremony attended by a quarter of a million people. Her body is enshrined at the church of Our Lady of Grace in Nettuno.

Thought for the Day: The heroism of St. Maria Goretti is the heroism of a young girl with a conscience. Her situation is not much different from that of many young girls today, and her kind of fortitude is a powerful lesson in an age where conscience is often laid aside for the most trivial reasons. She is the modern saint for the young woman of today.

From 'The Catholic One Year Bible': ". . . I firmly believe in the Jewish law and everything written in the books of prophecy; and I believe, just as these men do, that there will be a resurrection of both the righteous and ungodly. Because of this I try . . . to always maintain a clear conscience before God and man." —Acts 24:14-16

Blessed Benedict XI (*JULY 7*)

On September 7, 1304, William of Nogaret and Sciarra Colonna, henchmen and councillors of King Philip the Fair of France, burst into the papal residence at Anagni, demanded that the pope, Boniface VIII, resign because of crimes they accused him of, publicly insulted him, and threatened to kill him. One of the two cardinals who were by the pontiff's side was Nicholas Boccasini, former master-general of the Dominicans and cardinal-archbishop of Ostia. When Boniface died three days later in Rome, Boccasini was chosen to succeed him.

Nicholas Boccasini became a Dominican when St. Thomas Aquinas was teaching at Paris and was educated at Venice and Bologna. He entered the Dominicans in 1254, was provincial of Lombardy from 1282 to 1296, and master-general of the order in 1296. He kept the Dominicans loyal to Boniface VIII, was sent by Boniface on diplomatic missions to England and France, and went as papal legate to Hungary to bring peace to that troubled nation.

He stood by Boniface's side during his troubles with Philip the Fair and was elected pope within two weeks of Boniface's death, taking the name of Benedict XI. His first effort was to bring peace between the Holy See and the French king, and this was helped by his universal reputation for holiness and wise administrative talents. His first act was to modify the rigid interpretation of Boniface's bull *Clericos Laicos*, which had so angered the French king, thus reconciling Philip the Fair with the papacy. But he refused to absolve Nogaret and Colonna for their public insult to Boniface.

Although Blessed Benedict XI was pope for only eight months, he brought peace to the Church and died in Perugia on July 7, 1304, loved and revered for his holiness and his humanity. He was honored as a saint from the time of his death and was beatified by Clement XII in 1736.

Thought for the Day: Blessed Benedict had to undo many of the harsh policies of his predecessor and yet not weaken the authority of the Church. He did this with unusual tact and firmness, without losing the prestige of the papal office. It was his own genuine holiness and gentleness that accomplished the task. Gentleness can often accomplish wonders in the hearts of human beings.

From 'The Catholic One Year Bible': [Paul said:] ". . . I demand my privilege of a hearing before the Emperor himself. . . . *I appeal to Caesar.*" Festus conferred with his advisors and then replied, "Very well! You have appealed to Caesar, and to Caesar you shall go!" —Acts 25:11-13

Raymond of Toulouse was a rare man who furthered Jewish-Christian relations at a time when Jews were often the victims of Christian brutality and prejudice. As a boy, as was the custom of the time, he was consecrated by his parents to religious life; but when he came of age, he decided to marry and lived happily with his wife until her death.

He saw around him poverty and suffering of all kinds and determined to do what he could to relieve it. Moreover, he helped everybody, including the Jews of the area, who were often the victims of prejudice and intolerance. He built a hospital and a college for poor priests and even built two stone bridges over the Garonne River for the safety of travelers.

St. Raymond of Toulouse was remembered as a man who did much, put his hand to every kind of charitable work, and even helped to build a stone church to enshrine the relics of St. Sernin. St. Sernin's was a collegiate church, with a community of canons, and after his wife's death, he was accepted as a canon of this church, devoted to the care of one of France's most famous shrines.

He left a deep impression on his fellow canons that was fresh a century after his death, when his life was written by one of the canons of St. Sernin's. He had a cheerful, enthusiastic disposition and seemed delighted to tackle projects that would help others or further the cause of religion. He died in 1118.

In 1652, an epidemic struck the city of Toulouse and was ended, it was believed, through the intercession of Raymond and his protection of the city. He was never formally canonized, but his tomb at Toulouse became noted for its many miraculous cures, and his veneration as a saint was approved in that year.

Thought for the Day: Some people seem to have a gift for just doing good, doing it constantly, cheerfully, and without ever seeming to tire of helping others. Motivated only by a love of others, they always find new ways to make others happy. They take the Gospel at its face value and realize in the deepest part of their beings that whatever they do to others, they do to Christ.

From 'The Catholic One Year Bible': . . . "Would to God that whether my arguments are trivial or strong, both you and everyone here in this audience might become the same as I am, except for these chains." — Acts 26:29

On June 26, 1572, in the battle for independence from Spain, the Calvinist "Sea Beggars" took the city of Gorkum in the Netherlands and imprisoned the Catholic religious of the city. Hatred for Spain and for Catholicism was widespread because of Spain's hold on the Netherlands, and the religious — Franciscans, Augustinians, Dominicans, Premonstratensians — and four secular priests were treated cruelly.

On the order of Admiral Lumaye, Baron de la Marck, they were ordered to Briel and were marched half-naked in a procession lasting several hours. They were interrogated and promised their freedom if they would abandon their faith in the Blessed Sacrament and in the primacy of the pope. This they refused to do and they were imprisoned in a deserted monastery outside of Briel to await execution.

Oddly enough, some of the most fervent among them apostatized and two who had lived less than exemplary lives went gladly to their deaths. In a nearby turf shed, there were beams and upon these they were hanged one by one. Two of the Franciscans were ninety years old and two others were over seventy. The Franciscan guardian, St. Nicholas Pieck, was one of the first to be hanged and died encouraging the others to face death boldly. Their bodies were mutilated before they were cold, and the brutality of the execution shocked even some of the Calvinists. Afterward, their bodies were thrown into ditches where they remained until 1616 when, during a truce between Spain and the Netherlands, the remains were dug up and brought to the Franciscan church in Brussels.

We have an eyewitness account of the martyrdoms from a nephew of Nicholas Pieck. There were nineteen martyrs in all. Before their deaths, the city officials of Gorkum objected to the imprisonment of the religious and priests, and the prince of Orange ordered their release. They were killed out of sheer hatred for their faith and for their refusal to deny that faith. They were canonized in 1867 by Pope Pius IX.

Thought for the Day: We have no way of knowing whether we will ever be asked to give our lives for our faith and we need not worry about whether we would have the strength to endure martyrdom. Such strength comes from God, not from ourselves, and if that supreme sacrifice were ever asked of us, the strength would be given.

From 'The Catholic One Year Bible': Arrangements were finally made to start us on our way to Rome by ship; so Paul and several other prisoners were placed in . . . custody. . . . We left on a boat which was scheduled to make several stops along the Turkish coast. — Acts 27:1-2

SS. Anthony and Theodosius Pechersky *(JULY 10)*

The great monastery of Mount Athos off the coast of Greece has been the seedbed of saints since it was founded in the year 963, and it was from Mount Athos that Byzantine monasticism was brought to Russia through the influence of SS. Anthony and Theodosius Pechersky.

As a young man, Anthony, born in 983 at Lubech, near Chernigov, Russia, began to live a solitary life; but, realizing that he needed training in this form of life, he made a pilgrimage to Mount Athos and became a member of one of its monasteries. After a few years, he was ordered by the abbot to go back to his own country to lead others.

He began to live in a cave near Kiev, beside the Dnieper River, and was soon joined by others. The community grew, and when a prince of the region offered them land above the caves where they lived, they built a wooden monastery and church, dedicated to the Mother of God. Anthony died there in 1073 at the age of ninety.

In 1032, the young Theodosius came to the Kiev monastery and it was he who was the real organizer of the monastery founded by Anthony. He succeeded as abbot about the year 1040, enlarged the buildings, and established the monastic rule of St. Theodore the Studite as the rule of the monastery. A hospital was built close to the monastery as well as a hospice for travelers and pilgrims. Like St. Basil, he insisted on works of mercy as part of monastic life and even took part in the evangelization of the region. The influence of the "Caves of Kiev" monastery was felt all over Russia.

Theodosius became the champion of the poor and oppressed and faced tyrants boldly when they oppressed their people. It was he who began the tradition of the *staretz*, the monk spiritual director, so characteristic of Russian monastic life. He invited everyone, regardless of age, sex, or station, to come to him with their problems.

In 1074, Theodosius celebrated Easter with his monks and a week later he was dead. He was buried in one of the caves, but in 1091, his body was taken to the principal church of the monastery. He was canonized in 1088 by the bishops of the Kiev province.

Thought for the Day: Saints like Anthony and Theodosius Pechersky had a great love of people, and everyone sensed this. They were called *prepodobny*, the "ones very like Christ," and this was the basis for their whole attraction. When we truly imitate Christ, we reflect something of His kindness and mercy, and make Christ Himself live in the world.

From 'The Catholic One Year Bible': . . . Julius wanted to spare Paul, so . . . he ordered all who could swim to jump overboard and make for land, and the rest to try for it on planks and debris from the broken ship. — Acts 27:43-44

Benedict was a Roman, born in the town of Norcia, not far from Rome. His twin sister, Scholastica, vowed herself to God at a very early age, and brother and sister were very close. The young Benedict was sent to Rome to be educated, but the state of the city in the wake of the barbarian invasions was anything but Christian, and the young man fled the city, horrified at the vice and moral corruption that was fast becoming the city's way of life.

In his search for a haven where he could live according to his conscience, he began to live a solitary life, going deeper and deeper into the wilderness near Subiaco. He found in a life of prayer and contemplation the spiritual security he had been seeking. He became known in the area as a man of deep spirituality, and his reputation for holiness and independence of spirit brought him to his life's work.

A community of monks in the neighborhood asked him to be their abbot. At first he refused, since it was clear that his views of what it meant to be a monk and theirs were very different. They persisted until he consented, but he soon gave up the task, since several of the monks were plotting to poison him.

St. Benedict went back to his own hermitage, and after a few years others started to join him. Soon there were too many in the wilderness, and so he organized them into twelve monasteries and ruled over them as their superior and spiritual father.

When jealousy and slander threatened to destroy the small work he had begun, Benedict retired once again into solitude, this time in the wilderness near the ancient town of Casinum, called Monte Cassino. Here again disciples gathered around him, and this time he gathered them into one monastery, organized their monastic life into the form that Benedictine monasticism has had since that time, and wrote the first draft of what would become the *Rule of St. Benedict.*

He died sometime after the year 546 and was buried beside his sister, St. Scholastica, in the Oratory of St. John the Baptist at Monte Cassino.

Thought for the Day: All great things begin in silence, and St. Benedict founded that way of life that is built upon silence. We all need a secret place where we can be silent, collect our thoughts, and begin to listen to the voice of God. From Benedict's silence came Benedictine monasticism; from our silence great things can arise.

From 'The Catholic One Year Bible': Paul lived for the next two years in his rented house and welcomed all who visited him, telling them with all boldness about the Kingdom of God and about the Lord Jesus Christ; and no one tried to stop him. — Acts 28:30-31

St. John Gualbert *(JULY 12)*

John Gualbert lived in the days when vendettas were a way of life in Italy and vendetta murders were common. Revenge for wrongs done was the order of the day, and as a member of the Visdomini family he was caught up in this immense pride in family honor. He was born in Florence, and his older brother, Hugh, was killed by a friend of the family.

St. John Gualbert considered it his duty to avenge the death of his brother. When about to kill the man who had killed his brother, the man fell on his knees and begged forgiveness in the name of Christ. Young John was so moved by this plea in the name of Christ that he forgave the man and, shocked by his own inhumanity, decided to consecrate his life to God.

He became a monk at St. Miniato monastery in Florence. In 1027, he visited St. Romuald at Camaldoli and decided to found a monastery of his own, more austere than St. Miniato and aimed at Church reform. In 1030, in Vallis Umbrosa, near Fiesole, he founded a monastery based on the rule of St. Benedict but with special statutes of his own. He also originated the concept of the lay brother, which became common in other orders.

From Vallambrosa, John founded and reformed other monasteries, and to each of these monasteries was attached a hospice for the poor and the sick. When Pope St. Leo IX was elected pope, he consulted John on his way to Rome, and it was due to his efforts that simony, which was so much a part of ecclesiastical life at the time, was almost wiped out. This brought him into conflict with the simoniac archbishop of Florence, Peter Mezzabarba.

Deeply revered for his holiness and love of the poor, John died at the abbey of St. Michael the Archangel, Passignano, on July 12, 1073. He was canonized by Pope Celestine III in 1193.

Thought for the Day: Often, totally un-Christian practices are accepted casually by Christians, and in St. John Gualbert's day these were blood revenge and simony. His own brush with the first brought about his conversion, and he risked his life to root out the second. Sometimes we have to take the risk of following Christ, whatever the consequences.

From 'The Catholic One Year Bible': . . . Through Christ, all the kindness of God has been poured out upon us undeserving sinners; and now he is sending us around the world to tell all people everywhere the great things God has done for them, so that they, too, will believe and obey him. — Romans 1:5

Husband-and-wife saints are rare in history, but St. Henry the Emperor and his wife, St. Kunigunde, are two of the most outstanding. They ruled the Holy Roman Empire together, helped reform the Church, founded monasteries, and established the great see of Bamberg, for which they built a great cathedral.

Henry was born at Hildesheim, the son of Duke Henry the Wrangler of Bavaria. He was educated at Hildesheim and by Bishop Wolfgang of Regensburg. In 998, he married Kunigunde, a member of the noble Luxembourg family. In 1002, he succeeded to the throne after the death of Otto II. He worked to stabilize the empire, putting down feuds and fighting rival claimants to the throne. In 1014, he was crowned emperor by Pope Benedict VIII in Rome.

His first concern after consolidating the empire was the restoration and progress of religion. He repaired and restored the episcopal sees of Hildesheim, Magdeburg, and Strasbourg and generously endowed others. He provided liberally for the poor in all of these places, setting up foundations to support a wide variety of charitable works.

During his absences, his queen, Kunigunde, founded monasteries and provided for the financial stability of the see of Bamberg from her own dowry. The couple collaborated in the governing of the empire and in the work of furthering the work of religion and Church reform.

It was through the superb management skills of Henry that the empire was placed on a solid footing, preparing the way for the great Hohenstaufen period that followed. He was a great admirer and friend of the abbey of Cluny and supported its efforts at Church reform. He was notable specifically as a Christian statesman and soldier and is considered one of the great rulers of the Holy Roman Empire.

Henry died at Gottingen in 1024 and is buried in the cathedral at Bamberg, together with his wife, Kunigunde. He was canonized by Pope Eugene III in 1146.

Thought for the Day: Emperors do not live like monks, and the holiness of an emperor is quite different from that of a monk. St. Henry was first of all an emperor, and it was as an emperor that he became a saint. He was shrewd in diplomacy, astute in politics, and a superb statesman. Genuine holiness can blossom anywhere.

From 'The Catholic One Year Bible': . . . They brought the Ark of God into the special tent that David had prepared for it, and the leaders of Israel sacrificed burnt offerings and peace offerings before God. — 1 Chronicles 16:1

Blessed Kateri Tekakwitha *(JULY 14)*

Kateri Tekakwitha is one of the first fruits of the Jesuit mission to North America and the first beatified American Indian. Like St. Thérèse of Lisieux, she died at the age of twenty-four after a life of great austerity and holiness. She was born in New York state, near what is now Auriesville, and so she is indeed a native-born American saint.

Her mother was a Christian Algonquin who had been captured by the Iroquois and taken to Auriesville, where she was made the wife of a Mohawk chief. Kateri was the oldest child of the marriage and together with a younger brother was brought up among the Mohawks. When her father, mother, and brother died in a smallpox epidemic, she was taken into the home of an uncle. She had the disease also, and it left her disfigured for the few remaining years of her life.

In 1667, she met Jesuit missionaries who visited the home of her uncle. Very shy by nature, Kateri did not receive any Christian instructions for a long time, partly from fear of her uncle. She finally approached one of the missionaries, Father Jacques de Lamberville, who gave her instructions in the Christian faith and baptized her in 1676. For her baptism, she took the name Katherine, or Kateri.

Her conversion brought about fierce opposition from her family, and so Father Lamberville advised her to go to the Christian village of Sault St. Louis, on the St. Lawrence River, where she could live her Christian faith without hindrance. After traveling two hundred miles through the wilderness, Blessed Kateri Tekakwitha arrived at the village in 1677, where she received her First Communion.

Taking one of the Jesuits for her spiritual director, she began to live an exemplary Christian life, noted especially for her devotion to prayer and to works of charity. In 1679, she took a private vow of virginity, something most unusual for an Indian woman who depended upon a husband for her complete support. She became an inspiration to the Indian community and when she died in 1680, she was revered as a saint. In 1980, three hundred years after her death, she was beatified by Pope John Paul II.

Thought for the Day: For Blessed Kateri Tekakwitha holiness was a very lonely path, but she realized that great sacrifices had to be made if she were to be faithful to God. The Christian faith was a totally new revelation to her and gave meaning and purpose to her whole life. She became a living example of that faith and led others as well to holiness.

From 'The Catholic One Year Bible': ". . . I accept your promise, Lord, that I and my children will always rule this nation. And may this bring eternal honor to your name as everyone realizes that you always do what you say. They will exclaim, 'The Lord of heaven is indeed the God of Israel!' " —1 Chronicles 17:23-24

St. Bonaventure *(JULY 15)*

As a small boy, St. Bonaventure fell seriously ill and was restored to health by the intercession of St. Francis. He was born at Bagnoregio near Naples in 1217, and his parents were Giovanni di Fidanza and Maria di Ritello. He was educated by the friars at Bagnoregio and then studied in Paris where he became a master of arts. He joined the Franciscans in Paris and studied theology under Alexander of Hales.

In 1248, he became a bachelor of Sacred Scripture and stayed on to teach in Paris. It was during these years that the mendicant friars, both Franciscan and Dominican, were under severe attack by the secular masters of the university, who resented their entrance into the teaching profession. For this reason, Bonaventure's reception of the doctorate was delayed until 1257, when, on direct orders of Pope Alexander IV, he and St. Thomas Aquinas were granted their doctorates in that year. In that year also, Bonaventure was elected minister-general of the Franciscan Order, on the resignation of John of Parma.

As minister-general, Bonaventure began a series of visitations of the whole Franciscan Order to acquaint himself with its problems but continued as well to write mystical and theological works, among the most notable, *The Journey of the Mind to God,* which he wrote at La Verna where St. Francis had received the stigmata. He codified the statutes of the Franciscan Order, drew up a new set of constitutions, and wrote his biography of St. Francis for the guidance of his order.

In 1273, he was created cardinal-bishop of Albano by Pope Gregory X and after his consecration worked with the pontiff to prepare for the Council the pope had called at Lyons in 1274. It was en route to this council that Bonaventure's friend Thomas Aquinas had died.

Bonaventure himself died while the council was still in session, on July 15, 1274. He was deeply mourned and buried the same day in the Franciscan church in Lyons. He was canonized in 1482 and declared a Doctor of the Church in 1588.

Thought for the Day: St. Bonaventure, known as the Seraphic Doctor, was a mystic in the midst of activities, a contemplative who ruled his order with firmness and wisdom. It is possible to be very busy and still be deeply absorbed in God, and that is the secret of saints like Bonaventure. The saint finds God everywhere.

From 'The Catholic One Year Bible': "This is a terrible decision to make," David replied, "but let me fall into the hands of the Lord rather than into the power of men, for God's mercies are very great." — 1 Chronicles 21:13

St. Marie Madeleine Postel *(JULY 16)*

Julie Postel was a precocious young woman with a mind of her own and when she was only eighteen she set up a school for poor children. She had a good education herself and saw the need for education all around her. She carried on her work for five years and then the French Revolution burst upon France; in 1790, when the National Assembly passed a law requiring the clergy to uphold the civil constitution, the Church in France was torn by schism, with some priests taking the oath and others refusing.

In Julie Postel's home village, the priests who took the oath to uphold the constitution were in the majority. Julie and others refused to attend their Masses, and she built a chapel in her home where the "nonjuring" priests could celebrate Mass. The dangers for her were very great, and in these times of great danger she gave herself to prayer with fervor and intensity.

After the Revolution, she worked to undo the damage done to religion. She taught, she prepared children for the sacraments, and she organized works of mercy. Gradually an idea began to form: she would found a congregation of sisters to do this kind of work. She went to Cherbourg, met the Abbé Cabart, who helped her to rent a house, got her pupils, and encouraged three other young women to join her. In 1807, the four took vows and Julie took the religious name Marie Madeleine. Within three years, her nuns were instructing two hundred little girls.

In 1816, St. Marie Madeleine Postel moved her community to Tamerville and then in 1832 she established her headquarters in the abandoned abbey of St.-Sauveur-le-Comte, which has remained the motherhouse ever since. Within a year, she had ten postulants and the community began to grow. She broadened the curriculum of the schools of her time and was an educational pioneer by her methods and ideas.

When she died in 1846 at the age of ninety, her congregation had one hundred fifty members. Pope Pius X beatified her in 1908, and she was canonized by Pope Pius XI in 1925.

Thought for the Day: Saints always show great originality in doing God's work and amaze others by their energy, their great courage, and their refusal to be discouraged. They tackle what seem to be impossible tasks because their confidence in God is unlimited. They can encourage us in our own work for God and that is why they are given to us as examples.

From 'The Catholic One Year Bible': By this time David was an old, old man, so he stepped down from the throne and appointed his son Solomon as the new king of Israel. . . . He commanded his son Solomon to build a temple for the Lord God of Israel. — 1 Chronicles 23:1, 22:6

The French Revolution broke out in 1789 and a year later all religious orders in France were suppressed, except those devoted to nursing and teaching. Among those suppressed were the cloistered Carmelites. At the convent in Compiègne, the sisters were driven from their monastery, their property impounded, and they were forced to wear secular dress. The community divided into four groups and lived in different houses close to St. Anthony's Church in the city. The nuns kept in touch with each other but had to be very careful that they were not reported to the authorities.

In 1794, they were arrested for continuing their religious lives and plotting against the Republic and were imprisoned in a deserted Visitation convent. In 1790, they had taken an oath to uphold the Republic, but when this oath was condemned by the Catholic bishops, the nuns formally retracted the oath before the mayor of the city. They were publicly abused and insulted, sent to Paris, and brought before the judges of the Republic. They were allowed no legal defense and the charges against them proved to be frivolous.

Condemned as "fanatics" for their devotion to their religion, they were taken in open carts to the guillotine in the Place du Trone Renverse, the nuns singing the *Miserere*, the *Salve Regina*, and the *Te Deum* as they were carted off to their execution. There were ten professed choir nuns, including the prioress (Blessed Teresa Ledoine), one novice, three lay sisters, and three extern sisters. Their bodies were thrown into a pit with other victims of the Revolution.

The oldest of the nuns was seventy-eight and the youngest, twenty-nine. As each nun mounted the scaffold, she asked for the blessing of her superior and chanted the *Laudate Dominum* as she went to her death. They were beatified on May 27, 1906.

Thought for the Day: There are martyrs in every age, and the Martyrs of Compiègne were no exception. In Poland, in Albania, in Russia and Czechoslovakia, there are those imprisoned for their faith and those who die for their faith. Our witness of the Christian faith may not lead to death, but we should profess it boldly and openly.

From 'The Catholic One Year Bible': It is clear, then, that God's promise to give the whole earth to Abraham and his descendants was not because Abraham obeyed God's laws but because he trusted God to keep his promise. — Romans 4:13

St. Pambo *(JULY 18)*

Pambo was one of the early monastic founders, a disciple of St. Anthony of Egypt and the instructor of the Tall Brothers, who were persecuted for their support of Origen. St. Pambo was one of the founders of the Nitrian group of monasteries, one of the great monastic centers of Egypt.

As a young man, Pambo took to heart anything that was taught him and was known for an incident that became famous among the desert monks, containing as it did a powerful lesson in wisdom. When he sat down at the feet of his first monastic, the text to be expounded was Psalm 39: "I said: I will watch my ways, so as not to sin with my tongue." Pambo said, "That will do for today," and went off to think about it. When he had meditated on this text for about six months, he came back to his teacher for a second lesson.

When St. Melania visited him in the desert and made him a gift of three hundred pounds of silver, he told her that it would be of great benefit for the poorer monasteries but did not thank her. She reminded him of the value of the gift. Pambo merely replied: "He to Whom you have offered this gift has no need for you to tell Him its value."

His was no narrow-minded asceticism, and he once reminded two monks who were arguing over whether it was better to give up a fortune or to use it to help the poor, "There are other roads to holiness besides being a monk." When two other monks were congratulating themselves on their great austerities, he told them: "These are not the things that make a good monk. Don't offend others and you will be saved."

Pambo died while he was making a basket for one of his disciples. "I have worked for everything I have eaten," he told his disciple, "and now I have to go to God before I have even begun to serve Him." Melania, who was there when he died, provided for his funeral and took away his unfinished basket as a relic. He died about the year 390.

Thought for the Day: All vocations are not the same, as St. Pambo well realized, and God judges the heart rather than the way of life. We have to place our feet on some pathway to God, and that is what a vocation is: a pathway to God. The important thing is to seek Him and serve Him well. With his salty remarks, Pambo understood this.

From 'The Catholic One Year Bible': . . . Abraham never doubted. He believed God, for his faith and trust grew ever stronger, and he praised God. . . . He was completely sure that God was well able to do anything he promised. — Romans 4:20-21

St. Macrina the Younger *(JULY 19)*

Macrina was the older sister of St. Basil of Caesarea and was the dominant influence upon him and their brothers St. Gregory of Nyssa and St. Peter of Sebastea. Her mother educated her carefully, taught her to use her talents well, and grounded her in the strong Christian spirit the family inherited from St. Gregory the Wonderworker.

When St. Macrina the Younger was twelve years old, she was betrothed; but when the young man died, she refused all offers of marriage. She had a dominant hand in the education of her brothers, and when Basil returned from the universities a very conceited young man, she taught him the meaning of humility and turned his mind to loftier matters than a university or court career.

Basil used his father's estate to found a convent for his mother and sister, and they were soon joined by other women seeking a consecrated life. Macrina is thus looked upon as one of the founders of women's monasticism. When her mother died, she gave her estate to the poor and earned her living by the labor of her hands.

Basil went on to become bishop of Caesarea in Cappadocia, one of the giants of the Eastern Church, and Gregory is considered the greatest master of mysticism that the early Church produced. Macrina was a powerful influence on both Basil and Gregory throughout their lives and both wrote memoirs of her. When Basil died in 379, she herself became ill, and Gregory of Nyssa, on visiting her found her very sick and close to death. Her cheerfulness and the great devotion she showed in the face of death deeply impressed him, and Gregory was with her when she died.

Macrina died at the hour of the lighting of lamps, greatly mourned by her community and by crowds pouring into the church for her funeral. At the request of a monk named Olympius, Gregory wrote her life, and her popularity spread throughout the East.

A competent theologian in her own right, Macrina was known also as a spiritual directress of great skill and was long remembered for her spiritual insight and counsel. She is revered especially in the Greek, Egyptian, Syrian, and Arab Churches.

Thought for the Day: Each and every one of us, like St. Macrina the Younger, has the power of personal influence. What we are and what we say can have a critical influence on others. Do we ever reflect on just how our lives influence others? Or are we concerned about that at all? It is something to ponder.

From 'The Catholic One Year Bible': David was king of the land of Israel for forty years; seven of them during his reign in Hebron and thirty-three in Jerusalem. He died at an old age, wealthy and honored; and his son Solomon reigned in his place. — 1 Chronicles 29:26-28

Around 1585, word of a "mystery man" began to leak into Mexico City, a strange hermit who lived out in the lonely valley of Guestaca, who walked miles to go to Mass, lived penniless, and had traveled from the shrine of Our Lady of Guadalupe in Spain to the shrine of Our Lady of Guadalupe in Mexico. Disturbed by the wagging tongues of the day, and the story becoming exaggerated with the telling, the archbishop of Mexico set up an investigating commission to look into the matter. What they discovered was quite remarkable, and Blessed Gregory López had to find a new place to hide.

He had been a page in the court of Philip II in Spain and while visiting the shrine of Our Lady of Guadalupe in Estramadura had heard of the shrine of the same name in Mexico. He went to Mexico convinced that God would show him what to do, sold his possessions, gave his money to the poor, then went off to find a place to live as a hermit. He found a suitable place in Guestaca, walked twenty-four miles for Mass on Sundays and great feasts, and caused a lot of gossip by his unusual way of life. To quiet the tongues, he lived on a plantation for a while to attend Mass regularly, but after the earthquake of 1566 he returned to his hermitage.

He was convinced to try the Dominicans, but he found that community life was not for him and returned to his solitude. When the archbishop approved of his way of life, and Gregory became too popular, he went to work in a hospital and wrote a book on pharmacy for the nursing brothers. In 1589, a priest-friend let him set up a hermitage near his church, then joined him in his life of solitude. They spent time in scriptural study, spent long hours in prayer, and became spiritual advisers to the people of the area.

Gregory remained something of a loner all of his life, and when he died in 1596 at the age of fifty-four, miracles were attributed to him, and his priest-friend wrote his life. Gregory was simply a most unusual man who took his own path to holiness and stuck to it to the end of his life. He has not been formally beatified but has been highly revered since his death, his fame reaching as far as England, France, and Germany.

Thought for the Day: There are no patterns for the saints, and the genuine saints break all molds. God is interested in us right where we are, and our own particular circumstances are as good a place as any to be a saint. Holiness is within the reach of all of us. It is impossible to say where our pathway may lead.

From 'The Catholic One Year Bible': King David's son Solomon was now the undisputed ruler of Israel, for the Lord his God had made him a powerful monarch. —2 Chronicles 1:1

St. Lawrence of Brindisi *(JULY 21)*

His name was Julius Caesar, and he was born at Brindisi in the kingdom of Naples in 1559. Educated in Venice at the College of St. Mark, he entered the Capuchins and was given the name Lawrence. Finishing his studies at the University of Padua, he showed a flair for languages, mastering Hebrew, Greek, German, Bohemian, Spanish, and French, and showed an extraordinary knowledge of the text of the Bible.

While still a deacon, St. Lawrence of Brindisi became known as an excellent preacher and after his ordination startled the whole of northern Italy with his amazing sermons. Sent into Germany by the pope to establish Capuchin houses, he became chaplain to Emperor Rudolf II and had a remarkable influence on the Christian soldiers fighting the Muslims when they were threatening Hungary in 1601. Through his efforts, the Catholic League was formed to give solidarity to the Catholic cause in Europe. Sent by the emperor to persuade Philip III of Spain to join the League, he established a Capuchin friary in Madrid. He also brought peace between Spain and the kingdom of Savoy.

His compassion for the poor, the needy, and the sick was legendary. Elected minister-general of his order in 1602, he made the Capuchins a major force in the Catholic Restoration, visiting every friary in the thirty-four provinces of the order and directing the work of nine thousand friars. He himself was a dominant figure in carrying out the work of the Council of Trent and was described by Pope Benedict XV as having earned "a truly distinguished place among the most outstanding men ever raised up by Divine Providence to assist the Church in time of distress."

In 1619, he undertook a journey to see King Philip III of Spain on behalf of the oppressed people of Naples who were ruled by a tyrannical governor. Lawrence reached Lisbon where the king was residing, and it was there that his last illness overtook him. His body was carried back to Spain and buried in the church of the Poor Clares at Villafranca del Bierzo.

Lawrence was canonized by Pope Leo XIII in 1881 and declared a Doctor of the Church by Pope John XXIII in 1959.

Thought for the Day: St. Lawrence's compassion for the poor moved him to make a dangerous trip to Spain to oppose an oppressive tyrant. He realized that evil has to be opposed and that if good men do not oppose it, the evil will continue. Our voice — individual or collective — should be heard in the cause for truth and justice.

From 'The Catholic One Year Bible': So the Temple was finally finished. Then Solomon brought in the gifts dedicated to the Lord by his father, King David. They were stored in the Temple treasuries. . . . And . . . the glory of the Lord, coming as a bright cloud, filled the Temple. . . . — 1 Chronicles 5:1, 14

St. Mary Magdalene *(JULY 22)*

The feast of St. Mary Magdalene is considered one of the most mystical of feasts, and it is said that of all the songs of the saints, that of Mary Magdalene is the sweetest and strongest because her love was so great. That love was praised by Jesus Himself who said that because much was forgiven her, she loved much.

Where she is buried, no one knows. Legend has her dying in Provence, France, in a cavern where she spent her last days, and her body resting in the chapel of St. Maximin in the Maritime Alps. Another has her buried in Ephesus where she went with St. John after the Resurrection. This latter view is more likely, and St. Willibald, the English pilgrim to the Holy Land in the eighth century, was shown her tomb there.

She was the first witness to the resurrection of Jesus, His most ardent and loving follower. She had stood with Mary at the foot of the Cross on that brutal Good Friday afternoon and had been by the side of Mary during these difficult hours. On Easter morning, she went with the other women to the tomb and it was there, in the garden near the tomb, that Jesus appeared to her. It was she who brought the news of the Resurrection to the Apostles, and Peter and John raced to the tomb to see what had happened.

She was from Magadala, a small fishing town on the Sea of Galilee, between Capernaum and Tiberias. She was known to be a "great sinner," a woman of the streets who heard Jesus speak of the mercy and forgiveness of God and changed her life completely. Her matter-of-fact witness to the Resurrection moved Peter and John to go and see for themselves: "I have seen the Lord and these things he said to me." Jesus had chosen her to bring the news to them and she simply told them what had happened.

She has always been the example of great love and great forgiveness, one of those close to Jesus who grasped the truth of God's love for human beings and spent her life bearing witness to that love.

Thought for the Day: St. Mary Magdalene seized the moment of truth when it came, and she did not hesitate to make a spectacle of herself to show her sorrow for her past life. We all need moments of conversion, when we must do something about our lives and our standing before God. In this Mary Magdalene is a model for all of us.

From 'The Catholic One Year Bible': As Solomon finished praying, fire flashed down from heaven and burned up the sacrifices! And the glory of the Lord filled the Temple. . . . All the people worshiped . . . and thanked the Lord. "How good he is!" they exclaimed. — 2 Chronicles 7:1, 3

St. Bridget of Sweden *(JULY 23)*

Bridget of Sweden, with St. Catherine of Siena, worked for the return of the popes from Avignon to Rome, but she died before that work was accomplished. She was a Swedish princess, visionary, and mystic, pilgrim to the Holy Land, foundress of a religious order, and the mother of St. Catherine of Sweden. Her order, the Bridgettines, almost disappeared at the time of the Reformation, but a few convents of nuns survived and Bridgettine brothers have recently been organized in the United States.

As a young girl, St. Bridget of Sweden was a lady-in-waiting at the court of Magnus II of Sweden and at the age of fourteen she married Ulf Gudmarsson. The couple had eight children, among them St. Catherine of Sweden. From her early childhood, Bridget experienced visions and revelations and these were put into writing before her death.

After her husband's death in 1344, she lived as a recluse near the Cistercian monastery of Alvastra. In 1346, King Magnus endowed a monastery for her at Vadstena, and it was here that she established her order. In 1349, she went to Rome and remained there for the rest of her life, except for pilgrimages in Italy and a long journey to the Holy Land in 1371. She worked for the reform of the Church, advised kings on political matters, and denounced the abuses of bishops and abbots.

For twenty years, she continually admonished the pope of Avignon to return to Rome, but her words were not heeded. When she died in 1373, she left to her daughter her mission and her concern for Church reform, and it was during her daughter's lifetime that the papacy did return to Rome.

Her visions and revelations made Bridget something of a celebrity and after her death they were the subject of much comment and thorough examination of the Church. They were declared free from error, even though everything in them has not been fully approved or accepted.

After her death, Bridget's body was taken back to Sweden and buried in the convent church at Vadstena.

Thought for the Day: St. Bridget's maid told others after the saint's death that she was "kind and meek to every creature and that she had a smiling face." Truly holy people are gentle with others, eminently kind, and compassionate toward all, and this is the first sign of genuine holiness. How I treat others is pretty much a reflection of how much I love God.

From 'The Catholic One Year Bible': When the Queen of Sheba heard of Solomon's fabled wisdom, she came to Jerusalem to test him. . . . And Solomon answered all her problems. Nothing was hidden from him; he could explain everything to her. — **2 Chronicles 9:1-2**

SS. Boris and Gleb *(JULY 24)*

These two saints are responsible for the recognition of a special category of saint, called *strastoterptsy* in Russian (literally, "passion-bearers"), innocent persons unwilling to die but rejecting violence, who accept suffering and death in the spirit of Christ. SS. Boris and Gleb were the sons of the first Christian prince of Russia, St. Vladimir of Kiev, and with their brother Syvatopolk were heirs to their father's kingdom after his death. They became, however, the victims of a dynastic murder, their brother unwilling to share the throne with them.

Boris was returning from a military expedition when the news of his brother's intentions reached him, and his soldiers offered to defend him. But he dismissed them saying that "it is not right that I should raise my hand against an older brother who now stands for me in the place of my father. It is better for me to die alone than to be the cause of many others dying."

He sat down by the side of the River Alta to wait for the death that was sure to come, meditating on the sad fate that waited for him. He asked God's forgiveness for his brother and prayed through the night. Next morning, the soldiers sent by his brother found him and ran him through with spears and finished him with their swords.

The younger brother, Gleb, unaware of the assassination of Boris, was sent for by Syvatopolk. While he was on his way by boat, a gang of men boarded and began to surround him with their swords. Gleb begged for his life, but when they refused, he did not resist. "I am in your hands," he told them. "I don't know why I have to die, but God knows. Who would think that brother would kill brother? I am betrayed, O Lord, as You Yourself were."

Five years after their deaths in 1015, the bodies of the two princes were found incorrupt and they were reinterred in the church of St. Basil at Vyshgorod. Their tomb quickly became a place of pilgrimage, and they were so widely venerated that the ecclesiastical authorities canonized them. Their canonization was confirmed by Pope Benedict XIII in 1724.

Thought for the Day: SS. Boris and Gleb were not martyrs, since they did not die for the faith, but they were the innocent victims of violence who accepted their deaths in union with Christ. Some are called merely to suffer, with no apparent reason. It is good to know that there are such saints and that there can be holiness in suffering unjust violence.

From 'The Catholic One Year Bible': . . . The Holy Spirit helps us with our daily problems and in our praying. For we don't even know what we should pray for, nor how to pray as we should; but the Holy Spirit prays for us. . . . — Romans 8:26

St. James the Greater *(JULY 25)*

In Spain, he is called El Señor Santiago, the patron saint of horsemen and soldiers, and his great shrine at Santiago de Compostela in that country has been a place of pilgrimage for centuries. He is one of those that Jesus called Boanerges, "son of thunder," the brother of John the Evangelist and the son of Zebedee the fisherman from Galilee.

St. James the Greater and his brother John were apparently partners with those other two brothers, Peter and Andrew, and lived in Bethsaida, on the north shore of the Sea of Galilee. How and where James first met Jesus, we do not know; but there is an old legend that makes Salome, his mother, a sister of Mary, and if this were the case, he would have known Jesus from childhood.

Along with Peter and his brother John, James was part of the inner circle of Jesus, who witnessed the Transfiguration, were witnesses to certain of His miracles, like the raising of the daughter of Jairus, and accompanied Him to the Garden of Gethsemani. Like his brother, he was active in the work of evangelization after the death of Jesus, and one legend, very unlikely, even has him going to Spain after Jesus' resurrection.

His prominence and his presence in Jerusalem must have been well known, for scarcely a dozen years after the Resurrection, he became involved in the political maneuverings of the day and was arrested and executed by King Herod Agrippa. This was followed by the arrest of Peter also, so his death must have been part of a purge of Christian leaders by Agrippa, who saw the new Christian movement as a threat to Judaism.

Jesus had foretold this kind of fate when He prophesied that James and his brother John would "drink of the same chalice" of suffering as Himself. The two brothers had asked to be seated at the right of Jesus and at His left in His kingdom, and Jesus told them that they would be with Him in a far different way than they expected.

James's death is the only biblical record we have of the death of one of the Apostles, and he was the first of that chosen band to give his life for his Master.

Thought for the Day: St. James the Greater's ambition for being someone of importance was changed to a different kind of ambition as he came to know Jesus better. He became the great Apostle, spreading the knowledge of Christ and dying for his efforts. In all of us, our water is turned into wine when we get close to Jesus Christ.

From 'The Catholic One Year Bible': God's laws are perfect. They protect us, make us wise, and give us joy and light. God's laws are pure, eternal, just. They are more desirable than gold. They are sweeter than honey dripping from a honeycomb. — **Psalm 19:7-10**

SS. Joachim and Anne *(JULY 26)*

Who does not know about the great shrine of Ste. Anne de Beaupré in Canada, where miracles abound, where cured cripples leave their crutches, and where people come from thousands of miles to pray to the grandmother of Jesus? At one time, July 26 was the feast of St. Anne only, but with the new calendar the two feasts of the parents of the Blessed Virgin Mary have been joined and are celebrated today.

Our information about Mary's parents comes from an apocryphal Christian writing, the *Protoevangelium Jacobi* (or *Gospel of James*), written about the year 170. According to this story, Joachim was a prominent and respected man who had no children, and he and his wife, Anne, looked upon this as a punishment from God. In answer to their prayers, Mary was born and was dedicated to God at a very early age.

From this early Christian writing have come several of the feast days of Mary, particularly the Immaculate Conception, the Nativity of Mary, and her Assumption into Heaven. Very early also came feast days in honor of SS. Joachim and Anne, and in the Middle Ages numerous churches, chapels, and confraternities were dedicated to St. Anne. The couple early became models of Christian marriage, and their meeting at the Golden Gate in Jerusalem has been a favorite subject of Christian artists.

Anne is often shown in paintings with Jesus and Mary and is considered a subject that attracts attention, since Anne is the grandmother of Jesus. Her two great shrines — that of Ste. Anne d'Auray in Britanny, France, and that of Ste. Anne de Beaupré near Quebec in Canada — are very popular. We know little else about the lives of Mary's parents, but considering the person of Mary, they must have been two very remarkable people to have been given such a daughter and to have played so important a part in the work of the Redemption.

There is a church of St. Anne in Jerusalem and it is believed to be built on the site of the home of SS. Joachim and Anne, when they lived in Jerusalem.

Thought for the Day: The importance of parents in the life of a child! Who can measure it? They not only give life to their child but mold as well the character and moral personality of the child. The home is still the first and most important school, and in the home the most dominant influence is most certainly the parents. Nothing shows more the dignity of parenthood.

From 'The Catholic One Year Bible': . . . It is by believing in his heart that a man becomes right with God; and with his mouth he tells others of his faith, confirming his salvation. — Romans 10:10

She was born not far from the ancestral home of the Gonzagas and felt a special kinship with St. Aloysius Gonzaga. Aloysius had been drawn to teaching children in the streets of Rome, and very early in her life St. Bartholomea Capitanio found herself doing the same thing. When she was eleven, she entered the Poor Clares but did not find her vocation there and returned home in 1824 to open a school for children in her own home.

She looked around and saw all kinds of things to do. Her father was a heavy drinker, but she won him over by sheer kindness and, since her vocation was not to any religious life that she saw, she found herself a spiritual director and vowed herself to God privately. In 1826, she started a much-needed hospital in Lovere, which she directed with unusual energy and practicality, and became something of a home nurse for many of her patients.

Noticing the need for education, she very early obtained a teacher's certificate and gathered the young about her. When the young people left her, she continued to correspond with them, her letters filled with all kinds of practical advice and spiritual programs of every kind. She conceived the idea of a religious community dedicated to all kinds of charitable works and looked around for some way to do it.

Around 1830, she met St. Vincenza Gerosa who had been thinking along similar lines, and in 1832 they dedicated themselves to God in a new religious congregation called the Sisters of Charity of Lovere. Bartholomea worked prodigiously to spread the work of the new congregation, in her spare time continuing to write the letters that were so prized by those who received them. After her death, her *Scritti spirituali* filled two huge volumes and her letters, also published, numbered over three hundred.

She died in 1833 at the young age of twenty-six, her ideas and energy inspiring others long after she was gone. She was beatified in 1926 by Pope Pius XI and canonized, together with Vincenza Gerosa, by Pope Pius XII in 1950. Her influence on the young people of her time was extensive and her letters are still read by those looking for insight into the education and spiritual direction of the young.

Thought for the Day: St. Bartholomea Capitanio was a contemporary of John Henry Newman's, who had his own brilliant ideas on the education of the young. She was a pioneer in a much neglected field and by her very interest found creative things to do and say. She shows that the opportunity for good works is never lacking, if we will only look around us.

From 'The Catholic One Year Bible': If you won't plow in the cold, you won't eat at the harvest. Though good advice lies deep within a counselor's heart, the wise man will draw it out. Most people will tell you what loyal friends they are, but are they telling the truth? — Proverbs 20:4-6

St. Samson of Dol *(JULY 28)*

Caldey Island off the southern coast of Wales today houses a Trappist monastery, but it was the site of monastic life centuries before when Welsh monks settled on the island and founded a small monastery. It was a monastery in the Welsh tradition of St. Illtud, austere in its discipline and strict in its observance. The most notable saint of these early years is Samson, born in Gwent, not far from the ruins of Tintern abbey. His father was Amon and his mother was Anna. He was born in the year 485 when monasticism flourished in Wales.

He was dedicated to God when he was five years old and was trained by Illtud himself, whose monastery at Llantwit in Glamorgan was called "a nursery of saints." St. Samson of Dol became so outstanding as a monk and scholar at a very young age that two brothers, nephews of Illtud who thought he might succeed their uncle as head of the monastery instead of themselves, tried to poison him.

To avoid further conflict, Samson received permission from Illtud to go to Caldey Island. Here he was joined later by his own father and uncle and became abbot of the monastery at the death of its abbot, Piro. Samson is responsible for sending monks into Ireland and influencing monasticism there, and several Irish saints are said to have traveled to Wales to study under him and receive their monastic formation. The influence of Welsh monasticism on Ireland was great in these years.

He did not remain abbot very long and, resigning his office, he and his father and several other monks lived as hermits near the Severn River. Soon after, he was consecrated bishop, evangelized Cornwall, and made his way to Britanny across the English Channel where many Britons had fled when the Angles and Saxons invaded Britain. He became a veritable dynamo of activity: founding churches and monasteries, putting rightful kings on their thrones, becoming a peacemaker, and even visiting Paris and attracting the notice of King Childebert, who chose him to be bishop of Dol.

Samson signed the Acts of the Council of Paris in 557 and left his name on churches throughout Britanny. He died peacefully among his monks in 565 and is one of the most popular of Welsh saints. One of the Scilly Islands still bears his name.

Thought for the Day: Spiritual men and women seek solitude, and it is in solitude that their characters are formed and their spirits are strengthened. When they put their hand to active works, they accomplish great things and touch the lives of millions. Having loved solitude, they carried their solitude with them, and this is the secret center from which they work.

From 'The Catholic One Year Bible': Oh, what a wonderful God we have! How great are his wisdom and knowledge and riches! How impossible it is for us to understand his decisions and his methods! For who among us can know the mind of the Lord? — **Romans 11:33-34**

St. Martha *(JULY 29)*

Martha is the lady of Bethany who welcomed Jesus into her home and, together with her sister, Mary, and her brother, Lazarus, were dear and close friends of Jesus. Today, in Bethany, there is a church built over the site of their home, which Pope Paul VI visited on his trip to the Holy Land. Today, if you visit there, little Bedouin children will come begging coins and point up the hill to what is believed is the site of Lazarus's tomb.

It was for St. Martha and her sister that Jesus performed one of His greatest miracles: the raising of their brother to life. It was at their home that He stopped on the way to Jerusalem, or when He was in the area. It was in Martha's house that He defended Mary's contemplative leisure, gently chiding Martha that there were more important things in life than mere busyness. And it was to Martha that He spoke those stirring words that are spoken at every Christian burial: "I am the resurrection and the life, whoever believes in Me, even if he dies, shall live, and whoever is alive and believes in Me, will never die."

It is not generally known that Jesus had no home in Jerusalem and that His nights were spent either on the Mount of Olives, where all Galileans stayed on visits to Jerusalem, or at Martha's home in Bethany, just over the hill from the Mount of Olives. It is also probable that this is where Mary, Jesus' mother, stayed when she was in Jerusalem at the time of His crucifixion.

Martha's closeness to Jesus is shown by her words at the time of Lazarus's death: "Lord, if You had been here, my brother would never have died," and the Gospel says very clearly that "Jesus loved Martha and her sister and Lazarus very much."

Early Christian legend has Martha traveling to France with St. Mary Magdalen, but this is doubtful. Her home probably became an early Christian meeting place, and she would undoubtedly have been active in the first Christian community, giving hospitality to the Apostles as she gave hospitality to Jesus Himself.

Thought for the Day: Hospitality is an ancient Christian virtue and one that draws down blessings on the hospitable. Jesus did not reproach St. Martha for her hospitality but for her excessive busyness. We have to find ways of finding leisure in God, even in the midst of activity, and hospitality to others should not take us away from the joy we should find in Him.

From 'The Catholic One Year Bible': Don't just pretend that you love others: really love them. . . . Love each other with brotherly affection and take delight in honoring each other. Never be lazy in your work, but serve the Lord enthusiastically. — Romans 12:9-11

St. Peter Chrysologus *(JULY 30)*

In the fifth century, Ravenna, not Rome, was the capital of the Roman empire in the West, and Ravenna itself became a metropolitan see. St. Peter Chrysologus was one of the most distinguished archbishops of that see.

Peter was born in Imola about the year 400 and studied under Cornelius, bishop of that city, who ordained him deacon. In 433, the archbishop of Ravenna died, and when a successor had been chosen by the clergy and people of Ravenna, they asked Bishop Cornelius to obtain confirmation of their choice from Pope Sixtus III. On his trip to Rome, Cornelius took his deacon, Peter, as his companion; upon seeing Peter, the pope chose him for the see of Ravenna instead of the one selected by the clergy and people of Ravenna.

Peter was consecrated and was accepted somewhat grudgingly at first by both the clergy and the people. Peter, however, soon became the favorite of Emperor Valentinian III, who resided at Ravenna and was also highly regarded by Pope St. Leo the Great, the successor of Pope Sixtus.

There were still traces of paganism in Peter's diocese, and his first effort was to establish the Catholic faith everywhere, rooting out abuses and carrying on a campaign of preaching and special care of the poor. Many of his sermons still survive, and it is on the basis of these that he came to be known as "the golden word."

In his concern for the unity of the Church, Peter Chrysologus opposed the teaching of Eutyches, condemned in the East, who asked for his support. Peter also received St. Germanus of Auxerre to his diocese and officiated at his funeral.

Knowing that his own death was near, Peter returned to his own city of Imola and after urging great care in the choice of his successor he died at Imola about the year 450 and was buried in the church of St. Cassian. In 1729, Pope Benedict XIII declared him a Doctor of the Church.

Thought for the Day: Good preachers are rare, but good preachers are treasured and listened to. Many a person has been converted to a better life by the words of a good preacher, and we all have profited from the words of others. St. Peter Chrysologus was called "the golden word" because of his eloquence and because his words changed those who listened. Good listening is as important as good preaching.

From 'The Catholic One Year Bible': Wake up, for the coming of the Lord is nearer now than when we first believed. The night is far gone, the day of his return will soon be here. — Romans 13:11-13

St. Ignatius of Loyola *(JULY 31)*

Ignatius was born in the castle of Loyola in the Basque country of Spain about 1491, the youngest of eleven children. Like his brothers, he was trained to be a soldier, and it was while fighting against the French at Pamplona in 1521 that his military career was cut short by a cannonball that broke his leg.

His leg was set poorly and had to be broken again, and Ignatius on his bed of pain tried to amuse himself by reading. The only books in the castle were a life of Christ and stories of the saints. These two books brought about a complete change in his life: he determined to dedicate his life to God, and when he was well, he went to make a retreat at Manresa, near the great abbey of Montserrat. It was here, in prayer and reflection, that St. Ignatius of Loyola began his *Spiritual Exercises*, the manual of his own spiritual life that was to become the backbone of Ignatian spirituality.

In 1523, he made a trip to the Holy Land and, after returning, began studies for the priesthood at Barcelona and Alcala. In 1528, he went to Paris to complete his studies and gathered around him six followers who would become the founding members of the Society of Jesus. After dedicating themselves to the service of God, they headed for Italy to go to the Holy Land. When this was impossible because of the war between the Venetians and the Turks, they went to Rome and offered themselves to the pope for any service he wished to assign them.

With the foundation of the Society of Jesus thus laid, Ignatius made his headquarters in Rome where he directed the work of the society and completed the constitutions of the order. Within a few short years, the Jesuits, as they were called, had spread throughout Europe and the world, and it was through their efforts that the reevangelization of Europe began. When Ignatius died in 1556, the Jesuits numbered over one thousand, scattered throughout nine European countries and provinces as well as India and the New World.

Ignatius died on July 31, 1556, and was canonized in 1622. Pope Pius XI declared him the patron of spiritual exercises and retreats.

Thought for the Day: The power of a good book! St. Ignatius of Loyola was converted by reading the lives of the saints and wondering why he could not be like them. His life before was anything but religious; reading about our Lord and the saints, however, changed his life. But for that book, Ignatius would not have founded the Society of Jesus, and the world would have been deprived of the power for good that the Jesuits became.

From 'The Catholic One Year Bible': . . . The important thing for us Christians is not what we eat or drink but stirring up goodness and peace and joy from the Holy Spirit. If you let Christ be Lord in these affairs, God will be glad; and so will others. — **Romans 14:17-18**

THE SAINTS OF AUGUST

St. Alphonsus Liguori *(AUGUST 1)*

Alphonsus Liguori, born in 1696, was the son of an ancient Neapolitan family, his father an officer in the royal navy. At the age of sixteen, Alphonsus received his doctorate in both canon and civil law and for nearly ten years practiced at the bar. When he found that one of the legal cases he was defending was not based on justice but on political intrigue, he gave up the practice of law and dedicated his life to God.

Ordained to the priesthood in 1726, St. Alphonsus Liguori joined a group of secular priests dedicated to missionary activities. He involved himself in many kinds of pastoral activities, giving missions and organizing workers, and had a part in the founding of an order of contemplative nuns.

In 1732, he founded the Redemptorists, a congregation of priests and brothers, to work especially among the country people of Italy who often lacked the opportunity for missions, religious instruction, and spiritual retreats. Strangely, his first companions deserted him; but Alphonsus stood firm, and soon vocations multiplied and the congregation grew.

The Redemptorists were approved by Pope Benedict XIV in 1749, and Alphonsus was elected superior general. In 1762, he was appointed bishop of Sant' Agata dei Goti and as bishop he corrected abuses, restored churches, reformed seminaries, and promoted missions throughout his diocese. During the famine of 1763-64, his charity and generosity were boundless, and he also carried on a huge campaign of religious writing.

In 1768, he was stricken with a painful illness and resigned his bishopric. During the last years of his life, problems in his congregation caused him much sorrow and when he died on August 1, 1787, at Pagani, near Salerno, the Redemptorists were a divided society. He was beatified in 1816, canonized in 1839, and declared a Doctor of the Church in 1871.

Thought for the Day: St. Alphonsus Liguori devoted himself to the most uneducated and unlettered people of Italy and used his huge talents to bring the Gospel to the poor. He recognized the ' universal call to holiness" and saw that every human being is beloved of God. It is a conviction that we should all have.

From 'The Catholic One Year Bible': May God who gives patience, steadiness, and encouragement help you to live in complete harmony with each other — each with the attitude of Christ toward the other. And then all of us can praise the Lord together with one voice, . . . — Romans 15:5-6

St. Eusebius of Vercelli *(AUGUST 2)*

Eusebius was the founder of the canons regular, priests living under a religious rule and dedicated to pastoral work. It was the immediate result of the rise of monasticism in the East, and St. Eusebius of Vercelli saw the possibilities of the new movement for the clergy. His example was imitated all over the West and brought about a renewal of clerical life.

He was born in Sardinia and as a child was taken to Rome, where he became a member of the Roman clergy under Pope Julius. Consecrated for the see of Vercelli in 344, he gathered his clergy into a community life, founding also the dioceses of Turin and Embrun. In 355, he attended the Council of Milan as legate of Pope Liberius, which defended St. Athanasius against those Western bishops intimidated by the emperor. When Eusebius was ordered along with other bishops to condemn Athanasius, he refused, insisting instead that they all sign the Nicene Creed. When threatened by the emperor, Eusebius stood his ground and told the emperor he had no right interfering in Church matters.

In anger, the emperor sent Eusebius into exile in Palestine, where he was severely mistreated by the Arians. He was moved around from place to place and after his release by the Emperor Julian he consulted with Athanasius in Alexandria on the Arian crisis. Returning to Italy, he joined with St. Hilary of Poitiers in opposing the Arian bishop of Milan and returned to Vercelli amid the rejoicing of his people.

Eusebius is considered by many to be the author of the Athanasian Creed, and a copy of the Gospels written in his own hand is preserved in the cathedral at Vercelli. He died on August 1, 371, and his courage in suffering for the faith inspired other bishops to oppose the Arian heresy.

Thought for the Day: St. Eusebius of Vercelli refused to "go along with the crowd," even when threatened by an emperor, and he suffered long and cruelly for his convictions. Sometimes we have to oppose others, especially in matters that are important, and *how* we do it is as important as *that* we do it. We should never lose our Christian kindness and gentle manner, even in opposing others, but it should be very clear where we stand.

From 'The Catholic One Year Bible': Will you be my prayer partners? For the Lord Jesus Christ's sake, and because of your love for me — given to you by the Holy Spirit — pray much with me for my work. Pray that I will be protected in Jerusalem from those who are not Christians. — Romans 15:30-31

St. Germanus of Auxerre *(AUGUST 3)*

In 429, Roman Britain had been overrun by the Angles and Saxons of northern Germany, and the Christian population was devastated by the invasions, as well as deeply divided because of the Pelagian heresy. Concerned, the pope sent a delegation of Gallic bishops to combat the heresy and strengthen the faith of the Christians of Britain. The leader of the delegation was St. Germanus of Auxerre, former governor of the province of Armorica in Gaul and a fearless leader of the Gallic Church.

He was born at Auxerre, studied law and rhetoric in Rome, and after his marriage was sent to Gaul as governor. On the death of St. Amator, bishop of Auxerre, he was chosen, against his own wishes, to be bishop of the city, and, like St. Ambrose before him, changed his life completely and dedicated his life to God and to his pastoral duties.

In Britain, he not only strengthened the faith of the British Christians but also organized them to resist the invading Saxons and brought about a complete rout of the invaders at a battle near Flintshire, by the simple tactic of having the whole army shout "Alleluia!" at the top of their voices. The Saxons were turned back without bloodshed.

On returning to Gaul, he faced a similar threat. The Roman general Aetius had sent an army led by a barbarian, Goar, to put down a revolt near Auxerre, and, knowing the army would ravage the province, Germanus went out to meet the barbarian leader, riding up to him and taking hold of the bridle of his horse. At first Goar refused to talk with the bishop, but Germanus persisted and the barbarian leader agreed not to devastate the province until the matter had been referred to Aetius. In return, Germanus had to go to Ravenna to obtain an imperial pardon for Goar's people, and the province was spared.

It was on this trip to Ravenna that Germanus died in 448. His body was taken back to Auxerre with great honor, and after a magnificent funeral he was buried in the abbey of St. Germanus.

Thought for the Day: In the early Church, bishops were not only spiritual leaders but often civic leaders as well, when the people had no other champions against the oppression of governments. St. Germanus fought for his people and became their champion and their defender. Like the Good Shepherd, he was willing to lay down his life for his sheep.

From 'The Catholic One Year Bible': I commit you to God, who is able to make you strong and steady in the Lord, just as the Gospel says, and just as I have told you. . . . To God, who alone is wise, be the glory forever through Jesus Christ our Lord. Amen. — **Romans 16:25-27**

The Curé of Ars, St. John Vianney, is one of the most beloved saints of the Catholic Church, and the spiritual revolution that he brought about in his parish at Ars was one of the marvels of nineteenth-century France.

He was born at Dardilly, near Lyons, in 1786, when the French Revolution was at its height and received very little formal education. Because of the unsettled times, he had to make his first confession and First Communion secretly and at the age of eighteen began his studies for the priesthood under the Abbé Balley, pastor at Ecully.

Discouraged by his lack of scholastic ability, John Vianney made a pilgrimage to the shrine of St. John Regis at La Louvesc and was then called up for military service. Through a strange set of circumstances, his unit left without him, and after the general amnesty of 1810 he began formal studies for the priesthood but found the subjects difficult to master. Nevertheless, because of his goodness and common sense, he was ordained at Grenoble in 1815 and was sent as an assistant to his former teacher, the Abbé Balley.

In 1818, he was assigned to Ars and remained there for the rest of his life. He fasted and prayed, visited every family in his parish, taught catechism, and by his preaching led his people back to the practice of their religion. In eight years, he thoroughly restored religion in the parish, organized religious guilds, and fostered truly Christian homes.

His greatest fame was as a confessor, and people came from all over France by the thousands to be his penitents. He was usually in the confessional all day, from midnight to early evening, except for meals and the celebration of Mass. For thirty years, he was disturbed by strange phenomena attributed to the devil.

Worn out by work and austerities, John Vianney died on August 4, 1859, at the age of seventy-three. He was beatified by Pope St. Pius X in 1905 and canonized by Pope Pius XI in 1925. In 1929, he was declared the patron of parish priests.

Thought for the Day: By hard work and prayer, and his own living example, St. John Vianney transformed his whole parish into a model Christian community. To bring about change, wishing is not enough: we have to work, to pray, and to become living models of the Christian life ourselves.

From 'The Catholic One Year Bible': I can never stop thanking God for all the wonderful gifts he has given you, now that you are Christ's: he has enriched your whole life. . . . What I told you Christ could do for you has happened! —1 Corinthians 1:4-6

Peter Julian Eymard was born in 1811 in the diocese of Grenoble, France. Peter worked at his father's trade — that of a knifemaker — until he was eighteen. He was ordained at Grenoble in 1831 and received the permission of his bishop in 1839 to enter the Marist Fathers. During his seventeen years in the Marists, he acted as provincial superior and rector of the college at La Seine-sur-Mer.

In 1851, he made a pilgrimage to Notre-Dame de Fourvieres and wrote later: "The idea haunted me . . . that Jesus in the Blessed Sacrament had no religious institute to glorify His mystery of love, whose only object was entire consecration to Its service."

On the advice of his superiors, St. Peter Julian Eymard put off his plan for founding such an institute until the idea had matured. During this time, he received encouragement from Pope Pius IX and from Venerable John Colin, founder of the Marists. In 1856, Father Eymard submitted his plan for an institute of priest-adorers of the Blessed Sacrament and it was approved by the archbishop of Paris. The archbishop put a house at his disposal and Father Eymard began his institute with one companion. Vocations were slow, but soon two other houses were established and a regular novitiate set up.

The institute suffered many difficulties, particularly from detractors who criticized Father Eymard for leaving the Marists. His only reply was: "They are doing me a service." St. John Vianney, who knew Father Eymard, said of him: "He is a saint. . . . His work . . . will do great things for the glory of God."

During the last four years of his life, Father Eymard suffered from very painful illnesses and insomnia. In July of 1868, his health broke completely and his doctor ordered him to leave Paris. On July 21, he arrived in his hometown of La Mure, weak and partially paralyzed. On August 1, he died. He was beatified in 1925 and canonized in 1962, during the Second Vatican Council.

Thought for the Day: Devotion to the Blessed Sacrament was the heart of St. Peter Julian Eymard's life. "Without it," he said, "I should have been lost." This *tantum sacramentum*, as St. Thomas Aquinas called the Blessed Sacrament, is the very center of the Christian life and should be the center of our existence.

From 'The Catholic One Year Bible': . . . It is from God alone that you have your life through Jesus Christ. He showed us God's plan for salvation; he was the one who made us acceptable to God; he made us pure and holy and gave himself to purchase our salvation. — 1 Corinthians 1:30

St. Hormisdas (AUGUST 6)

Hormisdas was pope during the Acacian Schism in the sixth century and was a widower and a deacon of the Roman Church. He has the distinction of having his son, St. Silverius, also elected pope and thus there have been a father and son as the successors of St. Peter.

The Acacian Schism came about during the Monophysite crisis, in the period following the Council of Chalcedon, when certain Eastern bishops refused to accept the council with its proclamation of "one person and two natures" in Christ. In facing the problem, St. Hormisdas insisted that the authority of the Council of Chalcedon be accepted as well as the *Tome of Pope Leo*, which clarified the issue for the council.

In 519, legates from the pope were sent to Constantinople to act as the pontiff's representatives in terminating the schism, and the statement signed by all the bishops called by the emperor was called the Formula of Hormisdas. It definitively ended the Acacian Schism that had divided Rome and Constantinople for thirty-five years. It unfortunately also alienated still further the Syrian, Jacobite, and Coptic Churches, which held that God became incarnate in one nature, thus bringing about the first great division in the Christian Churches and the establishment of the Monophysite Churches.

Pope Hormisdas lived in troubled times, with the Vandals occupying Roman Africa and the Ostrogoths soon to occupy Italy. His son, who followed him as pope in 536, inherited these troubles and was himself martyred in a dispute with the Empress Theodora.

Hormisdas died in 523, revered as a wise peacemaker, and was buried in the portico of St. Peter's. Over a hundred of his letters are preserved, and he is considered one of the greatest of the early popes who furthered the unity of the Church by strengthening bonds with the see of Peter.

Thought for the Day: Faith in Jesus Christ as the Incarnate Son of God is the very foundation of the Christian faith, and it was St. Hormisdas's task as pope to clarify that faith and strengthen that belief. The substance of that faith is expressed in the Nicene Creed, which we proclaim every Sunday, and it is well to reflect upon its meaning as we profess it.

From 'The Catholic One Year Bible': . . . No mere man has ever seen, heard or even imagined what wonderful things God has ready for those who love the Lord. But we know about these things because God has sent his Spirit to tell us, and his Spirit searches out and shows us all of God's deepest secrets. — **1 Corinthians 2:9-10**

In the early centuries, the Church was shaken by several violent persecutions, the most violent begun under the Emperor Decius in 250 and continued by his successor, the Emperor Valerian. St. Sixtus II was pope during the persecution under Valerian.

There was not only the persecution itself to face but also a division among bishops over the baptism given by heretics. The bishops of North Africa, under St. Cyprian, refused to recognize the baptism by heretics, but Rome, beginning with the pontificate of St. Stephen I, did recognize them. Sixtus succeeded Stephen and had to face the division in the Church.

Valerian's persecution began in 257 and there were many Christian martyrs. One of the most illustrious of the martyrs of this period was St. Lawrence, whose feast day is celebrated on August 10. Cyprian in Africa took note of the martyrdom of Sixtus in a letter to the African bishops: "You are to understand that Sixtus suffered in a cemetery upon the 6th of August, and with him four deacons. The officers of Rome are very keen on this persecution. . . . Pray that we may think of immortality rather than death. . . . We know that soldiers of Christ are properly not killed, but crowned."

The pope and his clergy were hunted out by the soldiers of the emperor and were found gathered in one of the catacombs that also served as a cemetery for the Christians. The pontiff was arrested while he was speaking to the gathered Christians and was taken away to be beheaded, along with the clergy with him. He was buried in the cemetery of St. Callistus on the Appian Way.

He is the most highly venerated pope martyred after St. Peter, and his name is mentioned in the Roman Canon of the Mass. One of his deacons, St. Lawrence, was martyred four days later.

Thought for the Day: Some people have to suffer simply for doing good, and that in itself is a kind of martyrdom, even though it does not end in death. There is a price to pay for following Christ, and following Christ means precisely going about doing good. We should not be surprised if we are criticized for the good we do and we should not be discouraged if others do not understand.

From 'The Catholic One Year Bible': God, in his kindness, has taught me how to be an expert builder. I have laid the foundation and Apollos has built on it. . . . And no one can ever lay any other real foundation than that one we already have — Jesus Christ. — 1 Corinthians 3:10-11

St. Dominic *(AUGUST 8)*

The fame of St. Dominic is not only in the order he founded, the Order of Preachers, but also in the place he had in the development of the Rosary, one of the most popular prayers of Catholics.

Dominic was born in 1170 in Calaruega, Spain. While still a student, he was made a canon of the cathedral at Osma and after ordination to the priesthood lived there in community following the rule of St. Augustine.

In 1204, he accompanied his bishop to Sweden to arrange a marriage for King Alfonso IX of Castile and on this trip passed through the Languedoc region of France, then riddled with the Albigensian heresy. After their mission to Sweden was completed, Dominic and his bishop went to Rome to obtain permission to work in the missions of Russia. Instead, the pope commissioned them to preach among the Albigensians in Languedoc. It was while carrying on this preaching mission that Dominic conceived the idea for the Order of Preachers.

He gathered around him a small band of preachers and worked effectively to convert the Albigensians. In 1214, he gathered these preachers into a community and received the approval for his community from Fulk, archbishop of Toulouse. Accompanying Fulk to the Council of the Lateran in Rome, he obtained provisional approval for his order from Pope Innocent III. A year later, after drawing up his own constitutions based on the rule of St. Augustine, the Order of Preachers was approved by a decree of Pope Honorius III. The basic pattern of the order was apostolic activities flowing from contemplation. Since its founding, it has remained one of the great forces for good in the Catholic Church, giving birth to a multitude of saints.

Dominic saw his order grow rapidly and together with the Franciscans become the dominant religious force in thirteenth-century Christendom. He died at Bologna on August 6, 1221, at the age of fifty-two, surrounded by many of his followers. When he died, there were Dominicans in Italy, France, England, Spain, Scandinavia, Poland, and the Holy Land. His friend Cardinal Ugolino, elected pope as Gregory IX, canonized him in 1234 declaring that he no more doubted the sanctity of Dominic than that of SS. Peter and Paul.

Thought for the Day: Besides his eminent kindness, St. Dominic had a liking for apples and turnips, which shows a human side to his holiness. Ascetic and austere, he radiated around himself a gentleness and thoughtfulness that made him remembered for years. There is no reason why holiness has to be cold and forbidding.

From 'The Catholic One Year Bible': . . . When the Lord comes, he will turn on the light so that everyone can see exactly what each one of us is really like, deep down in our hearts. . . . At that time God will give to each one . . . praise. . . . —1 Corinthians 4:5

St. Oswald of Northumbria

(AUGUST 9)

Oswald was the son of Ethelfrid, the Anglo-Saxon king who was killed in battle in 616 and whose kingdom was taken over by Edwin. When Edwin himself was killed in the battle of Hatfield Chase in 633, Oswald returned to do battle for his kingdom against the Britons and the Mercians to the south, defeating them at Heavensfield, near Hexham, in 634, and thus regaining his kingdom.

He became king of the whole of Northumbria. After settling himself in the family fortress at Bamburgh, on the North Sea, St. Oswald of Northumbria sent to St. Columba's monastery at Iona, off the western coast of Scotland, for a bishop for his people. The bishop who was sent was St. Aidan, who made his own headquarters at Lindisfarne, an island close to Bamburgh, and the evangelization of Northumbria began.

The king sent Aidan twelve young Anglo-Saxons to be the future spiritual leaders of his people, accompanied the bishop on his preaching tours around his kingdom, and worked with the bishop for the religious development of his people, even translating Aidan's sermons into English, since Aidan spoke only Celtic. Through the king's efforts, another monastery was founded on the mainland, in what is now southern Scotland, and it was from this monastery, Melrose, that the most famous saint and bishop of Northumbria would come, Cuthbert.

Oswald constantly had to defend his kingdom against enemies to the south and west, and less than ten years after his own victory he was killed at the battle of Maserfelth, where he was defeated by the combined forces of Britons and the southern Anglo-Saxon kingdoms. This was on August 5, 642, and his enemies devastated his kingdom, causing misery that would be remembered for a hundred years.

For a time, Oswald's bones were kept at the abbey of Bardney. He was one of the most revered saints of northern England, and his life was written in St. Bede's *History of the English Church and People.* With St. Cuthbert, he is one of the major saints of Northumbria.

Thought for the Day: St. Oswald of Northumbria was known for the nobility of his life, for his concern for the religious life of his kingdom, and for bravery in battle. Kings, too, can be saints, even though the temptations of power will always be present. Oswald overcame the temptations and became one of the first Christian heroes of medieval England.

From 'The Catholic One Year Bible': Just as water is turned into irrigation ditches, so the Lord directs the king's thoughts. He turns them wherever he wants to. We can justify our every deed but God looks at our motives. — Proverbs 21:1-2

St. Lawrence *(AUGUST 10)*

Lawrence was one of the most beloved deacons of the early Church, whose martyrdom and charity to the poor became one of the great legends of early Christendom. He lived during the persecution of the Emperor Valerian, which was during the pontificate of St. Sixtus II, and the account of his martyrdom has become one of the stories of the saints repeated down through the centuries.

As deacon, St. Lawrence was in charge of the administration of charity to the poor and served in this office under Pope St. Sixtus. When Sixtus and four other deacons were arrested in the catacombs and were being led away to their martyrdom, Lawrence met them on the way and said to the pope: "Father, where are you going without your deacon?" The Holy Father answered: "My son, I do not leave you. You will follow me in three days."

When Lawrence himself was brought up before the prefect of Rome, he was asked to hand over the Church's treasures to the Roman authorities. Asking for time to gather together the Church's treasures, Lawrence rounded up the poor of the city whom he had fed and befriended and brought them before the prefect. "These are the treasures of the Church," Lawrence told him.

Angered, the prefect ordered Lawrence to be stripped and bound upon a gridiron to be roasted to death. Halfway through this torturous death, he was supposed to have said to the executioner: "Turn me over, I am done on one side already." What is clear is that he went to his death cheerfully, was the marvel of all those who watched him die, and the story of his martyrdom spread throughout the Christian world, inspiring others also to lay down their lives for their faith.

His tomb became a favorite spot for pilgrimages in Rome, at his burial place on the Via Tiburtina. After the Peace of Constantine in 312, the emperor himself built a chapel on the site of Lawrence's burial, and this in later years became the basilica of St. Lawrence-Outside-the-Walls. It is the fifth most important basilica in Rome and is still one of the most revered of martyrs' tombs.

Thought for the Day: Generosity to the poor has always been an important Christian practice. This means not only sharing our surplus with them, but even our substance. In this we are most like Jesus Himself, who blessed such generosity and made it one of the marks of His disciples. What have I given to the poor lately?

From 'The Catholic One Year Bible': Don't you know that some day we Christians are going to judge and govern the world? So why can't you decide even these little things among yourselves? Don't you realize that we Christians will judge and reward the very angels of heaven? So you should be able to decide your problems down here on earth. . . . —
1 Corinthians 6:2-3

"The Lady Clare, shining in name, more shining in life, most shining in conversation, was a native of Assisi, noble of birth but nobler by grace, a maiden most pure in heart, young in years, strong in determination, steadfast in purpose, but wise and meek and a marvelous lover of Christ." Thus is St. Clare described by her contemporaries. Born in 1193, she was taken with the dream and vision of St. Francis of Assisi and became the foundress of the "Poor Women of Assisi," known today as the Poor Clares.

On Palm Sunday of the year 1212, she ran away from home and went out to St. Francis' church of the Portiuncula, where he lived with his community. The meeting had been prearranged, and Francis and his brethren met her at the door of the chapel of Our Lady of the Angels with lighted tapers. They led her to the altar where she cut off her hair and put on the penitential habit of Francis. The founder of the Franciscans then placed her in the convent of the Benedictines in Assisi, until he had built a convent for her. When the news reached Assisi, the whole town was up in arms, and Clare's relatives stormed the convent to "rescue" their daughter from the "madness" of Francis.

She held out, and Francis gave Clare the church of San Damiano. So powerful was her example that her mother and two sisters joined her. Thus began the adventure of the Poor Clares, the companions of Francis in his great love for God.

After the death of Francis, Clare herself became a powerful spiritual force in Italy, having for friends bishops, cardinals, and popes. In 1253, she fell ill and was visited by Pope Innocent IV on her deathbed. She died at San Damiano surrounded by her nuns and some of Francis' own companions. She passed to heaven in great joy. She was sixty years old and had lived her life of poverty for forty-two years. Two years later, she was canonized by Pope Alexander IV, and her body rests today in the chapel of the Poor Clare convent in Assisi.

Thought for the Day: St. Clare was caught up in the great spiritual adventure begun by St. Francis and never lost that vibrant love of God that she shared with him. All of us need a vision that cuts through the commonplace of our existence and shows us far horizons. Clare lived that adventure till her dying day and left an imperishable memory.

From 'The Catholic One Year Bible': " *'If you sin, I will scatter you among the nations; but if you return to me and obey my laws . . . I will bring you back to Jerusalem. For Jerusalem is the place in which I have chosen to live.'* " — Nehemiah 1:8-9

St. Maximus the Confessor *(AUGUST 12)*

In the year 626, the Persians invaded the Byzantine empire, including the Holy Land, and many of the holy places were destroyed. Many monasteries were also endangered, one of them the monastery at Cyzicus, south of Constantinople, where the abbot and monks had to flee the invading Persians. The abbot was St. Maximus the Confessor, one of the great champions of the faith during the Monothelite heresy, who opposed the emperor who furthered the heresy.

He was born at Constantinople about 580 and became secretary to the Emperor Heraclius. Retiring from the court, he became a monk first at Chrysopolis and then at Cyzicus. Fleeing the Persians, he made his way to Crete and Cyprus and then to Africa. At Carthage, he took part in the debate over Monothelitism, attended the Lateran Synod of 649 that condemned the heresy and, together with Pope St. Martin I, was arrested by the Emperor Constans for his opposition to the emperor, who had commanded silence on the matter.

Brought to Constantinople, Maximus was accused of treason, exiled to Thrace, then imprisoned in a monastery at Rhegium. A commission from the emperor was sent to force him to change his views, but he remained firm and was threatened with even greater suffering. Even though he was a very old man, he was beaten, his hands were cut off, and to make sure that he would not openly profess his beliefs, his tongue was cut out. Together with several other monks who refused to submit to the emperor, Maximus died a few weeks after suffering these tortures.

He has always been revered as a great theologian, a lover of the unity of the Church, and a firm defender of sound doctrine. Like Pope Martin, he opposed the authority of the emperor in matters of faith and died bearing witness to the divinity of Christ by his opposition to the Monothelite heresy. He is venerated in both the Eastern and the Western Churches and is considered one of the great mystical writers of the East.

Thought for the Day: We find it hard to understand the mixture of religion and politics that was so much a part of early Christianity. St. Maximus, an obedient citizen but holding firmly to the witness of his own conscience, opposed Emperor Constans when the emperor tried to interfere in matters of faith. We, too, may sometimes have to suffer for our beliefs and for holding firm to the witness of our own conscience.

From 'The Catholic One Year Bible': Steady plodding brings prosperity; hasty speculation brings poverty. Dishonest gain will never last, so why take the risk? Because the wicked are unfair, their violence boomerangs and destroys them. — **Proverbs 21:5-7**

"Brothers Boys" all over the world rejoiced in 1968, when a Christian Brother, Benildus Romançon, was canonized by Pope Paul VI. He had died a little over a century before, a beloved teacher and friend to generations of boys.

He was born Peter Romançon in the village of Thuret in 1805. As a young boy, he was sent to be educated by the Christian Brothers at Riom and in 1820 entered their novitiate at Clermont-Ferrand. When he received the religious habit, he took the name of Benildus.

He began his life of teaching at Riom and then was made superior at Billom. In 1841, he was sent to open a Brothers' school at Saugues and there he remained for the rest of his life. His effect upon his pupils was remarkable, and he was one of the few teachers who could speak about religious truths and not bore his students. He prepared himself for his classes by a thorough study of theology and the art of teaching, and his whole work was permeated with prayer. His students worked hard, and he gave special attention to those who found their studies difficult.

His example attracted vocations to the Christian Brothers, and many of his pupils joined him in his vocation. In 1855, Brother Benildus became ill and had to remain in bed and then was struck down with a serious rheumatic disease. For seven years, he was given various treatments, with no success, and in the early months of 1862 it was clear that he could not last much longer. His boys carried on a campaign of prayer for him, but he told them: "God is calling me. . . . I will pray for you in heaven." He died on August 13, 1862, surrounded by his community.

From the moment of his burial, his grave became a place of pilgrimage. In 1896, the cause for his canonization was begun, and in 1968 he was proclaimed St. Benildus, a model teacher, a friend, and a living example of generations of students.

Thought for the Day: How precious is a good teacher! All of us have had them and have reason to be grateful for them. For most of us, our lives would have been very different without the powerful influence of a good teacher. We should thank God for those who have influenced and fashioned our own lives.

From 'The Catholic One Year Bible': A man is known by his actions. An evil man lives an evil life; a good man lives a godly life. It is better to live in the corner of an attic than with a crabby woman in a lovely home. An evil man loves to harm others; being a good neighbor is out of his line. — Proverbs 21:8-10

St. Maximilian Kolbe *(AUGUST 14)*

Maximilian Kolbe, the martyr of Auschwitz, not only died a martyr's death but was one of the most remarkable priests of the twentieth century. His apostolic works under the banner of Mary Immaculate made him a household word in his native Poland, where his City of the Immaculate (or, in Polish, Niepokalanow) housed over seven hundred Franciscans, carrying on a press apostolate of staggering proportions.

He was born in Zdunska Wola, Poland, in 1894 and became a Franciscan when he was sixteen. Sent to Rome for studies, he was appalled by the boldness of the enemies of the Church and decided to organize a militia of Mary to combat modern godlessness. Returning to Poland after his ordination in 1918, he received his superiors' reluctant permission to begin his work, obtaining a piece of land from a Polish prince.

In spite of ill health, he began a printing and publishing campaign that transformed the Catholic mission in Poland and after meeting with Japanese students on a train decided to inaugurate a similar work in Japan. Arriving at Nagasaki in 1930, he set up printing presses and founded a community to carry on his work, returning to Poland in 1936.

In 1939, the Nazis invaded Poland, and in 1941 St. Maximilian Kolbe was arrested with several of his friars. After the occupation of Warsaw, he was released and allowed to return to his friary. Because of his activities, he was arrested again and sent to Auschwitz, and it was here that his heroism shone for all to see.

He was the strength and comfort of everyone in that terrible camp; he was beaten, abused, and insulted, but his response was only gentleness and kindness. Finally, when ten prisoners were randomly selected to die after an attempted escape, he offered to take the place of another prisoner. Left to die in an empty barracks, he was finally given an injection of carbolic acid to hasten his death. It was August 1941. Word of his death spread throughout the camp, and the "saint of Auschwitz" became the living symbol of the triumph of good over evil. He was canonized by Pope John Paul II in October 1982.

Thought for the Day: When evil is rampant, God raises up saints. St. Maximilian Kolbe brought the presence of God to the terrible death camp of Auschwitz. By his very life, he proclaimed the existence of God. Something of God should shine in our own lives.

From 'The Catholic One Year Bible': I am an apostle, God's messenger, responsible to no mere man. I am one who has actually seen Jesus our Lord with my own eyes. . . . If in the opinion of others, I am not an apostle, I certainly am to you, for you have been won to Christ through me. — 1 Corinthians 9:1-3

Tarcisius was a twelve-year-old acolyte during one of the fierce Roman persecutions of the third century, probably during that of Valerian. Each day, from a secret meeting place in the catacombs where Christians gathered for Mass, a deacon would be sent to the prisons to carry the Eucharist to those Christians condemned to die. At one point, there was no deacon to send and so St. Tarcisius, an acolyte, was sent carrying the "Holy Mysteries" to those in prison.

On the way, he was stopped by boys his own age who were not Christians but knew him as a playmate and lover of games. He was asked to join their games, but this time he refused and the crowd of boys noticed that he was carrying something. Somehow, he was also recognized as a Christian, and the small gang of boys, anxious to view the Christian "Mysteries," became a mob and turned upon Tarcisius with fury. He went down under the blows, and it is believed that a fellow Christian drove off the mob and rescued the young acolyte.

The mangled body of Tarcisius was carried back to the catacombs, but the boy died on the way from his injuries. He was buried in the cemetery of St. Callistus, and his relics are claimed by the church of San Silvestro in Capite.

In the fourth century, Pope St. Damasus wrote a poem about this "boy-martyr of the Eucharist" and says that, like another St. Stephen, he suffered a violent death at the hands of a mob rather than give up the Sacred Body to "raging dogs." His story became well known when Cardinal Wiseman made it a part of his novel *Fabiola*, in which the story of the young acolyte is dramatized and a very moving account given of his martyrdom and death.

Tarcisius, one of the patron saints of altar boys, has always been an example of youthful courage and devotion, and his story was one that was told again and again to urge others to a like heroism in suffering for their faith. In the *Passion of Pope Stephen*, written in the sixth century, Tarcisius is said to be an acolyte of the pope himself and, if so, this explains the great veneration in which he was held and the reason why he was chosen for so difficult a mission.

Thought for the Day: Mere boys can become saints, and youth is no barrier to holiness. The call to holiness begins at baptism, and we do not have to wait for old age and gray hair to serve God. Youthful saints tell us something about sanctity, and their example is especially luminous as they dedicate their young lives to God.

From 'The Catholic One Year Bible': In a race, everyone runs but only one person gets first prize. So run your race to win. To win the contest you must deny yourselves many things that would keep you from doing your best. — **1 Corinthians 9:24-25**

He was the pagan son of a pagan king, and when his father and all his nobles were baptized, mostly as a matter of expediency, the ten-year-old prince was likewise baptized and given the name Istvan (Stephen). When he succeeded to the throne of Hungary, he had already married the Christian sister of Emperor Henry II (himself a saint) and he fashioned his kingdom of Hungary into a truly Christian commonwealth.

He unified the country under his leadership and then consulted Pope Sylvester II about the ecclesiastical organization of his people. The pontiff not only approved of what he had done but also had him crowned king. Stephen worked to establish episcopal sees, set up his own headquarters at Szekesfehervar, and founded monasteries, particularly the great abbey of St. Martin, which even today is the motherhouse of the Hungarian Benedictine Congregation.

St. Stephen of Hungary worked to abolish violence and bloodshed in his kingdom, founded parish churches, and changed his people from a seminomadic nation to a stable, settled one. He saw in the Christian religion the only unifying force that would unite his people.

He codified the law of his people and had them promulgated through his kingdom. He was, as historians claim, the founder and architect of the Hungarian people and nation, and intended to pass on this legacy as well as his crown to his son, Emeric. But Emeric died in a hunting accident and is himself considered Blessed.

During Stephen's last years, he had to face disputes over the succession. He died on the Feast of the Assumption, 1038, and was buried beside his son. His tomb soon became the scene of miracles, and forty-five years after his death, at the order of the pope, his relics were enshrined in a chapel in the great church of Our Lady of Buda. He was canonized in 1083, less than fifty years after his death.

Thought for the Day: The young King Stephen saw a remarkable power in the Christian religion to give stability and purpose to his people, but he first stabilized his own life by making his religion the very backbone of his personal life. It was this example that endeared him to his people, for whom he is still an inspiration and a model.

From 'The Catholic One Year Bible': . . . I try to please everyone in everything I do, not doing what I like or what is best for me, but what is best for them, so that they may be saved. And you should follow my example, just as I follow Christ's. — **1 Corinthians 10:33—11:1**

Blessed Joan Delanoue *(AUGUST 17)*

This was a lady whose family made money selling religious bric-a-brac to pilgrims who came to the shrine of Our Lady of Ardilliers. The trade was good, and her parents managed to raise twelve children on the profits of their business. When her widowed mother died, Joan was left the small religious shop and a little capital and she proceeded to set up business for herself. She worked the pilgrim's trade for all it was worth, even opening her shop on Sundays and holy days.

Then something happened. She befriended a strange pilgrim who went from shrine to shrine, and something that this old lady did or said struck home to Blessed Joan Delanoue. She found a priest to talk to, the Abbé Geneteau, and he simply advised her to close her shop on Sundays.

Through her experience with the old pilgrim, Joan gradually began to see her vocation as one of serving the poor, and this new understanding so baffled and bewildered her that she began giving away her possessions. Then, on the advice of the old pilgrim, she went to care for six poor children who lived in a stable in St.-Florent — and her remarkable vocation began. She still kept her shop, filling her cart with food, clothing, and blankets two or three days a week, but then, in 1698, she closed up her shop: her vocation was to give, not to take.

Joan set up a kind of hospice, which people called Providence House, and money seemed to come out of nowhere. When a serious accident demolished the house and one of the children was killed, she moved to another place, took in beggars and the poor. She sought the advice of St. Louis de Montfort, who at first severely criticized her but soon became convinced of her special mission and gave her his blessing.

Unwittingly, she founded a religious congregation to carry on her work, the Sisters of St. Anne, which soon began to grow. She worked tirelessly until she was seventy years old, expanding her work and making foundations. She died on August 17, 1736, poor as a pauper herself but considered a saint by everybody. No one had ever done so much with so little. She was beatified by Pope Pius XII in 1947, the same year that Louis de Montfort was also canonized.

Thought for the Day: Seeing only profit to be made from the poor, Blessed Joan Delanoue began to see them as a treasure far greater than money. She discovered her vocation in a strange and unusual way and found she could do the work of armies. Her faith in Divine Providence never wavered, and Divine Providence never disappointed her.

From 'The Catholic One Year Bible': A man who loves pleasure becomes poor; wine and luxury are not the way to riches! The wicked will finally lose; the righteous will finally win. — **Proverbs 21:17-18**

It is to St. Helena that we owe the recovery of the holy places in Jerusalem, and as the mother of the Emperor Constantine she used her position to rebuild the ancient Christian sites in the land of Jesus.

An innkeeper's daughter, she married a general who later became the Emperor Constantine Chlorus, the father of Constantine. When he became emperor, he repudiated her, but she had already given birth to the son who would succeed him.

Constantine remained a catechumen until his deathbed, but his mother became a Christian and took a special interest in the church-building activities of her son. She involved herself in the building of great Christian churches in Rome, in Constantinople, and in the Holy Land. It was while visiting Jerusalem, directing the restoration of the city as a Christian center, that Helena is said to have discovered the True Cross, under the rubble on Mount Calvary, after the Roman city built by the Emperor Hadrian had been excavated and the spots sacred to Christians restored: the hill of Calvary, the Holy Sepulcher, the cave at Bethlehem, and other sites of our Lord's life.

At the age of eighty, she carried out Constantine's orders to build a great church over the site of the resurrection of Jesus, and thus the church of the Holy Sepulcher was begun, still the most sacred spot in Christendom. She is responsible also for the building of churches in the West, notably at Trier, where the Western emperor resided, and in Cologne, Xanten, and Bonn. According to the historian Eusebius, Helena spent her last days in the Holy Land. She was noted for her love of the poor, the adornment of churches, and the freeing of prisoners.

She died about the year 330, and her body was taken to Rome where it rested in a splendid mausoleum on the Via Labicana but later was taken to Constantinople. In the ninth century her relics were taken to the abbey of Hautvilliers. She is honored as the patron saint of Trier, Bamberg, and Basel.

Thought for the Day: Reverence for holy places is part of the Christian instinct, especially those associated with the life of our Lord and the saints. It was through the efforts of St. Helena that Christian buildings began to rise in the East and West. Pilgrimages and visits to holy places have always been part of Christian devotion.

From 'The Catholic One Year Bible': . . . On the night when Judas betrayed him, the Lord Jesus took bread, and when he had given thanks to God for it, he broke it and gave it to his disciples and said, "Take this and eat it. This is my body, which is given for you. Do this to remember me." — 1 Corinthians 11:23-24

St. John Eudes *(AUGUST 19)*

John Eudes was born in Normandy, that part of France famous for Mont-St.-Michel, Caen, Lisieux, and Bayeux. He was sent to the Jesuit college at Caen to be educated, took minor orders in 1620, and joined the Congregation of the Oratory founded by Pierre de Berulle. Ordained in 1625, he began a preaching career that would last his whole lifetime.

When an epidemic of the plague broke out in his home diocese in 1627, St. John Eudes volunteered to care for the sick and heroically saved the lives of the victims of the plague. His special ministry was parish missions, and he began to see that the spiritual renewal of France was impossible without an educated and holy clergy. He tried to set up a seminary in Caen but was opposed by the local Oratorian superior, and so he separated himself from the Oratory and began his own order, the Congregation of Jesus and Mary, popularly called the Eudists.

His congregation was dedicated to the formation of priests, and through his efforts seminaries were established at Caen, Coutances, Lisieux, Rouen, Evreux, and Rennes. He also founded a congregation of nuns to reclaim fallen women, the Congregation of Our Lady of Refuge.

He was noted for his devotion to the Sacred Hearts of Jesus and Mary and was a voluminous spiritual writer. He was the first to compose a liturgical office for the Sacred Hearts of Jesus and Mary, and his last years were spent on his most famous spiritual treatise, *The Admirable Heart of the Most Holy Mother of God*.

He preached his last mission at St.-Lo in 1675, where he preached in the open air for nine weeks. His health broke from this ordeal, and he realized his active days were over. He died on August 19, 1680, and was beatified in 1909. In 1925, he was canonized by Pope Pius XI. In one of his books, he summed up the principle of his own life and works: "Our wish, our object, our chief preoccupation must be to form Jesus in ourselves, to make His spirit, His devotion, His affections, His desires and His disposition live and reign there. All our religious exercises should be directed to this end."

Thought for the Day: St. John Eudes saw religious life around him in shambles and determined to do something about it. To do this, he had to start out in an entirely new direction. Sometimes the old ways do not work anymore and we have to find something new. This ability to take an entirely new direction is part of Christian wisdom.

From 'The Catholic One Year Bible': There are different kinds of service to God, but it is the same Lord we are serving. There are many ways in which God works in our lives, but it is the same God who does the work in and through all of us who are his. —1 Corinthians 12:5-6

He was a young man who threw everything away for God when he was scarcely out of his teens, became a leader of men before he was twenty-five, and became the conscience of the West for a whole generation. He was known as the Harpist of Mary, Our Lady's Troubador, and the Panegyrist of the Mother of God.

He was born in 1090, six years before the first crusade, and his father was Tescelin Sorrel, a noble belonging to a prominent Burgundian family. Tescelin and his wife, Aletha, had many sons and daughters, and the sons of the family were dedicated to arms. Bernard found a different kind of adventure, and when he was twenty-two, having gathered an army of friends and relatives to follow him, he entered the abbey of Citeaux, the strictest monastery of the day. His coming revitalized the monastery, and before he died there were over three hundred Cistercian monasteries, scattered from England to Palestine.

At the age of twenty-five, St. Bernard became abbot of Clairvaux and began there a preaching and teaching mission that made him the symbol of his age. He became embroiled in political and theological controversies, battled the dubious teaching of men like Peter Abelard, and attacked the soft living of the monks of his day who had settled into a comfortable way of life. He became the adviser of kings, princes, cardinals, and even the popes themselves when one of his monks became Pope Eugene III.

In the midst of his travels, Bernard wanted to remain at Clairvaux and called himself the riddle of his age, since he had to spend so much time outside his monastery. It was said that mothers hid their sons and wives hid their husbands when Bernard was in the territory, since so many followed him into the cloister.

For over forty years, he was the light of the Church, and when he died in 1153 he had influenced every major figure in his century. His memory is kept alive in the Cistercian Order, and the Church honors him as the "Honey-Tongued Teacher," the one who spoke so sweetly and so eloquently of God and His mysteries. Dante enshrined him in his *Divine Comedy* and made him the spokesman for the mystical life and for those who love and honor Mary.

Bernard was canonized in 1174 and was declared a Doctor of the Church in 1830.

Thought for the Day: "Look to the Star, Look upon Mary," St. Bernard wrote, "and she will rescue you from every sin, temptation and misery." This shining devotion to the Mother of God is at the very heart of Catholic devotion, and Bernard best exemplifies this childlike love of the Mother of God. It is something to be imitated.

From 'The Catholic One Year Bible': If I had the gift of being able to speak in other languages without learning them, . . . If I gave everything I have to poor people, and if I were burned alive for preaching the Gospel but didn't love others, it would be no value whatever. — 1 Corinthians 13:1, 3

St. Pius X *(AUGUST 21)*

Giuseppe Sarto was born in the village of Riese, near Venice, in 1835, the second of ten children. His family was poor, and as a schoolboy he walked each day five miles to and from the grammar school at Castelfranco. He entered the seminary at Padua and was ordained a priest at the age of twenty-three. For seventeen years, he was curate and pastor, then was made spiritual director of the seminary and chancellor of the diocese. In 1884, he was appointed bishop of Mantua.

His success as bishop in a difficult diocese brought him to the attention of Pope Leo XIII, and in 1892 he became cardinal-archbishop of Venice. He was noted for his spirit of poverty, pastoral zeal, concern for divine worship,and Catholic Action.

On the death of Leo XIII, he was elected pope and, in the face of the growing apostasy from religion in the modern world, adopted as his motto "to restore all things in Christ" and took the name Pius X. He applied Christian teaching to every area of social, cultural, and political life, furthered Catholic education and promoted social justice and charity.

The most serious problem he had to face was that of Modernism, which in its hard-core conviction was a denial of the sovereignity of God and the supernatural order, and he struck the deathblow to the heresy with his encyclical *Pascendi* in 1907. His influence on the interior life of the Church was extensive, especially with his decree on frequent Communion, his *motu proprio* on sacred music, his establishment of the Pontifical Biblical Institute, and his order for the codification of canon law.

St. Pius X lived to see the opening of World War I and died just after hostilities broke out on August 20, 1914, saddened by the terrible destruction of the war. He was beatified by Pope Pius XII in 1951 and canonized in 1954. The German historian Ludwig von Pastor wrote of him: "Everyone was moved by his simplicity and angelic kindness. Yet it was something more that carried him into all hearts: and that 'something' is best defined by saying that all who were ever admitted into his presence had the deep conviction of being face to face with a saint."

Thought for the Day: St. Pius X realized that self-sacrifice is the very basis of holiness, and even as a young boy he tackled the hardships necessary to get an education. This followed throughout his life. Without sacrifice, there is no genuine virtue and nothing worthwhile is accomplished.

From 'The Catholic One Year Bible': There lived in the land of Uz a man named Job — a good man who feared God and stayed away from evil. He had a large family of seven sons and three daughters, and was immensely wealthy. . . . He was, in fact, the richest cattleman in that entire area. — **Job 1:1-3**

Around the year 1315, rumors spread in Siena and the surrounding countryside of a group of madmen haunting the region of Mont' Amiata, near Ancona, and news of them came to the attention of Pope John XXII at Avignon. They were summoned to Avignon to give an account of themselves, and the pope, much to his surprise, found that the "madmen" were a group of hermits led by Blessed Bernard Tolomei, a former lawyer and *podesta* of Siena. Impressed, the pontiff told them to draw up a rule for themselves and put themselves under the authority of a bishop.

This was the beginning of the Olivetan Benedictine congregation, one of the strictest and most notable of Benedictine families. The members were distinguished by their simplicity of life, white habits, and a strongly centralized government. After their meeting with John XXII, they began to grow in numbers and in 1344 their order was confirmed by Pope Clement VI.

About 1346, an epidemic of the plague broke out in Siena, and the Olivetans became the saviors of Siena: they devoted themselves completely to the care of the sick and suffering, to the burial of the dead, and it seemed that they were miraculously preserved from contagion themselves. As the Black Death spread through Italy, the Olivetans were strangely immune, until one of their numbers was struck down with the disease: it was their founder, Bernard Tolomei.

As a young man, Bernard Tolomei had wanted to become a monk but was prevented by his parents, so he became a soldier, a law student, and a man dedicated to public service. Scheduled to give a public lecture on philosophy in Siena, he gave instead a sermon on the vanity of all things, left the city, and began to live in solitude in the wilderness outside of Siena. Soon he was joined by two others who had been impressed by his example. When the pope called them from their solitude, they began a revolution in religious life that saw the birth of a new religious family.

The Olivetan Benedictines still exist today, one of the most active of Benedictine congregations, and have several houses in the United States.

Thought for the Day: At some time, we have to face the fact of our own mortality and the overpowering reality of eternity. It does not mean that we have to leave the world like Blessed Bernard Tolomei, but it may require a drastic change in our own way of living. Somewhere and somehow, we have to begin to take God seriously.

From 'The Catholic One Year Bible': "Oh, that my sadness and troubles were weighed. For they are heavier than the sand of a thousand seashores. . . . For the Lord has struck me down with his arrows; he has sent his poisoned arrows deep within my heart." — **Job 6:2-4**

St. Rose of Lima *(AUGUST 23)*

Rose of Lima was the daughter of Gaspar Flores, a Spanish conquistador from Puerto Rico, and María de Oliva, and she was born in Lima, Peru, in 1586. She was baptized Isabel but received the name Rose as a nickname and it became her given name.

She belonged to a group of Peruvians associated with the Dominicans during the archbishopric of St. Turibius de Mogrovejo who carried on a vast program of social work in early Lima, the others being St. Martin de Porres and Blessed Juan Massias. She wanted to become a nun, but this was denied her, so she remained at home and contributed to the support of her family by selling flowers.

When St. Rose of Lima was twenty, like her patroness, St. Catherine of Siena, she became a member of the Third Order of St. Dominic and wore the religious habit at home, sometimes placing a crown of thorns on her head. She lived in a small hermitage she had built on her family property and in one of the rooms set up an infirmary to care for destitute children, old people, and the sick.

She was known for her severe penances and austerities and for extraordinary mystical graces; moreover, she was known and loved throughout Lima by rich and poor alike, who looked to her for protection from calamity and for the protection of God by her prayers. The last three years of her life were spent in the home of Don Gonzalo de Massa, a government official whose wife was very fond of Rose. It was here that she was stricken with her last illness in 1617, dying after a long and painful illness on August 24 of that year at the age of thirty-one.

City officials and senators carried her body to its grave, and she was revered as a saint from the moment she died. It was impossible to hold the funeral for several days because of the crowds, and she was finally buried privately in the cloister of St. Dominic's Church as she had requested. Her body was later moved into the church where it still rests, under an altar in the crypt.

She was canonized by Pope Clement X in 1671 and was proclaimed the patroness of all Peru.

Thought for the Day: St. Rose of Lima found her plans to become a nun frustrated by others, but this did not stop her from seeking God in her own way. Although not wealthy, she enriched others by her love and service. We may have to find our own unique pathway to God and if we are sincerely interested in living for Him, we will find a way.

From 'The Catholic One Year Bible': I passed on to you right from the first what had been told to me, that Christ died for our sins just as the Scriptures said he would, and that he was buried, and that three days afterwards he arose from the grave just as the prophets foretold.
— 1 Corinthians 15:3-4

Very little is known about St. Bartholomew, beyond the fact that he is listed among the Apostles. His name in Aramaic means "son of Tolmei," and since this seems to be a family name, or what we would call his last name, many scholars believe he is to be identified with the Apostle Nathaniel, mentioned in St. John's Gospel. He is called Bartholomew in the list of Apostles given in the Gospels of Matthew, Mark, and Luke, and also in the Acts of the Apostles where he is present at the election of Matthias to replace Judas.

In the Gospel of John, he is associated with Philip, and it is Philip who brings Nathaniel to Jesus. In the other three Gospels, Bartholomew is paired with Philip, so it seems they are the same person. If this identification is correct, Bartholomew received great praise from Jesus Himself who called him "a true Israelite in whom there is no guile."

In the *Roman Martyrology*, Bartholomew is said to have preached the Gospel in India, then went to Armenia where he converted many to the Christian faith. He is also mentioned preaching the Gospel in Ethiopia and Persia. Eusebius, the early Church historian, records that an Alexandrian traveling in India discovered a copy of the Gospel of Matthew written in Hebrew, left there by Bartholomew, whose death took place, according to these early records, at Albanopolis in Armenia, on the Caspian Sea, where he was flayed alive, then beheaded at the order of King Astyages.

His relics are venerated at Benevento in Italy and in the church of St. Bartholomew-on-the-Tiber in Rome. It is possible that his relics were brought West during the crusades when relics of the early Church were prized in Europe. Bartholomew is represented in art with a skin over his arm and a knife in his hand, the symbols of his martyrdom.

Thought for the Day: Like many others who served Christ, St. Bartholomew is just a name in history, his life lost in legend. But that does not really matter; what really counts is that he was an Apostle and follower of Jesus and gave his life for the preaching of the Gospel. Like the other Apostles, he "drank the chalice of the Lord and became the friend of God."

From 'The Catholic One Year Bible': So, dear brothers, since future victory is sure, be strong and steady, always abounding in the Lord's work, for you know that nothing you do for the Lord is ever wasted as it would be if there were no resurrection. —**1 Corinthians 15:58**

St. Louis (AUGUST 25)

The long reign of King Louis IX, 1226-70, is the period of a cultural explosion in France and Europe, at the height of the "Thirteenth, the Greatest of Centuries," the age of remarkable saints and remarkable leaders: St. Francis of Assisi, St. Thomas Aquinas, St. Dominic, Innocent III, Stephen Langton, St. Albert the Great, and Emperor Frederick II. St. Louis was at the very heart of this development and has been looked upon as the model Christian king.

He was the son of Louis VIII of France and Blanche of Castille and was born on April 15, 1214. At his father's death in 1226, he was only twelve years old and so his mother became regent of the kingdom. When he was nineteen, he married Margaret of Provence and they had ten children.

Louis is best known from his crusades and from the memoirs of him written by one of his officers, the Sire de Joinville. Louis took the cross in 1244 and remained in the East for ten years, returning in 1254. He is remembered as a fair, wise, and loving monarch who ruled his people with justice and firmness, negotiated treaties, and fostered religion, learning, and the arts.

In 1270, he led a second crusade to deter Muslim advances in Syria. His brother, Charles of Anjou, already master of Italy, convinced Louis to attack Charles's enemy, the emir of Tunis, before heading for the East. The attack was a failure, the crusader army struck by typhus. Louis himself caught the disease and he died on August 24, giving last instructions to his sons on how they should behave as kings.

His army returned to France carrying his bones, which were enshrined in the abbey church of St. Denis. His tomb quickly became the scene of miracles of healing, and he was canonized less than thirty years after his death, in 1297. He built the Ste. Chapelle in Paris to house the Crown of Thorns and was very fond of the cathedral of Chartres, where he had been baptized. As husband, father, and king, he showed himself not only an exemplary Christian but also a remarkable human being who never lost the human touch and sat on the seat of power with rare humor and humility.

Thought for the Day: St. Louis was known for his horror of offending God and for his uprightness in dealing with others. He never used his position to take unfair advantage of others and he looked upon his kingship as one of service. He never threw his weight around and that example alone is something worth pondering and imitating.

From 'The Catholic One Year Bible': ". . . I know that my Redeemer lives, and that he will stand upon the earth at last. And I know that after this body has decayed, this body shall see God! Then he will be on *my* side! Yes, I shall see him, not as a stranger, but as a friend! What a glorious hope!" —Job 19:25-27

St. Elizabeth Bichier *(AUGUST 26)*

The French Revolution was a difficult time for Catholics, especially since the Civil Constitution of the Clergy demanded priests to take an oath of loyalty to a government hostile to the Church. Since most priests would not take the oath, they went underground, carrying on their priestly ministry in secret. St. Elizabeth Bichier was one of those Catholics who supported the priests who carried on their work in secret.

She was born near Poitiers in 1773, the daughter of a public official. Her uncle was a priest, and she was strongly influenced by his spiritual direction when she was still a young girl. She had thought about entering the Trappistines but was persuaded not to by St. André Fournet who saw in her a genius for active work. Father Fournet suggested that she found a congregation to care for the sick and educate the poor, and following his directions she entered the Carmelite novitiate to prepare for her work. "Your work is in the world," he told her. "There are ruins to be rebuilt and ignorance to be remedied."

With five companions, she began her first community at La Guimetiere, where they began to teach children and give shelter to the sick and the aged. Five years later their rule was approved by diocesan authorities and their congregation was named the Daughters of the Cross.

Despite many setbacks, the congregation began to flourish and during two years, 1819-20, thirteen new convents were opened. By 1830, there were sixty convents. Elizabeth traveled constantly, saw her congregation well established, and faced the terrible loss of Father Fournet, who died in 1834.

She carried on for two more years, but her health began to fail in 1836. She was completely exhausted, suffered from erysipelas, and was in acute pain most of the time. In August of 1838, it was clear her end was near. She died peacefully on August 26, admired even by those who were hostile to the faith, who marveled at her energy, her patience in the face of seeming insurmountable obstacles, and her grim determination to carry on her work. She was canonized in 1947 by Pope Pius XII.

Thought for the Day: Mother Teresa of Calcutta has predecessors in such remarkable women as St. Elizabeth Bichier who helped to rebuild religion after the shambles of the French Revolution. Their faith enabled them to face any difficulties, tackle any task, and accomplish amazing things. The power of faith can still accomplish marvels and will until the end of time.

From 'The Catholic One Year Bible': What a wonderful God we have — he is the Father of our Lord Jesus Christ, the source of every mercy, and the one who so wonderfully comforts and strengthens us in our hardships and trials. —**2 Corinthians 1:3-4**

Who has not heard of the mother of St. Augustine, whose persistence and prayers won the grace of conversion for her son, giving the Church and human civilization one of its greatest minds and one of the most enduring of saints? In his *Confessions*, Augustine himself paints an unforgettable picture of her, and her influence on him was deep and lasting.

St. Monica followed his career with genuine pride, unhappy only that he had wandered from God into immoral living, and she followed him from Africa to Rome and Milan, hoping that a good marriage would change his life and settle him down. She almost despaired of his conversion, but when she poured out her heart to a bishop of her concern for her son, he told her: "It is not possible that a son of so many tears should perish."

Finally, through the influence of St. Ambrose in Milan, and her own persistence and prayers, a change came over Augustine. She stayed with him at a villa in the country where he went to prepare himself for baptism and to carry on discussions with his friends. Monica joined in these conversations and showed herself something of a philosopher and scholar in her grasp of the Scriptures.

Finally, the great day came and Augustine was baptized by Ambrose at Easter, 687, together with several of his friends. A great change had come over Augustine and he prepared to return to Africa to begin his new life, stopping off at the port city of Ostia before embarking for his homeland. It was there that Monica carried on those conversations with her son that Augustine records in his *Confessions* and it was there that she died, her son beside her, her whole being looking forward to the eternal life for which she longed.

Her passing was a beginning and an end for Augustine. He carried his memory of her to his grave, realizing the great debt that he owed her, cheered in later years by the memory of her holiness.

Thought for the Day: Persistence in prayer! If St. Monica is a model of anything, she is a model of this. Her love moved her to storm heaven for her son and she would not give up until the prayer was answered. There is no problem that cannot be conquered by prayer and no difficulty that cannot be unraveled by insistent prayer. Hers is a powerful lesson.

From 'The Catholic One Year Bible': It is this God who has made you and me into faithful Christians and commissioned us apostles to preach the Good News. He has put his brand upon us — his mark of ownership — and given us his Holy Spirit in our hearts as a guarantee that we belong to him, . . . — 2 Corinthians 1:21-22

Yesterday, the mother; today, the son. It is perhaps more apropos than coincidental that the commemoration of St. Augustine should follow that of his mother, St. Monica. The two names are linked in the history of holiness and Augustine remains the prime example of the converted sinner and the great Doctor of Grace — the first truly great theological mind in Western Christendom.

He was born in Tagaste, in North Africa, near the ancient city of Carthage, then one of the great Christian centers of the ancient world. His father was Patricius, a pagan, and his mother, as we have mentioned, was Monica. Augustine was inscribed among the catechumens as a child and educated a Christian by his mother, but a passion for learning and for the honors that went with learning attracted him early and he never took the Christian religion seriously.

After a short interest in Manicheism, Augustine plunged into a life of dissipation, meanwhile looking for a patron to sponsor his career. He found it in a certain Romanianus who sponsored his studies at Carthage, where he lived a wildly immoral life, living with a woman who bore him a son.

He did have a first-class mind, however, and studied the best thinking of the day, pondered the Christian Scriptures, and became profoundly impressed with the spiritual doctrine of the Neoplatonists. Leaving Carthage for Rome, and then for Milan he came under the influence of St. Ambrose, and his remarkable conversion took place, ending forever his hopes for a career and every worldly ambition.

He returned to Africa, began to live a life of seclusion with his friends, was ordained a priest against his will, then consecrated auxiliary bishop of Hippo. When he succeeded as bishop on the death of his patron, Valerius, a new page in the history of Christianity began and Augustine's battles with Donatism, Manicheism, and Pelagianism became part of doctrinal history.

His death in 430 saw the end of the patristic age and the beginning of the Middle Ages. The next one thousand years of Christian thought are but a commentary on the massive work of Augustine, and he remains the classical thinker and teacher of Christian truth. He had been a Christian for forty-three years and a bishop for thirty-five. His writings have become classics of Christian thought and his *Confessions* an enduring monument to the mercy of God and the power of His grace.

Thought for the Day: Once he saw the truth, St. Augustine gave himself to it completely and devoted his whole life to its service. Having been in darkness so long, he never ceased to be grateful for the light. Our faith is the truth by which we live, and its power should illumine our minds and transform our lives.

From 'The Catholic One Year Bible': . . . Thanks be to God! For through what Christ has done, he has triumphed over us so that now wherever we go he uses us to tell others about the Lord and to spread the Gospel like a sweet perfume. —2 Corinthians 2:14

José Miguel Serra was born on the island of Majorca in 1713, the son of poor farmers. He joined the Franciscans in 1730 and took the religious name of Junípero. In 1738, he became professor of philosophy for his province and after receiving his doctorate from Lullian University was appointed to the Duns Scotus chair of philosophy at that university. In 1749, he sailed for Mexico.

While assigned to teach at the Apostolic College of San Fernando in Mexico City, he carried on mission work in the dioceses of Mexico, Puebla, Oaxaca, Valladolid, and Guadalajara. In 1767, when the Jesuits were exiled from California, he was appointed prefect of the Lower California missions. When Upper California was colonized by the Spanish, Blessed Junípero Serra accompanied a military expedition north and founded his first mission at San Diego in 1769.

As Spanish colonization progressed north, he founded missions along the coast of California, making his headquarters at San Carlos Mission, which was located at Monterey-Carmel. In his missionary work, he had frequent conflicts with the military authorities over the treatment of the native Indians and in 1773 wrote his *Representación* to the viceroy in Mexico City, with thirty-two points for a change of policy. In spite of illness, he carried on extensive missionary journeys, was deeply devoted to the Indians, and did much to improve their lot. He introduced them to methods of agriculture, educated them in trades, and worked to improve their standard of living. He is considered the founder and father of the California missions, a remarkable achievement in so short a time.

He died at Carmel on August 28, 1784, and is buried at this mission. In 1931, his statue was placed in the Hall of Fame in Washington, D.C. His cause for beatification was begun in 1934, and he was beatified by Pope John Paul II on September 25, 1988.

Thought for the Day: Blessed Junípero Serra started out as a professor of philosophy but found himself plunged into a totally new work. With trust in God, he tackled his new task and found himself not only a founder of missions but a champion of the Indians. We have no way of knowing where the will of God will lead us, but we must be prepared to follow it, wherever it leads.

From 'The Catholic One Year Bible': . . . That first glory as it shone from Moses' face is worth nothing at all in comparison with the overwhelming glory of the new agreement. So if the old system that faded into nothing was full of heavenly glory, the glory of God's new plan for our salvation is certainly far greater, for it is eternal. — 2 Corinthians 3:10-11

St. Pammachius *(AUGUST 30)*

Pammachius, a boyhood friend of St. Jerome's, was a member of the Roman nobility and the heir to vast estates and great wealth. He met Jerome when the future biblical scholar came to Rome for studies, and they remained friends for the rest of their lives. In 385, St. Pammachius married Paulina, the daughter of St. Paula, another friend of Jerome's, and on her death in 397 he devoted his life to works of charity and the study of his faith.

His friendship with Jerome became strained during the Jovinian controversy, with Jerome's negative statements about marriage, but the breach was healed by Pammachius, who would not let rhetoric destroy a friendship. After his wife's death, he began to live something of a religious life and to care for the sick and the poor. Together with St. Fabiola, likewise a friend of Jerome's, he built a large hospice in Rome for pilgrims, especially those who were sick and poor.

Since he had no children, Pammachius made the poor his heirs and became known in Rome as the benefactor of the blind, the moneyless, and the handicapped. Whenever he went out into the streets, the poor flocked around him and no one was ever disappointed or refused. His concern for religion led him to the study of theological questions, and when Jerome and his friend Rufinus became bitter opponents in their disagreement over Origen, Pammachius tried to soften their controversy and bring about a reconciliation. He received a letter from St. Augustine thanking him for his support during the Donatist Schism and was also a friend of St. Paulinus of Nola, who wrote Pammachius a touching letter on the death of his wife.

Pammachius died in 410 at the time of Alaric's sack of Rome, and it is possible that this terrible destruction brought about his death. The site of his home in Rome is now occupied by the church of SS. John and Paul on the Coelian Hill. Since he was one of the first Romans of senatorial rank to become a Christian and involve himself in Christian causes, his works of charity were remembered for centuries; more important, he is a powerful example of the effect of Christian teaching upon a person of rank.

Thought for the Day: St. Pammachius felt that he had to take his faith seriously and looked for ways to put it into practice. For a wealthy man, there are all kinds of opportunities to help others, and Pammachius looked upon his works of charity as an obligation of his Christian conscience. He took the words of our Lord seriously.

From 'The Catholic One Year Bible': We are pressed on every side by troubles, but not crushed and broken. We are perplexed because we don't know why things happen as they do, but we don't give up and quit. We are hunted down, but God never abandons us. — 2 Corinthians 4:8-9

St. Aidan *(AUGUST 31)*

In the year 635, a monk from St. Columba's monastery on the island of Iona, off the western shore of Scotland, after sailing the Firth of Lorne and the Sound of Jura, went on foot across what is now southern Scotland and followed the old Roman road south to the city of Bamburgh on the North Sea. He had come at the request of the Northumbrian King Oswald to be bishop to the peoples scattered over Northumbria, and his coming was a momentous event in the history of England.

The monk was St. Aidan, founder of Lindisfarne monastery and first bishop of Northumbria, who with his monks evangelized northern England and brought about a religious and cultural revolution that enriched medieval Europe. He did not set up his see at York, which was the largest city in Northumbria, but, according to Celtic custom, in a monastery, and that monastery was a royal foundation, built in the shadow of the king's fortress and protected by the armies of the king.

King Oswald, himself a saint, had been educated on Iona and when he recovered his kingdom in the battle of Heavensfield, his first concern was for the religious welfare of his people. He sent to Iona for a bishop, and Aidan — noted for his kindness and his discretion, his simplicity and his love of the poor — was sent to Northumbria.

From his island monastery of Lindisfarne, Aidan evangelized the whole territory, founding monasteries and churches. He was the friend of king and peasant, courteous to people of all classes, going on foot on his preaching missions, the friend even of rival kings who looked upon him as a spiritual father and a saint.

A few years after Aidan's arrival, King Oswald was killed in a fierce battle with his enemies to the south, and the whole country was ravaged. Aidan was the peacemaker and gave stability to the people during these days of darkness.

When Aidan died in 651 in his little royal church at Bamburgh, the Christian religion was firmly established in the region and the effects of his work would endure for centuries. After him came St. Cuthbert, St. Wilfrid, St. Bede, St. Boniface, and Blessed Alcuin.

Thought for the Day: St. Aidan had a great love of people and walked among the poor and the rich with the same openness and simplicity. He encouraged the rich to help the poor and the poor to better themselves, and he educated the poor in his monasteries. His was an overflowing Christian charity that touched the life of everyone.

From 'The Catholic One Year Bible': . . . We must all stand before Christ to be judged and have our lives laid bare — before him. Each of us will receive whatever he deserves for the good or bad things he has done in his earthly body. — **2 Corinthians 5:10**

THE SAINTS OF SEPTEMBER

St. Fiacre *(SEPTEMBER 1)*

That bearded statue of a saint often seen in gardens is not St. Francis, it is St. Fiacre, the patron saint of gardeners. In Paris, the horse-drawn cabs are called *fiacres*, since the first such cabs came from the Hotel St. Fiacre, with a huge picture of Fiacre over the door. But he was Irish, not French, even though it was in France that he would become famous.

He was born in Ireland at the beginning of the seventh century, when monasticism was flourishing in Ireland. Looking for greater solitude, he crossed the English Channel to France and arrived at the city of Meaux, where the bishop, St. Faro, gave him a place of solitude in the forest of Breuil. According to legend, Faro gave him as much land as he could plow in a day, and Fiacre, it was said, used his staff for a plow. He cleared away the trees, made himself a hermitage with a garden, and built a small chapel as well as a hospice for pilgrims. The hospice later developed into the village of St. Fiacre in Seine-et-Marne.

His hospitality became legendary. He listened to all who came to him, served them with his own hands, and sometimes restored the sick to health. It was said that he knew how to grow plants of every kind, produced the most extraordinary vegetables and flowers, and grew herbs to use for medicine.

Over thirty churches were dedicated to him in France, and his feast is celebrated at Meaux with great festivity and huge floral decorations. His shrine has always been a place of pilgrimage, and Anne of Austria, the wife of Louis XIII of France, made a pilgrimage on foot there after the recovery of her husband through Fiacre's intercession.

St. Vincent de Paul had a special devotion to Fiacre because of his love of the poor and made a pilgrimage to his shrine. In France, Fiacre is not only the patron saint of gardeners and horticulturists, he is also the patron saint of cabdrivers.

Thought for the Day: Saints seemed to have compassion and a love for the poor, and it is for this that many are especially remembered. There is nothing so attractive as kindness, especially to those who can give nothing in return. There is something God-like about love of the poor, and so it has the special blessing of God.

From 'The Catholic One Year Bible': . . . God was in Christ, restoring the world to himself, no longer counting men's sins against them but blotting them out. This is the wonderful message he has given us to tell others. — **2 Corinthians 5:19**

Martyrs of September *(SEPTEMBER 2)*

The French Revolution brought terror in the form of massacres and other atrocities into the civil and political life of France, and some of the first victims of this terror were priests and religious, those in particular who refused to take the oath prescribed by the Civil Constitution of the Clergy. The Martyrs of September were a group of priests, bishops, and religious who were dragged from their prisons during a time of mob violence and cruelly executed.

The first prison attacked was that of the Abbaye, a former monastery where those considered the enemies of the new state were imprisoned. The mob dragged the priests from the prison, held a mock trial, ordered them to take the prescribed oath, and when they refused, were killed on the spot. One, Blessed Alexander Lenfant, had been the confessor of the king, and this was especially held against him. Five minutes before his own death, he heard the confession of another man doomed to die.

The mob then made for the Carmelite church in the Rue de Rennes, where over one hundred fifty bishops and priests were held. Breaking into the prison, priests were slaughtered right and left. Again, a mock trial was held and those who refused the oath were hacked to pieces.

On September 3, the mob came to the Lazarist seminary of St.-Fermin, which was also used as a prison. Here, their first victim was a sixty-year-old Jesuit, Blessed Peter Guerin. When he refused to take the oath, he was thrown from a window and stabbed when he hit the ground. On this day, over ninety were killed, among them Blessed Louis Joseph François, superior of the seminary, who was given a chance to escape but chose to die with his fellow prisoners.

When the Martyrs of September were beatified in 1926, one hundred ninety-one were mentioned by name, but there were hundreds of others, unknown and unheralded, who gave their lives for their faith amid the horrors of the Revolution. Among the victims were an archbishop and two bishops. So thorough was the massacre that at the prison of La Force where other prisoners were kept, there was not one survivor to describe the last moments of the martyrs.

Thought for the Day: These martyrs died for the same faith that we profess, and the profession of that faith brought them terrible sufferings and death. It is something to ponder. Do we realize what the profession of our faith means and that someday we might be called upon to die for it?

From 'The Catholic One Year Bible': There is a right time for everything: / A time to be born; / A time to die; / A time to plant; / A time to harvest; / A time to kill; / A time to heal; / A time to destroy; / A time to rebuild; / A time to cry; / A time to laugh; / A time to grieve; / A time to dance. — Ecclesiastes 3:1-4

St. Gregory the Great *(SEPTEMBER 3)*

Like St. Ambrose, St. Gregory the Great had a career in public service before taking on the reins of Church government; as pope he embodied in himself the best instincts of good government and a talent for leadership that set the pace for the future pontiffs of the Middle Ages.

He was born in Rome, received an excellent education, was trained in law, and as prefect of the city presided over the Senate and provided for the defense, food supply, finances, and the civil order of the city. About 575, he retired from public life to become a monk and turned his home on the Coelian Hill into a monastery.

In 579, he was sent as papal representative to the court at Constantinople where he gained wide experience involving the problems of the empire. Recalled to Rome in 586, he served as counselor to the pope. In 589, he was elected to succeed Pope Pelagius II who had died of the plague, and his first problem was the plague itself, which was killing thousands. His fatherly concern lifted the spirits of the people, and Gregory used the occasion to turn their minds toward God.

When the Lombards threatened Rome, Gregory became the savior of the city, working tirelessly for peace. From this time on, the people of Italy looked to the pope as their protector, and the foundation was laid for the creation of the Papal States in the years to come. His energy, vision, and concern for all peoples were seen in his policies of government for the papal patrimony, those estates administered by the pontiff in Italy and Sicily, by his reform of the liturgy and the publication of the Gregorian Sacramentary, by his synodical letters to the patriarchs of Constantinople, Alexandria, and Antioch, by the linking of the Churches in the West to the see of Peter, and by his missionary delegation to Anglo-Saxon England.

By his writings, Gregory is one of the Four Fathers of the Latin Church, and the influence of his writings dominates the whole Middle Ages. His *Pastoral Care* became the pastoral manual of later centuries and his *Moralia* laid the foundation for medieval spirituality.

In his thirteen years as pope, he crowded a lifetime. He died in 604, sick and worn out, still dictating letters on his deathbed. He was buried in St. Peter's, and his epitaph called him the great "consul of God."

Thought for the Day: St. Gregory shows the critical importance of leadership and the fantastic things that a good leader can accomplish. He influenced every aspect of religious life and is with good reason called "the Great." His life shows how important one man's witness can be.

From 'The Catholic One Year Bible': He who loves money shall never have enough. The foolishness of thinking that wealth brings happiness! The more you have, the more you spend . . . so what is the advantage of wealth. . . ! — **Ecclesiastes 5:10-11**

St. Rose of Viterbo *(SEPTEMBER 4)*

In thirteenth-century Italy, loyalties were divided between emperor and pope, between the Guelfs and the Ghibellines, and the politics of the day revolved around these two loyalties. The popes were Innocent III and his successors and the emperor was Frederick II, who fought the pontiffs and divided the loyalties of the people.

St. Rose of Viterbo was born in the midst of this political turmoil and as a very little girl had experienced the terrible state into which her city had been thrown by this divided loyalty. At the age of twelve, something of a child prodigy, she began to speak out for loyalty to the pope and spent four years in the streets of Viterbo urging her people to oppose the emperor.

In the beginning, her father told her to stay in the house and threatened to beat her, but she boldly faced up to him. She became the center of political controversy, crowds rushed to hear her, and the emperor became so concerned about her influence that he ordered the *podestà*, or mayor, of the city to put her to death. Fearing the crowds of her admirers, the *podestà* refused but did banish Rose and her family from the city.

She went on to other towns — Soriano, Vitorchiano — and continued her preaching. In December 1250, she announced that the emperor would die, and he died in mid-December of that year at Apulia as she had announced. She returned home in triumph. Her mission completed, she asked to enter the convent of St. Mary of the Roses at Viterbo but was refused. She was even turned out of a small chapel that had been built for her and her companions near the convent.

Rose returned to her father's house, where she remained until she died at the age of seventeen in 1252. She was buried in the church of Santa Maria di Podio, but her relics were later transferred to the very convent where she was refused admittance. When the church burned down in 1357, her body was preserved and each year is carried in procession through the streets of Viterbo, still incorrupt. She was canonized in 1457.

Thought for the Day: Some saints have a most unusual mission that at first seems to have little to do with sanctity. But all things are under God's providence and He has purposes that He does not reveal to us. Like St. Rose of Viterbo, we have to do God's will as we see it and not worry about what others think of us.

From 'The Catholic One Year Bible': . . . You are going to die and it is a good thing to think about it while there is still time. Sorrow is better than laughter, for sadness has a refining influence on us. Yes, a wise man thinks much of death, while the fool thinks only of having a good time now. — Ecclesiastes 7:2-4

In the lagoon of Venice, on the island of Alga, sits the monastery of San Giorgio, until recently a Benedictine monastery, but now an artistic monument. It was to this monastery, at that time a monastery of Augustinian canons, that St. Lawrence Justinian came in 1400 at the age of nineteen. A few months earlier he had passed through a spiritual crisis that moved him to consecrate himself to God and he became noted in the community for his austerities.

Ordained to the priesthood in 1406, he was elected superior at Vicenza and then at San Giorgio. In 1424, he was elected general of the congregation. In 1431, he was chosen by Pope Eugene IV to be bishop of Castello and in 1451 became archbishop and the first patriarch of Venice.

What impressed everyone about this priest and archbishop was his great simplicity of life and his liberality with the poor. He took care of beggars, was the friend of the rich and the poor, and showed a genius for apostolic works. His writings parallel his work, and he saw the secret of pastoral zeal in the pursuit of eternal wisdom. According to Lawrence, pastoral work is nothing more than the communication of divine wisdom and it is from this intense center that all pastoral work flows; the substance of one's life and effort is given to the pursuit of wisdom, and apostolic activity is the overflow of this love of wisdom. In his writings, he explains the unity of his own life and the principle of his own activity.

When Lawrence was seventy-four years old, he was struck down with fever and as death approached he asked to be laid on a bed of straw. The whole city of Venice came to pass in procession before him and he insisted on having the beggars of the city come in as well. When his favorite disciple, Marcello, wept at his impending death, Lawrence said to him: "I'm going first, but you will follow shortly. We will meet again at Easter." And Marcello, in fact, died the following Lent.

Lawrence died on January 8, 1455, but his feast is kept on the date of his consecration as bishop. He was canonized in 1690.

Thought for the Day: Some people burn with a fire that seems to burn deep inside them and gives light and warmth to every life they touch. There is something about the love of God that makes a person luminous and bright, bringing joy wherever such a person goes. Some of this fire should burn in our own lives, too.

From 'The Catholic One Year Bible': Yes, remember your Creator now while you are young, before the silver cord of life snaps, and the gold bowl is broken, and the pitcher is broken at the fountain, and the wheel is broken at the cistern; and the dust returns to the earth as it was, and the spirit returns to God who gave it. — Ecclesiastes 12:6-7

Raymond Lull is the Don Quixote of saints, a strange, mystical man who lived the life of a spiritual troubador; he was a student of Arabic and the compiler of mystical encyclopedias who wandered over the world singing of Christ and the love of God. His most notable written work, *The Book of the Lover and the Beloved*, is a mystical work in the Franciscan tradition and was widely read in the late Middle Ages.

He was born around 1235 in Majorca of wealthy parents. He married young and had a son and a daughter. He was shameless in his pursuit of women, but one night as he was writing a poem to his latest conquest, he had a vision of Jesus Christ hanging on the Cross. His conversion was not immediate, but when it happened, it was complete.

He made a pilgrimage to Compostela in Spain to ask for guidance, made provision for his family, gave the rest of his wealth to the poor, and after a period spent in solitude and prayer began intense studies to prepare himself for the conversion of the Muslims. He learned Arabic and wrote in that language, and with the help of King James II of Majorca he founded a school for the training of missionaries to convert Islamic adherents.

Blessed Raymond Lull wrote endless books, tried to join the Dominicans but was turned down, and finally became a Franciscan tertiary and in 1292 boarded a ship bound for Africa to do missionary work among the Muslims. He did preach in the streets of Tunis but so enraged the Muslim officials that they imprisoned him and then put him on a ship bound for Naples.

His dream was to convert the followers of Islam, but every attempt he made to work among them failed. He appealed to popes, sailed to Cyprus to meet the khan of Tartary, lectured in Paris, and once more sailed for North Africa. Again he was imprisoned and deported. He was shipwrecked on the way home and returned to Africa a third time where he was stoned and left for dead. Rescued by Genoese sailors, he died aboard ship in sight of his native Majorca on June 29, 1316.

An amazing man! His life is a record of continual disappointments and incredible literary activity. His feast is celebrated by the Franciscans, and he is mentioned with great respect by Pope Pius XI in his encyclical *Orientalilum Rerum*. He desired a martyr's death and is considered by some to be a martyr because of the manner of his death.

Thought for the Day: Blessed Raymond Lull was a strange man, but he was also a holy one. Eccentrics can be saints, too, and sanctity is open to everyone. We should be careful about judging and criticizing others because they are different from us. We may be criticizing a saint.

From 'The Catholic One Year Bible': "My beloved said to me, 'Rise up, my love, my fair one, and come away. For the winter is past, the rain is over and gone. The flowers are springing up and the time of the singing birds has come. . . . Arise, my love, my fair one and come away.' " — Song of Solomon 2:10-13

The Merovingian kings, those who succeeded Clovis as kings in France, were violent, savage men, intent on power and wealth, and ruthless in the murder of anyone who was a threat to their thrones. Their history is a brutal, bloody story of murder, intrigue, dynastic violence, and unscrupulous treachery. St. Cloud was born in the midst of this violence and bloodshed, escaped with his life, and became a saint in the process.

He was the grandson of Clovis, the first Christian king of the Franks, and was brought up by his grandmother, Clotilde, Clovis's widow, along with his two older brothers. They were the sons of Chlodomer, one of the four sons of Clovis who had divided their father's kingdom among them. Chlodomer was killed in a battle to win Burgundy, after murdering Sigismund, king of Burgundy. Since the three princes were underage, their uncle Childebert administered the kingdom.

But Childebert had his eye on keeping the kingdom for himself and plotted with another king to kill the young princes and take the kingdom for themselves. The two older boys were taken prisoner and brutally murdered, but Cloud escaped, most probably with the help of his grandmother, and fled the kingdom.

This terrifying experience when he was only eight years old made a powerful impression on the young prince, and even when he came of age he did not try to regain his kingdom. Instead, he turned his thoughts inward, found himself a hermit's cell, and began to live a life of prayer and seclusion. He put himself under the discipline of another hermit and spent his time in meditation and prayer. Later, he moved to a spot on the Seine River near Nogent and built himself a hermitage which still bears his name, St.-Cloud.

Ordained a priest, he carried on missionary work among the native peoples and died in the year 560 at the age of thirty-six. Out of the violence of that age, saints were born, and Cloud has left a memory that has endured the centuries. In France, he is the patron saint of nail-makers.

Thought for the Day: With his brothers murdered, St. Cloud could have spent his life in bitterness, seeking revenge. Instead, he left the world of politics behind and turned to God. Even tragedy can be turned to good and the sons of murderers can become saints.

From 'The Catholic One Year Bible': . . . God, who gives seed to the farmer to plant, and later on, good crops to harvest and eat, will give you more and more seed to plant and will make it grow so that you can give away more and more fruit from your harvest. —2 Corinthians 9:10

Clonmacnoise was one of the great monastic centers of Ireland; its founder, revered through the whole of Ireland, was Kieran, one of seven children. His father, Beoit, was a cartwright and his mother, Darerca, belonged to the bardic clan of Glasraige. As a boy, Kieran was tutored by a deacon named Justus and later studied under St. Finian at Clonard and at Aran under St. Enda. Kieran was offered a master's chair at Clonard but had other plans for himself.

Choosing a spot where the ancient chariot road through Ireland crosses the River Shannon, St. Kieran of Clonmacnoise set about building a monastery. When a local tribesman named Diarmuid MacCearbhail came sailing down the river, Kieran said to him: "Come here, for you are a king, and stake out the church. . . ." "I am not a king," Diarmuid told him. "You will be tomorrow," Kieran replied, and so it happened.

After Armagh, Clonmacnoise became the greatest monastic school of Ireland and at one time had ecclesiastical jurisdiction over half of Ireland. It was a center of learning and literature, the cradle of saints. From Clonmacnoise, Irish monks went to England, Germany, Iceland, and Austria. It was believed that Kieran would bring safely to heaven anyone buried at Clonmacnoise, and therefore many of the kings of Ireland were buried there. The monastery was sacked by the Vikings during the great Viking raids of the eighth and ninth centuries and then permanently destroyed by the Anglo-Normans in the twelfth century after they plundered it.

Kieran died soon after founding Clonmacnoise and was buried in his Eclais Beg (or Little Church), which became one of the most sacred spots in Ireland. Kieran's name is linked with many of the other great monastic founders, and he is numbered among the Twelve Apostles of Ireland.

Thought for the Day: The fragrance of a holy life lives down through the centuries, and this is true of St. Kieran, whose spirit lived on at Clonmacnoise and inspired generations of monks. There is something strong and wonderful about these early Irish founders, something that rubs off on anyone who studies them.

From 'The Catholic One Year Bible': . . . The children I raised and cared for so long and tenderly have turned against me. Even the animals — the donkey and the ox — know their owner and appreciate his care for them, but not my people Israel. — Isaiah 1:2-3

The slave trade was one of the most disgraceful and barbarous practices of the Christian nations, and the fact that it went on so long is a terrible commentary on the Christianity of these nations. It took a bloody civil war in the United States to bring an end to this social evil.

St. Peter Claver, known as the "saint of the slave trade," did his work at one of the most notorious slave centers in the New World: Cartagena, Colombia, in South America. He and his Jesuit colleagues could not convince the Spanish colonists of the massive evil of slavery, and he dedicated himself to the physical and spiritual welfare of the miserable victims of slavery.

He was born in Verdu, Spain, in 1580 and entered the Society of Jesus in 1602. While studying philosophy in Majorca, he met the remarkable Jesuit lay brother St. Alphonsus Rodríguez, who formed Peter Claver's spirituality and encouraged him in his missionary vocation. In 1610, after theological studies in Barcelona, Peter was sent to Cartagena, one of the great trading ports of the New World. There he met Alfonso de Sandoval, whose writings on the evils of slavery were the first systematic attacks on the system.

Peter shared the convictions and indignation of his fellow Jesuit, but his work was in a different direction. After his ordination, he turned his attention to the slaves themselves, armed with medical skills and superb teaching ability. He went fearlessly into the disease-infested holds of the slave ships where sickness and despair had taken their toll. In this miserable atmosphere, he cured the slaves' sores, bandaged their wounds, and brought them a bit of comfort and compassion.

From the beginning of his work he was considered a saint, and the story of his miracles spread through the slave grapevine. In his last years, he suffered from paralysis and complete neglect, dying in 1654 as the news of the pope's condemnation of the slave trade reached him. He was canonized by Pope Leo XIII in 1888 at the same time as his friend and mentor, Alphonsus Rodríguez.

Thought for the Day: The barbarism and inhumanity of human beings sometimes cannot be stopped, but there are those who stem the tide of inhumanity by their devotion and compassion. It is hard to believe that Christians could have anything to do with slavery, and it is good to know that people like St. Peter Claver helped bring about its end.

From 'The Catholic One Year Bible': He will send a signal to the nations far away, whistling to those at the ends of the earth, and they will come racing toward Jerusalem. . . . They [will] roar like lions and pounce upon their prey. — Isaiah 5:26, 29

St. Nicholas of Tolentino *(SEPTEMBER 10)*

Born in 1245, St. Nicholas of Tolentino was a child prodigy who so impressed the bishop of Fermo that he was given minor orders and made a canon of the cathedral when he was scarcely a teenager. Moved by a sermon of a Father Reginald, he decided to become an Augustinian friar and made his profession at the age of eighteen.

Ordained a priest when he was twenty-six years old, Nicholas was sent to Tolentino four years later and there spent the rest of his life. The town had been in turmoil for years because of the continual battle between pope and emperor and the moral life of the city was in shambles. The results of the civil war had brought about alienation from the Church, civil discord, and every kind of crime and immorality. Nicholas began to go out among the people, talking to them of God and the things of heaven. His very manner and personality attracted them and he was listened to.

Those hardened in their crimes made fun of him, but Nicholas would not be intimidated, even though soldiers would unsheathe their swords and fence while he was speaking. Nicholas was kindness itself, going into the slums of Tolentino, visiting the sick and bedridden, settling family feuds, caring for children, and even chatting with the criminals who went about the city, begging them not to be cruel to others. Gradually, his manner worked, and even some of the hardened criminal types came around. Nicholas was also known for his devotion to the souls in purgatory and is sometimes known as the patron of the holy souls.

Nicholas's final illness lasted almost a year and toward the end was not able to rise from his bed, except to hear the confession of a man who would confess only to him. He died on September 10, 1305. It was about this time that the pope moved his headquarters to Avignon, and so Nicholas's canonization did not take place until 1446. His body lies enshrined in a basilica built for it in Tolentino, adorned with beautiful frescoes of his life.

Thought for the Day: St. Nicholas of Tolentino had a remarkable power of persuasion and he gently worked to change others by simple persuasion and the power of his own personality. Roughness, especially with those who are hardened in vice or crime, does very little good, for it betrays a certain self-righteousness. Gentleness accomplishes much.

From 'The Catholic One Year Bible': . . . I have faced grave dangers from mobs in the cities and from death in the deserts and in the stormy seas. . . . I have lived with weariness and pain and sleepless nights. — **2 Corinthians 11:26-27**

Louis of Thuringia was the husband of St. Elizabeth of Hungary, a remarkable man in his own right, dearly loved by his wife, beloved of his people: husband, father, a just and astute ruler, and a courageous soldier. Born in 1200, he was the oldest son of Herman I and, as was often the custom in those days, when he was eleven years old he was betrothed to Elizabeth, the four-year-old daughter of Andrew II of Hungary. Elizabeth grew up in the Hungarian court, and when Louis succeeded his father in 1221 the marriage took place.

It was an idyllic and happy marriage, and Blessed Louis of Thuringia showed a remarkable tolerance for the innovative charities of his wife. Once he found a leper in his bed and instead of being angry recognized in the leper the person of Jesus Christ and paid for the building of a leprosarium in Wartburg. When his treasurer complained about Elizabeth's many charities, fearing that so much expenditure would drain the treasury, Louis replied: "Let her be as generous as she wants, as long as she leaves me a house to live in and a roof over our heads."

So fond was Elizabeth of her husband that when he returned from military campaigns or service with the emperor, she would ride out to meet him on her finest horse, dressed in her loveliest gown. The bond between them was strong and sweet. They had three children and one of them, Gertrude of Altenberg, is also Blessed.

In 1227, Louis volunteered to accompany the emperor on a crusade and on June 24 of that year set out for Jerusalem, in command of the Central-German forces. He met the emperor at Troja, and in September the whole army took to sea. Three days later, when the ships put in at Otranto, Louis caught malaria and soon was on the point of death. In his last hours, he was in a delirium and thought his room was full of white doves. "I must fly away with the white doves," he said, and died. When news of his death reached Elizabeth, she cried: "The world is dead to me and all that was pleasant in it."

He was buried in the Benedictine abbey of Reinhardsbrunn.

Thought for the Day: The marriage of Blessed Louis of Thuringia and St. Elizabeth was an almost perfect marriage, for they loved each other dearly and tenderly, and their only concern was to make the other happy. That is the only solid basis for a happy marriage, something that some married couples never learn. Happiness is found in making others happy.

From 'The Catholic One Year Bible': . . . Unto us a Child is born; unto us a Son is given; and the government shall be upon his shoulder. . . . His everlasting, peaceful government will never end. — Isaiah 9:6-7

St. Guy of Anderlecht *(SEPTEMBER 12)*

Guy of Anderlecht was a Christian Dick Whittington, poor as a pauper, wandering around what is now Belgium, finding jobs where he could, free as a bird, and loving his freedom. He was called the "Poor Man of Anderlecht" and was loved and revered as a kind of St. Francis, his home the great outdoors.

Although he had very little himself, he shared what he had with the poor, and would feed others and fast himself. A priest in a country church gave him a job as sacristan, and St. Guy of Anderlecht made the church shine with the care he gave it, endearing himself to everyone as he swept and cleaned the floors.

The Dick Whittington side of his character came out when a merchant from Brussels convinced him that if he invested his money in a merchant vessel, he would make a big profit and would have more money to share with the poor. Guy thought about it and it seemed like a good idea, so he became a partner of the man from Brussels and invested all his money in the ship. Unlike Dick Whittington, however, the ship sank going out of the harbor and Guy was left without a job and without money, since he had quit his job as sacristan to become a partner with the man from Brussels.

Realizing he had been a little foolish, Guy decided to make a pilgrimage to Rome and to Jerusalem and went on a seven-year pilgrimage to the holy places. When he returned, he was sick and worn out; reaching Anderlecht, he was struck down by exhaustion and fatigue. He died in a hospital in Anderlecht and was buried in the cemetery of a local church. So many miracles began to be worked at his grave that his body was moved to a shrine that soon became a place of pilgrimage.

Thought for the Day: There are some people who seem to go through this world like children, totally dependent on God and lacking for nothing. Although they often seem to others to be impractical and foolish, they live by a wisdom that is not of this world. We call them "saints," and would that a little bit of their "foolishness" rub off on us.

From 'The Catholic One Year Bible': The Lord will dry a path through the Red Sea, and wave his hand over the Euphrates, sending a mighty wind to divide it into seven streams that can easily be crossed. He will make a highway from Assyria . . . just as he did for all of Israel long ago when they returned from Egypt. —**Isaiah 11:15-16**

St. John Chrysostom *(SEPTEMBER 13)*

John Chrysostom was the son of a Latin father and a Greek mother; his mother, Anthusa, was widowed at the age of twenty, soon after his birth. Putting aside all thought of remarriage, Anthusa gave all of her attention to her son: she gave him the best classical education of the day, and enrolled him as a catechumen when he was eighteen. He came under the influence of Meletius, patriarch of Antioch, who sent him to the monastic school of Diodore, then baptized him and ordained him lector.

At this time, St. John Chrysostom decided to take his future into his own hands and became a monk-hermit, living in a cave, studying the Scriptures, and putting himself under the discipline of an old hermit named Hesychius. However, his health broke under this austere regimen and he returned to Antioch, was ordained a priest, and began his remarkable career as a preacher.

During the next twelve years, he electrified Antioch with his fiery sermons, filled with a knowledge and an eloquence that were astonishing. It was during this period that he received the nickname Chrysostom, or golden mouth, for his words seemed to be pure gold. In 397, when the see of Constantinople became vacant, the Emperor Arcadius appointed John patriarch, and since it was feared that he would refuse the honor, he was lured to Constantinople and consecrated bishop of the city in 398.

John found himself in a nest of political intrigue, fraud, extravagance, and naked ambition. He curbed expenses, gave lavishly to the poor, built hospitals, reformed the clergy, and restored monastic discipline. But his program of reform made him enemies, in particular the Empress Eudoxia and the Patriarch Theophilus of Alexandria. The city in turmoil, his life threatened, John was exiled by the emperor in the year 404.

The papal envoys were imprisoned, and John — defended by the pope and ordered restored to his see — was sent further into exile, six hundred miles from Constantinople, across the Black Sea. Worn out and sick, he died of his hardships at Comana in Pontus. His last words were, "Glory to God for all things."

Thought for the Day: The result of doing good is sometimes opposition and suffering, and St. John Chrysostom suffered for trying to do what was right. We should not be surprised if this happens to us. He died in exile, exhausted and ill. We may have to suffer only sharp words and disapproving looks.

From 'The Catholic One Year Bible': I pray that you will live good lives, not because that will be a feather in our caps, proving that what we teach is right; . . . Our responsibility is to encourage what is right at all times, . . . Be happy. Grow in Christ. Pay attention to what I have said. Live in harmony and peace. —**2 Corinthians 13:7-8, 11**

In 602, the Persians under Chosroes II invaded the Byzantine empire. Antioch was taken in 611 and Jerusalem fell in 614. The holy places were destroyed, the patriarch of Jerusalem, Zachary, taken prisoner, and the True Cross was taken to Persia (modern-day Iran). In a series of brilliant campaigns, the Emperor Heraclius drove the Persians out of Turkey and Armenia, led his armies into Persia, deposed Chosroes, and returned the True Cross to Jerusalem. It is the commemoration of this event that is celebrated today, when the emperor himself, with the Patriarch Zachary beside him, carried the True Cross into Jerusalem with great rejoicing, solemnity, and celebration.

According to the story, the emperor was determined to carry the Cross himself through the gates of the city, with great pomp and ceremony. But at the entrance to the city, he found that he could not go forward, stopped by some unseen force. The Patriarch Zachary suggested that the imperial splendor was scarcely in keeping with the simplicity with which Jesus Himself had carried the Cross. The emperor then laid aside his royal robes and, dressed in simple clothes and barefoot, carried the Cross and returned it to the church of the Holy Sepulcher.

The holy places destroyed by the Persians were restored by the monks of Jerusalem and through the generosity of St. John the Almsgiver, patriarch of Alexandria. The church of the Nativity had remained untouched by the Persians in respect for the great figures of the Magi, which were painted on the walls of the church, dressed like Persian astrologers. The return of the True Cross was the last step in the restoration of the city and a triumph for the emperor who had carried out a difficult campaign to defeat the Persians and drive them from his empire.

This Feast of the Exaltation of the Holy Cross is one of the great feasts of the Eastern Church and also commemorates the dedication of the basilicas in Jerusalem built by Constantine. In certain monastic orders, this date marks the beginning of the "Black Fast," the great monastic fast that lasts from September 14 until Easter.

Thought for the Day: The Cross symbolizes our redemption and the price paid for our salvation and so has always been a revered symbol. The wood of the Cross itself, discovered by St. Helena, has always had a special place in the devotion of Christians and its return in triumph to Jersualem has always been a memorable feast day.

From 'The Catholic One Year Bible': May peace and blessing be yours from God the Father and from the Lord Jesus Christ. He died for our sins just as God our Father planned, and rescued us from this evil world in which we live. All glory to God through all the ages of eternity. — Galatians 1:3-5

St. Catherine of Genoa (SEPTEMBER 15)

Catherine Fieschi was the youngest of five children; her father was viceroy of Naples and her mother came from an ancient, noble family of Genoa. In 1461, when St. Catherine of Genoa was fourteen, her father died, and two years later, her mother arranged a marriage for her with a powerful rival family, the Adornos. She was married to Giulano Adorno, a man of weak character, loose morals, and spendthrift habits, who was never at home, continually unfaithful to her, and ill-tempered.

Catherine, on the other hand, was witty and intelligent, a lover of people and parties, deeply religious and scrupulously honest. After five years of utter loneliness, deep in desperation she made a full confession of her life to a priest, went through a complete spiritual transformation, and had a vision of Jesus crucified.

Her husband, Giulano, at the same time, found himself bankrupt, brought about a complete change in his life, and became a Franciscan tertiary. The couple gave away their property and possessions and moved to a small house near a hospital to dedicate their lives to the service of the sick and the poor.

At first, they simply worked without pay, then in 1490 took over the administration of the hospital, and Catherine's heroism in the epidemic of 1493 made her famous throughout the city.

Her life of prayer during twenty-five years was extraordinary and intense, but it was something that she carried on without direction. Then, in 1499, after the death of Giulano, she met Don Cattanto Marabotto, who had become chaplain of the hospital, and she placed herself under his direction.

Her sayings and conversations were written down after her death by a lawyer friend, Ettore Vernazza, and the collection entitled *Treatise on Purgatory* is her most notable mystical writing. She remained right up to her death in 1510 a wise and witty woman, noted for her happy spirit and love of people, a sparkling conversationalist and a deep and devoted friend.

She was canonized in 1737 and her name was added to the *Roman Martyrology*.

Thought for the Day: Out of her loneliness, St. Catherine of Genoa discovered God, and in God she found all the happiness she could ever want. She then tried to find ways to share that happiness and became the Florence Nightingale of her time. It is good to know that she was witty and had a good sense of humor.

From 'The Catholic One Year Bible': . . . Disaster is roaring down upon you [Babylon] from the terrible desert, like a whirlwind sweeping from the Negeb. I see an awesome vision: oh, the horror of it all! God is telling me what he is going to do. I see you plundered and destroyed.
— Isaiah 21:1-2

This is one of the great heroes of the early Church: a bishop, a martyr, a theologian and teacher, primate of the North African Church, and beloved bishop of Carthage, who preceded St. Augustine as the teacher of North Africa.

He was born a pagan, was a teacher of rhetoric and an advocate in the courts, one of the most educated men of his day, was a prominent figure in the civil and political life of Carthage, and until middle age was deeply involved in the public and social life of the city.

Then, when he was about fifty, something happened. St. Cyprian met an old priest named Caecilian, and the truth of Christianity struck him full force. Awed and astonished at what he now understood, he took a vow of celibacy, was baptized, and turned his mind to the study of the Scriptures and the Christian thinkers who had preceded him.

He was ordained a priest, and in 248 the bishopric of Carthage became vacant and he was appointed, much against his will. But when he became bishop, he fulfilled his pastoral charge with unusual energy, goodness, and courage, showing himself as remarkable a leader in the Church as he had in public life.

A year after he became bishop, the Decian persecution struck, and Cyprian went into hiding, not from cowardice but in an effort to strengthen and encourage his flock. When the crisis was over, Cyprian became involved in a controversy with the pope over baptism by heretics, and the controversy threatened to bring about a breach between Rome and North Africa, a controversy that would later break out and create the Donatist Schism.

But another persecution under the Emperor Valerian broke out, and Cyprian was exiled to Curibis; a year later he returned to Carthage for trial. He could have fled again but did not, wanting to give his people an example of martyrdom to encourage them in their own resistance. He was tried, condemned, and beheaded on September 14, 258, and immediately became the martyr-saint of North Africa and an example of Christian fortitude under persecution.

Thought for the Day: St. Cyprian met Christian truth, and it transformed and illumined his whole life and became his life's study. He felt so loyal to it that he was willing to die for it and gave his life as a witness (martyr). What kind of witness do we give to the truth of what we believe?

From 'The Catholic One Year Bible': I have been crucified with Christ: and I myself no longer live, but Christ lives in me. And the real life I now have within this body is a result of my trusting in the Son of God, who loved me and gave himself for me. — **Galatians 2:20**

bert Bellarmine was the nephew of Pope Marcellus II from uscany in northern Italy. At the age of eighteen, he entered the Jesuits in Rome, studied theology at Padua, and then was sent to teach at the University of Louvain in Belgium. Louvain at this time, just after the Council of Trent, was in the forefront of Catholic scholarship in the face of the Reformation, and Bellarmine became the chief Catholic scholar of his time, skilled in languages, patristics, Sacred Scripture, Church history, and the teachings of the reformers themselves.

In 1576, Pope Gregory XIII requested that he teach at the Roman college, and St. Robert Bellarmine's lectures there appeared in three volumes in 1586. He put Catholic scholarship in order in confronting the arguments of the reformers, avoiding polemics and facing their arguments fairly and squarely.

In 1588, he became spiritual director of the Roman college and had St. Aloysius Gonzaga as one of his penitents. The effect of Aloysius upon Bellarmine was profound, and he carried the memory of this luminous young man to his grave.

In 1599, Bellarmine was created cardinal and served on a number of Roman congregations. In 1602, he was made archbishop and appointed to the see of Capua where he reformed the diocese and impressed all by his preaching and charity to the poor. In 1605, he was recalled to Rome.

In 1616, he became involved in the Galileo controversy and admonished Galileo to temper his views. As a cardinal, he was noted for his poverty, generosity to the poor, and devotion to duty. He died on September 17, 1621, the great champion of the Catholic faith, whose learning and writings provided a bulwark against the teaching of the Reformation. He was canonized in 1930 and was declared a Doctor of the Church a year later. His body, along with that of Aloysius Gonzaga, lies in St. Ignatius Church in Rome.

Thought for the Day: St. Robert Bellarmine made himself informed about the sources of his faith, its history, and its meaning. He recognized that learning must come to the defense of truth but that attacks upon the faith must be faced fairly. Always a gentleman in controversy, he treasured truth more than victory.

From 'The Catholic One Year Bible': O Lord, I will honor and praise your name, for you are my God; you do such wonderful things! You planned them long ago, and now you have accomplished them, just as you said. — Isaiah 25:1

St. Joseph of Cupertino *(SEPTEMBER 18)*

Joseph of Cupertino has become something of a legend because of his feats of levitation, which bewildered his community, delighted his admirers, and caused him to be shut away by Church authorities. The Church has made him the patron saint of fliers, not without a touch of humor.

He was born Joseph Desa at the small village of Cupertino in Brindisi, Italy, in 1603. As a child, he was looked upon as something of a nuisance and became the butt of village jokes. He was apprenticed to a shoemaker but was a complete failure at the trade; when he was seventeen, he applied for admission to the Franciscans and then to the Capuchins. Both dismissed him for his absentmindedness and unreliability.

Through the influence of an uncle, he was finally accepted by the Franciscans as a servant, given the habit of a tertiary, and sent to work in the stables. Something came over him, and he became a zealous religious and was accepted as a novice. He did poorly at studies and was accepted for ordination to the priesthood by sheer accident. After his ordination, his gift of levitation became evident as well as miracles of healing. During Mass and the Divine Office, he would sometimes be lifted off his feet, and this was witnessed by hundreds of people. His community was so disturbed by these phenomena that St. Joseph of Cupertino was forbidden to celebrate Mass in public and was kept hidden away for fear of public ridicule.

His last years were spent with the Capuchins at Pietrarossa where he lived in strict seclusion. But pilgrims flocked to the place and he had to be moved elsewhere. Until the end of his life, he was moved from place to place, his notoriety following him. On August 10, 1663, he fell sick and knew that he was going to die. Five weeks later, on September 18, he died at the age of sixty. His canonization took place in 1767.

Thought for the Day: In his own eyes, St. Joseph of Cupertino seemed a complete failure, an embarrassment to his order and something of an oddity. But his love of God was evident to everyone and it was this, rather than his strange gifts, that endeared him to so many. For all his oddity, he was a saint and that is what is important.

From 'The Catholic One Year Bible': . . . The Lord God says, See, I am placing a Foundation Stone in Zion — a firm, tested, precious Cornerstone that is safe to build on. He who believes need never run away again. — Isaiah 28:16

In 664, during the great plague that struck England, the archbishop of Canterbury died, leaving the most important see in England vacant. The kings of Northumbria and Kent chose a new archbishop and sent him to Rome to be consecrated by the pope. But he, too, died. The pontiff, St. Vitalian, finally chose a remarkable man to fill the see, a Greek priest from Tarsus named Theodore.

During his twenty-two years as archbishop of Canterbury, St. Theodore united the Church in England by his farseeing policies and wise decisions. He held synods and divided dioceses, placing dedicated bishops in every see. It was he who restored St. Wilfrid to the archbishopric of York and it was he, too, who appointed St. Cuthbert bishop of Lindisfarne.

St. Theodore of Canterbury was sixty-six years old when he came to England, and when he died at the age of eighty-eight, Christianity was flourishing everywhere. He established at Canterbury a theological school that drew students from all over Europe and was the first archbishop of Canterbury whose authority was recognized all over England. He drew up a set of canons for the Catholic Church in England that gave unity and stability to the whole country and united the Catholics of England by common faith and customs. However, when he tried to divide Wilfrid's great see of York, Wilfrid objected, appealed to the pope, and made a long journey to Rome. But Theodore's decision held and Wilfrid never recovered his authority over all the northern dioceses.

When Theodore arrived in England, the country was divided in loyalty to Celtic customs, Welsh sympathies, and Roman allegiance. When he died in 690, he left a united Christian people. In the words of St. Bede the Venerable: "The English churches prospered more during the pontificate of Theodore than they had ever done before." His feast day is observed in the dioceses of England and among the English Benedictines.

Thought for the Day: Under St. Theodore, Canterbury became a beacon of learning for the whole of England. He realized the critical need of knowledge for the progress of the faith and for its firm establishment. Piety is not enough — knowledge is essential. How much do I prize a deep and clear knowledge of what I believe?

From 'The Catholic One Year Bible': Look, a righteous King is coming, with honest princes! He will shelter Israel from the storm and wind. He will refresh her as a river in the desert and as the cooling shadow of a mighty rock within a hot and weary land. Then at last the eyes of Israel will open wide to God, . . . — Isaiah 32:1-3

Emily de Rodat was a lively, precocious child, born during the French Revolution. She was brought up by her grandmother, who instilled in her a genuine religious spirit and a great love of the poor. In 1804, she met the Abbé Antoine Marty, who directed Emily to teach catechism classes to the poor. She tried several religious orders but found her vocation in none of them.

Listening to a conversation of poor women in Villefranche complaining that there was no one to teach their children, Emily proposed to Abbé Martin that she become their teacher. She rented a house and started a free school in May of 1816. Eight other young women joined her, and the Congregation of the Holy Family was begun.

Several foundations followed as well as a broadening of the nuns' work. They visited prisons, established orphanages, and took care of aged religious. Realizing that active work needed the support of prayer, St. Emily de Rodat founded a convent of cloistered nuns, making her congregation attractive to a wide variety of vocations.

Her life was not always tranquil. She often differed with the Abbé Martin in her views and usually followed her own judgment. "She was a saint," someone said of her, "but a headstrong saint." She insisted on simplicity in religious life and a commonsense attitude to religious life itself. "Religious vocations are brought about by the grace of God," she said, "not by any words of ours."

She had always been troubled with ill health, and in April 1852 her eyes became afflicted with cancer. She resigned her office as mother-general and realized that the end was near. Her sufferings increased, and for three weeks in September of that year she patiently waited for the end, which came on September 19. She was beatified in 1940 and canonized in 1950.

Thought for the Day: St. Emily de Rodat realized that nothing is done without difficulty and faced difficulties courageously and with humor. There is no such thing as a tranquil existence, and every life has its hardships and frustrations. Courage is not only necessary for saints, it is the necessary quality for any well-lived life.

From 'The Catholic One Year Bible': . . . When the Holy Spirit controls our lives he will produce this kind of fruit in us: love, joy, peace, patience, kindness, goodness, faithfulness, gentleness, and self-control; . . . Those who belong to Christ have nailed their natural evil desires to his cross and crucified them there. — **Galatians 5:22-24**

Matthew was a tax collector, a despised profession among the Jews, and he probably was stationed at Capernaum because of its importance as a fishing and trading center. Whether he was a Galilean, we are not sure, but he did live in Capernaum and had a house there.

His call to follow Jesus is mentioned in the three Synoptic Gospels. As a tax collector, he would have been well-to-do, which is indicated by the banquet that he hosted for Jesus after his call.

We do not know the circumstances that led up to his call, whether there had been any preparation on the part of Jesus or whether they had ever met. The call in the Gospels is abrupt, and so it seems that there had been some preparation. Jesus at this time had made Capernaum His residence, and His work and miracles were well known in the city.

The first Gospel is attributed to St. Matthew, but little else is known about his life or his ministry. He is mentioned in the list of Apostles in the three Synoptic Gospels and in the Acts of the Apostles. His symbol among the Evangelists is the Man, since he begins his Gospel with the human genealogy of Jesus. Early Christian tradition has him preaching in Judea and then going to evangelize Ethiopia, Partha, and Persia. He is venerated as a martyr, but nothing is known of the time, place, or circumstances of his martyrdom.

His chief claim to fame is his Gospel, which alone gives us the story of the visit of the Magi to Bethlehem, King Herod's slaughter of the Innocents, and the Flight into Egypt. It is in his Gospel also that we have the Sermon on the Mount. His gift of storytelling has made his Gospel memorable, and his Gospel is noted also for its wide knowledge of Jewish law and custom.

Thought for the Day: St. Matthew was deeply involved in the making of money and saw something in Jesus which made all of that meaningless. His is the classical example of a "vocation," a call to follow Jesus. He left all behind to follow the Master. A vocation can come at any time, in any place, to anyone.

From 'The Catholic One Year Bible': Share each other's troubles and problems, and so obey our Lord's command. If anyone thinks he is too great to stoop to this, he is fooling himself. . . . Each of us must bear some faults and burdens of his own. For none of us is perfect! — Galatians 6:2-3, 5

St. Thomas of Villanova *(SEPTEMBER 22)*

This St. Thomas was born at Fuentellana in Castile, Spain, in 1486 but received his name from the town where he was brought up, Villanueva de los Infantes. His father was a miller, and it was the outgoing generosity of the family that gave Thomas his charitable disposition. At the age of sixteen, he went to the University of Alcalá for studies; he became a master of arts and licentiate in theology and, when he was twenty-six years old, a professor of philosophy. In 1516, he joined the Augustinians at Salamanca, was ordained a priest, and gave lectures in theology.

Elected provincial in 1533, he sent Augustinian missionaries to the New World and saw his order established in Mexico. Emperor Charles V appointed him to the archbishopric of Granada, but he refused. Later, accidentally named for the archbishopric of Valencia, he tried to turn it down but was not able to do so. He was consecrated in Valladolid and went to Valencia on foot and took possession of his cathedral in 1545.

Choosing to live in absolute simplicity, St. Thomas of Villanova became a dynamo of activity in his archdiocese. The see was immensely wealthy, and he used the wealth for the benefit of the poor and his many charities. Each day several hundred poor came to his door and each one was fed and given money. He took destitute orphans under his care and set up dowries for poor girls. He paid his servants to find abandoned infants and took care of them. When a nearby town was plundered by pirates, he sent money to rebuild the town and ransom captives.

He tried to resign several times, but his request was refused. In August of 1555, he had a heart attack and prepared for the end. He ordered that all he owned be given to the poor and that after he died his bed be given to the local jail. When he was dying, Mass was offered in his presence and he died peacefully on September 8.

He was known as "the model of bishops," "the almsgiver," and "the father of the poor"; he was buried in the church of the Augustinian friars in Valencia. Several universities, including one in the United States, are named after him. He was canonized in 1658.

Thought for the Day: The overwhelming generosity of the saints! Their trust in Divine Providence is so great that they give away anything and everything they have, not counting the cost. They know they will be provided for. Generosity with the poor is the mark of the Christian, and almsgiving has always been a genuine Christian practice.

From 'The Catholic One Year Bible': . . . All praise to God for his wonderful kindness to us and his favor that he has poured out upon us, because we belong to his dearly beloved Son. . . . He took away all our sins through the blood of his Son, . . . — Ephesians 1:6-7

St. Adamnan of Iona *(SEPTEMBER 23)*

When St. Bede was a boy of fifteen in the monastery of Jarrow in northern England, Jarrow had a strange visitor. His head was shaved at the top and the rest of his hair fell to his shoulders and he spoke the strange, Celtic tongue of the Irish monks. His name was Adamnan and he was abbot of Iona, an island monastery off the western coast of Scotland; he was the ninth successor of St. Columba and was *coarb*, or superior, of all the Irish monks in Scotland.

As abbot of Iona, Adamnan continued the tradition of welcoming young Englishmen to Iona and educating them, and one of the students who sought refuge in his monastery was Prince Aldrid, son of King Oswy of Northumbria who had been born in Ireland and was in exile in Iona during the reign of his half-brother Egfrid. Adamnan had educated the young man, and in 685 Aldrid succeeded his father and his brother as king of Northumbria.

St. Adamnan of Iona was in England to visit his former student and to ask for the release of Irish captives, taken in a raid by King Egfrid in Ireland. His visit to Jarrow was part of his visit to England, since Jarrow, too, was noted for its love of learning and scholarship.

Bede later remembered the Irish abbot and described him as "a good and wise man, remarkably learned in the Scriptures." Adamnan also wrote a life of Iona's founder, Columba, and edited one of the most popular books of his day, an account of the holy places in Jerusalem, which were described to him by a Frankish bishop shipwrecked on the island monastery.

Back in Ireland, Adamnan was responsible for the passing of "Adamnan's Law," which decreed that women would not be allowed to take part in warfare and that women and children should not be taken prisoners in war.

His humanity and learning endeared him to the people of Scotland, who preserved his memory for many generations. He failed to convince the monks of Iona that they should adopt the Roman date for the celebration of Easter, and he died on September 23, 704, sad at the lack of harmony in the Church. He is the most notable successor of Columba as abbot of Iona.

Thought for the Day: What he could not accomplish by gentleness, St. Adamnan of Iona would not try to accomplish by harshness, and, for him, the keeping of peace was more important than the date of Easter. He was known as a lover of peace and of the brethren, a good description of what every Christian should be.

From 'The Catholic One Year Bible': . . . You are no longer strangers to God and foreigners to heaven, but you are members of God's very own family, citizens of God's country, and you belong in God's household with every other Christian. — **Ephesians 2:19**

King John of England was neither a good man nor a good king, but he had a wholesome respect for holiness; and because of this respect, Blessed Robert of Knaresborough was one of those who could talk back to the king.

Like Richard Rolle, the Hermit of Hampole, Robert was likewise a hermit. He had entered the Cistercian monastery at Newminster together with his brother, but he soon realized that he was called to the hermit's vocation. He gave up his inheritance and began to live in a cave by the River Nidd, near Knaresborough. He found the cave was inhabited by a soldier hiding from the king. Later, the soldier moved on and Robert occupied the cave by himself.

He moved to various hermitages, trying always to find a deeper solitude. When someone gave him a barn, the local sheriff accused him of hiding thieves and burglars and tore his barn down. The sheriff had a change of heart after a terrifying dream and gave Blessed Robert some land, horses, oxen, and cows for his upkeep. Another of Robert's brothers (who was mayor of York and a successful merchant) was embarrassed by Robert's notoriety and sent men to build a chapel beside the cave where Robert lived.

The hermit's reputation for holiness spread, and people came from everywhere to seek his advice and ask for his prayers. Robert also became the champion of the poor and the oppressed, which he considered one of the first duties of a hermit. When King John was staying at Knaresborough Castle, he visited Robert and asked if he needed anything. Robert showed him an ear of corn and asked the king if he could create anything like it, which naturally the king couldn't. He asked King John for a piece of plowland next to his own for the poor, and the king gave it to him.

When he lay dying, the monks of Fountains Abbey offered to clothe him in the Cistercian habit, but he refused and gave directions that he was to be buried in his own chapel. He was mourned by the local people as a "devout, debonair, and discreet man." In later years, his body was moved to the church of the Trinitarian Order in Knaresborough.

Thought for the Day: Blessed Robert of Knaresborough had a very strong sense of where God wanted him to be and he never swerved from it, even for something that was considered more perfect. He followed his own unique pathway to God and found God in his own way. There is something to be said for this kind of single-mindedness.

From 'The Catholic One Year Bible': . . . Glory be to God who by his mighty power at work within us is able to do far more than we would ever dare to ask or even dream of — infinitely beyond our highest prayers, desires, thoughts or hopes. — Ephesians 3:20

St. Albert of Jerusalem *(SEPTEMBER 25)*

This saint is considered the legislator of the Order of Mount Carmel, for it was he who drew up the community's primitive rule at the request of the hermits living on Mount Carmel in the thirteenth century. But his coming to Jerusalem was itself remarkable and is part of the fascinating and tragic story of the crusades.

When Godfrey of Bouillon set up the Latin kingdom in Jerusalem after the first crusade, the Greek bishops were driven from the main cities, and thus there originated the Latin patriarch of Jerusalem, an office that exists to this day. The first Latin patriarchs were scarcely worthy of their office and were often as deeply involved in political intrigue and personal ambition as any nobleman. In 1203, the canons of the Holy Sepulcher and the king of Jerusalem asked Pope Innocent III to send a worthy and holy bishop to fill the office, one who would be a true shepherd of souls. The man chosen was Albert, bishop of Vercelli.

He was a skilled diplomat, close to the pope, and was known as a peacemaker, having brought peace between Parma and Piacenza in 1199. In 1205, Pope Innocent invested him with the pallium and sent him to Jerusalem.

Jerusalem had been taken by the Muslims in 1187, and so the patriarch set up his headquarters at Acre. St. Albert of Jerusalem found himself in an almost impossible position, trying to keep peace between the warring Frankish factions and working for peace as well with the Muslims, who came to respect him.

About 1210, St. Brocard, prior of the hermits on Mount Carmel, asked him to draw up a rule for the community, and Albert drew up a rule in sixteen chapters, which became the foundational rule of the Carmelite Order.

On the Feast of the Exaltation of the Holy Cross, during a procession through the city, Albert was assassinated by a disgruntled hospitaler whom he had deposed from office. He never accomplished his dream to get to Jerusalem, but his memory as a peacemaker lived on. He is considered the first legislator of the Order of Mount Carmel, and his feast is also celebrated by the canons regular of the Lateran.

Thought for the Day: Under obedience, St. Albert of Jerusalem set out into the unknown, his life suddenly taking a totally new direction. All of us have to face the unknown and the unexpected, and it is a measure of our confidence in God how well we face something entirely new. Our stability is not in ourselves but in God.

From 'The Catholic One Year Bible': Some of us have been given special ability as apostles; to others he has given the gift of being able to preach well; some have special ability in winning people to Christ, . . . still others have a gift for caring for God's people as a shepherd does his sheep, leading and teaching them in the ways of God. — Ephesians 4:11

SS. Cosmas and Damian *(SEPTEMBER 26)*

This is one of the most ancient feasts of the Church, and these two martyrs have been honored in the East and West in many ways, including the building of churches in their honor in Rome and Constantinople. Along with St. Luke, they are the patron saints of doctors. Little is known of their true history, but the legend that has come down to us is of very early origin.

SS. Cosmas and Damian were venerated in the East as the "moneyless ones" because they practiced medicine gratis. According to the legend, they were twin brothers, born in Arabia, who studied in Syria and became skilled physicians. They were supposed to have lived on the Bay of Alexandretta in Cilicia, in what is now Turkey.

Since they were prominent Christians, they were among the first arrested when the great persecution under Diocletian began. Lysias, the governor of Cilicia, ordered their arrest, and they were beheaded. Their bodies, it was said, were carried to Syria and buried at Cyrrhus.

What is certain is that they were venerated very early and became patrons of medicine, known for their miracles of healing. The Emperor Justinian was cured by their intercession and paid special honor to the city of Cyrrhus where their relics were enshrined. Their basilica in Rome, adorned with lovely mosaics, was dedicated in the year 530. They are named in the *Roman Martyrology* and in the Canon of the Mass, testifying to the antiquity of their feast day.

The great honor in which they are held and the antiquity of their veneration indicate some historical memory among the early Christians who came out of the great persecutions with a new cult of Christian heroes. Cosmas and Damian were not only ideal Christians by their practice of medicine without fee, they also symbolized God's blessing upon the art of healing and that respect for every form of science, which is an important part of Christian tradition.

Thought for the Day: A Christian is generous: with his time, with his talents, with his money. SS. Cosmas and Damian practiced medicine free, looking upon this as a Christian service to others. I may not be able to imitate them in this, but my own spirit of generosity should be a clear part of my Christian witness.

From 'The Catholic One Year Bible': Listen to me, my people, my chosen ones! I alone am God. I am the First; I am the Last. It was my hand that laid the foundations of the earth; the palm of my right hand spread out the heavens above; I spoke and they came into being. — Isaiah 48:12-13

Vincent de Paul was ordained a priest at the unusual age of twenty and at first does not seem to have had any lofty ambitions. He became chaplain to Queen Margaret of Valois and also was abbot *in commendam* of a small abbey, which meant he enjoyed the revenues of the monastery.

On a visit to Paris, he met Cardinal Berulle, founder of the French Oratorians, and through Berulle's influence he began to see his priesthood in a new light. He became tutor to a wealthy family and gradually became aware of the terrible spiritual state of the peasants of France. He quit his comfortable chaplaincy and became a pastor.

Returning to Paris, he became an itinerant pastor to the galley slaves and began to make the rounds of the prisons. With the help of his wealthy patron, he also began to work among the peasants working for the great landowners, working as well in the prisons and galleys to alleviate the sufferings of the prisoners.

In the midst of his work, St. Vincent de Paul became friends with St. Francis de Sales and St. Jeanne de Chantal, and was chaplain to the Visitation nuns in Paris. When Jansenism arose in France, he became its most vigorous opponent and was largely responsible for its defeat. He had gathered around him a number of priests interested in working among the poor country people, and in 1626 he gathered them into a religious congregation, the Congregation of the Mission. In 1632, Vincent made his headquarters in the priory of St.-Lazare, and in France his congregation was known as the Lazarists.

With the help of St. Louise Marillac, he founded the Daughters of Charity in 1633, dedicated to working among the poor. He completed the rules for his congregations in 1658 and with the death of St. Louise Marillac in 1660 he realized that his work was over. He died on September 27, 1660, and his body lies at the motherhouse of his congregation in Paris.

His works of charity inspired thousands of others throughout the Church. In 1833, Frederic Ozanam founded the St. Vincent de Paul Society to work among the poor, inspired by the example of Vincent himself.

Thought for the Day: St. Vincent de Paul was shocked by the religious state of the country people of France and found himself thrust into his life's work. Sometimes, something just has to be done and there is no one else to do it. If we look around, we can find all kinds of ways to lead others to God.

From 'The Catholic One Year Bible': . . . It was our grief he bore, *our* sorrows that weighed him down. And we thought his troubles were a punishment from God, for his *own* sins! . . . He was wounded and bruised for *our* sins. — Isaiah 53:4-5

St. Wenceslaus *(SEPTEMBER 28)*

This is the "good King Wenceslaus" whom we sing about at Christmas time, whose charity to the poor was famous during his lifetime. He was not really a king but a duke, the duke of Bohemia, in what is now Czechoslovakia, of which he is the patron saint.

He was born near Prague about 907, the oldest son of Ratislav, ruler of Bohemia. His grandmother was St. Ludmilla, wife of the first Christian duke of Bohemia, and she brought up her grandson to be a devout Christian. When Ratislav died, leaving Wenceslaus the throne, his mother became regent, with disastrous results for the country.

With pagan and Christian factions at war, Ludmilla in 621 urged her grandson Wenceslaus to take over the rulership himself. The queen-regent, fearing Ludmilla's influence over the young prince, had her murdered, but the nobles of the country sided with Wenceslaus, and the power of the mother was broken.

The young king tried to make peace between the warring factions, allied his country with Emperor Henry I of Germany, and set about trying to restore order to the country. His younger brother, Boleslaus, hoping to capture the throne for himself, allied himself with those opposed to Christian rule and who resented Wenceslaus's close ties with the clergy. When St. Wenceslaus married and had a son, Boleslaus saw his chance of succession disappear and plotted the murder of his brother.

In September of the year 929, Boleslaus invited his brother to Stara Boleslav to celebrate the feast of SS. Cosmas and Damian. On the morning of September 28, while Wenceslaus was on the way to Mass, he was stabbed and killed by Boleslaus. His last words were, "May God forgive you, brother."

He was immediately acclaimed as a martyr by the people, and by the end of the century his feast was being observed throughout the country. His shrine became a place of pilgrimage where miracles occurred. He is the patron saint of the Bohemian people and of Czechoslovakia.

Thought for the Day: Good example lives on. St. Wenceslaus's generosity to the poor was legendary and his goodness known everywhere. The principle that those who help the poor will "themselves be blessed" spread that good example. What kind of a Christian example do we give?

From 'The Catholic One Year Bible': May God give peace to you, my Christian brothers, and love, with faith from God the Father and the Lord Jesus Christ. May God's grace and blessing be upon all who sincerely love our Lord Jesus Christ. — Ephesians 6:23-24

SS. Michael, Gabriel, and Raphael *(SEPTEMBER 29)*

This is the ancient feast of Michaelmas, one of the few feast days with the contracted form of the word Mass in its name (the others are Christmas, Candlemas, and Martinmas). It was an ancient feast dedicated to St. Michael the Archangel, but in recent times it has become the common feast of the three archangels mentioned in the Scriptures: SS. Michael, Gabriel, and Raphael.

St. Michael was long venerated in the West as the head of the heavenly armies and patron saint of soldiers. Popular veneration of this heavenly patron began with an apparition of Michael at Gargano in southern Italy in the fifth century, during an invasion by the Goths. His veneration at Mont-St.-Michel in France and at Mount St. Michael in Cornwall, England, is based on a similar apparition. Today's feast has its origin in the dedication of a church at Gargano in Italy.

St. Gabriel, the angel of the Annunciation and in the prophecy of Daniel, was long venerated in the Eastern Church along with SS. Michael and Raphael. He appears uniquely as the herald of the Most High, majestic in appearance, bringing God's message to men. In 1951, Pope Pius XII proclaimed Gabriel the patron of the communication arts, especially television.

St. Raphael appears in only one book of the Bible, the Book of Tobias, or Tobit, and his name means "God has healed." He appears as the envoy of God, sent to answer prayers and bring healing. Because of his role in the Book of Tobias, he is the patron saint of travelers. In his own words, he was "one of the seven angels who are ever ready to enter into the presence of the Lord's glory."

The three archangels are symbols of God's care and providence and His intimate concern for His people. Their representations show them to be figures of power and beauty, aiding in the battle against evil and protecting those who call upon them. Raphael is usually portrayed accompanying travelers, and Gabriel is pictured in the classical paintings of the Annunciation. Sir Jacob Epstein's sculpture, *St. Michael and the Devil,* on the porch of Coventry Cathedral in England, is a superb modern portrayal of the place of Michael in Christian tradition.

Thought for the Day: We are surrounded by wonders, and angels are among the most wondrous. "We believe in one God, . . . maker of all that is seen and unseen," we profess in the Nicene Creed. The angels bring God close to us and help us to realize that we are not alone in the universe.

From 'The Catholic One Year Bible': May you always be doing those good, kind things which show that you are a child of God, for this will bring much praise and glory to the Lord. — Philippians 1:11

St. Jerome

This is a saint of great likes and dislikes. As a young man, he made friendships that lasted a lifetime, but his thunderous invectives against his enemies and critics are also famous, and he is seen to be the most human of saints and one of the most powerful forces for good in the history of the Church.

St. Jerome was born around the year 342 in what is now Yugoslavia, and at the age of twelve he was sent to Rome to study under the famed grammarian Donatus. There he met Rufinus of Aquileia whose friendship he kept until late in life, and Pammachius, a Roman patrician whose friendship he kept to the end.

He traveled with student-friends to Trier and there discovered monasticism and joined a community of would-be monks. In 371, he began his travels, journeying as far as Antioch, and then tried the life of a hermit in the Chalcis region of Syria. Returning to Antioch, he studied under some of its most eminent teachers, was ordained a priest, and went to Constantinople to study under St. Gregory Nazianzus and St. Gregory of Nyssa, and to read Origen, whose scriptural work he greatly admired.

In 382, he traveled to Rome where he became secretary to Pope Damasus and spiritual director to several Roman families. On the death of the pope, in the company of his brother and several monks, he left for the East. He toured the monastic centers of Egypt with St. Paula, a wealthy Roman matron, and finally settled in Bethlehem where he spent the rest of his life.

In Bethlehem, he began a new translation of the Scriptures, using the original Hebrew and Greek, producing the Latin *Vulgate*, the most influential book of the ancient Christian world. Scriptural commentaries and historical studies came forth from his pen, and as the most learned man of his time he took an active part in the theological controversies of his day.

He died in the year 420, an old man, and was buried under the church of the Nativity. His body was later taken to Rome where it rests today in the church of St. Mary Major.

Thought for the Day: "To know the Scriptures is to know Christ," wrote St. Jerome, and he made the Scriptures his life's study. He found there not only occupation for his mind but also wisdom for his life and a pattern of holiness that leads to God. The Scriptures should be our light and our life.

From 'The Catholic One Year Bible': Your attitude should be the kind that was shown us by Jesus Christ, who, though he was God, did not demand and cling to his rights as God, but laid aside his mighty power and glory, taking the disguise of a slave and becoming like men.
— Philippians 2:5-7

THE SAINTS OF OCTOBER

St. Thérèse of Lisieux *(OCTOBER 1)*

One of the most popular saints of modern times, the "star" of the pontificate of Pope Pius XI, the saint whose *Story of a Soul* brought holiness close to millions and whose "Little Way" made her loved all over the world is St. Thérèse of Lisieux (also called Thérèse of the Child Jesus).

But she was no plaster-cast saint, in spite of the efforts of many admirers to make her so. Her holiness was hard won, "at the point of a sword," she said, and her sanctity had a toughness to it that shines through her letters and authentic sayings.

She was the youngest of the children of Louis and Zélie Martin, born at Alençon, France, in 1873, and she followed two sisters and several cousins into the religious life. Two other sisters also became religious. Thérèse was a lively, affectionate child, attached to her two sisters who entered Carmel before her and was the joy of her father after their mother's death.

Determined to enter the Carmel at Lisieux at the early age of fifteen, she even appealed personally to Pope Leo XIII for permission to enter underage, which she eventually did, in 1888, remaining the rest of her life behind its walls. In spite of turmoil within the convent and political factions within the community, she concentrated on her spiritual growth, living a life of heroic regularity and fidelity, completely unnoticed by those around her. When, after her death, her autobiography burst upon the world, the most surprised readers were the members of her own community.

In 1893, she was appointed acting mistress of novices and she showed a mature wisdom and rare discretion far beyond her years. Hers was a fresh and vigorous expression of the essentials of holiness, and her "Little Way," in the words of Pope Benedict XV, "contained the secret of sanctity for the entire world."

Eighteen months before her death, she showed signs of a tubercular condition and during her final illness was often fatigued, racked with pain, and plunged into interior darkness. She died on September 30, 1897, twenty-four years of age. She was beatified in 1923 and canonized in 1925.

Thought for the Day: St. Thérèse's great discovery was that holiness is the normal condition willed by God for every human being, and the cultivation of a personal relationship with God is the essence of sanctity. First, she taught this to herself and then she taught it to the rest of the world.

From 'The Catholic One Year Bible': Whatever happens, dear friends, be glad in the Lord. I never get tired of telling you this and it is good for you to hear it again and again. — **Philippians 3:1**

St. Leodegar of Autun *(OCTOBER 2)*

Leodegar was one of the saints caught in the web of Merovingian politics, after the conversion of the Franks under Clovis. He was born near Arras in 678, descended from a noble Frankish family. He was sent to the court of Chlotar II to be educated, and the king sent him to his uncle, the bishop of Poitiers, who ordained him a deacon. After ordination to the priesthood, he was made abbot of St.- Maixent, which he ruled for six years.

He was recalled to the court by St. Bathildis, the British slave girl who became queen, and in 663 was appointed bishop of Autun. It was a difficult assignment, since the see had been vacant for two years and political factions were everywhere.

With the death of King Chlotar II and the queen's retirement to a convent, the kingdom was thrown into chaos, and St. Leodegar of Autun sided with those who opposed Ebroinus, mayor of the palace. With the exile of Ebroinus, Leodegar was accused of plotting against the new king, Childeric II, and was exiled to Luxeuil. When the king was assassinated, Leodegar returned to his see, but the bitter infighting in the kingdom continued, and Leodegar found his see city besieged and the demand that the bishop be turned over to those now in power.

Leodegar gave himself up to prevent the sack of the city. Accused of having a hand in the assassination of King Childeric, Leodegar was blinded and his tongue cut out. He then was taken before a synod of bishops, his robes of office torn off his back, and was dragged off to the forest of Sarcing where he was beheaded.

When the kingdom was returned to normalcy, another synod of bishops exonerated Leodegar and proclaimed him a martyr. His remains were taken to his abbey of St.-Maixent, and a basilica was built to enshrine his relics. Invoked for diseases of the eye, he is venerated in the dioceses of Autun and Poitiers.

Thought for the Day: St. Leodegar of Autun was a victim of the barbarous politics of the day, when it was difficult to remain neutral in the midst of dynastic murders. In spite of his best efforts, he was drawn into the intrigue and, although a holy man, died the victim of circumstances. It is good to know that even saints sometimes have to face things beyond their control.

From 'The Catholic One Year Bible': Heaven is my throne and the earth is my footstool: What Temple can you build for me as good as that? My hand has made both earth and skies, and they are mine. Yet I will look with pity on the man who has a humble and contrite heart, who trembles at my word. — Isaiah 66:1-2

St. Thomas of Cantelupe *(OCTOBER 3)*

When the Normans conquered England, William the Conqueror divided up the country and gave it to his followers, who became the new nobility and the owners of great estates. The Cantelupes were one of these new noble families. The father of Thomas was a steward in the household of King Henry III and his mother was the dowager countess of Evreux and Gloucester. He was born in 1218, one of five sons and three daughters, and he was sent to study at Oxford when he was nineteen. In 1245, he accompanied his father to the Council of Lyons and was ordained a priest by Pope Innocent IV.

After studying at Orléans and Paris, St. Thomas of Cantelupe returned to England and became chancellor of Oxford. He was at one time chancellor of England. In 1275, he was chosen bishop of Hereford, a much neglected diocese, and took over his duties with a firm hand. He excommunicated nobles who tried to interfere with his spiritual administration. He loved children and the poor and was known to be a deeply spiritual man and a devoted shepherd of souls.

In a battle with the archbishop of Canterbury over jurisdiction, he found himself excommunicated and went to Rome to plead his case before the pope. Received very kindly by Pope Martin IV at Orvieto, he withdrew to a nearby village to await the pontiff's decision.

But the long journey from England had been too much for him, and he died on August 25, 1282. He was buried at Orvieto, but later his relics were returned to Hereford and interred in the Lady-Chapel of the cathedral. His shrine was the site of pilgrimages from all over England, and miracles of healing were reported. He was canonized in 1320, the last Englishman to be canonized in the Middle Ages.

Thought for the Day: St. Thomas of Cantelupe was simply a hardworking bishop who had to fight injustice and greed from destroying the cause of religion. He found that it was his example and his efforts that made a difference and, as bishop, he was often the only advocate for the poor and the victims of injustice. We all have to stand up for what we believe.

From 'The Catholic One Year Bible': Always be full of joy in the Lord; I say it again, rejoice! Let everyone see that you are unselfish and considerate in all you do. Remember that the Lord is coming soon. — Philippians 4:4-5

Francis Bernadone, the gifted young man who dreamed of knighthood and nobility, tasted the bitter disillusionment of war in all its ugly reality. Sick at heart, he sensed that there was something greater to aim for and found it in the knighthood of the spirit and the service of Christ the King.

He was born and baptized Giovanni Bernadone, but his father called him by the nickname Francesco, the "little Frenchman." His parents' pride and joy, he went off to war and came back sick in body and spirit, his whole world having crumbled around him. During his weeks of recuperation, St. Francis of Assisi discovered his soul and his God, threw caution to the winds, and took up the life of a beggar, choosing to be a fool for Christ.

Francis became the talk of the town of Assisi after his change of heart, and the young men of the city gathered around him as they had when he was the troubador of the town. He organized them into the "poor men of Assisi," a strange religious brotherhood quite unlike any religious life at the time. As the numbers of his group grew, Francis rebuilt ruined churches around Assisi and went to Rome to receive approval for his "friars minor" from Pope Innocent III. The Portiuncula chapel near Assisi became the cradle of his order and it was there that he invested St. Clare with the Franciscan habit and founded the Poor Clares.

Dreaming of martyrdom, he embarked on a ship for the East to convert the sultan of Egypt, but the sultan let him go with a smile, recognizing the obvious holiness of the little man from Assisi. Returning to Italy, he presided at the Chapter of Mats in 1221, his order now three thousand in number.

On Mount Alvernia in 1224, he received the stigmata — the wounds of Christ — in his body. During his last two years, he was blind and seriously ill and he died at the Portiuncula on October 3, 1226. He was canonized two years after his death, and a great basilica was built for him at Assisi to enshrine his remains. His body was solemnly interred in the crypt of the basilica in 1230 where it has remained ever since.

Thought for the Day: "You are a fountain of life to Your creatures," St. Francis of Assisi sang in his "Canticle of Brother Sun." Everything is a gift of God, and this realization made a saint out of Francesco Bernadone. We need only look around us to see the goodness of God.

From 'The Catholic One Year Bible': Christ is the exact likeness of the unseen God. He existed before God made anything at all, and, in fact, Christ himself is the Creator who made everything in heaven and earth, the things we can see and the things we can't; . . . He was before all else began. . . . — **Colossians 1:15-17**

Blessed Raymond of Capua

Raymond of Capua was the confessor and spiritual director of St. Catherine of Siena and was assigned the task by the Dominican general chapter when Catherine's notoriety was beginning to reflect upon the Dominican Order, of which she was a tertiary.

He was of the distinguished Della Vigne family of Capua, entered the Dominicans when he was a student at Bologna, and served as prior of the Dominican house in Rome, as lector in Florence, and then as regent of studies at Siena, where he met Catherine of Siena. He was appointed her spiritual director in 1374.

Their first task together was to help victims of the Black Plague, which struck Italy, and they worked together also to reconcile the city of Florence and the Tuscan League with the pope. He collaborated with her also in bringing about the pontiff's return from Avignon to Rome. When the returning pope, Gregory XI, died, he was succeeded by Urban VI. Urban was a difficult man, and after they left Rome the cardinals elected an antipope; this was the beginning of the Great Western Schism, with two and then three claimants to the papal throne.

Pope Urban sent Blessed Raymond of Capua on a mission to France to preach against the antipope, but his mission failed when he was refused admittance to France, his life threatened by soldiers of Clement. He returned to Pisa, hoping for another chance. In April 1380, Catherine died in Rome, and Raymond took over the direction of her small group of followers, at the same time working strenuously to end the schism.

About the time of Catherine's death, Raymond was elected master-general of the Dominicans and led a reform movement within the order to restore primitive observance. He also began to write his life of Catherine of Siena. While on a visitation to Nuremberg, Germany, in 1399, he died and was buried at St. Dominic's in Naples. He is known best for his association with Catherine of Siena who found in him the light and support that she needed in carrying out her mission to the Church.

Thought for the Day: Spiritual direction is a very difficult art but a badly needed one. To guide other people to God presupposes sound judgment and a sensitivity to the ways of God in others. We all need spiritual advice sometimes, and it is good to know that there are gifted priests and spiritual directors to whom we can turn.

From 'The Catholic One Year Bible': Let your roots grow down into him [Christ] and draw up nourishment from him. See that you go on growing in the Lord, and become strong and vigorous in the truth you were taught. Let your lives overflow with joy and thanksgiving for all he has done. — Colossians 2:7

St. Bruno

(OCTOBER 6)

Bruno is the founder of the Carthusians, one of the great teachers of the age, and one-time chancellor of the archdiocese of Rheims.

He was born in Cologne and received the best education the age had to offer, finishing his studies at the cathedral school at Rheims. When he was twenty-seven years old, he was invited to head the school of grammar and theology at Rheims, and many of the most noted scholars in Europe studied under him, including the future Pope Urban II.

In 1075, St. Bruno was appointed chancellor of the diocese and became involved in the ecclesiastical politics of Rheims. At that time Rheims had as archbishop the simoniacal Manasses, who drove Bruno from the city, confiscating his property. Through Bruno's efforts, Manasses was finally deposed and when Bruno was offered the archbishopric, he refused. He had had enough of politics and had been seeking the advice of St. Robert of Molesmes, one of the holiest men of the time and future founder of the Cistercians.

Like Robert, Bruno determined to seek God in solitude, setting up the first Carthusian monastery in the mountains of Grenoble. The order received its name from the name of this isolated mountain, La Grande Chartreuse.

But he did not remain long in his solitude. In 1089, his former pupil was elected pope as Urban II and the Holy Father called him to Rome as his adviser. When the pontiff had to flee Rome, which was a stronghold of the antipope, Bruno went with him, seeking the protection of the Normans in southern Italy, who were loyal to Urban. Here the king, Roger of Sicily, gave him a fertile piece of land in the wilds of Calabria, and Bruno received the pope's permission to return to solitude.

In September of 1101, Bruno became sick and died on October 6. He was buried in the hermitage cemetery of his monastery of Santa Maria La Torre and his body was later transferred to the church of San Stefano.

Thought for the Day: We are all so busy! St. Bruno realized that "only one thing is necessary," and that to obtain that pearl of great price he had to flee everything else, however important. Something of that spirit has to be part of all of us.

From 'The Catholic One Year Bible': . . . In Christ there is all of God in a human body; *so you have everything when you have Christ,* and you are filled with God through your union with Christ. He is the highest Ruler, with authority over every other power. — Colossians 2:9-10

Our Lady of the Rosary *(OCTOBER 7)*

In 1571, Christian Europe was threatened by an invasion of the Turks as it had been several times in its history. Turkey was the dominant power of the Mediterranean Sea, and Turkish vessels had been making raids on Italy ever since the fall of Rhodes in 1522.

In 1570, the Turks demanded the surrender of Cyprus; so, to resist the Turkish advances, the Christian armies of Europe were organized under Don John of Austria. Two hundred six ships were organized from Venice, Naples, Genoa, Spain, Malta, and the Papal States. They met a Turkish force of two hundred thirty ships at the Bay of Lepanto, off the western shore of Greece.

In Rome, Pope Pius V, realizing the critical importance of the battle for Christian Europe, prayed the Rosary to Our Lady of Victory. At the same time the pontiff was praying, vigils of prayer and processions were made in the churches of Rome, pleading for a victory. The Rosary became the Christian weapon in the battle, and thousands joined the pope in saying the beads asking for Mary's intercession.

It was a hard-fought battle, the Christian forces fighting against tremendous odds. Nine thousand Christian soldiers were killed in the battle and dozens of ships were lost, but the Christian forces won the battle and twelve thousand Christians were released from slavery to the Turks.

The Holy Father ordered that every year there should be celebrated a feast in honor of Our Lady of Victory, to commemorate the victory. Later, Pope Gregory XIII changed the name of the feast to Our Lady of the Rosary and ordered it to be celebrated on the date of the victory itself, the first Sunday of October. Recently, the date was fixed for October 7.

Thought for the Day: The Rosary is the ancient prayer to our Lady that has become the most popular prayer of the Catholic. It is called *Mary's Psalter* and is one of the easiest forms of prayer. With its fifteen mysteries, it is also a complete course on the life of Christ and the events of Mary's life. Millions pray the Rosary every day.

From 'The Catholic One Year Bible': Let the peace of heart which comes from Christ be always present in your hearts and lives, for this is your responsibility and privilege as members of his body. — Colossians 3:15.

St. Louis Bertrand *(OCTOBER 8)*

Louis Bertrand was born in Valencia, Spain, in 1526 and was a distant relative of St. Vincent Ferrer. He entered the Dominicans when he was eighteen and was ordained by St. Thomas of Villanova when he was twenty-one.

At first, St. Louis Bertrand was not distinguished for his preaching, but he worked at it and soon became one of the most outstanding preachers in Spain. During a pestilence in 1557, he worked heroically among the sick and helped to bury the dead.

In 1562, he went to the New World and landed at Cartegena, Colombia, where he did missionary work. He was active in what is now Panama and the nearby islands and once was almost poisoned by the Carib Indians. He was shocked by the savagery and greed of the Spanish colonists but felt powerless to do anything about it. After a mission of six years, he was recalled to Spain.

After serving as prior at San Onofre, he was elected master-general of the Dominicans and then returned to Valencia where he trained other preachers and directed novices. His own preaching was accompanied by miracles, and he is reported to have had the gift of tongues. His life was noted for its austerity and penitence, and he seemed to have the power to touch even the most hardened sinners.

In 1579, he was struck with a painful illness but continued his work of preaching. In 1580, after preaching in the cathedral of Valencia, he collapsed in the pulpit and had to be carried to his monastery where he remained bedridden until his death. He died on October 9, 1581, at the age of fifty-five.

Louis Bertrand was canonized by Pope Clement X in 1671 and is the patron saint of Colombia.

Thought for the Day: The power of a good preacher! We all know the power of words and the value of good preaching. What would we do without the words of preachers to lure us back to God and open our minds to the riches of our faith? The mission of preachers is one of the most important in the Church, and good preachers are a treasure.

From 'Thc Catholic One Year Bible': Make the most of your chances to tell others the Good News. Be wise in all your contacts with them. Let your conversation be gracious as well as sensible, for then you will have the right answer for everyone. — Colossians 4:5-6

St. John Leonardi *(OCTOBER 9)*

Giovanni Leonardi was an assistant to a pharmacist and besides his holiness and other achievements is known also for being given the care of St. Philip Neri's cat. The cat was famous in Rome and went with a house in Rome that Philip had given to the order founded by St. John Leonardi.

John became a priest in the troubled times of the Counter-Reformation, when religious reform was in the air and the Jesuits were beginning to reevangelize Europe. As a young priest, he worked in hospitals and prisons and gathered a group of young men around him to join in the work. Their headquarters was the church of Santa Maria della Rosa in Lucca.

He formed his followers into a religious congregation, which was approved by Pope Gregory XIII in 1580 and became a powerful force for good in the whole of Italy. John wrote one of the very early catechisms for the instruction of children, and it was still in use right up into the last century. The state of religion in Italy at the time was desperate, with thousands never hearing a preacher and thousands of others completely neglecting the practice of their faith.

John's priests spread out over Italy, founding houses throughout the Papal States. He also began four other religious congregations and was commissioned by the pope to reform several others. He early conceived the idea of a seminary for the foreign missions that eventually became the College de Propaganda Fide under Pope Urban VIII.

In the year 1609, an influenza epidemic swept through Italy and John Leonardi worked tirelessly among those stricken with the disease, nursing especially his own religious brothers. In October of that year he caught the illness himself and died on October 9. He was beatified in 1861 and canonized in 1938. His relics are enshrined in the church of Santa Maria Campitelli in Rome.

Thought for the Day: Care of the sick has always been close to the heart of the saints. They see in the sick and the suffering an image of the suffering Jesus and realize also the redemptive power of suffering. Compassion is a native Christian virtue and the sick are important members of the Mystical Body of Christ.

From 'The Catholic One Year Bible': . . . We speak as messengers from God, trusted by him to tell the truth; we change his message not one bit to suit the taste of those who hear it; for we serve God alone, who examines our hearts' deepest thoughts. —1 Thessalonians 2:4

St. Francis Borgia *(OCTOBER 10)*

He was the duke of Gandia, grandee of sixteenth-century Spain, a cousin to Emperor Charles V, loving husband, and the father of eight sons. In 1539, he was named viceroy of Catalonia and in 1542 succeeded his father as duke of Gandia.

Born in 1510, St. Francis Borgia might have lived an uneventful life, filled with the duties of state, if he had not met the newly founded Jesuits in Barcelona and determined to build them a college in Gandia. This started his mind working in a new direction, and on the death of his wife in 1546 he wrote to St. Ignatius about entering the Society of Jesus. Allowed to take vows secretly as a Jesuit in order to administer his estate and provide for his children, he studied theology at his own university, receiving his doctorate in 1550.

After receiving his doctorate, he made a pilgrimage to Rome and there arranged with Ignatius for his formal entrance into the Jesuits. Ordained a priest in 1551 in Spain, he began his work as a Jesuit in Ignatius' own home province of Guipuzcoa. He became commissary general of the Jesuits in Spain and in 1565, with the Jesuits growing rapidly, was appointed assistant general of the order for Spain and Portugal. On the death of Ignatius' successor, Diego Lainez, Francis was elected general of the Jesuits. It is in this office that he was most notable and is considered by some the second founder of the order.

His term of office saw new activities and expansion of the Society of Jesus, with Francis starting new missions in the Americas, consolidating the work in the Far East where St. Francis Xavier had labored and furthered the training of priests at the German college for assignments in the countries ravaged by the Reformation. He established new colleges throughout Europe and directed the work of the Roman college which later became the Gregorian university.

In 1571, he was sent by the pope on a mission to Spain and attracted crowds everywhere wanting to get a glimpse of the "Duke become a Jesuit." Worn out by fatigue, he returned to Rome in 1572 by way of Ferrara where his cousin Duke Alfonso sent him on a litter to Rome. He died two days after his arrival, sending word to his children and grandchildren before he died. He was canonized in 1671.

Thought for the Day: Francis Borgia was not born a saint and he had to fight all the temptations of wealth, position, and honors to work at it. He gave his huge talents and his huge heart to God and so among all those with the name of Borgia, only his has *Saint* before his name.

From 'The Catholic One Year Bible': . . . Night and day we pray on and on for you, asking God to let us see you again, to fill up any little cracks there may be yet in your faith. —1 Thessalonians 3:10

James of Ulm was born on October 11, 1407, and died as a very old Dominican lay brother on his birthday in 1491. He was born in Ulm, and his family were the Griesingers, still well known in that part of Germany. When he was twenty-five, he left home to become a soldier in Italy, but camp life so shocked him by its roughness and immorality that he took a job as secretary to a lawyer in Capua.

He was so loyal and so efficient in his work that when he wanted to return home, his employer would not let him leave. He slipped away secretly, joined the army again in Bologna, and became a friend of the Dominicans there. When he asked to join the Dominicans as a lay brother, he was accepted and he spent the next fifty years as a Dominican.

It was in the Dominicans that the artistic talent of Blessed James of Ulm blossomed. The Dominicans had a long tradition of nourishing artists and employed artists for the decoration of their own churches and convents. James became a master of painting on glass, influencing the development of art in the fifteenth century and teaching a number of remarkable pupils whose work still endures. Notable among these pupils were Fra Anastasio of Como and Fra Ambrogino of Soncino. James has a prominent place in the history of Christian art, and it is felt that he must have developed the talent before he entered the Dominicans, perhaps training as an apprentice to an artist during his early years.

He was noted also as ready to obey at the slightest suggestion; on one occasion he prepared to take off for Paris on a moment's notice at the direction of a superior. He asked only that he be allowed to go and get his hat and walking stick.

After his death in 1491, he became the patron saint of glass painters and glaziers. He was beatified by Pope Leo XII in 1825.

Thought for the Day: Beauty is one of the names of God, and art — in the words of Dante — is, as it were, God's grandchild. The masterworks of religious art are mighty hymns to the glory of God and communicate something of His wonder and beauty. Christian artists like Fra Angelico and Blessed James preach by their artistic creations.

From 'The Catholic One Year Bible': . . . Blessed is the man who trusts in the Lord and has made the Lord his hope and confidence. He is like a tree planted along a riverbank, with its roots reaching deep into the water. . . . Its leaves stay green and it goes on producing its luscious fruit. — Jeremiah 17:7-8

St. Wilfrid of York

Wilfrid of York was the fiery bishop of the seventh century whose troubles and tribulations never seemed to end. He was born in Northumbria, around 635, and as a young man went to the court of King Oswy at Bamburgh where he became a favorite of the queen. He was trained at Lindisfarne under St. Aidan, but at the age of sixteen, helped by the queen, went to Rome to be educated and to become familiar with European traditions.

He arrived back in England in 658, was given land for a monastery by King Oswy's son, Alchfrid, who ruled part of Northumbria under his father, and at the Synod of Whitby in 664 urged the adoption of Roman customs throughout England and influenced King Oswy in deciding in favor of Rome.

Nominated bishop of York, he went to France to be consecrated and returned to find his see given to another. He retired to his monastery at Ripon, near York, and made his monastery the architectural marvel of England. Restored to his see by Theodore, archbishop of Canterbury, he governed as sole bishop of Northumbria until the division of dioceses in 678, when he contested the division and was driven from his see by the king.

The rest of his life was spent evangelizing England, building his monasteries at Ripon and Hexham, and going back to Rome trying to recover his see. St. Wilfrid of York did recover his see for a short time in 685 but lost it again and spent the rest of his life as abbot of Ripon.

His life, written by Eddius Stephanus, is the first biography of an English saint and is a colorful document of English ecclesiastical life in that period. His monasteries at Ripon and Hexham were remarkable for their architecture and innovative designs, attesting to Wilfrid's influence on the development of architecture in England. He introduced the rule of St. Benedict and Gregorian chant to England and was one of the most learned men of his time.

He died on a visitation to one of his monasteries in 709 and was buried in his monastic church at Ripon.

Thought for the Day: St. Wilfrid of York had all of the problems of a pioneer. He was the forerunner of Roman traditions in England and had a great love of ritual and pageantry, quite contrary to the spirit of his times. He was willing to fight for his convictions and had to suffer exile and imprisonment many times. Anything not worth suffering for is not worth having.

From 'The Catholic One Year Bible': That day of the Lord will come unexpectedly like a thief in the night. . . . So be on your guard, not asleep like the others. Watch for his return and stay sober. — 1 Thessalonians 5:2, 6

In Westminster Abbey, set as a gem in this historic shrine, is the tomb of St. Edward the Confessor, once the wonder of England. It is a monument to the great king, the founder and builder of the abbey and one of England's greatest monarchs.

He came as king after a line of Danish monarchs, Harold Harefoot and Hathacanute, and the English people were glad to have an English king at last. He became one of the most beloved kings in English history, and his shrine at Westminster Abbey is evidence of this.

He was the son of King Ethelred II and was reared at Ely Abbey until the Danish invasions sent him into exile in Normandy. He was elected king in 1042. Surrounded by a divided people and hostile nobility, he kept his position by a combination of gentleness and caution.

He had made a vow to make a pilgrimage to the tomb of St. Peter if he obtained his throne and, since the journey became impossible after his accession, he built and endowed an abbey close to London at Thorney, which came to be called the "west minster" to distinguish it from St. Paul's in the east of London.

He married Edith, daughter of Earl Godwin, but he left no heir. He was criticized for his close links with the Normans, and he did make a promise of his throne to William, duke of Normandy.

On the Feast of Holy Innocents, 1065, the new choir at Westminster Abbey was consecrated, with most of the nobles of England attending. The king was too ill to be present and he died a week later. There was great mourning at his death, since he was deeply loved and revered by his people. It was also suspected that there would be a battle for the succession, further dividing the country. That expected battle was the battle of Hastings, which changed the course of English history forever. St. Edward was buried at his new abbey and canonized in 1161.

Thought for the Day: St. Edward the Confessor, even though a king, was noted for his gentleness, a quality not usually associated with kings. Gentleness has to do with the way we treat others and is based on an innate respect for their persons. Since they deeply reverenced God, the saints deeply reverenced the image of God closest to them: other human beings.

From 'The Catholic One Year Bible': Timely advice is as lovely as gold apples in a silver basket. It is a badge of honor to accept valid criticism. A faithful employee is as refreshing as a cool day in the hot summertime. One who doesn't give the gift he promised is like a cloud blowing over a desert without dropping any rain. — Proverbs 25:11-14

Callistus I was an early pope who governed the Church from 217 to 222. He was a Roman by birth and was a slave of the imperial household, owned by a Christian named Carpophorus. He was put in charge of a bank by his master and lost the money deposited by other Christians. He fled from Rome, was captured, and sentenced to the mines of Sardinia. He was later released and lived at Anzio.

Under Pope Zephyrinus, St. Callistus I — now a freeman — was made a deacon and put in charge of the cemetery (which would later be named after him) on the Appian Way, where many of the early pontiffs were buried. He was a close friend and confidante of the pope's, and when Zephyrinus died in 217, Callistus was elected to the chair of Peter.

The followers of St. Hippolytus, however, objected to the election and elected Hippolytus, claiming that Pope Callistus was too lax in enforcing Church discipline. This schism in the Church at Rome would last until after Callistus's death and be resolved only in 235.

Callistus is credited with stabilizing the Saturday fast and originating the observation of the Ember Days. He also taught that the Church had the power to absolve from all sins and should adopt a policy of mercy toward those who fell away from the faith in time of persecution. His enemies accused him of laxism and this further divided the Church in Rome.

Callistus was killed in a popular uprising in Rome and was buried on the Aurelian Way. In 1960, his tomb in the cemetery of Calepodius on the Appian Way was discovered in the remains of an oratory erected there by Pope Julius I in the fourth century. The crypt is decorated with paintings portraying his martyrdom. He lived in a time when critical decisions had to be made in the Church and he made several decisions that have been part of Church discipline and teaching ever since.

Thought for the Day: For his "quality of mercy," St. Callistus I was accused of laxism by the rigorists of his day. In this he imitated the gentleness of Christ Himself. To be harsh and demanding of others is completely contrary to a Christian ethic, and we should watch our own behavior that it conforms to that of Christ.

From 'The Catholic One Year Bible': May our Lord Jesus Christ himself and God our Father, who has loved us and given us everlasting comfort and hope which we don't deserve, comfort your hearts with all comfort, and help you in every good thing you say and do. — 2 Thessalonians 2:16

St. Teresa of Ávila *(OCTOBER 15)*

When Teresa of Ávila was a little girl, she ran away from home with her brother, hoping to be martyred by the Muslims in North Africa. They were found by an uncle before the day was through and carried back to their home. This childish act was typical of the woman who became St. Teresa of Ávila, and she has delighted the Church ever since with her wit, her spiritual doctrine, and her amazing adventures as a foundress of convents.

She was born in Ávila, Spain, in 1515, and lost her mother at the age of fifteen. When she was twenty years old, she entered the Carmelite monastery of the Incarnation in Ávila, where she became the center of a wide circle of friends whom she charmed by her winsome ways and delightful sense of humor.

She was forty years old before she began in earnest the task of pleasing God and was the recipient of communications from God that make her the classic Christian mystic. She was able to put her experiences into writing, and these writings have become spiritual classics and the basis for her being named a Doctor of the Church.

Teresa began her reform of the Carmelites in 1560, with the advice of St. Peter of Alcantara and the Jesuits, and her first reformed convent was established in 1562. She was given permission by the Carmelite general to establish reformed convents as well as a reformed branch of men, for which she recruited St. John of the Cross. Her work brought her many opponents and critics, and she once complained that her life was like a "night in a bad inn."

In 1580, Teresa was sixty-five years old and broken in health; she had only two more years to live. She made her last foundation at Burgos in July of 1582 and en route to Ávila stopped off at Alba de Tormes where she died on October 5. The next day, the Gregorian calendar came into force dropping ten days from the calendar, and so the date of her death became October 15. She was buried at Alba de Tormes, canonized in 1622, and declared a Doctor of the Church by Pope Paul VI in 1970.

Thought for the Day: "God save us from sad-faced saints," is one of St. Teresa's characteristic sayings. She hated gloom and radiated around herself cheerfulness and good spirits. In spite of her sufferings and problems, she kept her sense of humor, and her writings are filled with lightheartedness and profound insights into human nature.

From 'The Catholic One Year Bible': . . . We trust the Lord that you are putting into practice the things we taught you, and that you always will. May the Lord bring you to an ever deeper understanding of the love of God and of the patience that comes from Christ. —2 Thessalonians 3:4-5

St. Margaret Mary Alacoque *(OCTOBER 16)*

Margaret Mary Alacoque is the saint of the Sacred Heart, and it is from the revelations given to her that the modern devotion to the Sacred Heart has arisen. She was a contemplative nun of the Order of Visitation at Paray-le-Monial in France, and it was here that the revelations took place between 1673 and 1675.

She was the fifth of seven children, and her father was Claude Alacoque, a royal notary. She was educated in the home of her grandmother. Her early life was spent at home, mistreated by her relatives and suffering from rheumatism. When she was twenty-four years old, she entered the Visitation convent at Paray-le-Monial and spent the remainder of her life there.

The revelations given to her asked her to spread devotion to the Sacred Heart of Jesus as the symbol of His love culminating in the great revelation on the Feast of Corpus Christi in 1675 when He told her, showing her His Sacred Heart: "Behold the heart which has so loved men that it has spared nothing, even exhausting and consuming itself in testimony of its love."

The revelations brought her nothing but suffering and humiliation and made her the object of ridicule and hostility, and it was not until a Jesuit, Blessed Claude de la Colombière, was assigned as her confessor that St. Margaret Mary Alacoque found an understanding mind. He became convinced of the genuineness of her experiences and gave her every assurance of their authenticity. The hostility within her community continued, however, until she was appointed mistress of novices and began to spread devotion to the Sacred Heart.

She became sick in 1690 and a week later asked for the Last Sacraments. She died on October 17 of that year and was canonized by Pope Benedict XV in 1920. In 1765, a liturgical celebration honoring the Sacred Heart was approved and in 1856 this celebration became a feast day of the Church.

Thought for the Day: The love of God is the power behind creation and the backbone of the universe. Devotion to the Sacred Heart is devotion to the love of God embodied in the human heart of Jesus Christ and therefore the living symbol of His love. It is God's way of saying, "I love you," and a constant reminder of that love.

From 'The Catholic One Year Bible': Glory and honor to God forever and ever. He is the King of the ages, the unseen one who never dies; he alone is God, and full of wisdom. — **1 Timothy 1:17**

Ignatius of Antioch was the magnificent man of the early Church, the fiery lover of Christ who "wished to be ground by the teeth of wild beasts that I may become the pure bread of Christ." His example has lived through the centuries and made him one of the most beloved of saints.

We know him chiefly through the letters that he wrote to the Christian churches while on his way to Rome to be martyred. He was bishop of Antioch, condemned to death during the reign of the Emperor Trajan. He was a Syrian, a convert from paganism and the third bishop of Antioch.

En route to Rome, he wrote his letters and was visited by his fellow Christians in the ports along the way. He began his journey in chains, and his one fear was that his fellow Christians would bring about his release and he would be denied the glory of martyrdom. In his letters, St. Ignatius of Antioch encourages his fellow Christians in their faith, gives them warnings about the dangers of the times, and speaks of himself and his coming martyrdom.

His journey took him from Antioch to Smyrna to Troas, then through Macedonia and Illyria to Rome. His guards were eager to get to Rome for the games, for which he would be a prize attraction. St. Polycarp, himself a future martyr, visited him in Smyrna, and Polycarp attests to Ignatius' martyrdom in his Epistle to the Philippians. When he approached Rome, Roman Christians went out to meet him and wanted to work for his release. This he begged them not to do, and he was taken to the Flavian amphitheater and during the gladiatorial games was killed by two lions.

His letters were treasured in the early Church and give us many details about Christian teaching and organization at this point in history. Ignatius himself lives in his letters, and it is this deep personal note that makes them so attractive. His words "I am God's wheat and I am to be ground by the teeth of wild beasts that I may be found the pure bread of Christ" show something of his spirit, which had found its fulfillment in Christ and its home in His promise of eternal life.

Thought for the Day: St. Ignatius of Antioch was one of the first Christian heroes and became the model of martyrs. We all need heroes, especially the young, and without them life soon becomes dull and commonplace. God gives us our heroes in the saints and martyrs, and we should keep them before our eyes constantly.

From 'The Catholic One Year Bible': Pray . . . for kings and all others who are in authority over us, or are in places of high responsibility, so that we can live in peace and quietness, spending our time in godly living and thinking much about the Lord. — 1 Timothy 2:2

Luke is called by St. Paul "our dear and glorious physician," and in the Epistle to Philemon he describes him as his "fellow worker." He was a close associate of Paul's in his missionary journeys and was the aged Apostle's only companion shortly before his death.

It seems certain that St. Luke was not a Jew but a Greek who encountered Paul on his second missionary journey and accompanied him until the end of his life. Tradition attributes the third Gospel and the Acts of the Apostles to Luke and are considered two parts of a history of Christian beginnings.

From the "we" sections of the Acts of the Apostles, it is concluded that Luke met Paul at Troas, rejoined him at Philippi sometime later, accompanied him to Jerusalem, and stayed with him during his imprisonment in Caesarea and Rome. "Luke alone is with me," Paul says in his Second Epistle to Timothy. Deserted by all, his "dear and glorious physician" stayed with him to the end.

We have few certain facts about Luke's life. Early legends say he was a painter, and an early icon of our Lady was attributed to him. That he was well educated and literate is clear from his two writings and, according to St. Jerome, of all the Evangelists, "Luke was the most learned in the Greek language." Another tradition says that he was unmarried, worked chiefly in Greece, and died at the age of eighty-four in Boeotia. Around 360, Emperor Constantius I ordered Luke's relics brought from Boeotia to Constantinople.

In Christian iconography, Luke is portrayed as a man, a writer, or an ox. It is in Luke's Gospel that we have the account of the Annunciation as well as the *Magnificat* and the Presentation of Jesus in the Temple. In writing his Gospel, it was Luke's intention to relate "all that Jesus began to do and teach" so that others could understand the foundations of their faith and be led to a living faith in Jesus Christ.

Thought for the Day: Our faith is built upon facts and deals with real people and real events, and the more knowledge we have of these people and events, the more solid our faith. The Gospels are written for our instruction and should be pondered and read often. It is from a knowledge of Jesus Christ that our faith grows.

From 'The Catholic One Year Bible': I will make an everlasting covenant with them, promising never again to desert them, but only to do them good. I will put a desire into their hearts to worship me, and they shall never leave me. — Jeremiah 32:40

The deaths of the North American martyrs were among the most barbaric in the history of martyrdom, and their heroic deaths were the seed of Christians in the New World. Six were Jesuit priests and two were lay volunteers. St. Isaac Jogues and St. John de Brébeuf are the best known of the priests; René Goupil was the best known of the volunteers. The other priests were Antoine Daniel, Gabriel Lalemant, Charles Garnier, and Noel Chabanel. The second volunteer was John Lalande.

The first group — Goupil, Jogues, and Lalande — were killed at Auriesville in New York state by Mohawk and Iroquois Indians. St. René Goupil was martyred when the flotilla he was traveling on was captured by the Iroquois. He underwent barbaric torture and then was tomahawked to death. St. Isaac Jogues, after being captured and brutally tortured, escaped, then returned three years later on a peace mission. He and St. John Lalande were put to death by a Mohawk war party that captured them.

St. Antoine Daniel was killed when his mission at Huronia was attacked by the Iroquois. Riddled with arrows, his body was thrown into the burning chapel of the mission.

St. John de Brébeuf and St. Gabriel Lalemant were martyred at the town of St. Ignace when the Iroquois attacked and captured them. They were tied to stakes and brutally tortured, their bodies literally torn apart while they were still alive.

St. Charles Garnier was killed when the Iroquois attacked the mission of St. Jean. He was struck with two bullets, then axed to death. He could have fled but instead remained at his post as the Indians swarmed through the mission.

St. Noel Chabanel was killed by an apostate Indian who blamed his newfound faith for his misfortunes. His murderer admitted that he had killed Father Chabanel out of hatred for the Catholic faith.

The Jesuit Martyrs of North America were beatified in 1925 after their stories were unearthed from nearly three centuries of obscurity, and they were canonized by Pope Pius XI in 1930.

Thought for the Day: Their faith in Jesus Christ meant so much to these Jesuit martyrs that they were willing to risk every hardship and even death to bring the Gospel to savage tribes of Indians. They undertook the hardships and gladly took the risk. They will live in the annals of faith until the end of time.

From 'The Catholic One Year Bible': . . . Exercise yourself spiritually and practice being a better Christian, because that will help you not only now in this life, but in the next life too. — 1 Timothy 4:8

Bertilla Boscardin is a relatively recent saint (she died in 1922) and is remembered as something of a Florence Nightingale at the hospital in Treviso, Italy, where she worked and died. She was canonized only thirty-nine years after her death and there are people still alive who remember her.

Annetta Boscardin was born of a poor peasant family in 1888 near Verona, Italy, and as a child suffered much from her father's heavy drinking. Everyone called her "the goose," for she was considered not very bright, even by her parish priest. When she was sixteen, she was accepted by the Sisters of St. Dorothy at Vicenza and put to work in the scullery, the bakehouse, and the laundry.

She was sent to be trained as a nurse at Treviso, and there is where "the goose" began to shine. In 1907, she was assigned to the children's ward of the hospital, and her devotion to the sick soon became the talk of the town.

In 1915, during World War I, the Treviso hospital was taken over by the Italian army, and in 1917 the hospital was on the front line of attack. St. Bertilla Boscardin worked heroically among the frightened patients and was evacuated with them to a military hospital near Como.

Her untiring service made her admired and loved by the soldiers, and so a jealous superior banished Bertilla to the laundry. The mother-general of the congregation, hearing of this, recalled her to Treviso and after the war put her in charge of the children's ward at Treviso.

Her health had never been good, and in 1921 she had to undergo an operation. She never recovered and on October 20, 1922, she died. She was considered an angel of mercy by the people of Treviso, and crowds flocked to her tomb. A plaque in the hospital described her as "a soul of heroic goodness," and miracles of healing were attributed to her intercession. She was beatified in 1952 and canonized in 1961.

Thought for the Day: Some people find their mission in service to others, and their every gift or talent seems destined for doing good to others. St. Bertilla Boscardin was an obscure nursing sister in a large hospital, but there was something special about the way she touched the lives of others. That special ingredient is called sanctity and it is something that everyone recognizes.

From 'The Catholic One Year Bible': In a vision you spoke to our prophet and said, "I have chosen a splendid young man from the common people to be king — he is my servant David! I have anointed him with my holy oil. I will steady him and make him strong. — Psalm 89:19-21

Hilarion, the first Palestinian monk, passed on the tradition of St. Anthony, which he had learned directly from that patriarch of monks, when Hilarion was a boy of fifteen. He was born in the Gaza strip, at Tabatha, and was sent to study at Alexandria, where he was baptized. The dominant figure in his new faith at the time was the Coptic Anthony, and Hilarion went into the desert to meet him. He stayed with him for two months, then returned to Gaza, where he began to imitate the life of Anthony.

St. Hilarion lived in the greatest simplicity, loving the joys of solitude and building himself a small hermitage in the wilderness. He grew his own vegetables, and his way of life soon began to be imitated by other monks. He was respected and loved by the Bedouins who inhabited the desert with him, and they revered him as a holy man. He converted many of them and helped them build their churches.

Although he did not found monasteries himself, Hilarion inspired others to do so and soon was revered as the father of Palestinian monks. He was disturbed by this notoriety and suddenly left Palestine for Egypt, where Anthony had recently died. He made a pilgrimage to the places where Anthony had lived.

Because of the crowds that still flocked to him, Hilarion left Egypt for Sicily, where he thought he would be unknown. But his fame followed him and he left for what is now Yugoslavia. But the novelty of his way of life attracted attention, and he took a ship to Cyprus where he finally found the solitude he craved on the most inaccessible part of the island. There, at the age of eighty, he died.

In his last days, Hilarion was visited by St. Epiphanius, bishop of Salamis, who gave information about him to St. Jerome who wrote his life. One of his disciples, Hesychius, carried his body to his home in Gaza and buried it there.

His tradition of monastic life was passed on to St. Euthymius, who in turn influenced the Celtic monasticism of St. Ailbe and St. Kieran of Saigher.

Thought for the Day: St. Hilarion longed for a solitude that continually escaped him, the price of being a pioneer. But he persisted and finally found the solitary life he was looking for. We all have to be alone with God sometimes, and although we may have trouble doing it, it is worth the time and trouble. God seeks after those who seek Him.

From 'The Catholic One Year Bible': Oh, Timothy, you are God's man. . . . Fight on for God. Hold tightly to the eternal life which God has given you, and which you have confessed with such a ringing confession before many witnesses. — **1 Timothy 6:11-12**

Blessed Severinus Boethius *(OCTOBER 22)*

Boethius is considered by some to be a martyr for the faith, but his sainthood is doubted by others. However, he is listed in *Butler's Life of the Saints* as a martyr, and his story is interesting because of his influence on the thought of the later Middle Ages. He is certainly one of the most outstanding Christian thinkers of the early Christian centuries, and his *Consolation of Philosophy* has inspired saints and martyrs through the centuries.

Blessed Severinus Boethius was one of those rare minds that can assimilate knowledge and pass it on in an understandable form. He planned to translate the whole of Plato and Aristotle into Latin to share the Greek wisdom with his contemporaries. He also wrote a treatise on the Trinity that is considered a major work of Western theology.

He was born when Odoacer, the Ostrogoth, had become ruler of Italy, and when Boethius was thirteen, Odoacer was overthrown by Theodoric. He entered public life in the footsteps of his father and in 510 was made consul by Theodoric.

Theodoric began to suspect that certain of his nobles were plotting with the emperor in Constantinople to overthrow his government, and Albinus, an ex-consul and friend of Boethius', was charged with treason. Boethius defended Albinus in court, was himself accused of being part of the plot, and imprisoned. It was in prison that he wrote his best known work, *The Consolation of Philosophy*. He found no defenders, even among his friends, and not even his father-in-law, Symmachus, stood up for his innocence.

Boethius was cruelly tortured and died a violent death. He was buried in the cathedral at Ticinium, and his relics are now in the church of St. Peter at Pavia.

He was honored as a martyr, since Theodoric was Arian, but the most that can be said is that he died unjustly. The reflective manner in which he faced death was an inspiration to others, and his works were one of the important sources of writings throughout the Middle Ages. He died in the year 524.

Thought for the Day: Blessed Severinus Boethius reflected on the fleetingness of life, how fast it passes, and how unstable human existence is. This made him look beyond his death to a more enduring life. That is a profoundly Christian message, and it is obvious from his life and death that he lived it fully.

From 'The Catholic One Year Bible': Hold tightly to the pattern of truth I taught you, especially concerning the faith and love Christ Jesus offers you. Guard well the splendid, God-given ability you received as a gift from the Holy Spirit, who lives within you. — 2 Timothy 1:13-14

St. John Capistrano *(OCTOBER 23)*

This is the saint of the swallows who come back to the mission named after him on the feast of St. Joseph each year. St. John Capistrano was a Franciscan preacher and papal diplomat. He was born in Abruzzi, Italy, studied law at Perugia, and in 1412 became governor of the city. He married the daughter of a prominent citizen. During a war between Perugia and the Malatesta family, he was imprisoned. There he had time to think about his life and decided to become a religious despite the fact that he was married.

How John settled the problem of his marriage is not known, but at the age of thirty he presented himself to the Franciscans at Perugia and in 1420 was ordained to the priesthood. He soon became one of Italy's most popular preachers and also worked hard to end the division in the Franciscans, with the order split into two camps over the issue of poverty.

In 1443, John became vicar general of his branch of the Franciscans, the Observants, and he worked for the canonization of St. Bernardine of Siena, who had been one of his teachers.

His diplomatic missions for the pope, which took him to Austria, Hungary, and Bohemia, began in 1451. He was commissioned by the Holy Father to preach a crusade against the Turks who were threatening Eastern Europe and was credited with an important part in the victory of the Christian forces led by John Hunyadi. His intense labor began to wear him down, and soon after the siege of Belgrade he fell ill from an infection and arrived at Ilok, Hungary, very close to death. His last letter before his death gave instructions for all his personal effects to be returned to Capistrano. He died on October 23, 1456.

The process for John's canonization was begun the year after his death but was opposed by those who thought him unduly severe in his work as inquisitor. He was canonized by Alexander VIII on October 16, 1690, and is honored with the title Apostle of Europe. It was through his efforts that the Turkish advance on Western Europe was halted in the fifteenth century.

Thought for the Day: It took a stay in prison for St. John Capistrano to think about the affairs of his soul, an enforced solitude that made him realize he had to change his life. Most of us do not take the trouble to think about how we stand with God, and so misfortune sometimes is a blessing. "Look to yourself" is a good piece of advice.

From 'The Catholic One Year Bible': Take your share of suffering as a good soldier of Jesus Christ, just as I do, and as Christ's soldier do not let yourself become tied up in worldly affairs, for then you cannot satisfy the one who has enlisted you in his army. — 2 Timothy 2:3-4

St. Anthony Mary Claret *(OCTOBER 24)*

Anthony Mary Claret, the founder of the Claretians, was born in the north of Spain in 1807. The son of a weaver, he worked in textile mills as a weaver and designer, and in his spare time studied Latin and printing. Ordained in 1835 after studying at Vich, he entered the Jesuits in Rome, but his health broke down and he was advised to work at the evangelization of his own country. By 1840, he was one of the most popular preachers in Spain.

After several years of preaching missions and retreats, St. Anthony Mary Claret founded the Missionary Sons of the Immaculate Heart of Mary, popularly known as Claretians, and in 1850 was appointed archbishop of Santiago, Cuba. It was a difficult assignment, as there was widespread immorality, even among the clergy, and he brought about much-needed reforms. He encouraged sound farming methods and credit unions for the poor and did everything to promote Christian family life.

In 1857, he returned to Spain to become confessor to Queen Isabella II and resumed his preaching mission and did much to further popular religious press. He founded societies to publish and spread free Catholic literature, much of it written by himself. While rector of the Escorial, the royal residence, he founded a science laboratory, a museum of natural history, a music school, and a language school. He furthered every area of education that would contribute to the development of a solid Christian culture.

Because of his closeness to the royal family, he was attacked in the press and was forced to leave Spain in the revolution of 1868, when the queen was exiled. He went to Rome and took part in the Vatican Council of 1870 at which he spoke in defense of papal infallibility.

He died at the Cistercian monastery of Fontfroide in France, a tired and sick man, on October 24, 1870. He was canonized by Pope Pius XII in 1950.

Thought for the Day: St. Anthony Mary Claret realized the critical importance of education to further the Christian life, and he saw ignorance at the root of much immoral living. Good books and sound teaching have changed many a life and fashioned many a saint. Books are certainly one of the great gifts of God.

From 'The Catholic One Year Bible': The whole Bible was given to us by inspiration from God and is useful to teach us what is true and to make us realize what is wrong in our lives; it straightens us out and helps us do what is right. — 2 Timothy 3:16

Blessed Thaddeus MacCarthy

Thaddeus MacCarthy was a bishop who never ruled his see, even though he was appointed to two of them. He lived in a time when Ireland was in turmoil, when clans were warring against one another, and when dynastic jealousies disturbed the peace of the Church.

He belonged to the royal clan of the MacCarthys in Munster. His father was the lord of Muskerry and his mother was the daughter of the lord of Kerry. He studied under the Franciscans at Kilcrea and then went abroad for further study. In 1482, he purportedly was appointed bishop of Ross by Pope Sixtus IV, but politics intervened and he never took possession of his see.

In 1485, Henry VII became king of England, Ireland, and Scotland, and his party wanted to have its own representative as bishop of Ross. The temporalities of the see were seized, and Blessed Thaddeus MacCarthy was declared an intruder. The case was brought to Rome, and the rival claimant, Hugh O'Driscoll, was given the see. Thaddeus, however, was appointed bishop of the united dioceses of Cork and Cloyne, which had no bishop.

When he arrived back in Ireland, he found his cathedral occupied and someone else claiming his bishopric. Thaddeus returned to Rome to appeal to the pope, and this time the pontiff defended his rights and sent him with papers to the lord deputy of Ireland to assist the bishop in securing his see. Fearing danger to his life from his enemies, Thaddeus set out for Ireland as a pilgrim, stopping at the famous monastery of St. Bernard's at the foot of the Alps. The next morning he was found dead in his bed.

When news of the death of the bishop traveling in disguise spread, crowds flocked to the cathedral of Ivrea for his funeral. His tomb became a local shrine, and in 1895 the Holy See recognized Thaddeus as Blessed. His feast is kept in the dioceses of Ross, Cork, and Cloyne, and in Ivrea, where he was buried.

Thought for the Day: Sometimes what we look upon as failure is success in God's eyes. Blessed Thaddeus never was able to do his work as a bishop, and everything seemed to go against him. But in the midst of that failure, he was a success in God's eyes. We cannot always control outward circumstances, but we can live our lives for God.

From 'The Catholic One Year Bible': . . . Preach the Word of God . . . at all times, whenever you get the chance, in season and out, when it is convenient and when it is not. Correct . . . your people when they need it, . . . encourage them to do right, . . . — 2 Timothy 4:2

Cedd belonged to a family of brothers, and all six of them were chosen by King Oswald of Northumbria to be trained by St. Aidan to be monks and missionaries. This was in 635, when Aidan came from the monastery of Iona in Scotland to become bishop of King Oswald's kingdom. One of St. Cedd's brothers was St. Chad, who was the first bishop of York and then bishop of Lichfield.

In 653, Peada, king of the Middle Angles, asked Aidan's successor at Lindisfarne for a bishop for his diocese, and St. Finan chose four monks from Lindisfarne to evangelize Peada's people. Later, the king of the East Saxons, whose chief city was London, also asked for a bishop, and Finan called Cedd to Lindisfarne and consecrated him bishop of London.

Cedd founded three monasteries of his own, the best known being Lastingham, where he died of the plague in 664. St. Bede has a beautiful story of Cedd's founding of Lastingham: Cedd spent forty days in prayer and fasting in a remote spot given to him by King Ethelwald.

In 664, Cedd was present at the Synod of Whitby and was a member of the Irish party, those wishing to retain the Irish date for Easter. But when the synod decided in favor of the Roman date, Cedd accepted the decision, not wanting to cause any further disunity in the English churches.

After the Synod of Whitby, a plague struck England, and Cedd was among those who died from the plague. At the news of his death, thirty monks came from London to spend their lives where their founder had died. But they, too, caught the plague and were buried near the little chapel that had been erected in Cedd's memory.

Cedd was the second bishop of the city of London; the first was Mellitus, who came with St. Augustine and later became archbishop of Canterbury. Mellitus was driven from the see by the king of the East Saxons in 616, and London was without a bishop until Cedd's arrival about 654.

Thought for the Day: St. Cedd was trained by a saint and he himself trained others to holiness. A good teacher teaches mostly by what he is; and, if he is a good teacher, the things that are important to him become important to those he teaches. Good teachers fashion the souls of others by contact with their own soul.

From 'The Catholic One Year Bible': . . . I have been sent to bring faith to those God has chosen and to teach them to know God's truth — the kind of truth that changes lives — so that they can have eternal life, which God promised them before the world began. . . . — Titus 1:1-2

Contardo Ferrini is a good example of that combination of holiness and learning that is so much a part of the Catholic tradition. He follows in the footsteps of St. Thomas Aquinas, St. Anselm, and that other great mind of the nineteenth century, John Henry Newman.

As a youngster, Blessed Contardo Ferrini had a passion for study, and this is not surprising, since his father was a mathematician, physicist, architect, and civil engineer. His spiritual guide as a young man was Don Adalbert Catena and one of his early teachers was Msgr. Anthony Ceriani, prefect of the Ambrosian Library in Milan. From Msgr. Ceriani, he learned Hebrew together with a sound piece of scholarly advice: "Don't trust too much in secondhand information. . . . Go directly to the sources of truth."

He was born in 1859 in Milan and in 1876 entered the law school of Borromeo College in Pavia. He helped to form student societies, and one of the societies he founded exists to this day. He earned his doctorate in 1880 and then went to study at the University of Berlin. Puzzled about what vocation he might be called to, and after much thought and prayer, the young scientist and jurist in 1881 made a vow of lifelong celibacy.

He returned to Italy in 1883 and plunged himself into study and research, visited libraries in Paris, Florence, Rome, and Copenhagen and developed his remarkable fluency in languages (he knew German, Latin, Greek, French, Spanish, Dutch, Hebrew, Syriac, Coptic, and Sanskrit). He taught Roman law at the University of Pavia, meanwhile becoming a Franciscan tertiary and cultivating a deep life of prayer and a wide circle of friends. He was given professorships at Messina and Modena and made important contributions to the study of law.

In 1902, hoping to overcome his fatigue from his intense work by mountain climbing, he came back feeling worse than better. On October 5, he went to Mass, came home, and collapsed. After several days in a coma, he died of typhus on October 17 at the age of forty-three and was beatified on April 15, 1947.

Thought for the Day: Blessed Contardo Ferrini pioneered a way of life now recognized by the Church as a secular institute, in which the Christian professional carries on his work in a Christian spirit, ordering his whole work to God. Pope Pius XII approved of this way of life as a state of perfection, and Contardo was one of its pioneers.

From 'The Catholic One Year Bible': . . . Let everything you do reflect your love of the truth and the fact that you are dead earnest about it. Your conversation should be so sensible and logical that anyone who wants to argue will be ashamed of himself because there won't be anything to criticize in anything you say! —Titus 2:7-8

These two Apostles have been linked in name since the early days of Christianity, and some believe that this is because they were relatives of Jesus.

St. Simon in the Gospels is called "the Zealot," and this may indicate that he belonged to that military group of Jews called the Zealots, the last of whom committed suicide on Masada rather than surrender to the Roman legions. Legend has Simon evangelizing the area around Edessa in Syria, where later a great school of theology arose. It is also said that after preaching in Egypt, he joined St. Jude in Mesopotamia and that they both went as missionaries to Persia and were martyred there. Undoubtedly, their names are linked because of this association.

Jude was most certainly a relative of Jesus and is mentioned in the lists of the "brothers of the Lord." He is sometimes also called Thaddeus. He is considered by most scholars to be the brother of James, the first bishop of Jerusalem and the leader of the early Christian community there.

Jude is the patron of "hopeless cases," and devotion to him as the advocate of impossible causes is widespread throughout the Church. He is the author of the Epistle of Jude in the New Testament, one of those called the "Catholic Epistles."

An early Christian historian, Hegisippus, mentioned that Jude's grandsons were arrested during the persecution of the Emperor Domitian about the year 80 because they were "descendants of David," but that they were released because their poverty and obscurity were no threat to the empire.

At the Last Supper, it was Jude who asked Jesus why He did not manifest Himself to the rest of the world, and Jesus answered that He and the Father would visit all those who loved Him, saying, "We will come to him and make our abode with him." These two Apostles are honored in both Eastern and Western Churches.

Thought for the Day: The lives of the Apostles SS. Simon and Jude are obscure and uncertain, but they were very close to Jesus Christ and shared in the great work of redemption. It is not necessary to be known in order to be close to God, and happiness comes from following closely in the footsteps of Jesus, not in being known.

From 'The Catholic One Year Bible': . . . When the time came for the kindness and love of God our Savior to appear, then he saved us . . . by washing away our sins and giving us the new joy of the indwelling Holy Spirit whom he poured out upon us with wonderful fullness. . . . — Titus 3:4-6

After the suppression of Catholicism under Queen Elizabeth of England, it was not possible to train priests to take care of the spiritual needs of English Catholics, scattered as they were throughout England, under threat of death and persecution, and faced with a hostile government.

In 1568, the English college was founded at Douai in France by William Allen, later named cardinal, and it was there that English priests were trained and sent to take part in the difficult and dangerous English mission. They began to arrive in England in 1574, and immediately the laws of England were tightened and legislation against them was passed. They were considered traitors and fugitives, and during the next hundred years over one hundred sixty of them were put to death in England and Wales. Eighty of these have been beatified, and their heroic lives and deaths were the strength and support of English Catholics during these difficult times.

The first among these martyrs was Blessed Cuthbert Mayne, who was executed at Launceston in 1577. The heroism of these martyrs and the difficulties of English Catholics have been dramatized in the historical fiction of Msgr. Robert Hugh Benson, *Come Rack, Come Rope, By What Authority?* and others. Some of these notable martyrs are St. Edmund Campion, Blessed Ralph Sherwin, Blessed Alexander Briant, Blessed John Paine, and Blessed Luke Kirby. Some of them were converts who returned to England with a price on their heads.

During the French Revolution, with the Catholic religion proscribed in France, the college at Douai was transferred to England itself, becoming two colleges, St. Edmund's in the south and St. Cuthbert's at Ushaw in the north. The prayer for the feast of these Douai martyrs reads: "Kindle in us, Lord, the spirit in which the blessed martyrs of Douai labored, so that filled with this spirit, we may love what they loved and do as they taught."

Thought for the Day: Nowadays the practice of our religion brings with it no danger and no threat, and it is possible that not having to suffer for it we may become less fervent in our faith. It is good to reflect on what others suffered, if only to make us realize what a precious gift we have.

From 'The Catholic One Year Bible': I always thank God when I am praying for you, . . . because I keep hearing of your love and trust in the Lord Jesus and his people. And I pray that as you share your faith with others it will grip their lives too, as they see the wealth of good things in you that come from Christ Jesus. — **Philemon 1:4-6**

Alphonsus Rodríguez is a good example of the power of teaching, when it is embodied in a living person. He was the adviser and confidante of St. Peter Claver, and it was his teaching and example that inspired Peter Claver in his own life and work. When the astonishing labors of Peter Claver are considered, the amazing influence of St. Alphonsus Rodríguez, a simple Jesuit lay brother, is seen in all its grandeur. One saint fashions another saint.

Alphonsus, the son of a wool merchant, was born in Segovia, Spain, in 1532. He studied at the Jesuit college at Alcala, and after the death of his father returned home to help his mother in the family business. In 1558, he married and had a daughter and two sons.

When his business failed, and on the death of his wife and two of his children, he sold his business and went into seclusion. At the death of his second son, he tried to enter the Society of Jesus but was refused because of ill health. For a time, he considered living as a hermit.

In 1571, he was accepted as a Jesuit lay brother and sent to the Jesuit college on Majorca. There he was the house porter for forty-six years and was remembered for his patience, humility, gentleness, and mystical absorption in prayer. He became a favorite of the Jesuit students, gave them timely advice and spiritual counsel, and planted in them his own deep devotion to the Mother of God. His influence on Peter Claver was especially remarkable, and this "Apostle to the Slaves" treasured the notes he had made of Alphonsus' counsels and kept them with him to his dying day.

In May of 1617, Alphonsus became deathly sick; he suffered a prolonged agony, which lasted several months, before he died in October of that year. His funeral was attended by the Spanish viceroy, the bishop of Majorca, and hundreds of the poor and sick whom he had befriended. He was canonized in 1888 by Pope Leo XIII together with his spiritual son, Peter Claver.

Thought for the Day: It is not necessary to be rich and famous to be influential. St. Alphonsus Rodríguez lost his business, was turned down for the priesthood, and yet influenced hundreds of students by his holiness of life and deep wisdom. Personal influence is the overflow of a good life, and if we take care of the tree, we do not have to worry about the quality of the fruit.

From 'The Catholic One Year Bible': Long ago God spoke in many different ways to our fathers through the prophets. . . . But now in these days he has spoken to us through his Son to whom he has given everything, and through whom he made the world. . . . — Hebrews 1:1-2

St. Wolfgang *(OCTOBER 31)*

Wolfgang was one of those rare young men who were attracted to the great abbeys of Germany, became excellent students and scholars, and went on to found schools of their own. He was born about the year 930 and was sent to the abbey of Reichenau, set on an island in Lake Constance. The abbey was founded by Charles Martel in 724 and flourished as a center of learning under Walafrid Strabo and later under Herman Contractus.

One of St. Wolfgang's fellow students was Henry, brother of the bishop of Wurzburg, and Henry persuaded Wolfgang to accompany him to Wurzburg to study under the Italian grammarian Stephen. When Henry himself became archbishop of Trier in 956, he took Wolfgang with him and made him head of the cathedral school there.

On Henry's death in 964, Wolfgang became a monk at Einsiedeln, was ordained, and did missionary work in Hungary. In 972, he was appointed bishop of Regensberg. Here, he showed himself a reformer, corrected abuses, and recommended the division of his own diocese to form the diocese of Prague, he himself selecting one of his disciples to be bishop there. His reforms spread to other dioceses, and he was the driving force of a widespread religious and pastoral renewal in that part of Germany. During the duke of Bavaria's rebellion against Emperor Otto II, Wolfgang lived as a hermit in Salzburg but returned to his see when the turmoil was over. From this hermit period arose the legend that he had lived on the Abersee, at a place even now called Sankt Wolfgansee in upper Austria.

He was taken ill while traveling down the Danube and died at Puppingen, not far from Linz. He was buried in Sankt Emmeram and was canonized by Pope St. Leo IX in 1052. His feast is celebrated in the dioceses of Germany and also by the canons regular of the Lateran, since he restored the canonical life of the clergy in his own time.

Thought for the Day: Pastors like St. Wolfgang were not only the shepherds of their flock but influenced cultural and social life as well. They set up centers of education, educated future emperors and bishops, and restored stability and tranquillity to the regions where they worked. That is why they are often remembered for centuries, and the memory of their good deeds lives on in legends and folk tales.

From 'The Catholic One Year Bible': . . . It was right and proper that God, who made everything for his own glory, should allow Jesus to suffer, for in doing this he was bringing vast multitudes of God's people to heaven; for his suffering made Jesus a perfect leader, one fit to bring them into their salvation. — **Hebrews 2:10**

THE SAINTS OF NOVEMBER

All Saints *(NOVEMBER 1)*

The Feast of All Saints seems to have originated in Ireland and was brought by the Irish monks of Iona to Northumbria, where it was celebrated in all the churches founded by the Irish monks. From Northumbria, it spread to the continent, when Alcuin was the schoolmaster of the Franks under Charlemagne. About 835, Pope Gregory IV asked Emperor Louis the Pious to extend the celebration throughout the whole of the Frankish empire. It was the great abbey of Cluny that made the feast popular and joined to it the celebration of All Souls' Day.

Every day of the year, as this book shows, we celebrate the feast day of some saint, but there are only three hundred sixty-five days in the year and only that many can be commemorated. Besides, there are many more saints in heaven than those beatified or canonized, many millions more unknown or unremembered, who are yet a part of the communion of saints and the family of God. The Feast of All Saints — All Hallows, as it was called in Old English — celebrates the army of holy ones who stand before the throne of God, the multitude of saints and angels who stand forever before His face.

There has been such a commemoration from the beginnings of Christianity, and the first was the commemoration of all the martyrs observed in Edessa in the fourth century. From a sermon by St. John Chrysostom, we know that the Church at Antioch commemorated the martyrs on the first Sunday after Pentecost. In 609, Pope Boniface IV dedicated the ancient Pantheon in honor of the martyrs, when he received it from the Emperor Phocas, that "the memory of all the saints might from this time on be honored in the place which had formerly" been devoted to the worship of the Roman gods.

The prayer for the feast indicates the purpose for this annual celebration: "Almighty, ever-living God: we are celebrating with joy the triumph of Your grace in Your saints. With so vast a multitude praying for us, may we receive from You the fullness of mercy we have always desired."

Thought for the Day: We belong to the communion of saints, and all those who have gone before us into heaven are our close and dear friends, concerned about us and praying for us. It is a fellowship we should be aware of, and our bonds with this army of holy ones should be a source of strength and joy to us.

From 'The Catholic One Year Bible': . . . Jesus was faithful to God who appointed him High Priest, just as Moses also faithfully served in God's house. But Jesus has far more glory than Moses, just as a man who builds a fine house gets more praise than his house does. — Hebrews 3:2-3

The Feast of All Souls is a twin feast with All Saints and originated at the great abbey of Cluny in France, where it began under the fifth abbot of Cluny, St. Odilo. After the solemn celebration of All Saints, the monastery bell was tolled, and the monks offered prayers for the souls of the departed. November 2 was chosen so that the joining of the two feast days would proclaim the Catholic belief in the communion of saints.

The Church has never been satisfied with a mere remembrance of the dead. The belief in the communion of saints is expressed in customs and devotions that bring home the reality of our common bond with God. Catholics are encouraged to pray on this day, and the Church has centered its own commemoration of the dead in the sacrifice of the Mass itself. Priests are permitted to offer three Masses on this day for the souls of the dead, and the whole Church is keenly conscious of the reality of death and the need that the dead have for our prayers.

Every nation or culture has its festival of the dead. In Japan, it is known as *Odori-Obon* and occurs in late August. Japanese gather before their family shrines, adorning them with scrolls inscribed with the names of the dead; then they gather at the edge of the lake or the sea, fill miniature boats with food — symbolic of the journey the dead have taken — and send them with prayers into the unknown.

For the Christian, however, remembering the dead is more than an empty memory. It is part of the Church's teaching on the communion of saints. We are all one family in God, separated for a time by death but who will be together again some day.

On All Souls' Day, the family of God gathers in one mighty army to remember and pray for those who have died in the one faith, children of the one Lord. It is a "holy and wholesome thought to pray for the dead" — holy because the dead are with God, still bound to us by bonds of faith; wholesome because we are reminded of our own death and our own ultimate meeting with God.

Thought for the Day: All Souls' Day celebrates the oneness that we have in God and in Christ, and the fact that our prayers will help to bring our beloved dead into the presence of Christ. The Feast of All Souls also celebrates the hope we have in our own immortality and that the "sadness of death gives way to the bright promise of immortality."

From 'The Catholic One Year Bible': . . . There is a full complete rest *still waiting* for the people of God. Christ has already entered there. He is resting from his work, just as God did after the creation. Let us do our best to go into that place of rest, too. — Hebrews 4:9-11

St. Martin de Porres *(NOVEMBER 3)*

Martin de Porres was the son of a Spanish nobleman and a black mother, one of the many "half-castes" of the city of Lima, Peru, in the sixteenth century. Running wild in the streets of Lima, he might have grown up something of a juvenile delinquent, but his mother taught him kindness and gentleness, and he learned to be sensitive to the suffering of others and generous with the few possessions he had.

To make sure he would have a future, his mother apprenticed him to to a barber and surgeon, and he carried on a medical work of mercy among the poor. Impressed with the charity of the Dominicans in Lima, he applied to be accepted as a lay helper. Seeing his fidelity and devotion, the Dominicans, after nine years, received him as a lay brother.

After this, Martin became the marvel of Lima, during the days when St. Rose of Lima and Blessed John Massias carried on their own work among the poor. His love of everyone, even of animals, made him a figure not unlike that of St. Francis of Assisi, and in St. Martin de Porres the extraordinary was ordinary. He was a mystic of the highest order, with the gift of bilocation and other marvels. He had remarkable theological knowledge and was famous for his miraculous cures. He spent long nights in prayer and penance, and during the day took care of the sick, looking after the poor and showing God's goodness to everyone. He was the friend of all: of rich and poor, the simple and the great, bishops, governors, men, women, and children.

Once, when his Dominican priory was deeply in debt, he offered to sell himself to raise money in payment. He seemed to come up miraculously with money when it was needed for the poor and yet was an ingenious, practical agriculturist who taught skilled farming methods to the poor.

He died at Rosary Priory in Lima on November 3, 1639, and his pallbearers were the bishops and nobility of Peru. Beatified in 1837 and canonized in 1962, Martin de Porres is the patron saint of social justice.

Thought for the Day: The closer a person gets to God, the more love he seems to have for others. St. Martin had a thirst for God that drove him to spend his nights in prayer, and that love overflowed into amazing activities for the good of others. We need never fear that prayer will limit our power to do good; it only intensifies everything we do.

From 'The Catholic One Year Bible': . . . Even though Jesus was God's Son, he had to learn from experience what it was like to obey, when obeying meant suffering. It was after he had proved himself perfect in this experience that Jesus became the giver of eternal salvation to all those who obey him. — Hebrews 5:8-9

St. Charles Borromeo *(NOVEMBER 4)*

Charles Borromeo was the nephew of Pope Pius IV and could have lived a life of splendor as a noble churchman. Instead, he became a driving force for reform in the Church after the disaster of the Reformation and a pastoral genius who pioneered the decrees of the Council of Trent in Italy and created farseeing pastoral policies as cardinal-archbishop of Milan.

St. Charles Borromeo was born in 1538, and his mother was Margherita de' Medici. He was tutored at Milan by Francesco Alciati and earned a doctorate in civil and canon law at the University of Pavia. When his uncle was elected pope as Pius IV, Borromeo was called to Rome and held a number of important positions in the Roman curia. He was created a cardinal in 1560, was prefect of the secretariat of state for his uncle during the third session of the Council of Trent, and was ordained to the priesthood in 1563.

Already as a member of the Roman curia, he worked at the spiritual renewal of the people of Rome, promoted the catechism of the Council of Trent, helped to found the Roman seminary, and published an edition of the writings of the Church Fathers.

In 1560, he was made administrator of the archdiocese of Milan, and in 1566 took up permanent residence in the city. He began a program of pastoral renewal in Milan that had considerable influence in the whole Catholic world. He called six provincial councils and eleven diocesan synods, founded a seminary and staffed it with Jesuits, promoted cultural and social institutions in his diocese, set up hospices for the homeless, and founded orphanages, hospitals, and schools. His zeal and energy seemed boundless, and Milan would feel his influence for centuries to come.

Several times he was in danger of death by assassination from those who opposed his reforms, but he succeeded admirably, making Milan a model diocese. In 1584, returning from a retreat, he was struck down with a fever, brought home on a stretcher, and died in the middle of the night between the third and fourth of November. He was only forty-six years old and was canonized in 1610.

Thought for the Day: It was the death of his brother, Federigo, that brought about a change in St. Charles Borromeo, turned him to God and the affairs of his own soul. From this beginning, he became a dedicated priest, a zealous and energetic bishop, and a saint of God. That should make all of us ponder our own lives.

From 'The Catholic One Year Bible': This certain hope of being saved is a strong and trustworthy anchor for our souls, connecting us with God himself behind the sacred curtains of heaven, where Christ has gone ahead to plead for us. . . . — Hebrews 6:19-20

St. Bertilla of Chelles *(NOVEMBER 5)*

This remarkable abbess had two queens as her religious subjects in the abbey of Chelles and it was to her abbey that St. Hilda of Whitby planned to come when she was thinking of entering a convent.

St. Bertilla of Chelles was born near Rouen, France, around 635, and through the encouragement of St. Ouen, bishop of Rouen, she entered the Columban monastery of Jouarre. Trained in the Celtic traditions of prayer and hospitality, she was in charge of the monastery hospice and was given the care of pilgrims, the poor, and the sick.

When St. Bathildis, the English slave girl who became the queen of Clovis II, decided to found the abbey of Chelles, she asked the abbess of Jouarre to send a colony of nuns from Jouarre to form the first community. Bertilla was chosen to head this community. Under her rule, the monastery of Chelles became known for its observance, spirit of prayer, and holiness of life, and attracted vocations even from England.

After the death of Clovis II, Bathildis herself took the religious habit at Chelles and put herself under the rule of Bertilla, even though she (Bathildis) was the foundress of the abbey. The other queen who entered was Hereswith, widow of the king of East Anglia. Chelles became the model for other convents on the continent, and Bertilla the model for abbesses. It is quite possible that Hilda herself came to Chelles to study its monastic life before she founded her own monasteries at Hartlepool and Whitby.

The two monasteries founded by royalty — one on the continent and one in England — were oases of humanity in cruel and barbarous times, and the leading figure in pioneering this monastic life for women was Bertilla, who ruled Chelles for almost fifty years and inspired women like Hilda to do the same thing in their own countries.

Bertilla died at Chelles probably about 705, and her relics are preserved at Chelles-St.-André.

Thought for the Day: It says much for the sanctity of St. Bertilla of Chelles that two queens subjected themselves to her rule. She had first learned to obey and to serve others before she was chosen to rule others. Even as abbess, her humility, kindness, and consideration for others were paramount. She realized that as one who rules, she was called upon to serve.

From 'The Catholic One Year Bible': . . . Melchizedek was . . . a priest of the Most High God. . . . [He] placed a blessing upon mighty Abraham, and as everyone knows, a person who has the power to bless is always greater than the person he blesses. — Hebrews 7:1, 6-7

St. Theophane Vénard *(NOVEMBER 6)*

Theophane Vénard is known especially from the great devotion that St. Thérèse of Lisieux had to him and her delight in reading the letters from his prison in Indochina. He is one of the shining young men of the Paris Mission Society who inspired the founding of other missionary societies, such as Maryknoll and the Columban Fathers. He was only thirty-one years old when he died, martyred in Indochina, one of the most dangerous mission assignments of the nineteenth century.

St. Theophane Vénard was born in 1829, the son of a village schoolmaster in Poitou, France. He studied at Poitiers and then entered the seminary of the Paris Foreign Mission Society in 1852. After ordination, he was sent to Hong Kong where he studied languages for fifteen months, and then in 1854 he arrived in Tonkin where a violent persecution against the Church was raging.

He devoted himself to the spiritual needs of the suffering Vietnamese Catholics, often endangering his own life. He was expelled from Namdinh in 1856, sought refuge in Hanoi, and when the persecution reached Hanoi in 1858 he hid in caves, in the hulls of fishing boats, and in the homes of Catholics. On November 30, 1860, he was betrayed by a Christian and imprisoned in a bamboo cage, where he stayed until his death.

He knew what was coming and in one of his letters home wrote: "The order has come to seize all Christians, and to put them to death by what is called *lang-tri*; that is, by slow torture, cutting off first the ankles, then the knees, then the fingers, then the elbows, and so on until the victim is nothing but a mutilated trunk."

Toward the end, Theophane wrote: "These last days of my [imprisonment] pass quietly; all those who surround me are civil and respectful, and a good many love me. From the grand mandarin down to the humblest private soldier, everyone regrets that the laws of the country condemn me to death."

He was brought before the mandarins at Hanoi, tried, and sentenced to beheading. He was martyred on February 2, 1861. With nineteen others, he was beatified by Pope Pius X in 1909.

Thought for the Day: Every age of Catholic history has its martyrs, even our own. Today in Albania, Poland, Lithuania, and Czechoslovakia, people of all ages die for the faith. Many are young men like St. Theophane Vénard. We should pray that those who must die for their faith will be given the courage to endure to the end.

From 'The Catholic One Year Bible': . . . Jesus lives forever and continues to be a Priest so that no one else is needed. He is able to save completely all who come to God through him. Since he will live forever, he will always be there to remind God that he has paid for their sins with his blood. — **Hebrews 7:24-25**

St. Willibrord *(NOVEMBER 7)*

Of all the English monks who preceded St. Boniface to Germany, St. Willibrord is the most notable, even though his name is often confused with that of the brothers St. Winebald and St. Willibald. But Willibrord was the pioneer, the missionary genius who opened the German missions and paved the way for the even greater work of St. Boniface. He had a very interesting history.

Willibrord was born in Northumbria in the days of SS. Cuthbert, Benedict Biscop, Theodore of Canterbury, and Wilfrid. As a boy of seven, he was placed in the monastery of Ripon to be educated, where Wilfrid had recently established the Benedictine rule. When he was twenty, he joined two of his countrymen, Egbert and Wigbert, in Ireland to study in the Irish monastic schools, and it was there that he caught the missionary fever from his Irish masters.

He was thirty-one years old when he heard about the failure of his countryman Wigbert in the missions of Germany and decided to tackle the work himself, talking eleven other English monks into going with him. In 690, they landed at the mouth of the Rhine and received permission from the ruler of the country to evangelize Lower Friesland, between the Meuse and the sea, what is now the Netherlands.

Willibrord took off for Rome to receive the blessing of the pope, then returned to evangelize those lands that had been conquered by the Franks. Pepin of Herstal, the ruler of the Franks, wanted a bishop in the newly conquered territories. He sent Willibrord back to Rome to be consecrated bishop, with an official mandate from the pope. Willibrord then returned to Friesland and set up his headquarters at Utrecht.

He labored as far north as Denmark and in 714 baptized Pepin's son, Charles Martel. He was later joined by St. Boniface, who spent three years with him before setting out on his own missionary labors.

Willibrord founded the monastery of Echternach to retire to from time to time for prayer, and it was there that he died at the age of eighty-one on November 7, 739. He was buried in the abbey church, and his tomb has always been a place of pilgrimage. He was alive when St. Bede wrote his *History of the English Church and People,* and Bede notes that he was ruling the see of Utrecht at the time.

Thought for the Day: Europe as we know it today was evangelized by a number of remarkable Englishmen (among them St. Willibrord) who left home and country and formed a Christian people in the wilderness. It is hard to believe that it happened so long ago and that our faith has come down to us from these pioneers of the faith. We should be grateful.

From 'The Catholic One Year Bible': . . . Christ . . . is our High Priest, and is in heaven at the place of greatest honor next to God himself. He ministers in the temple in heaven, the true place of worship built by the Lord. . . . — **Hebrews 8:1-2**

Anthony Baldinucci was named after St. Anthony of Padua, to whom his father had a great devotion. By a strange coincidence, the Baldinucci family lived in the same house in Florence in which St. Aloysius of Gonzaga had lived, and Aloysius had a strong influence on the young Baldinucci. In 1681, at the age of sixteen, Blessed Anthony Baldinucci entered the Jesuits despite his poor health and was sent to the Jesuit novitiate of Sant'Andrea in Rome.

His dream was to go to India and follow in the footsteps of St. Francis Xavier, but because of his poor health he was assigned to preaching missions in the Italian provinces of Abruzzi and Romagna, working in Viterbo and Frascati. He spent twenty years at this work, concentrating his work among the poor and unlettered peasants of the region. To attract them, he became something of a showman, organizing processions of penitents wearing crowns of thorns and weeping as they walked through the streets of the towns. He often preached carrying a heavy cross and scourging himself, telling the people that he was doing penance for their sins.

After Anthony had the attention of the people, he would speak to them gently, trying to show them how their lives should be changed and how they could be better Christians. In most of the areas he served, the men were addicted to reckless gambling and heavy drinking, which ruined their family life, and Father Anthony would have public burnings of playing cards, his methods having a profound effect upon the people who heard him.

He was the most popular preacher in Italy at the time and usually arrived for his missions barefooted, wearing a tattered cassock and carrying his baggage on his back. In 1716, there was a famine in central Italy, and Anthony wore himself out relieving the poor.

He died exhausted from his tireless work on November 7, 1717. In 1710, he had stayed at the home of the Pecci family in Carpineto, and it was a descendant of this family, Pope Leo XIII, who beatified Anthony Baldinucci in 1893.

Thought for the Day: Some people have to be shocked into thinking about their own souls, and unless a good preacher is able to reach them they would never think about God. Good preachers bring medicine to the soul, and most of us have been influenced by good preachers. The living words of an effective preacher can change the whole direction of a life.

From 'The Catholic One Year Bible': . . . [Christ] went into that greater, perfect tabernacle in heaven, not made by men nor part of this world, and once for all took blood into that inner room, the Holy of Holies, and sprinkled it on the mercy seat; . . . — **Hebrews 9:11-12**

When St. Patrick was on his way to Tara, in that fateful year that he landed in Ireland, he passed a few days at the home of an Irish chieftain named Sechnan in Meath. The whole family was converted, and the chieftain's young son, Benignus, was so impressed with the Christian bishop that he sat by him while he slept, strewing flowers on him. When Patrick was leaving, the boy clung to his feet and asked to go with him. Patrick's followers objected, but Patrick told them: "Leave him alone, he will be the heir of my kingdom."

St. Benignus went with Patrick and became his dearest disciple and eventually his successor as bishop of Armagh. He was also a bard, sang with a lovely voice, and was nicknamed "Patrick's psalmodist." Patrick put him in charge of the music for the Mass, and as Benignus grew older, he became Patrick's right-hand man.

When he grew up, Benignus was ordained a priest, and his name is mentioned with Patrick's in the Irish code of law called Senchus Mor. He succeeded Patrick as bishop of Armagh and was his most devoted and beloved disciple and one of the first native-born Irish bishops. The evangelization of Clare and Kerry is attributed to Benignus.

During his growing up, Benignus was Patrick's constant companion and is mentioned in the *Tripartite Life* of Patrick in the legend of St. Patrick's Breastplate: "Patrick went with eight young clerics and Benignus a gillie with them, and Patrick gave them his blessing as they set out. . . . The enemy who were waiting to ambush them saw eight deer go past them, and behind them a fawn with a bundle on its back." The fawn was Benignus carrying his tablets on his back.

No one knows when Benignus died, but it is thought that he died after Patrick about the year 467. There is a legend that his relics were taken to Glastonbury in England, but it is most probable that he was buried at Armagh, where he succeeded Patrick as chief bishop of Ireland.

Thought for the Day: A young boy attaches himself to a saint and becomes a saint with him. How important it is to have the right teachers, and St. Benignus was fortunate in meeting St. Patrick when he was so young. It is a beautiful story, this tale of a boy and the great Apostle of Ireland and how the boy grew up to be the bishop of all Ireland.

From 'The Catholic One Year Bible': . . . Just as it is destined that men die only once, and after that comes the judgment, so also Christ died only once as an offering for the sins of many people; and he will come again, but not to deal again with our sins. — **Hebrews 9:27-28**

St. Leo the Great

Leo the Great is the first truly great pope of the early centuries and is remembered especially as one who confronted Attila the Hun and saved the city of Rome. He is the first pontiff fully conscious of the dignity and power of his sacred office and one of the few popes called "the Great."

He was a deacon of the Roman Church under Pope Celestine I and, like St. Lawrence, was entrusted with the care of the poor. He was sent to Gaul in 440 to reconcile two rulers, and during his absence the reigning pope died and Leo was elected in his place.

He looked upon preaching as one of his most serious duties, and the sermons he preached are luminous with doctrine, covering the great seasons and feast days and describing the activities of the Church in Rome during that period.

In 451, it was his *Tome to Flavian* that clarified for the Council of Chalcedon the issue of "nature" and "person" in Christ and condemned the Monophysite heresy. In 452, Attila and his Huns entered Italy, burning cities and slaughtering whole populations. After seizing Milan, the imperial capital in the West, Attila headed for Rome. Leo was the man of the hour.

Emperor Valentinian III and the senate ordered the pope to negotiate with Attila. St. Leo the Great left Rome surrounded by his priests and officials of the empire and met Attila near the present town of Peschiera. To everyone's surprise, Attila agreed to accept an annual tribute rather than enter Rome. Three years later, Rome was sacked by Gaiseric, but Leo was able to restrain the violence of the invaders to some degree.

Then the pope started rebuilding the city and aiding the victims. He sent priests to Africa to redeem captives and refused to be discouraged by the immense tasks he had to face. He died on November 10, 461, beloved by all, and mourned by rich and poor, emperor and citizen, Christian and non-Christian. His relics are still preserved in the Vatican basilica.

Thought for the Day: St. Leo the Great looked upon the office of the pope as that of Christ Himself and worked to make himself "all things to all men." He joined prayer to his immense labors and showed himself a true father of his people. He saw himself chiefly as a teacher, and his teaching remains one of the great monuments of his pontificate.

From 'The Catholic One Year Bible': . . . Christ gave himself to God for our sins as one sacrifice for all time, and then sat down in the place of highest honor at God's right hand, waiting for his enemies to be laid under his feet. — **Hebrews 10:12-13**

St. Martin of Tours *(NOVEMBER 11)*

Martin is called the glory of Gaul and the light of the Church in the fourth century. He was the first universally popular saint in Europe, and more churches are dedicated to him in Europe than to any other saint. He is one of the founders of monasticism in the West and influenced especially the development of the monastic way of life in Britain and in Ireland.

He was born a pagan and served in the Roman army in Gaul. It was while on duty as a soldier near Amiens that the incident happened which made him the subject of countless paintings. Passing a beggar on the road, shivering with the cold, Martin took off his cloak and cut it in two, giving one half to the beggar. Later that night, in a dream, he saw Jesus wearing the cloak and saying: "Martin, yet a catechumen, has covered me with his cloak."

St. Martin of Tours was discharged from the army by the Emperor Julian, was ordained lector by St. Hilary of Poitiers, visited his home where he converted his parents, then became a hermit on an island near Milan in Italy. When Hilary of Poitiers returned from exile, Martin went to France and founded what is considered the first monastery in the West, at Ligugé, in 361.

In 371, the people of Tours demanded Martin as their bishop, much against the wishes of the other bishops. He set up his headquarters at the monastery of Marmoutier, established parishes throughout his diocese, and endeared himself to all by his simplicity and kindness. He visited his parishes on foot, by donkey, or by boat, and was always going off on some errand of mercy. He begged for the lives of those condemned to death, had prisoners released, gave lavishly to the poor, and cured the sick with his power of healing.

While visiting a parish far from Tours, he became sick and realized that death was near. His priests begged him not to leave them, and he made his famous prayer: "Lord, if Your people still need me, I will not draw back from labor."

He died on November 8, 397, and was buried on November 11. A magnificent basilica was built over his grave at Tours to which pilgrims came from all over Europe. His feast day is the original Thanksgiving Day when God was thanked for a bountiful harvest and people feasted on "St. Martin's goose."

Thought for the Day: St. Martin of Tours was noted for his charity, shown by his kindness to the beggar. He believed literally that what he did to others, he did to Christ. He was not patronizing to the poor; he gave to them as he would to Christ Himself, and we should follow his example.

From 'The Catholic One Year Bible': . . . Since this great High Priest of ours rules over God's household, let us go right in, to God himself, with true hearts fully trusting him to receive us, because we have been sprinkled with Christ's blood to make us clean, . . . — Hebrews 10:21-22

Josaphat is one of those figures in history caught in a web of controversy where even good people find it hard to keep their heads. He was caught in a battle between Catholic and Orthodox, Latin and Byzantine, and found himself criticized and opposed on every side: by the Orthodox for being Catholic and by the Latıns for being Byzantine. He held firmly to Catholic unity against the Orthodox and just as firmly to Byzantine rights against the Latins. At that period of history, it was a no-win situation, and he is the great martyr to the cause of unity.

St. Josaphat was born in Lithuania about 1580 into a Catholic family and early promoted Catholic unity in a country divided between Orthodox and Catholic. He entered the Byzantine monastery of Holy Trinity in Vilna in 1604 and was elected Catholic archbishop of Polotsk in 1614. While clinging firmly to unity with Rome, he firmly opposed those Latins who saw unity only in Latin terms and would suppress Byzantine traditions in the name of Catholic unity. He firmly opposed the Latinization of his people and made enemies and severe critics among the Latin clergy of Poland.

Politically, the Catholic and Orthodox clergy were rivals in Lithuania, and the archbishopric of Polotsk was one of the contested sees. An Orthodox archbishop of Polotsk was appointed, and Josaphat was accused of taking office invalidly. Many of his Byzantine Catholics were won over to allegiance to Orthodoxy. Even the king of Poland wavered in his support of Josaphat, especially when Polish bishops accused him of betraying his faith by not Latinizing his diocese.

One of the hotbeds of trouble in Josaphat's diocese was Witebsk, and in November of 1623 he went there to bring about peace in his flock, preaching in the churches and trying to reconcile differences. On November 12, a mob broke into the house where he was staying, shouting hatred and violence. When he confronted them, he was struck in the head with a halberd and shot. His mangled body was dragged out and thrown into the river. He was canonized by Pope Pius IX in 1867.

Thought for the Day: It is important to say that there was a martyr for unity on the Orthodox side as well, and even good men were uncertain where truth and justice lay. St. Josaphat died working for reconciliation, and peacemakers often find themselves hated by both sides. It is part of the risk of being a true follower of Christ.

From 'The Catholic One Year Bible': What is faith? It is the confident assurance that something we want is going to happen. It is the certainty that what we hope for is waiting for us, even though we cannot see it up ahead. Men of God in days of old were famous for their faith. — Hebrews 11:1-2

St. Frances Xavier Cabrini *(NOVEMBER 13)*

Here is a lady very close to us, who lived and died in our century, and who was known as the "first American citizen saint." She has left her mark on these United States and left an imperishable memory wherever she went. She came here in 1889, a little nun in a black habit who spoke very little English but had a mandate from the pope in her hand.

She was born in Lombardy, Italy, in 1850, the youngest child of Agostino and Stella Cabrini. She was educated by the Daughters of the Sacred Heart and became a teacher. Because she had been sick with smallpox, she was refused admittance to the Daughters of the Sacred Heart, and so she taught in a private school at Vidardo and in 1874 was persuaded by Don Antonio Serrati to work at the House of Providence orphanage in Codogno. Here she took her religious vows in September 1877.

When the orphanage was closed by the bishop, he appointed her superior of the Missionary Sisters of the Sacred Heart, and this congregation was formally approved by Rome in 1888. In five years, there were seven houses of the congregation in northern Italy, and later a school and nursery were opened in Rome.

St. Frances Xavier Cabrini had hoped to do missionary work in China, following in the footsteps of her patron saint, but Pope Leo XIII persuaded her to go to the United States instead, to work particularly among Italian immigrants. In New York, she established schools and adult classes for the Italian immigrants, and in 1895 she founded Columbus Hospital.

In 1909, she became an American citizen and was elected superior general of her institute for life. She traveled across the United States founding convents, hospitals, schools, and orphanages, and established sixty-seven houses of her congregation throughout the world.

When Mother Cabrini died, her sisters numbered over fifteen hundred. She died of malaria in her hospital in Chicago on December 22, 1917, and was canonized by Pope Pius XII in 1946. Her accomplishments were amazing, and she left behind a flourishing congregation to continue the work she had begun.

Thought for the Day: A person who really wants to do good for others has unlimited possibilities, and the only limitations are really his or her own efforts. There is no limit to the good we can do, if we will just look around us. There is a great big harvest ready to be reaped.

From 'The Catholic One Year Bible': The people of Israel trusted God and went right through the Red Sea as though they were on dry ground. But when the Egyptians chasing them tried it, they all were drowned. — Hebrews 11:29

St. Lawrence O'Toole *(NOVEMBER 14)*

Lawrence O'Toole sounds like a man who might live down the street, but that is the English version of his name. His Irish name was Lorcan Ua Tuathail, he was descended from early Irish kings, and his grandfather was a prince of Kildare.

St. Lawrence O'Toole was born in 1128 and knew the turmoil of Irish politics from the time he was ten years old. When he was ten, he was given as a hostage to the king of Leinster, and when he was twelve, he was given into the care of the bishop of Glendalough. When the bishop was going to cast lots to see which of the O'Toole sons would serve the Church, Lawrence laughed and said that he would be happy to dedicate his life to God.

He spent the next twenty-two years at Glendalough as novice, student, and monk, and at the age of twenty-five was elected abbot. In 1161, when the archbishop of Dublin died, Lawrence was unanimously chosen bishop of Ireland's capitol, the first Irish archbishop of Dublin.

As archbishop, he organized his clergy into a community of canons regular and was a fearless defender of the rights of the Church. He set up synods to face the serious abuses in the country and in 1179 left Ireland to attend the Third Lateran Council. On his way to Rome, King Henry II of England tried to bully Lawrence regarding England's rights over Ireland, but in Rome he obtained the pope's protection for the see of Dublin. The Holy Father also appointed Lawrence papal legate for Ireland.

Before he left Ireland Lawrence tried to make peace between Henry II and a rebellious Irish chieftain and he tried again on his return in 1180, going to London to see the king. Angry, the king refused to let him return to Ireland, and Lawrence followed the king to Normandy, still trying to make peace between the king and the rebellious chief. Lawrence died at Eu in Normandy and never returned to Ireland. He was canonized by Pope Honorius III in 1225.

Thought for the Day: St. Lawrence O'Toole found himself in the middle of all kinds of trouble, none of it of his own making. But he remained calm and found that he could be a peacemaker. Instead of stirring up further trouble, he gave his efforts to reconciling enemies. This is still a noble Christian work.

From 'The Catholic One Year Bible': Keep your eyes on Jesus, our leader and instructor. He was willing to die a shameful death on the cross because of the joy he knew would be his afterwards; and now he sits in the place of honor by the throne of God. — Hebrews 12:2

He was known as the "teacher of everything there is to know," was a scientist long before the age of science, was considered a wizard and magician in his own lifetime, and became the teacher and mentor of that other remarkable mind of his time, St. Thomas Aquinas.

St. Albert the Great was born in Lauingen on the Danube, near Ulm, Germany; his father was a military lord in the army of Emperor Frederick II. As a young man Albert studied at the University of Padua and there fell under the spell of Blessed Jordan of Saxony, the Dominican who made the rounds of the universities of Europe drawing the best young men of the universities into the Dominicans.

After several teaching assignments in his order, he came in 1241 to the University of Paris, where he lectured in theology. While teaching in Paris, he was assigned by his order in 1248 to set up a house of studies for the order in Cologne. In Paris, he had gathered around him a small band of budding theologians, the chief of whom was Thomas Aquinas, who accompanied him to Cologne and became his greatest pupil.

In 1260, he was appointed bishop of Regensberg; when he resigned after three years, he was called to be an adviser to the pope and was sent on several diplomatic missions. In his latter years, he resided in Cologne, took part in the Council of Lyons in 1274, and in his old age traveled to Paris to defend the teaching of his student Thomas Aquinas.

It was in Cologne that his reputation as a scientist grew. He carried on experiments in chemistry and physics in his makeshift laboratory and built up a collection of plants, insects, and chemical compounds that gave substance to his reputation. When Cologne decided to build a new cathedral, he was consulted about the design. He was friend and adviser to popes, bishops, kings, and statesmen and made his own unique contribution to the learning of his age.

He died a very old man in Cologne on November 15, 1280, and is buried in St. Andrea's Church in that city. He was canonized and declared a Doctor of the Church in 1931 by Pope Pius XI. His writings are remarkable for their exact scientific knowledge, and for that reason he has been made the patron saint of scientists.

Thought for the Day: St. Albert the Great was convinced that all creation spoke of God and that the tiniest piece of scientific knowledge told us something about Him. Besides the Bible, God has given us the book of creation revealing something of His wisdom and power. In creation, Albert saw the hand of God.

From 'The Catholic One Year Bible': Since we have a kingdom nothing can destroy, let us please God by serving him with thankful hearts, and with holy fear and awe. For our God is a consuming fire. — Hebrews 12:28-29

St. Margaret of Scotland *(NOVEMBER 16)*

After the battle of Hastings, knowing that William the Conqueror's victory would be followed by the dynastic murders of any relatives of Edward the Confessor, several fled to Scotland. One of these was Margaret, daughter of Edward Atheling and Princess Agatha of Hungary. In 1070, she married King Malcolm Canmore of Scotland and was a leading figure in furthering the reforms of Pope Gregory VII in Scotland.

Her first influence was on her own husband, and his keen sense of justice together with a genuine concern for the welfare of his subjects was due to her influence. With the advice of Lanfranc, archbishop of Canterbury, St. Margaret of Scotland began a series of ecclesiastial reforms that transformed the religious and cultural life of Scotland. She encouraged education and religion, held synods and meetings of bishops and priests, and even organized women's guilds to provide vestments and linens for churches. She cared for the sick and the poor, set up hostels for pilgrims and travelers, and took a special interest in orphans and beggars.

She had six sons and two daughters; one son became King David I of Scotland; her daughter Matilda later married King Henry I of England. With the king, she founded Holy Trinity Abbey at Dunfermline and restored the great monastery at Iona.

In 1093, the king and his son Edward were killed by King William Rufus of England at Alnwick Castle, and four days later the queen herself died and was buried at Dunfermline. She was canonized in 1250 and in 1673 was declared the patron saint of Scotland.

Her remarkable character shows the powerful effect that a wife and mother can have on her husband, on her children, and, in the case of Margaret, upon a whole country. One of her sons, David, followed in his mother's footsteps, became king of Scotland in 1124, and is also honored as a saint. It was at his court that St. Aelred of Rievaulx spent his early years.

Thought for the Day: The most important ingredient in education is the formation of character, and when a strong moral character is placed in a position of influence, only good things result for everyone. St. Margaret of Scotland influenced a whole country, and one of her sons became a saint. That says something for the sheer power of goodness and its ability to transform lives.

From 'The Catholic One Year Bible': Continue to love each other with true brotherly love. Don't forget to be kind to strangers, for some who have done this have entertained angels without realizing it! Don't forget about those in jail. Suffer with them as though you were there yourself. — Hebrews 13:1-3

St. Elizabeth of Hungary *(NOVEMBER 17)*

At the age of four, Elizabeth, princess of the kingdom of Hungary, was brought to the castle of Marburg in Thuringia to be brought up with her future husband, Louis, prince of Thuringia, who was eleven years old at the time. Prince and princess grew up together and grew very fond of each other. When Elizabeth was fourteen and Louis was twenty-one, they were married, one of the happiest and most idyllic marriages in history. At the time of their marriage, Louis became ruler of Thuringia and Elizabeth began her remarkable works of charity that endeared her to the impoverished people of her kingdom.

She bore her husband three children and was deeply in love with him. When he would return from state business or a military campaign, she would rush out to meet him, dressed in her most beautiful gown. In 1227, Louis went to join the forces of Emperor Frederick II on a crusade, caught malaria, and died. When word of his death reached Elizabeth, she cried out: "The world is dead to me and all that is pleasant in it."

With Louis dead, his relatives tried to seize power for themselves and drove St. Elizabeth of Hungary and her children from their home. She was defended and helped by her aunt, abbess of Kitzingen; her uncle, bishop of Bamberg, finally regained her castle and her rights as the widow of Louis. She made provision for her children's future, then gave up all her possessions and received the habit of the Third Order of St. Francis. She built a hospital in honor of St. Francis and there took care of the poor, the sick, and the destitute, revered by all as a saint.

Her health finally gave way, and on November 17, 1231, she died among her poor. One of the hospital attendants found her singing shortly before her death and asked her why. "I heard a little bird singing," she said, "and it sang so sweetly, I had to sing, too." She was twenty-four years old.

After her death, a great church was built at Marburg to enshrine her body. She was canonized in 1235, less than four years after her death.

Thought for the Day: St. Elizabeth of Hungary became a saint as a wife and mother, and her husband's death only deepened her closeness to God and gave her new opportunities to help others. She loved her husband deeply and let everyone know it. Her love of God gave her a remarkable maturity and the kind of wisdom that is able to find God in everything.

From 'The Catholic One Year Bible': . . . Whatever is good and perfect comes to us from God, the Creator of all light, and he shines forever without change or shadow. . . . Through the truth of his Word . . . we became . . . the first children in his new family. — James 1:17-18

St. Rose Philippine Duchesne *(NOVEMBER 18)*

Rose Philippine Duchesne came to the wilds of North America when anything west of Pittsburgh was considered uncharted wilderness. She came up the Mississippi to Missouri and established a school at St. Charles as early as 1818, while St. Elizabeth Seton was doing her work in the eastern United States. She is the foundress of the American branch of the Society of the Sacred Heart.

She was born in Grenoble, France, in 1769, her father a successful businessman. She was educated by the Visitation nuns and, although her father opposed her decision, she entered the Visitation Order in 1788, in the middle of the French Revolution. She was not able to make her profession because of the disruption of the Revolution and had to return home when the Visitation sisters were expelled from their convents.

During the Revolution, she cared for the sick and poor, helped fugitive priests, visited prisons, and taught children. After the Revolution, she tried to reorganize the Visitation community but was unsuccessful, so she offered the empty convent to St. Madeleine Sophie Barat, foundress of the Society of the Sacred Heart, and entered the Sacred Heart Order herself. When the bishop of New Orleans, William Du Bourg, requested nuns for his huge Louisiana diocese, St. Rose Philippine Duchesne came to the United States, arriving in New Orleans in 1818.

She and her four nuns were sent to St. Charles, Missouri, where she immediately opened a school; then at Florissant, she built a convent, an orphanage, a parish school, a school for Indians, a boarding academy, and a novitiate for her order. In 1827, she was in St. Louis where she founded an orphanage, a convent, and a parish school. Her energy and ideas were prodigious. When she was seventy-two years old, she founded a mission school for Indian girls in Kansas and spent much of her time there nursing the sick.

Her last years were spent at St. Charles, a model and inspiration to those around her, facing all the hardships of pioneer work. She died on November 18, 1852, at the age of eighty-three and was canonized in 1988. She was truly the "missionary of the American frontier," one that her beloved Potawatomi Indians called *Quah-kah-ka-num-ad*, "Woman-who-prays-always."

Thought for the Day: Setback after setback after setback, even into old age! This woman of bronze — St. Rose Philippine Duchesne — let nothing stop her, nothing discourage her, nothing slow her down. We can do almost anything for God if we refuse to be discouraged and are willing to pay the price: the price is something called holiness.

From 'The Catholic One Year Bible': Dear brothers, how can you claim that you belong to the Lord Jesus Christ, the Lord of glory, if you show favoritism to rich people and look down on poor people? . . . God has chosen poor people to be rich in faith and the Kingdom of Heaven is theirs, . . . — James 2:1, 5

St. Odo of Cluny

(NOVEMBER 19)

Odo is the glory of the great abbey of Cluny, which was responsible for a huge program of monastic and clerical reform under this great abbot. He was the second abbot of Cluny but began his religious life as canon of St. Martin of Tours, to whom he always had a deep devotion. He was the son of Ebbo I, lord of Deols, and received his early education at the court of the duke of Aquitaine, then studied at Paris under Remigius of Auxerre.

While a canon of Martin of Tours, St. Odo of Cluny became acquainted with Blessed Berno, the founder of Cluny, and became a monk of the Cluniac monastery of Baume. In 927, he succeeded Berno as abbot of Cluny and it was he who obtained from Pope John XI the privilege of exemption and was authorized by him to reform the monasteries of France and Italy, where monastic observance was at a very low ebb.

So successful was he that he was called the "restorer of monasteries" and of the holy rule. It was Odo who established the Cluniac observance, which became the model of monasticism for over a century, and it was he who promoted an enthusiasm for the monastic life that would transform the religious life of Europe.

He was sent by the popes on peacemaking missions in Italy to reconcile two rulers who both had their eyes on ruling Italy. On returning from Rome in 942, he became sick and stopped at the monastery of St. Julian in Tours for the celebration of the feast day of St. Martin. He took part in the celebrations on November 11 and after a lingering illness died on November 18. During his last illness, he composed a hymn in honor of Martin.

Besides his work of monastic reform, Odo left a number of literary works and several pieces of liturgical music. His relics are kept at l'Isle-Jourdain in France.

Thought for the Day: Admiration for a saint can lead to sanctity. St. Odo of Cluny was deeply devoted to St. Martin of Tours and as a young student imitated Martin in his love of beggars. He always kept the example of Martin before his eyes and with such a model he found his own way to holiness.

From 'The Catholic One Year Bible': . . . The wisdom that comes from heaven is first of all pure and full of quiet gentleness. Then it is peace-loving and courteous. . . . It is wholehearted and straightforward and sincere. And those who are peacemakers will plant seeds of peace and reap a harvest of goodness. —James 3:17-18

St. Edmund the Martyr *(NOVEMBER 20)*

Bury St. Edmund's is the name of a town in England, a name most people have seen but have not the faintest idea what it means. It takes its name from the saint of today, Edmund, an English king, tortured to death by the invading Danes.

Edmund was king of East Anglia, that part of England that juts out into the North Sea. These were the days when the Vikings were ravaging Scotland, England, Ireland, and the coasts of France, and their biggest invasion came in 866, when Edmund was king of East Anglia. At first they were somewhat peaceable, demanding only horses. Swinging north, they took York, then marched south, plundering as they went.

They came into Edmund's kingdom, and he raised an army to meet them. But his army was soon overcome, and Edmund delivered himself into the hands of the Danes, hoping to save his people.

He was offered terms by the Danish leader, Ingvar, which he could not in conscience accept and was asked to deny his faith. St. Edmund the Martyr refused, was tied to a tree, and his body torn with whips. To amuse themselves, the Danish soldiers shot his body full of arrows till his body was "like a thistle covered with thorns." Ingvar then cut the ropes by which he was bound, dragged him from the tree, and beheaded him.

His body was buried at Hoxne and about the year 903 was taken to a town that was renamed St. Edmund's Borough, shortened to Bury St. Edmund's. During the reign of the the Danish King Canute, the monastery of Edmundsbury was founded to enshrine Edmund's body.

For centuries, Edmund was one of the most popular native saints in England and over forty churches were dedicated to him. Bury St. Edmund's became a great Benedictine abbey, famous for its manuscripts and works of art. It is one of the many examples of a town taking the name of the saint it honors.

Thought for the Day: It was said that St. Edmund read the psalter every day and learned it by heart so that in his kingship he could resemble King David. It was this religious devotion that prepared him for the terrible ordeal of martyrdom. Living religiously had prepared him well to die for the Christian faith.

From 'The Catholic One Year Bible': . . . What do you think the Scripture means when it says that the Holy Spirit, whom God has placed within us, watches over us with tender jealousy? . . . As the Scripture says, God gives strength to the humble, but sets himself against the proud and haughty. —James 4:5-6

St. Gelasius

Gelasius is one of those early popes who left his mark upon Church history, and this particular pontiff left a strong mark. It is the Gelasian theory of the "two powers" that has earned him a place in papal history. His letters to the Byzantine emperors set forth his views on the two powers that govern the world: the sacred authority of the bishops and the royal power of the emperor. He was telling the emperor plainly to stay out of Church affairs, since this imperial interference had been causing much trouble in the Church.

St. Gelasius was an African by birth and became archdeacon of the Church in Rome and assistant to the pope. He became the main spokesman in the papal quarrel with Constantinople known as the Acacian Schism and was a strong defender of papal primacy. It was he who applied the principles of papal authority laid down by Pope St. Leo I and applied these principles in a series of letters to the Eastern emperors.

An interesting side note to history is that Pope Gelasius insisted on Holy Communion under both kinds, a practice that was to die out in later centuries, only to be revived once again after the Second Vatican Council. His insistence on Communion from the cup was aimed at the Manichees who considered wine an unlawful drink and would not receive Communion from the cup.

Gelasius is the first pope to be greeted as vicar of Christ and it was he who rooted out the last vestiges of paganism in Rome. There is an early sacramentary called the Gelasian sacramentary; but, although Gelasius did write Mass formulas and treat of liturgical matters in his letters, this sacramentary came many decades after him.

His definition of papal authority and of the autonomy of bishops influenced canon law throughout the whole Middle Ages and contributed to a period in the development of canon law called the Gelasian Renaissance.

Gelasius died on November 21, 496, and was buried in St. Peter's, but the exact location of his grave is not known.

Thought for the Day: The Church today is free from the interference of governments, but it was not always so. Popes like St. Gelasius gradually freed the Church from its domination by political powers, and we now reap the benefits of their work. We should be grateful to the great pontiffs who have led the Church in difficult times.

From 'The Catholic One Year Bible': . . . If anyone has slipped away from God and no longer trusts the Lord and someone helps him understand the truth again, that person who brings him back to God will have saved a wandering soul from death, bringing about the forgiveness of his many sins. — James 5:19-20

St. Cecilia (NOVEMBER 22)

Cecilia is the patron saint of music and is one of the most celebrated of the early Roman martyrs. Nothing is known for certain about her life, but an early inscription refers to a church named after her. Her feast was celebrated in the sixth century at a church named after her in Rome, and an early legend gives an account of her martyrdom.

According to the legend, St. Cecilia was a Christian of noble rank in Rome engaged to a Roman nobleman named Valerian, whom she converted to Christianity, together with his brother, Tiburtius. When Valerian and Tiburtius were exposed as Christians, they were arrested and executed, most probably during the persecution under the Emperor Diocletian.

She was responsible for the conversion of over four hundred persons who were baptized in her home by Pope Urban. Arrested and brought before the Roman authority, she was condemned to be suffocated in a hot bath, but she was not harmed. She was then struck three times in the neck with a sword and lingered on for three days. After her death, her home was converted into a church and her body was buried in a crypt.

In 821, Pope Paschal I had her body removed from the crypt and placed under the altar in the basilica of St. Cecilia. In 1599, the tomb was opened and a sculptor named Maderna carved a statue of the saint, which was placed beneath the altar in her church.

Cecilia is named in the Canon of the Mass, and together with SS. Agnes, Lucy, and Agatha is one of the most revered of early women martyrs. She is usually portrayed with a small organ, since the legend about her says that she sang on the day of her scheduled marriage, asking God to help her in her trouble. Some scholars doubt that a martyr named Cecilia actually existed, since the legend about her is late, but her early veneration and her inclusion in the Canon of the Mass indicates some historical memory of such a martyr.

Thought for the Day: For the early Christians, their faith was an amazing revelation that brought light and joy into a world of gloom and uncertainty. It is hard for us to realize how startling the Christian faith was in those pagan times. We should reflect on what meaning that faith has for us and perhaps we will understand something of the joy of the martyrs.

From 'The Catholic One Year Bible': You love him even though you have never seen him; though not seeing him, you trust him; and even now you are happy with the inexpressible joy that comes from heaven itself. And your further reward for trusting him will be the salvation of your souls. — 1 Peter 1:8-9

St. Columban *(NOVEMBER 23)*

This great missionary abbot founded monastic centers in France, Switzerland, and Italy that became centers of evangelization and learning for the whole area. He was a monk of the monastery of Bangor in north Ireland, founded by St. Comgall, one of the notable monastic founders of Ireland.

At Bangor, sanctity and scholarship were prized, and St. Columban became a teacher in the monastic school there. He was born in Leinster, and after a youthful struggle he lived at Cluain Inis for a time. After thirty years at Bangor, he received Comgall's permission to spread the Gospel on the continent of Europe, and taking twelve companions with him he settled in Gaul where the devastation of the barbarian invasions had completely disrupted civil and religious life. Invited by the Merovingian King Childebert, he founded a monastic center in Burgundy at Annegray and two others at Luxeuil and Fontaines. From these three monasteries over two hundred foundations were made, and Columban composed for these monasteries two monastic rules.

With the zeal of a prophet, he attacked the immoral court life of the Merovingian kings, the lax local clergy, and introduced to the continent the Irish penitential system, which became the basis for private confession. Reproving a local king for his immoral life, Columban was expelled from Burgundy, traversed France and Germany, leaving disciples behind to found monasteries, and crossed the Alps to found his most famous monastery at Bobbio in Italy.

He was a firm opponent of Arianism, wrote letters to popes on the religious issues of the day, and left a legacy of writings that deeply influenced the monasticism that came after him.

He impressed his contemporaries as a giant of a man in mind and spirit, who revived religion on the continent and prepared the way for the Carolingian renaissance. He died at Bobbio on November 23, 615, and is buried in the crypt of St. Columban's Church there.

The St. Columban's Missionary Society took its name from him, recognizing in him a missionary genius with a uniquely Irish spirit.

Thought for the Day: St. Columban suffered for his outspokenness in the face of moral corruption and public depravity. He was exiled, but his words were remembered years later and many of his warnings heeded. He preached the word of Christ fearlesssly and was not afraid of the anger of kings. It is the kind of Christian courage we should have.

From 'The Catholic One Year Bible': . . . God called you out of the darkness into his wonderful light. Once you were less than nothing; now you are God's own. Once you knew very little of God's kindness; now your very lives have been changed by it. —1 Peter 2:9-10

St. Colman of Cloyne *(NOVEMBER 24)*

In Ireland, the clan of bards was highly regarded and the bard was part of the culture and the daily life of Irishmen. The bard was not only poet and minstrel, he was also the chronicler of his times or of his king, the genealogist, and something of a poet laureate. St. Colman of Cloyne was a native of Munster, a poet of great skill, and royal bard to the king of Cashel.

He was fifty years old before he became a Christian, and it happened in a strange way, in a manner typically Irish, a happening that is the stuff of legends.

St. Brendan of Clonfert, the navigator who himself is one of the great legends of Ireland, came to Cashel to settle a dispute over succession to the kingship. Saints were often called upon to be peacemakers, and since wars often resulted from disagreements, their peacemaking efforts prevented a lot of bloodshed.

While Brendan was in Cashel, the shrine and relics of St. Ailbe were found in a river, where robbers had drowned trying to carry them away. The finding of the relics was an awesome moment, since Ailbe was one of the patriarchal saints of Ireland, and the royal bard took part in the retrieval of the relics from the water.

When Brendan observed what had happened, he said to Colman: "Hands that have been hallowed by touching such holy remains should not remain the hands of a pagan." So Brendan baptized the bard and gave him the Christian name of Colman. Then he took him to St. Jarlath at Tuam, where he himself had studied, to begin studies for the priesthood, and sent him for counseling to St. Ita, who had reared Brendan himself.

He was ordained a priest, preached in Limerick and Cork, and in his old age taught the young St. Columba how to read. He founded a church at Cloyne and became its first bishop. He died about the year 606.

Thought for the Day: St. Colman received the gift of faith when he was over fifty years old but made up for lost time by a life of dedication and holiness. The lateness of the hour in which we are called makes no difference; what does matter is our dedication and devotion once the light has been given us. What return have I made for the light given me?

From 'The Catholic One Year Bible': . . . You should be like one big happy family, full of sympathy toward each other, loving one another with tender hearts and humble minds. . . . We are to be kind to others, and God will bless us for it. — 1 Peter 3:8-9

St. Peter of Alexandria *(NOVEMBER 25)*

In the early Church, there were three great centers of Christianity, the three major cities of the Roman empire: Rome, Alexandria, and Antioch; and these three centers, together with Contantinople after 330, would continue to influence Christianity in their region. Peter was bishop of Alexandria just before the Peace of Constantine, the last great bishop of that city before Christianity was given its freedom by Constantine.

He became bishop of Alexandria at the height of the persecution unleashed by the Emperors Decius and Diocletian and continued by their successor, in the year 300, and he would die a martyr's death before the Christian faith became acceptable.

St. Peter of Alexandria was chief shepherd of the Church in Egypt, and it was a time when thousands apostatized and thousands more were martyred. Peter laid down definite rules about how those who had lapsed should be received back into communion with the Church, and while holding firmly to the need for repentance he urged mercy for those who had acted under weakness.

For this he was accused of laxity by Meletius, bishop of Lycopolis, who considered Peter schismatic and would have no communion with him. This was the origin of the Meletian Schism that would plague Alexandria for another century.

The Roman authorities intensified the persecution of Christians, and Peter went into hiding for the sake of his flock. Peter was rounded up in a purge of Christians and with six hundred others, including four other bishops, was executed. He was the last martyr to be put to death in Alexandria, and his canonical decrees are considered milestones in early Church discipline.

After Peter came Achillas and Alexander, and then came St. Athanasius who brought the Church in Alexandria to its heights of glory. Peter was the forerunner who kept the faith alive in persecution and showed himself in every way a true father of his flock. He was martyred about the year 311.

Thought for the Day: In St. Peter's day, to die for the faith was common, and no one knew when that supreme sacrifice would be demanded. Heroism was the order of the day, and to be a Christian meant to be a hero. Some kind of heroism is demanded of all of us. What is important is that we are ready when it comes.

From 'The Catholic One Year Bible': . . . Try to live in peace even if you must run after it to catch and hold it! For the Lord is watching his children, listening to their prayers; but the Lord's face is hard against those who do evil. — **1 Peter 3:11-12**

St. John Berchmans *(NOVEMBER 26)*

This young saint of the Society of Jesus was born in Flanders, the oldest of five children. He grew up in an atmosphere of political turmoil caused by a religious war between the Catholic and Protestant sections of the Netherlands. He studied at the Gymnasium at Diest and worked as a servant in the household of Canon John Froymont at Malines in order to continue his studies.

In 1615, the Jesuits opened a college at Malines, and St. John Berchmans was one of the first to enter. He was an energetic student and was a leader among the students. In 1616, he entered the Jesuit novitiate at Malines and came under the influence of Father Antoine Sucquet. The young Berchmans developed a strong and deep spirituality based on the loving practice of fidelity. St. Aloysius of Gonzaga was his spiritual model, and he was influenced as well by the example of the Jesuit English martyrs.

It was his realistic appreciation for the value of ordinary things, a characteristic of the Flemish mystical tradition, that constituted his holiness. He was affable, kind, and endowed with an outgoing personality that endeared him to everyone. In 1618, he was sent to Rome to study philosophy and was an exceptional student. He requested after ordination to become a chaplain in the army, hoping to be martyred on the battlefield.

In the summer of 1619, the intense heat of Rome started to affect his health and he began progressively to get weaker. The doctors could not determine what was wrong, and for two years he was continually sick, requiring medical care, and as the summer of 1621 came, it was clear that he would not last long. He died peacefully on August 13, 1621, and numerous miracles were attributed to him at the time of his funeral.

He was beatified by Pope Pius IX in 1865 and canonized by Pope Leo XIII in 1888. His body lies in the church of St. Ignatius in Rome, where Aloysius of Gonzaga is also buried.

Thought for the Day: Like St. Thérèse of Lisieux, St. John Berchmans was not noted for anything extraordinary. He made kindness and courtesy as well as constant fidelity an important part of his holiness. The path to holiness lies in the ordinary rather than the extraordinary. That is a lesson that some learn only late in life.

From 'The Catholic One Year Bible': Feed the flock of God; care for it willingly, not grudgingly; not for what you will get out of it, but because you are eager to serve the Lord. . . . And when the Head Shepherd comes, your reward will be a never-ending share in his glory and honor. — 1 Peter 5:2, 4

St. Virgilius

(NOVEMBER 27)

Virgilius was a scientist before his time, and in his monastery of Aghaboe in Ireland he was known as "the Geometer" because of his knowledge of geography. In 743, he left Ireland for a pilgrimage to the Holy Land but got no farther than the court of Pepin, the father of Charlemagne. In 745, Pepin defeated Odilo, duke of Bavaria, and sent St. Virgilius to be abbot of the monastery of Sankt Peter and in charge of the diocese of Salzburg.

In accordance with the Irish custom, the bishop was subject to the abbot, who was the real head of the diocese. This was contrary to continental custom, and so Virgilius consented to be consecrated bishop. His most notable accomplishment was the conversion of the Alpine Slavs; moreover, he sent missionaries into Hungary.

In his first days at Salzburg, he was involved in controversies with St. Boniface, one over the form of baptism, which the pope decided in Virgilius's favor. Virgilius also expressed a number of opinions on astronomy, geography, and anthropology, which to Boniface smacked of novelty, if not heresy. He reported these views to Rome, and the pope demanded an investigation of the bishop of Salzburg. Nothing came of this and apparently Virgilius was able to defend his views.

Virgilius built a grand cathedral at Salzburg, baptized the Slavic dukes of Carinthia, and sent missionaries into lands where no missionary had yet gone. Returning from a preaching mission to a distant part of his diocese, he fell sick and died on November 27, 784. When the Salzburg cathedral was destroyed by a fire in 1181, the grave of Virgilius was discovered and this led to his canonization by Pope Gregory IX in 1233.

His feast is kept throughout Ireland and in the diocese of Salzburg.

Thought for the Day: St. Virgilius was not content to keep his faith to himself, but like many Irish monks at the time he wanted to share it with others. He looked for a ripe harvest and found it in Germany, where he labored for over forty years. If we look around, we can always find some way to share our faith with others.

From 'The Catholic One Year Bible': . . . We have not been telling you fairy tales when we explained to you the power of our Lord Jesus Christ and his coming again. My own eyes have seen his splendor and his glory: I was there on the holy mountain when he shone out with honor given him by God his Father, . . . —**2 Peter 1:16-18**

St. Catherine Labouré *(NOVEMBER 28)*

Zoé Labouré was the ninth of seventeen children; her father was Pierre Labouré, a successful farmer. Her mother died when she was eight, and when her older sister left home to become a Sister of Charity, Zoé took care of the household. She wanted to follow her sister into religious life, but her father opposed her and instead sent her to Paris to work in her brother's cafe. Unhappy in this work, she went to Châtillon-sur-Seine to stay with relatives and there entered the Sisters of Charity of St. Vincent de Paul in 1830.

She took the name of Catherine, and after her postulancy she was sent to the convent in Rue de Bac in Paris and there began to have a series of visions, indicating that she had a special mission to fulfill. In a second apparition in November of 1830, her mission was revealed when she saw a picture of Mary standing on the globe of the world with light streaming from her hands. Around the head of the Virgin were the words: "O Mary, conceived without sin, pray for us who have recourse to thee." After showing Catherine the medal, Mary commissioned her to spread devotion to it. Catherine confided the apparition to her confessor, who obtained permission from the archbishop of Paris to have the medal struck.

St. Catherine Labouré was sent to the convent of Reuilly in Paris and lived there for the next forty-six years. When the apparitions were investigated by the archbishop of Paris, she refused to appear and had pledged her confessor to secrecy regarding her identity. The apparitions were judged authentic, and devotion to the Miraculous Medal spread throughout the Church. For years, not even her superiors knew that she was the subject of the apparitions. She remained hidden and unknown to the end of her life.

She died on December 31, 1876, and her incorrupt body lies in the Sisters of Charity Motherhouse on Rue du Bac in Paris. She was beatified by Pope Pius XI in 1933 and canonized by Pope Pius XII in 1947.

Thought for the Day: Devotion to Mary is at the very heart of Catholicism, and from time to time we are reminded of this by our Lady herself: Guadalupe, Lourdes, Fátima, and by the apparitions to St. Catherine Labouré. This devotion is as ancient as the Church itself and is one of the qualities that marks a Catholic.

From 'The Catholic One Year Bible': . . . At Belshazzar's command, Daniel was robed in purple, and a gold chain was hung around his neck, and he was proclaimed third ruler in the kingdom. — Daniel 5:29

Joseph Pignatelli was a Jesuit at the time of the suppression of the order by Pope Clement XIV, and it was he who helped keep the spirit of the Jesuits alive during the long period of its suppression.

He was born in Saragossa, Spain, in 1737 and was left an orphan at the age of nine. His older brother took charge of the family, and Joseph and his younger brother became resident-students at the Jesuit college in Saragossa. He entered the Jesuits when he was sixteen, his younger brother, Nicholas, following him. During his student years, he contracted tuberculosis and was in poor health for the rest of his life.

After his ordination in 1762, St. Joseph Pignatelli served as chaplain to a prison and worked especially with those condemned to die. On April 3, 1767, the Jesuits were expelled from Spain by order of Charles III, and similar expulsions soon took place in Portugal and France. Young as he was, Father Joseph became the leader of the Spanish Jesuits and had gained a reputation for remarkable leadership in the Cloak and Sombrero Riots a few years earlier. All the Jesuits of Spain were taken to the port of Tarragona and banished from the country, their number filling thirteen flotillas. Refused entry to several port cities, they debarked at Corsica for a time, then found refuge in Ferrara.

When Pope Clement XIV formally suppressed the Jesuits in 1773, Father Joseph went to Bologna and, forbidden to exercise his priestly ministry, spent his time in prayer and scholarship. In 1797, the duke of Parma, with the encouragement of Joseph, received permission from the pontiff to establish a Jesuit province in his duchy. In 1798, Pope Pius VI, en route to exile in France, authorized Father Joseph to receive novices at Parma. Appointed Jesuit provincial of Italy, Joseph presided at the restoration of the society in Naples when Jesuits from all over the world came together, and in 1806 Pius VII restored the Gesu and the Roman college to the order. Joseph directed the restoration of the order before its official restoration by the pontiff in 1814.

Weakened by his tubercular condition, Father Joseph died on November 11, 1811, and was canonized in 1954. He is considered the savior and restorer of the Society of Jesus.

Thought for the Day: With the suppression of the Jesuits, St. Joseph Pignatelli saw his whole world collapse around him. He showed exceptional leadership in dark and difficult times and became the strength of thousands of others. This was the result of his deep life of prayer; it is this kind of prayer that makes saints.

From 'The Catholic One Year Bible': . . . A day or a thousand years from now is like tomorrow to the Lord. He isn't really being slow about his promised return, even though it sometimes seems that way. . . . The day of the Lord is surely coming, as unexpectedly as a thief, . . . —**2 Peter 3:8-10**

Andrew, the brother of St. Peter, was, like his brother, a native of Bethsaida in Galilee. He and Peter were fishing partners with James and John, the sons of Zebedee, and it was from their nets that Jesus called them, when He began His ministry in Galilee. The brothers had a house at Capernaum, where Jesus stayed when He was in that city.

When St. John the Baptist began his work, St. Andrew became his disciple, and it was Andrew who, after meeting Jesus, went to find his brother. Andrew was the first disciple called by Jesus. Later, the brothers went with Jesus to the marriage at Cana and witnessed His first miracle.

After the call of Jesus at Bethsaida, both Peter and Andrew accompanied Jesus on His preaching mission through Galilee, and then south to Jerusalem for the difficult days of the Passion and Crucifixion. Andrew was one of the witnesses to the risen Jesus and was in the upper room with the other Apostles when Jesus appeared to them on Easter night.

After the Resurrection, the New Testament is silent on Andrew. Early legends have him evangelizing Greece, Epirus, and Scythia, and there is a very strong tradition of his crucifixion at Patras around the year 70. Because of his close association with Greece, Andrew has been a popular saint among the Greeks and is the patron saint of the Church at Constantinople and of the Greek Orthodox Church.

Andrew is commonly represented with an X-shaped cross, on which he was crucified, and he is also the patron saint of Russia and Scotland (the great golf course at St. Andrew's is named after him). Among the Greeks, he is called the "Protoclete," or the first-called, since he was the first disciple called by Jesus.

Thought for the Day: St. Andrew was so excited about meeting Jesus that he brought his brother along so that he could also meet Him, and it was Andrew who introduced the Greeks to Jesus on Palm Sunday. He was a friend of the Master and his joy was in making Him known. What a wonderful description of a Christian: to make Jesus known. We can find no better model than Andrew.

From 'The Catholic One Year Bible': Christ was alive when the world began, yet I myself have seen him with my own eyes and listened to him speak. I have touched him with my own hands. He is God's message of life. . . . We guarantee that we have seen him; I am speaking of Christ, who is eternal Life. —1 John 1:1-2

THE SAINTS OF DECEMBER

St. Edmund Campion *(DECEMBER 1)*

Edmund Campion is the best known of the martyrs of the age of Elizabeth and was something of a John Henry Newman in the Anglican Church of his day. At fifteen, he was given a scholarship to Oxford, was made a junior fellow, and distinguished himself as a brilliant student and outstanding orator. Chosen to give an address of welcome to Queen Elizabeth when she visited Oxford in 1566, he won the patronage of the earl of Leicester, and the queen and William Cecil both expressed an interest in his future. He was the best-known Oxford figure of his day and was described by William Cecil as "a diamond of England."

In 1569, St. Edmund Campion went to Dublin to help found a university and there wrote his highly regarded *History of Ireland*, returned to London, and then crossed over to France where he was received into the Catholic Church. He received the subdiaconate at Douai, then went as a pilgrim to Rome and entered the Society of Jesus. After his novitiate, he was assigned to teach at Prague, where he was ordained in 1578.

In 1579, he was chosen to inaugurate a Jesuit mission to England. He landed in England disguised as a jeweler and, on reaching London, visited Catholics in prison. Soon after landing, he wrote his *Challenge to the Privy Council*, in which he indicated the purpose of his mission. He became the support and encouragement of Catholics in England, barely escaped capture countless times, and was pursued relentlessly by agents of the crown. He changed his name and his disguise frequently, wrote tracts challenging the Anglicans to debate, and became the symbol of Catholic resistance to the Church of England.

On June 30, 1581, he was betrayed, captured, and imprisoned in the Tower of London. He was tortured, forced into a theological debate, and on November 14, together with others, was condemned to death. At his trial, he told the judges: "In condemning us, you condemn all your own ancestors." On December 1, he was executed at Tyburn. He was beatified by Pope Leo XIII in 1886 and canonized by Pope Paul VI in 1970.

Thought for the Day: There are some people who have to live a hero's life, since they almost have no choice. To be true to their conscience, to their faith, they have to pour out their life or their blood for a cause. St. Edmund Campion was one of these. All of us may be called upon at some time to be heroes.

From 'The Catholic One Year Bible': Anyone who says he is walking in the light of Christ, but dislikes his fellowman, is still in darkness. . . . He who dislikes his brother is wandering in spiritual darkness and doesn't know where he is going, . . . —1 John 2:9, 11

Blessed John Ruysbroeck *(DECEMBER 2)*

John Ruysbroeck was a Flemish mystical writer who greatly influenced mystical teaching in the late Middle Ages and whose name is associated with the religious renewal in the Lowlands that also produced *The Imitation of Christ*. He was born near Brussels in 1293 and was raised by a devout mother who trained him in a life of holiness.

At the age of eleven, he went to Brussels to live with an uncle, John Hinckaert, a priest and canon of St. Gudule's. John Ruysbroeck studied for the priesthood and was ordained in 1317. Under his uncle's roof he continued to live a life of retirement and study and began the writings that were to be the basis of his spiritual teaching: *The Spiritual Espousals, The Kingdom of Lovers*, and *The Tabernacle*.

Together with his uncle and another canon, Francis van Coudenberg, Blessed John Ruysbroeck withdrew to a hermitage near Soignes for a life of greater solitude, and a number of disciples joined them. They decided to inaugurate a formal religious institute and adopted the rule of the canons of St.-Victor. John was made the prior of the new institute.

Excellent writings continued to come forth from his pen: *The Book of the Sparkling Stone, The Little Book of Enlightenment*, and *The Book of the Twelve Beguines*.

John Ruysbroeck's writings are considered classics of spirituality, anticipating the writings of St. John of the Cross in their clarity and doctrine. He strongly opposed the quietist tendencies of many of his contemporaries. His solid theological background and his ability to make clear the sure path of spiritual progress gave him a wide reading, and his books are lucid commentaries on the Augustinian doctrine of the life of grace.

For several years before his death, John lived in a small cell, just outside the cloister of his monastery. In his eighty-eighth year, he asked to be taken to the community infirmary, where he prepared himself for death. He died on December 2, 1381. He was beatified by Pope Pius X in 1908.

Thought for the Day: The contemplative life has always been treasured by the Church, and those living a life of seclusion are looked upon as "Treasures of the Church." We all need a little solitude once in a while, to put our life and our thoughts together, and dwell for a little while with the things of God.

From 'The Catholic One Year Bible': See how very much our heavenly Father loves us, for he allows us to be called his children — and we really *are*! . . . And we can't even imagine what it is going to be like later on. — 1 John 3:1-2

This amazing missionary — who evangelized the Far East — laid the foundation for Christianity in Japan and died with his eyes on the great harvest waiting in China. His name was on the lips of everyone in Europe after his *Letters* were published, and he inspired others to follow him in his great conquest of the world for Christ.

His beginnings did not reveal his future greatness. St. Francis Xavier was the pampered son of a Basque noble family, born near Pamplona in 1506. When he was eighteen, he was sent to Paris for study, and there at the college of St. Barbe, he met his fate in the person of St. Ignatius of Loyola. They roomed together during their studies, along with Peter Favre from Savoy.

Ignatius caught Francis Xavier in his trap of holiness, and Francis became one of the six who, together with Ignatius and Peter Favre, founded the Society of Jesus. He accompanied Ignatius to Rome, became his secretary and, when a missioner was requested by the king of Portugal to be sent to the Indies, the choice fell on Francis Xavier.

In 1541, he was appointed apostolic nuncio to the East by King John of Portugal and he embarked for India. Thirteen months later, he landed on Goa and carried on a short missionary activity there. He then set out for the Pearl Fishery coast and worked there for two years, laying the foundations of a Catholicism that has lasted to this day.

In 1545, he sailed for the Malay peninsula where he met a Japanese named Anjiro who told him about Japan. When other Jesuits arrived from Europe, he sent them across the Far East to establish missions and schools, then turned his eyes to Japan. He landed on Kagoshima in 1549, learned the language, and set out for Kyoto (which was then the capital of Japan), where the emperor resided. After laboring for two years, he left the Japanese mission in charge of another Jesuit and returned to Goa where he was appointed Jesuit provincial of India.

He then turned his eyes to China. Encountering difficulties entering that country, he sailed to the island of Sancian, just off the Chinese coast near Canton. There he caught a fever and, still waiting for permission to enter China, died on December 3, 1552. His body was returned to Goa and is enshrined in the Jesuit church there. He was canonized in 1622.

Thought for the Day: How much could we do for Christ if we did not count the cost? The difficulties and hardships that St. Francis Xavier had to face were unbelievable. He was often crushed with disappointment and faced with almost insurmountable obstacles. But he let nothing stop him. It is that kind of determination that makes a saint.

From 'The Catholic One Year Bible': . . . If our consciences are clear, we can come to the Lord with perfect assurance and trust, and get whatever we ask for because we are obeying him and doing the things that please him. — 1 John 3:21-22

St. John Damascene *(DECEMBER 4)*

This Doctor of the Church was born in Damascus, Syria, and his father was a government official under both the Byzantine emperor and the Muslim rulers of Damascus. Receiving an excellent classical education, and fluent in Arabic as well as Greek, St. John Damascene worked in the Muslim court until the hostility of the caliph toward Christianity caused him to resign his position, about the year 700.

He migrated to Jerusalem and became a monk at Mar Sabas monastery near Jerusalem. He taught in the monastery, preached many of his luminous sermons in Jerusalem, and began to compose his theological treatises.

It was about this ume that the iconoclast controversy shook the Churches of the East, when the Byzantine emperor ordered the destruction of images in Christian churches. John fought the heresy, bringing down upon himself the wrath of the emperor and the hatred of the iconoclast party.

He has left a rich legacy of writings, including his principal dogmatic work, *The Source of Knowledge*, which was a *summa theologica*, a refutation of heresy, an exposition of the Orthodox faith, and a study of contemporary religious issues. His writings on Mary constitute a true theology of the Mother of God, and his sermons of the saints, the liturgical feasts, and the Gospels show not only vast learning but also give us information about local customs and contemporary happenings.

Since he lived in the midst of political and theological turmoil, John wrote much to clarify true doctrine and to do his part in spreading the Gospel. The fact that he lived and worked in Jerusalem itself gives his sermons, delivered at many of the holy places, a special appeal.

He died at a very old age, some say one hundred four, in the midst of his labors, beloved by his fellow monks and revered by the people. He was buried at the monastery of Mar Sabas and was declared a Doctor of the Church in 1890.

Thought for the Day: St. John Damascene was concerned that erroneous doctrine would deceive people and wrote to clarify exactly what was sound teaching. He spent his life enlightening others and became a beacon of light in very difficult times. All of us should be bearers of light in some way.

From 'The Catholic One Year Bible': . . . Let us practice loving each other, for love comes from God, and those who are loving and kind show that they are the children of God, and that they are getting to know him better. —1 John 4:7

St. Sabas *(DECEMBER 5)*

Sabas, one of the great monastic founders, established several notable monasteries in Palestine, the most famous of which is Mar Sabas, near Jerusalem. He was born in Cappadocia and as a boy was given into the charge of an uncle, who treated him harshly. Unhappy at home, Sabas ran away to a monastery. Later, his uncle tried to persuade him to return to his family and marry, but Sabas decided to remain in the monastery.

When he was eighteen, St. Sabas went to Jerusalem to be trained by St. Euthymius, who sent him to the monastery of St. Theoctistus where Sabas remained for seventeen years. In 483, Sabas founded his own monastery in the Wadi en Nar. Because of his influence, he was persuaded by the patriarch of Jerusalem to be ordained a priest and became director of all the anchorites who inhabited Judea. He founded six other monasteries, four hospices for pilgrims to the Holy Land, and saw his disciples establish other monasteries and hospices.

His influence on the growth of monasticism in Palestine was considerable and his *typicon*, or rule, became the basis for many others.

In 511 and again in 530, he was sent as an emissary to Constantinople by the patriarch of Jerusalem and was received kindly by the Emperor Justinian. After his return from his second journey to Constantinople, Sabas fell sick and the patriarch himself cared for him. As his last hour approached, he appointed his successor and asked to be left by himself for the next four days so that he could be alone with his God.

Sabas died on December, 5, 532, ninety-four years of age. After the crusades, his relics were kept in Venice, but in recent years, at the command of the pope, his relics were returned to the monastery of Mar Sabas in Jerusalem. His *laura*, or monastery, still exists to this day in the Cedron Valley, just outside Jerusalem.

Thought for the Day: St. Sabas lived first what he later taught to others, and he became the spiritual father of generations of the monks down to the present time. We must first embody in ourselves the fullness of what we believe; and only then can we really influence others for good.

From 'The Catholic One Year Bible': I have written this to you who believe in the Son of God so that you may know you have eternal life. And we are sure of this, that he will listen to us whenever we ask him for anything in line with his will. —1 John 5:13-14

Nicholas and his legends have become associated with Christmas, and so it is fitting that his feast day should come in the month of December. Little is known of his true history, but legends fill in the story and explain why he has been linked to Christmas giving.

He was bishop of Myra in what is present-day Turkey, in the province of Patara, and was imprisoned in the persecution under Diocletion. He was also present at the Council of Nicaea in 325. This is all that is known of his true history, except that he died at Myra around 350.

The legends tell stories of his generosity: of providing dowries for poor girls, and his part in the release of three unjustly convicted army officers.

By the time of the Emperor Justinian in the sixth century, there was a church dedicated to St. Nicholas in Constantinople. When the Muslims conquered the Middle East, including St. Nicholas's city of Myra, soldiers from Italy took the relics to Bari, in southern Italy, and there they have rested since. A new church was built for them, and its dedication was attended by Pope Urban II. From Bari, devotion to Nicholas spread all over Europe, and there were over two thousand churches dedicated to him. In Holland, he was known as Sinter Klaas and he became associated with gift-giving at Christmas time. Sinter Klaas soon became Santa Claus, with no religious significance, and the Christian origins of the legend were forgotten.

Since Nicholas is the patron saint of sailors, sailors in the Aegean Sea customarily greet each other with: "May St. Nicholas hold the tiller." He very early became a patron saint for children, perhaps from the custom of the "boy bishop" on his feast day, when a young boy dressed as a bishop presided at the Mass.

Nicholas has shown himself to be one of the most lovable and endearing of the saints, and the fact that he appeals to so many differing kinds of people in so many different ways shows the richness of this tradition and the many ways that the saints become part of the lives of Christian people.

Thought for the Day: The simple generosity of a man lives on and is echoed through the centuries, inspiring others to a like generosity: thus, the influence of a holy life. Not only do the saints become immortal in heaven they also become immortal on earth by their imperishable memory.

From 'The Catholic One Year Bible': . . . I want to urgently remind you, dear friends, of the old rule God gave us right from the beginning, that Christians should love one another. If we love God, we will do whatever he tells us to. And he has told us from the very first to love each other. —2 John 1:5-6

Ambrose was a man who found his whole life going in a new direction, something he had not planned for and was totally unexpected. But he was admirably fitted for the job and carved a niche for himself in the history of the Western Church. His family belonged to the old Roman aristocracy, and at the time of Ambrose's birth, his father was praetorian prefect of the Gauls, one of the chief civil offices of the Roman empire.

St. Ambrose received an excellent education in the classics and in law, with a thorough training in Greek. In 365, he entered public life as an advocate and served also as a provincial governor, with his residence at Milan. His reputation as a talented leader made him popular in Milan, and when the Arian bishop of the city died, he was unanimously chosen bishop by the clergy and people of the city. This was a time when a bishop was a civic as well as a religious figure.

Since he was only a catechumen, he was first baptized, ordained, and then consecrated bishop. Taking his new office with deep seriousness, he gave his wealth to the poor, began to live a life of strict asceticism, and organized his episcopal household after a monastery. During his first years in office, Ambrose began a study of the Scriptures and the Greek Fathers and began also to share the results of his studies with the people of his diocese. He gave homilies rich in spiritual teaching, and his cathedral became a mecca for those wishing to deepen their knowledge of the Christian faith.

He opposed the old pagan aristocracy and strongly influenced the Western emperors in making Christianity the official religion of civic and public life. When the Arian Empress Justina demanded that a basilica in Milan be turned over to the Arians, Ambrose refused and occupied his cathedral, contesting the imperial order. When he was threatened with arrest, he carried on a perpetual vigil of prayer and sacred song, his cathedral filled with members of his congregation.

He was a promoter of the monastic life and of consecrated virginity, instructed and baptized St. Augustine, and worked for the establishment of a truly Christian society. He died in Milan in 397 and is one of the four Latin Fathers of the Church.

Thought for the Day: When he became a Christian and a bishop, St. Ambrose started to live in a way worthy of his calling. We should examine our own lives and see if there is anything about them inconsistent with our profession as Christians. Our first loyalty is to Christ.

From 'The Catholic One Year Bible': . . . Follow only what is good. Remember that those who do what is right prove that they are God's children; and those who continue in evil prove that they are far from God. —3 John 1:11

Blessed John Duns Scotus *(DECEMBER 8)*

John Duns Scotus is venerated as Blessed among the Franciscans and so it is fitting to include him here, on the Feast of the Immaculate Conception, since he had a major part in the development of the dogma.

He was born in Scotland and was trained by his uncle at the Franciscan friary at Dumfries, Scotland. When he was fifteen, he entered the Franciscans and was sent to Oxford to study. After ordination in 1291, he was sent to Paris for higher studies, then he returned to teach at Oxford. In 1302, he went to Paris again, received his doctorate of theology in 1305, and lectured there as regent master of the Franciscan chair at the university. In 1307, he was assigned to Cologne where he remained until his death.

Blessed John Duns Scotus was a superb philosopher and theologian and contributed to the development of a uniquely Franciscan theology in contrast to that of St. Thomas Aquinas and the Dominican school. The notion of an infinite being who is Love dominates his whole theology, and his ethics is characterized by the primacy of the will. He was a subtle and complex thinker who labored to give theology a unity of its own, apart from philosophy.

But his greatest theological achievement was his defense of the doctrine of the Immaculate Conception. The problem had been how to harmonize Mary's Immaculate Conception with the fact that she had to be redeemed like all descendants of Adam. Duns Scotus' solution was to hold that she had been redeemed beforehand, that, by the foreseen merits of Christ, she was preserved from original sin. It was a brilliant solution and provided the basis for the definition of the dogma by Pope Pius IX.

After his death in 1308, Duns Scotus was buried in the Franciscan church in Cologne, where his body lies today. He is venerated in the Franciscan Order and in the dioceses of Cologne and Nola.

Thought for the Day: From his sense of the eminent dignity of Mary, Blessed John Duns Scotus found the basis for the doctrine of the Immaculate Conception. This love of Mary was the heart of his spirituality, as it is the heart of any genuine Catholic spirituality. His love of Mary made his name immortal.

From 'The Catholic One Year Bible': . . . Build up your lives . . . upon the foundation of our holy faith, . . . Stay always within the boundaries where God's love can reach and bless you. Wait patiently for the eternal life that our Lord Jesus Christ in his mercy is going to give you. — Jude 1:20-21

St. Peter Fourier *(DECEMBER 9)*

Peter Fourier was born in Lorraine, France, in 1565 and was educated at the Jesuit university at Pont-a-Mousson. He entered the canons regular of St. Augustine in 1585 and was ordained to the priesthood in 1589. After receiving his doctorate in patristic theology in 1595, he was assigned to parish work at Mattaincourt, a morally lax parish, which he restored to the practice of the faith and to religious fervor.

St. Peter Fourier established religious organizations for men, women, and young people, labored to help the poor and victims of injustice, and in 1597 began a religious institute for women dedicated to teaching. He saw that the main reason for a lax religious life was lack of a sound and broad religious education, and his schools became models for their time.

He was ahead of his time in educational methods and pedagogical techniques, pioneering group instruction and the division of students according to their abilities in reading. In the work of religious renewal, it was said, Peter Fourier did more in six months than others had been able to do in thirty years. In 1616, his congregation received papal approval, and in 1628 his nuns took a fourth vow to devote themselves to the free education of children.

So successful was Peter Fourier in the work of religious renewal that in 1621 the bishop of Toul directed him to reform the canons regular of Lorraine. He was strongly opposed by the canons themselves, but he succeeded in establishing regular discipline and in 1632 was elected superior of the reformed congregations.

On the accession of Louis XIII, Peter went into exile to Franche-Comte, where he spent the last four years of his life. Serving as chaplain of a convent, he also established his last free school, and died on December 9, 1640. He was buried at Mattaincourt, and his shrine is even today the site of many pilgrimages. His canonization took place in 1897.

Thought for the Day: As a pastor, St. Peter Fourier saw the crying need for good schools and set about doing something about it. He had to start from scratch. We all have to put our hands to new and unexpected tasks for the Lord and we should not hesitate just because the task is new and different.

From 'The Catholic One Year Bible': See! He is arriving, surrounded by clouds; and every eye shall see him. . . . "I am the A and the Z, the Beginning and the Ending of all things," says God, who is the Lord, the All Powerful One who is, and was, and is coming again! — Revelation 1:7-8

St. Gregory III *(DECEMBER 10)*

At the funeral of Pope Gregory II in 731, there was a Syrian priest sitting among the attending clergy. He was well known for his learning and holiness and found himself suddenly acclaimed the new pope by clergy and people alike, much to his surprise. He took the name of the former pope and inherited many of his problems as well.

These were the days when the emperor in Constantinople was in the midst of his campaign against the veneration of images, called the iconoclast controversy. He was determined, on the basis of his own private bias, to root out the veneration of images in the Church and he had been just as strongly opposed by the popes, by St. John Damascene, and by other learned and holy leaders in the Churches of both East and West.

The new pope sent a strong letter to the emperor, but his messenger was seized by imperial officers and banished. St. Gregory III subsequently called a synod in Rome and excommunicated anyone who would oppose the veneration of images. Angry, the emperor sent ships with officers to arrest the pope and bring him to Constantinople, but the ships were lost in a storm. The emperor seized papal estates in southern Italy and Sicily and took the Baltic lands from papal jurisdiction and placed them under Constantinople.

In the face of Lombard attacks on Italy, Pope Gregory III appealed to the Frankish Prince Charles Martel, as if in anticipation of the future alliance between the papacy and the Franks.

Gregory III, who had expert knowledge of the Scriptures, was a polished and effective preacher, learned in both Latin and Greek, and was a lover of poverty and the poor. He died on December 10, 741. The *Liber Pontificalis* calls him "a man of deep humility and deep wisdom," and he was a worthy successor of the two pontiffs named Gregory who preceded him.

Thought for the Day: St. Gregory III did not hesitate to oppose even an emperor, when the emperor was wrong, risking imprisonment and death. That is the risk of responsibility, and he measured up to that responsibility. We, too, may have to take risks for the sake of truth and we should not hesitate to do so.

From 'The Catholic One Year Bible': . . . Every one who is victorious shall eat of the hidden manna, the secret nourishment from heaven; and I will give to each a white stone, and on the stone will be engraved a new name that no one else knows except the one receiving it. — Revelation 2:17

St. Damasus

Here is another pope, one of the greatest in the early Church, who was pontiff in the century that produced SS. Augustine, Jerome, Ambrose, and the Eastern Fathers, St. Basil and the two Gregories. A native of Spain, St. Damasus was a deacon under Pope Liberius and went with him into exile. He was elected pontiff in a stormy election, with an antipope also claiming the papal throne. But Damasus was the choice of both the clergy and the people and was consecrated in the Lateran basilica.

After his election a bloody battle took place between the supporters of Pope Damasus and the supporters of the antipope. The violence and turmoil continued into the first years of this pope's pontificate and the Holy Father himself was accused of a serious crime, of which he was exonerated by both the civil authority and a synod in Rome.

He had trouble with Arian bishops during his pontificate, but after St. Ambrose replaced the Arian bishop of Milan in 374, the Arian crisis lessened. It was during his papal reign that the Council of Constantinople was held in 381, and he is the first pope to call the see of Rome the apostolic see.

One of the most notable achievements of Damasus was his commission to St. Jerome to revise the Latin translations of the New Testament on the basis of the original Greek, and from this commission came the Latin *Vulgate* translation of the Bible. It was also during his pontificate that the emperors of both East and West proclaimed Christianity the official religion of the Roman empire. Damasus was a promoter of the cult of martyrs and restored and redecorated many of their tombs during his term of office.

Damasus died on December 11, 384, and was buried with his mother and sister in a small church he had built on the Via Ardeatina. His epitaph, which he wrote himself, expressed belief that "he . . . who gives life to the dying seeds of the earth . . . will make Damasus rise again from the dust."

Thought for the Day: It is to St. Damasus that we owe the translation of the Scriptures, which influenced so mightily the next fifteen hundred years. He felt that the word of God needed wide dissemination and he provided a genuine treasure for the Christian people. It is something for which we should all be grateful.

From 'The Catholic One Year Bible': "To everyone who overcomes — who to the very end keeps on doing things that please me — I will give power over the nations. You will rule them with a rod of iron just as my Father gave me authority to rule them; . . . I will give you the Morning Star!" — Revelation 2:26-28

The story of Juan Diego is the story of a very special child of God who listened to the beautiful lady and brought the love of God and the Christian faith to a whole people. Our Lady of Guadalupe is honored as the queen and mother of the Mexican people, and the story of her coming to Mexico is one of the loveliest in the history of the Church.

Juan Diego was an Indian who lived near Mexico City in the year 1531, not many years after Hernán Cortés had conquered Mexico. He was going to Mass one morning and passed near a hill called Tepeyac where he heard singing voices. Wondering what it was, he heard himself called by name and went to see who was calling him. At the top of the hill, he saw a lady, "her garments shining like the sun," and she asked him where he was going. He told her he was going to church. She told him she wanted a church built on the hill in her honor and to go to the bishop of Mexico City and tell him of her desire.

He did as he was told, and although the bishop received him kindly, he did not believe Juan's story. The next day, the lady was waiting for Juan on the hill and he told her what had happened. She told him to go back once more and that this time he would be listened to. The second time the bishop questioned him but said that he would need some kind of proof.

The next time he went to church, Juan Diego tried to avoid the lady, but she appeared to him anyway and gave him special instructions for the next visit: he was to climb the hill and gather some of the flowers that were there in his *tilma*, or cloak, and take them to the bishop.

When Juan came into the bishop's presence and opened his *tilma*, everyone in the room knelt, not at the miracle of flowers (it was the middle of winter), but at the image painted on the *tilma*: the image we know as Our Lady of Guadalupe.

The church was built and the image enshrined there. Recently, a new basilica was built to house the image, and this basilica is the center of the devotion of the Mexican people.

Thought for the Day: Our Lady appeared to the poorest and humblest of Indians and she appeared as an Indian, to show God's love for the Mexican people. She wanted them to realize that they, just as any other people, were important to God and that God was concerned about them. That message is also for us.

From 'The Catholic One Year Bible': "Look! I have been standing at the door and I am constantly knocking. If anyone hears me calling him and opens the door, I will come in and fellowship with him and he with me." — Revelation 3:20

St. Lucy *(DECEMBER 13)*

Lucy is one of those saints who have become part of the liturgy, and for centuries — before the reform of the calendar under Pope Gregory — her feast came at the winter solstice (thus, "This is the feast of St. Lucy Light; the shortest day and the longest night"). With the advent of the Gregorian calendar, her feast day lost that significance, but she is still considered the patron saint of those with ailments of the eyes.

We know only the barest facts about her history. She was a Sicilian maiden during the Diocletian persecutions who had vowed herself to God. She had been promised to a young man in marriage, and when she told him of her determination to remain unmarried, he accused her before the governor of Sicily of being a Christian. She was condemned to be burned, but since burning did not kill her, she was killed with a sword.

After the the Peace of Constantine, the body of St. Lucy was brought to Constantinople and, during the crusades, to Venice, where it now rests in the church of Santa Lucia. As Santa Lucia, she is the beloved saint of Italians, who usually have a great festival on her feast day.

In Scandinavian countries, Lucy Fires used to be burned on her feast day, and as the light-bringer, she heralded the coming of the True Light of the World at Christmas. She is also the patron saint of lamplighters and of the gondoliers of Venice, who made the song *Santa Lucia* popular by their singing of it as they rowed visitors through the lagoons of the city.

She is often portrayed with two eyes on a dish, with a palm of martyrdom or a lamp in her hand. She was venerated very early in the Church, along with the other two Sicilian martyrs, St. Barbara and St. Catherine, and her name was introduced into the Gelasian and Gregorian sacramentaries.

Along with St. Agatha, Lucy is mentioned in the Canon of the Mass. In the Middle Ages, she was one of the most popular saints in the Church and has been a favorite subject for Christian artists.

Thought for the Day: The heroism of a young girl dying for her faith made St. Lucy an early Christian heroine. At a time when Christians needed encouragement to suffer for their faith, her example led others to a like heroism. We all need heroes, and the saints are uniquely Christian heroes, showing us how to live, and sometimes how to die, for our faith.

From 'The Catholic One Year Bible': . . . The twenty-four Elders fell down before him and worshiped him . . . and cast their crowns before the throne, singing: "O Lord, you are worthy to receive the glory and the honor and the power, for you have created all things." — Revelation 4:10-11

St. John of the Cross *(DECEMBER 14)*

John of the Cross is the great mystical Doctor of the Church, whose writings have become the classical mystical literature and whose mystical theology has become almost an official doctrine. He was born in Spain in 1542, entered the Carmelite Order, and was associated with St. Teresa of Ávila in the reform of the Carmelites.

He was born Juan de Yepes on June 24, 1542, at Fontiveros, Spain. His father, the son of a wealthy silk merchant, was disowned by his family for marrying Catalina Alvarez, a poor weaver. Forced to live in poverty, Juan's father died soon after Juan, his third son, was born.

Young John was educated at Medino del Campo, where he was apprenticed in various crafts and also worked at a hospital before enrolling at the Jesuit college in the city. In 1563, at the age of twenty-one, he entered the Carmelite Order in Medina del Campo. After his novitiate, he was sent to the Carmelite college at Salamanca, for higher studies.

In 1567, he was ordained to the priesthood and in this year he met St. Teresa for the first time. He had been thinking of entering a stricter religious order and told her so. She convinced him to join the "reform" and in 1568, with two other friars, he made his profession according to the Carmelite primitive rule. The friars of the reform were called discalced, or shoeless.

In 1571, Teresa undertook the reform of her own monastery of the Incarnation at Ávila and appointed John confessor.

The reform was not accepted by other Carmelites, who resented the work of Teresa, and in 1577 St. John of the Cross was seized by the unreformed branch of the order, taken to Toledo, and ordered to renounce the reform. He refused and was imprisoned as a rebel. It was there that he wrote some of his greatest mystical poems. In 1578, he escaped miraculously, returned to the reform, and wrote his mystical writings upon which his fame is based.

In 1591, out of favor with the superiors of the reform, John was sent to a monastery in southern Spain. He became ill with fever, was sent to the monastery at Ubeda to recover, and died there on December 14, 1591. He was canonized in 1726 and declared a Doctor of the Church in 1926.

Thought for the Day: St. John of the Cross taught that only the possession of God can make us happy and that we should find our happiness in God alone. That is the essence of his mysticism, as it is the essence of the Christian faith. Love — and love alone — is the way to this possession.

From 'The Catholic One Year Bible': "The Lamb is worthy . . . the Lamb who was slain. He is worthy to receive the power, and the riches, and the wisdom, and the strength, and the honor, and the glory, and the blessing." — Revelation 5:12

Paolina Francesca di Rosa was born in Brescia, Italy, in 1813, the daughter of a wealthy landowner and public official. After her mother's death, she was educated by the Sisters of the Visitation and on leaving school took charge of her father's household, developing a skill for organization.

With her father's home as her base, she put her hand to a wide variety of charitable works, encouraged and supported by her spiritual director, the archpriest of the cathedral in Brescia. She was joined in her work by Gabriella Bornati, and they heroically cared for the sick during a devastating cholera epidemic in 1836.

It was due to her efforts that Brescia opened a school for the deaf, a home for wayward girls, passed laws to help indigent women, and instigated a program of social works. In 1840, she founded her religious congregation, the Handmaids of Charity, whose chief work was the care of the sick and the suffering. The foundress was scarcely thirty years old when others were soon inspired to join her.

Sister Maria Crocifissa became the angel of mercy for Brescia and the surrounding cities, especially when war broke out in northern Italy. Her sisters went onto the battlefields, nursing the wounded and dying; they staffed a military hospital and, with Sister Maria at their head, turned back a troop of unruly soldiers who tried to break into the hospital at Brescia.

In 1850, St. Maria Crocifissa di Rosa went to Rome to obtain papal approval for her congregation. Her congregation began to spread rapidly, and the foundress opened houses in Spalato and Verona. In 1855, at Mantua, she collapsed and was rushed to her motherhouse in Brescia. She died on December 15, 1855.

She was remembered for decades by those who knew her, for she had been a friend to all, ready to go at a moment's notice to look after the sick, sit at the bedside of the dying, or to comfort someone in trouble. Crowds flocked to her funeral, and she was buried in the chapel of the motherhouse of the Handmaids of Charity in Brescia. She was canonized by Pope Pius XII in 1954.

Thought for the Day: In her love of the crucified Christ, St. Maria Crocifissa di Rosa saw her mission in the suffering members of His Mystical Body. She made their sufferings her own and became the servant of all. How often do we see Christ in others, especially those who are sick and suffering?

From 'The Catholic One Year Bible': As I watched, the Lamb broke the first seal and began to unroll the scroll. Then one of the four Living Beings, with a voice that sounded like thunder, said, "Come!" — Revelation 6:1

Adelaide — the wife of two kings and the mother of another — lived in the midst of political intrigue, dynastic murders, and barbaric cruelty. She was the daughter of Rudolf II of Burgundy and at the age of two was betrothed to Lothair, son of Hugh of Provence. The marriage took place when she was sixteen and when Lothair was king of Lombardy. In 950, her husband died and was succeeded by a mortal enemy, Berengarius, who was suspected of poisoning Lothair.

Berengarius imprisoned Adelaide in a castle on Lake Garda after she refused to marry his son. When the German King Otto the Great led an army into Italy, he defeated Berengarius, released Adelaide from prison, and married her. Five children were born to them. In 962, Otto was crowned emperor at Rome and Adelaide returned with her husband to Germany.

In 973, Otto died and was succeeded by his son Otto II, Adelaide's oldest son. Persuaded by his Greek wife, the son treated his mother harshly, forcing her to seek refuge with her brother, Conrad, at Vienne. The abbot of Cluny brought about a reconciliation between son and mother. When Otto II died in 983, he was succeeded by his son, who was underage, and his mother, the Greek princess, became regent of the kingdom.

When the Greek princess died in 991, Adelaide herself became regent. She sought the best advisers to help her in her difficult task, among them SS. Wiligis of Mainz, Adalbert of Magdeburg, and Odilo of Cluny. St. Adelaide founded monasteries, sent missionaries to convert the Slavs, and showed herself kind and forgiving to those who had wronged her when she was out of power.

She impressed the people of her time as a woman of deep spirituality and Christian virtue, zealous for the cause of religion, and sensitive to the needs of her people. She died at the monastery she had founded at Seltz, near Strasbourg, on December 16, 999, and was canonized in 1097.

Thought for the Day: St. Adelaide had to live in the world, with all the turmoil and violence of political life, yet managed to live totally for God in the midst of her many occupations. She was wife, mother, queen, and empress, noble in every way. She is proof that sanctity can be achieved anywhere and that every way of life can be made holy.

From 'The Catholic One Year Bible': "They will never be hungry again, nor thirsty. . . . For the Lamb standing in front of the throne will feed them and be their Shepherd and lead them to the springs of the Water of Life. And God will wipe their tears away." — Revelation 7:16-17

Olympias is one of the glories of the Eastern Church, a friend of St. John Chrysostom's who suffered because of he disfavor into which he fell and gave an example of Christian charity in the Constantinople of the fourth century.

Heiress to a great fortune, St. Olympias was brought up by her uncle, Procopius, a friend of St. Gregory Nazianzus'. In 384, she married Nebridus, prefect of Constantinople, and Gregory wrote a poem for the wedding. In 386, with no children, her husband died and she began to devote herself to Christian service and works of charity.

Emperor Theodosius I urged her to remarry, but she refused and, since she had refused one of his kinsmen, he impounded her estate. Unperturbed, she continued to devote herself to charitable works, and after five years, the emperor had a change of heart. She was enrolled as a deaconess by the patriarch of Constantinople, and when John Chrysostom became patriarch, she put herself under his spiritual direction and built a convent next to the cathedral. In addition, she built a hospital, an orphanage, and a hospice for strangers.

John Chrysostom took her work and her followers under his protection, and she also became the friend of the brothers of SS. Basil, Gregory of Nyssa, and Peter Sebaste, encouraging Gregory in those writings that have made him the doctor of mysticism of the East.

During John Chrysostom's trouble with the emperor and with the patriarch of Alexandria, she stood by him with her strong support and underwent persecution because of him after he was exiled in 404. She refused to have anything to do with his successor because of the injustice to St. John and was sent into exile herself for this refusal.

She was still in exile when she learned of John Chrysostom's death in 407. When she died at Nicomedia the following year, she was scarcely in her mid-forties. Her body was taken back to Constantinople during the reign of Emperor Justinian I and buried in the convent that she founded.

Thought for the Day: Loyalty to friends is an important part of being a Christian, and St. Olympias suffered for her loyalty to St. John Chrysostom. Her friendship was a great comfort to him in his suffering, as his letters show, and his friendship was a support in her own sufferings. Friendship is something that even the saints cherished.

From 'The Catholic One Year Bible': O God, I beg two favors from you before I die: First, help me never to tell a lie. Second, give me neither poverty nor riches! Give me just enough to satisfy my needs! For if I grow rich, I may become content without God. And if I am too poor, I may steal, and thus insult God's name. — Proverbs 30:7-9

Winebald is one of those amazing English missionaries who evangelized Europe, leaving behind a flourishing Catholicism and a number of monasteries and laying the beginnings of Christianity in what is now Germany, France, Holland, Austria, Belgium, and Luxembourg.

St. Winebald was the son of a West Saxon nobleman, St. Richard, and the brother of St. Willibald. With his father and brother he made a pilgrimage to Rome in 721. His father died in Italy, and Winebald remained in Rome for further study, like his countrymen before him, St. Wilfrid and St. Benedict Biscop. He returned to England and brought back to Rome some of his relatives to begin a monastic life in the holy city.

When St. Boniface came to Rome in 739, he recruited Winebald for the German missions, ordained him a priest, and put him in charge of churches in Germany and Bavaria. His brother, Willibald, who was now bishop of Eichstätt, asked Winebald to found a monastery for the training of priests and as a center of learning. Their sister, St. Walburga, came from England to found a convent, and both the monastery and the convent were founded at Heidenheim.

He established the rule of St. Benedict in his monastery, and Heidenheim became an important center of learning in the missionary territory. Because of illness, Winebald was not able to carry on the missionary work that he desired and yearned to end his days at Monte Cassino.

In 761, Winebald visited St. Boniface's shrine at Fulda and on the way home to Heidenheim became very sick. When he reached Heidenheim, he became weaker and weaker and after giving his monks a few last words he died on December 18, 761. His tomb became a local shrine and the site of pilgrimages.

Thought for the Day: St. Winebald was strongly influenced by his father, St. Richard, and his brother, St. Willibald. Sometimes sanctity runs in the family, and the encouragement that the family members receive from one another is a large part of their holiness. Let us keep in mind that those we associate with have a powerful influence on our personality and character.

From 'The Catholic One Year Bible': O Lord, now I have heard your report, and I worship you in awe for the fearful things you are going to do. In this time of our deep need, begin again to help us, as you did in years gone by. Show us your power to save us. — **Habakkuk 3:2**

St. Macarius of Wurzburg *(DECEMBER 19)*

About 689, an Irish monk named Kilian was martyred at Wurzburg in Germany, where he had been commissioned a roving bishop by Pope Conon. His tomb at Wurzburg became the site of pilgrimages from Ireland and so many Irish pilgrims came over the centuries that in the year 1134 the bishop asked the Irish monks of St. James at Regensburg to establish a hospice there for these pilgrims.

The Irish monks from St. James established a monastery at Wurzburg and St. Macarius was named abbot. Like his predecessors, he was a man of deep learning and a calligrapher of great skill. He inaugurated at Wurzburg a remarkable literary activity and left behind at Wurzburg the largest collections of Irish manuscripts in existence, in the tradition of the *Book of Kells* and the *Book of Durrow.* The Irish monks were superb calligraphers and illuminators and produced some of the most beautiful manuscripts of the Middle Ages. Long before the invention of printing, they had large libraries and left their mark upon the learning of medieval Europe.

Macarius attracted to Wurzburg learned and talented monks from Ireland, among them David, a historiographer and head of the cathedral school, who became chaplain to the emperor. The influence of these Irish monks was remarkable and their monasteries were staffed with monks from Ireland until the year 1497, when they were driven out by Scottish monks.

Macarius died in 1153. In 1615, his body was exhumed and transferred to the abbey church. In 1818, his relics were moved to the Mariankapelle in Wurzburg. Like all the Irish monks, Macarius joined holiness of life to holy learning and worked not only for the establishment of religion but also for the creation of a uniquely Christian culture. To learning, they also joined a love of beauty, and the books they produced are considered masterpieces of the arts of illumination.

Thought for the Day: Belief is not enough: we have to embody that belief in works that bring the faith alive. St. Macarius realized that religion thrived where Christian literature flourished, and he produced beautiful books for the Christian people. His work lives on in his books and in the people whose lives he influenced.

From 'The Catholic One Year Bible': ". . . I will gather you together and bring you home again, and give you a good name, a name of distinction among all the peoples of the earth, and they will praise you when I restore your fortunes before your very eyes," . . . — Zephaniah 3:20

St. Dominic of Silos *(DECEMBER 20)*

St. Dominic, founder of the Order of Preachers, was named after this Benedictine abbot, who lived a century before him. According to Dominican tradition, St. Dominic of Silos appeared to Blessed Joan of Aza (the mother of the later St. Dominic), who made a pilgrimage to his shrine before the birth of her son, and named him after the abbot of Silos.

Dominic of Silos was born in Navarre, Spain, on the Spanish side of the Pyrenees, and was a shepherd boy, looking after his father's flocks. He acquired a love of solitude and as a young man became a monk at the monastery of San Millán de la Cogolla. He eventually became prior of the monastery and came into conflict with the king of Navarre over possessions of the monastery claimed by the king. The king drove Dominic out of the monastery, and Dominic went with other monks to Castille, where the king of Castille appointed Dominic abbot of the monastery of St. Sebastian at Silos.

The monastery was in terrible shape, spiritually and materially, and Dominic set about to restore the monastery and to reform the lives of the monks. He preserved the Mozarbic Rite (one of the variants of the Latin Rite) at his monastery, and his monastery became one of the centers of the Mozarbic liturgy. His monastery also preserved the Visigothic script of ancient Spain and was a center of learning and liturgy in that part of Spain.

Dominic of Silos died on December 20, 1073, about a century before the birth of his namesake, St. Dominic of Calaruega. Before the Spanish Revolution of 1931, it was customary for the abbot of Silos to bring the staff of Dominic of Silos to the Spanish royal palace whenever the queen was in labor and to leave it at her bedside until the birth of her child had taken place.

In recent times, great interest in Dominic of Silos has arisen since the literary treasures of the library of Silos have become known. The abbey had a profound influence on spirituality and learning in Spain. Today the monastery is an abbey of the Benedictine Congregation of Solesmes housing a library of ancient and rare manuscripts.

Thought for the Day: St. Dominic of Silos came to know God in the solitude of a shepherd boy. It was this love of solitude that drew him into monastic life where he could be alone with his God. Most of us are so busy we scarcely have time for Sunday Mass. We should cultivate a little solitude, too.

From 'The Catholic One Year Bible': . . . In heaven, the temple of God was opened and the ark of his covenant could be seen inside. Lightning flashed and thunder crashed and roared, and there was a great hailstorm and the world was shaken by a mighty earthquake. — Revelation 11:19

St. Peter Canisius *(DECEMBER 21)*

Peter Canisius, the remarkable Jesuit who almost single-handedly reevangelized Central Europe, founded dozens of colleges, contributed to the rebirth of Catholicism by his prodigious writings, and laid the groundwork for the Catholic Reformation north of the Alps.

He was born at Nijmegen, Holland, in 1521, and his father was an instructor to princes in the court of the duke of Lorraine. St. Peter Canisius was part of a movement for religious reform as a very young man and in 1543, after attending a retreat given by Blessed Peter Favre, joined the Jesuits and was the eighth professed member of the Society of Jesus.

He worked first in the city of Cologne, becoming a spokesman for the Catholic party. He became a consultor to the cardinal of Augsburg at the Council of Trent and in 1547 was called by St. Ignatius to Rome. He was sent to Sicily to teach, then after his solemn profession in Rome was sent back to Germany as the first superior of the German province of the Jesuits.

Peter then began to restore and found colleges, first in Vienna and Prague, and then in Munich, Innsbruck, and throughout northern Germany. He attracted vocations to the Jesuits, and the society began to flourish in Central Europe. He organized the Jesuits into a compact unit and made the society a leading force in the Counter-Reformation. He was in contact with all the Catholic leaders in Germany, and wrote fourteen hundred letters giving support to those laboring for reform. He was the adviser of the emperor and the confidante of three popes. He was consulted by papal legates and nunciatures and was a severe critic of religious and clerical life in post-Reformation Germany.

He recommended far-reaching reforms and had a profound effect upon the education and spiritual life of the clergy. Through his efforts, seminaries were founded, and the popes sent him on important diplomatic missions. In the midst of his many labors, he edited and published editions of the Fathers of the Church, catechisms, spiritual manuals, and textbooks that went into countless editions even in his own lifetime.

He died on December 21, 1597, at Fribourg, Switzerland, and was canonized and declared a Doctor of the Church in 1925.

Thought for the Day: Nothing discouraged St. Peter Canisius; he saw obstacles only as challenges, even though the obstacles were backbreaking. His confidence was in Christ and in his dream of conquering the world for Christ. With such an example before us, we should put our hand to our own task, with the same confidence in Christ.

From 'The Catholic One Year Bible': . . . I saw a woman clothed with the sun, with the moon beneath her feet, and a crown of twelve stars on her head. — Revelation 12:1

Blessed Marianus Scotus, Chronicler *(DECEMBER 22)*

There are two Irish Blessed by this name: one of them the founder of St. James Irish monastery at Regensburg, and the other, later in the century, known as the Chronicler for his most notable writing, a *Chronicle of the World*. This Marianus Scotus entered the monastery of Moville where he was educated, then left Ireland in 1056 and migrated to Cologne, becoming a monk at the Irish monastery of St. Martin's there.

In 1058, he went to St. Boniface's monastery at Fulda and was ordained in Wurzburg. At Fulda, he had a little cell where he lived a life of prayer, penance, study, and writing, walled off from the world but filled with his books.

In 1069, his abbot became archbishop of Mainz and brought Marianus with him; it was at Mainz that Blessed Marianus Scotus wrote his *Chronicle of the World*, a massive chronology of the world in three books, beginning with the creation of Adam to the year of Marianus's own death, 1082. It is considered an extraordinary work, displaying vast learning, and has been reprinted countless times. The Vatican has an eleventh-century manuscript of the work, and it indicates something of the scholastic ability of the Irish monks at this time.

This period of monastic history — and of Irish monastic history in particular — was not very widely known, and the Irish cultural influence on the continent of Europe had yet to be written. With their deep holiness, their wide learning, and their superb writing skills, the monks became the teachers of the continent for several centuries as well as missionaries and pedagogues to the great men of the period.

Many of these monks became tutors to princes and advisers to kings and helped to bring about the creation of a genuine Christian commonwealth. Marianus Scotus was one of these giants. He died on December 22, 1082, at the monastery of St. Martin in Mainz. In Irish, his name is Moel Brigte.

Thought for the Day: Blessed Marianus Scotus studied to see God's hand in history so that his readers could come to understand God's Providence through the ages. God is behind the universe and behind the world, directing it to His own ends and working for the salvation of the human race. To understand this is to look to God in everything.

From 'The Catholic One Year Bible': ". . . 'Judah shall be the Lord's inheritance in the Holy Land, for God shall once more choose to bless Jerusalem.' Be silent, all mankind, before the Lord, for he has come to earth from heaven, from his holy home." — Zechariah 2:12-13

St. John Kanty *(DECEMBER 23)*

John Kanty was born near Auschwitz, Poland, and studied at the University of Cracow. He was ordained a priest and became a professor of theology at the university. He was known for his generosity to the poor and to poor students in particular. He was so successful as a teacher and preacher that others at the university became jealous of his popularity and had him dismissed from the university and assigned to a parish in a nearby town.

He was not welcomed by his parishioners, but he threw himself into the new work and so won them over that when he left to return to the university a few years later, a crowd accompanied him along the road, sad to see him leave. "God does not want you to be sad," he told them. "If I have done any good for you all these years, sing a song of joy."

He was appointed professor of Sacred Scripture at the university, a position he held for the rest of his life. He had a wide circle of friends, among both the poor and the nobility, and once was turned from the house of a nobleman because of his shabby cassock. He gave lavishly to the poor, and any poor person in Cracow knew that he would never be turned away by St. John Kanty.

Everyone knew that he ate little, slept on the floor, and, when he made a pilgrimage to Rome, he walked all the way and back, his luggage carried on his back. He loved a good argument but told his pupils: "Fight all false opinions, but let your weapons be patience, sweetness and love. Roughness is bad for your own soul and spoils the best cause."

In 1473, when news got around the city of Cracow that he was dying, there was sadness everywhere. "My prison is falling apart," he told those who expressed sorrow at his passing. "Be happy for the soul that is about to leave it." He died on Christmas eve, 1473, at the age of eighty-three. He was canonized in 1767 and is one of the most beloved saints of Poland.

Thought for the Day: Sweetness of disposition wins more people than a sharp mind and roughness. Every human being is worthy of respect, even if his opinions are false and his attitudes wrong. We may be right in our opinions, but we are very wrong if we defend those opinions in an unkind and uncharitable way.

From 'The Catholic One Year Bible': . . . I heard a sound from heaven like the roaring of a great waterfall or the rolling of mighty thunder. It was the singing of a choir accompanied by harps. This tremendous choir — 144,000 strong — sang a wonderful new song in front of the throne of God. . . . — Revelation 14:2-3

St. Thorlak *(DECEMBER 24)*

Thorlak is a saint of Iceland, one of the few canonized saints of that remote island, even though for centuries, before the coming of the Viking, it was peopled by Irish monks who lived on the edge of the world on what they called Ultima Thule. The Vikings came in the eighth and ninth centuries, and by the beginning of the tenth century the country was divided into two dioceses.

Thorlak Thorhallsson was born at Fljotshilth, Iceland, in 1133 and was ordained a deacon when he was only fifteen. By the age of eighteen, he was ordained a priest and sent to England and France to study. While abroad, he became a canon regular of St. Augustine and returned to Iceland in 1161. Clerical life in Iceland at the time was rather lax, but St. Thorlak set up a religious regime for himself, and when a farmer died and left him land for a monastery, he established a monastery of canons regular, of which he became the abbot.

In 1178, he became bishop of Skalholt and set about to reform his diocese and improve ecclesiastical discipline. Clerical celibacy was not widely observed, there was constant lay interference in the affairs of the Church, and simony was rampant. He met with little success, faced opposition on all sides, and found little to encourage him in his efforts. Fortunately, he had the support of the Norwegian archbishop responsible for Iceland, who was trying to accomplish the same things in Norway, and Thorlak made some progress in raising the spiritual life of his diocese.

After fifteen years as bishop, he determined to resign his bishopric and return to his monastery, but he died on December 23, 1193, before he could carry out his intention. His work did not go unnoticed, however, and he was canonized by the Assembly of Iceland five years after his death. He is one of the three Icelandic saints venerated in Iceland. The other two are St. Jon Ogmundson and Blessed Guthmund the Good.

Thought for the Day: When things are falling apart, someone must hold them together. St. Thorlak was a pillar of stability in a lax and careless age, and the memory of his sanctity encouraged others to a holy life. He gave himself to God when he was fifteen years old and never took back the gift. His fidelity became a model for others.

From 'The Catholic One Year Bible': . . . All were holding harps of God, and they were singing the song of Moses, the servant of God, and the song of the Lamb: / "Great and marvelous / Are your doings, / Lord God Almighty. / Just and true / Are your ways, / O King of Ages." — Revelation 15:2-4

The *Roman Martyrology* thus announces the celebration of the Feast of Christmas:

In the 24th day of the month of December:
In the year 5,199 from the creation of the world, when in the beginning God created the heavens and the earth:
In the year 2,957 from the Flood:
In the year 1,510 from the going forth of the People of Israel out of Egypt under Moses:
In the year 1,032 from the anointing of David as king:
In the 65th week according to the Prophecy of Daniel:
In the 194th Olympiad:
In the year 752 from the foundation of the city of Rome:
In the 42nd year of the reign of the Emperor Octavian Augustus:
In the 6th age of the world, while the whole earth was at peace —

JESUS CHRIST,

Eternal God and Son of the Eternal Father, willing to consecrate the world by His gracious coming, having been conceived by the Holy Spirit, and the nine months of His conception being now accomplished. . . .

was born in Bethlehem of Judah,
of the Virgin Mary, made man.

THE BIRTHDAY OF OUR LORD JESUS CHRIST, ACCORDING TO THE FLESH.

The story begins with the simple lines of St. Luke's Gospel: "And Joseph also went up from Galilee . . . to the city of David which is called Bethlehem." In Palestine, in the reign of Caesar Augustus, a homeless couple was driven underground to escape from the night and the cold. And there, in silence and wonder a child was born. A child who was truly a human child but just as truly God. That is the mystery we celebrate today, and it is belief in that mystery that makes us Christians.

Thought for the Day: Christmas is the great window of the year, the great window that opens onto eternity and gives us a glimpse of immortality. Whatever it is that we experience at Christmas, this is back of it all. We may not know how to describe it, and sometimes we may be too choked up with feeling to define it ourselves, but that is the substance of the Christmas experience.

From 'The Catholic One Year Bible': "Take note: I will come as unexpectedly as a thief! Blessed are all who are awaiting me, who keep their robes in readiness and will not need to walk naked and ashamed." — Revelation 16:15

"Good King Wenceslaus went out, on the Feast of Stephen." This is the Feast of St. Stephen, the day after Christmas, when we commemorate the first disciple to die for Jesus: Stephen, the first martyr.

Stephen was one of the deacons chosen by the Apostles to serve the needs of the Greek-speaking members of the first Christian community in Jerusalem. He became the leader of these Greek-speaking Jews and, in contrast to some of the Hebrew-speaking Jews, spoke openly of Jesus as the Messiah and debated with those Jews who did not accept Jesus as the Savior.

Stephen's open profession of faith and fearless witness to Christ angered his opponents, and he was arrested and brought before the Sanhedrin on charges of blasphemy. Before the Sanhedrin, Stephen spoke even more boldly, accusing them of betraying their heritage by not recognizing Jesus as the Messiah.

When he also accused them of responsibility foı the death of Jesus, the Sanhedrin condemned him to death and incited the crowd against him. He was taken outside the city walls and stoned to death, the penalty for blasphemy. During the stoning, Stephen forgave his murderers, saw Jesus ready to receive him into Paradise, and died as a witness to faith in Jesus Christ. The Acts of the Apostles, which describes the scene, also adds: "The witnesses put down their clothes at the feet of a young man named Saul," thus opening the next phase of Christian history, which begins with St. Paul (as Saul after his conversion would later be known).

The death of Stephen brought about a persecution against the Christians in Jerusalem, and Saul himself was one of the leaders of the persecution. From this persecution, Christians went west to Caesarea and north to Antioch and Damascus. The Christian dispersion had begun, a dispersion that Saul himself would have a major part in. As in the case of all martyrs, the blood of Stephen was the seed of Christians.

Thought for the Day: With his dying breath, St. Stephen fulfilled one of the commands of Jesus: forgiveness of one's enemies. It was not easy for him, it is not easy for us, but that is the command of Christ. Can I think of anyone at this moment that I have not forgiven from my heart for some wrong — real or imagined — done to me?

From 'The Catholic One Year Bible': "Rejoice greatly, O my people! Shout with joy! For look — your King is coming! He is the Righteous One, the Victor! Yet he is lowly, riding on a donkey's colt! . . . His realm shall stretch from sea to sea, from the river to the ends of the earth." — Zechariah 9:9-10

St. John the Evangelist *(DECEMBER 27)*

John the Evangelist was the brother of James the Greater and the son of the fisherman Zebedee from Bethsaida in Galilee. Their mother was Salome, who may have been a sister of Mary's and if so, John was a cousin of Jesus'. They were fishing partners with Peter and Andrew, and John was also an early disciple of Jesus', after being a disciple of John the Baptist's.

John the Evangelist is identified by some as the "disciple whom Jesus loved," one of the inner circle of Jesus' close associates who were present at the Transfiguration, witnessed certain of His miracles, and accompanied Him to the Garden of Gethsemani.

Jesus called the two brothers the "sons of thunder," and this may indicate something of St. John the Evangelist's disposition. He and his brother asked to be seated at Jesus' right hand in His kingdom, but Jesus told them that they would share in His glory in a far different way.

It was John who stood by the Cross with Mary, and it was into his hands that Jesus entrusted His Mother. Legend has him caring for Mary after the Resurrection and becoming one of the pillars of the Jerusalem Church.

He is the author of the Gospel of John, the Book of Revelation, and three Epistles. Legend also has him going to Ephesus in his later years, being exiled to the island of Patmos by the Roman emperor and dying at Ephesus at a very old age.

His Gospel gives us information about Jesus found in no other Gospel and supplements the other three. The Gospel opens with the stirring Prologue bearing witness to the divinity of Jesus, together with the classical description of the Incarnation: "The Lord was made Flesh and dwelt amongst us."

The Church historian Eusebius describes John as the head of the Christian community at Ephesus, and early legends associate him with that city. His symbol among the Evangelists is the eagle because of his soaring theology, and his Gospel has been the favorite of scholars and mystics. Very early, there was a basilica dedicated to him in Ephesus.

Thought for the Day: After the Resurrection, St. John the Evangelist spent his life bearing witness to Jesus and saw in the Incarnation the living proof of God's closeness to His people. This faith was the very foundation of his existence, as it should be for ours, and each one of us, in our own way, should be an evangelist.

From 'The Catholic One Year Bible': After all this I saw another angel come down from heaven with great authority, and the earth grew bright with his splendor. He gave a mighty shout: "Babylon the great is fallen; . . ." —Revelation 18:1-2

In the Judea of King Herod the Great, it was dangerous to be a threat to the throne. In his fear of rivals to his throne, Herod had murdered his wife, two sons, uncle, mother-in-law, and several other relatives. Shortly before he died, he ordered all the eminent men in the kingdom to be gathered in the hippodrome at Jericho and killed. He knew that no one would mourn for him, and he wanted a nation in mourning at his death.

After Jesus' birth at Bethlehem and the journey of the Magi to Jerusalem searching for the "newborn king of the Jews," Herod again saw a threat to his throne. When the Magi had left Bethlehem, leaving the country secretly, Herod was determined to kill this child whom the Magi had acknowledged as king. Not knowing who the child was, he figured out a way to do away with Him: Herod would kill every male child in Bethlehem and, since he was not sure when the child was born, he ordered every boy two years old and under to be slaughtered.

The Gospel gives us the terrifying words given to Joseph in a dream: "Herod intends to search for this child and do away with him." Dynastic murders and other forms of mass killings have been common in every age and country, but this was one of the most brutal. In order to assure the death of one child, Herod ordered the death of many. The soldiers of Herod were quite accustomed to carrying out his orders for slaughter, and the slaughter of the Holy Innocents was not the first time they had been sent on a bloody mission. The order was carried out: every boy two years old and under was killed, and Bethlehem was transformed into a place of mourning.

The Holy Innocents are considered the first martyrs of the Christian faith, the first to give their lives for Christ, even if they did so unknowingly, and their feast day has been celebrated in the Church since the fifth century. Many beautiful customs have grown up around the feast, and the hymn for their feast day, *Salvete, Flores Martyrum,* is one of the loveliest in the liturgy, with its image of the Innocents before the throne of God, "playing with their palms and crowns."

Thought for the Day: The Holy Innocents were victims of injustice, and there are many such in the world today. Much injustice comes from a greed for power and an insensitivity to the rights and feelings of others. We should reflect at times on our own relationship with others and root anything resembling unfairness or injustice out of our lives.

From 'The Catholic One Year Bible': Then I heard again what sounded like the shouting of a huge crowd, or like the waves of a hundred oceans crashing on the shore, or like the mighty rolling of great thunder, "Praise the Lord. For the Lord, our God, the Almighty, reigns." — Revelation 19:6

Thomas Becket, the most illustrious martyr of England, was born in London about 1117, the son of Norman parents who were fairly well-to-do. He was educated at Merton Priory, in Paris, and may have studied law in Bologna. After his studies, he joined the household of Archbishop Theobald of Canterbury. In 1154, he was ordained deacon and appointed archdeacon of Canterbury, responsible for handling the archbishop's affairs. He was sent on several diplomatic missions by Theobald. As archdeacon, he came to the attention of King Henry II, who in 1155 appointed him chancellor of England.

While genuinely devout and scrupulously moral, St. Thomas Becket lived in a magnificent manner, rivaling even that of the king. At this time in his life, his ambitions seemed to be completely worldly, and he served his king with an unquestioning loyalty that endeared him to Henry but made him many enemies.

In 1161, Archbishop Theobald died, and Henry debated for a long time who to put in his place. He was just beginning to bring his kingdom under control, administratively and judicially, and the office of archbishop was a key position. Knowing Thomas's loyalty the king appointed him, against Thomas's own wishes and that of the monks of Canterbury, who had a voice in the selection.

From the moment of his election, Thomas was a changed man. His piety, devotion, and austerity of life were obvious, and he began to serve his God as faithfully as he had served his king. He opposed the king's interference in ecclesiastical matters, defended the rights of the Church, and insisted upon the rights of the see of Canterbury. This brought him into conflict with the king, who looked upon his actions as the height of disloyalty. In a play for power, the king demanded Thomas's condemnation by the other bishops, and Thomas fled the country, knowing his life was in danger.

After seven years in exile, still in conflict with the king, Thomas returned to England in 1170. In a fit of anger, the king expressed a wish to be rid of "this lowborn clerk," and some of his soldiers looked upon this as an order to kill Thomas. On December 29, they entered the cathedral of Canterbury where Thomas was about to assist at a Vespers service and brutally murdered him. The murder shocked England, and Thomas Becket was immediately honored as a martyr. Two years later, he was canonized.

Thought for the Day: Loyalty to Christ sometimes brings about suffering and sometimes martyrdom. Our lives may not end in martyrdom, but our loyalty to Christ and to our faith should be the most obvious thing in our life. We all have to bear witness to our faith in Christ and, like St. Thomas Becket, we should be bold in our loyalty to Christ.

From 'The Catholic One Year Bible': I saw the dead, great and small, standing before God; and The Books were opened, . . . And the dead were judged according to the things written in The Books, . . . — Revelation 20:12

Peter the Venerable is one of the most lovable figures of the twelfth century, a contemporary of St. Bernard's and Peter Abelard's, who gave Abelard a haven in his old age and brought about a rebirth of the great abbey of Cluny.

He was born in the Auvergne in 1092 and made his monastic profession at Cluny under St. Hugh. In 1109, he became prior at Vézelay and in 1122 was elected abbot of Cluny. At the time, there were four hundred monks at Cluny, and the abbey ruled two thousand dependencies. He showed himself a superb administrator, a remarkable scholar, a friend of popes, princes, and common people, and a person whose whole life was motivated by love.

Peter's predecessor had been a notorious abbot named Pontus, who had been a careless administrator, ambitious and worldly. In 1125, when Blessed Peter the Venerable was absent from Cluny, he took over the monastery, driving away anyone who opposed him. Peter and Pontus were called to Rome, the pope deciding in favor of Peter.

It was at this time that St. Bernard wrote his famous attack on Cluny, criticizing its monastic life, ridiculing its customs, and questioning the validity of its monastic observance. Peter began a correspondence with Bernard that lasted until the saint's death, and in his letters Peter shows himself a kind, loving, and humane man, quite in contrast to the severity of Bernard.

After the Council of Sens, in which Peter Abelard was condemned, with Bernard the power behind the condemnation, Peter brought about a softening of the condemnation on the part of the pope, gave Abelard a home at Cluny, and brought about his reconciliation with Bernard. A scholar himself, Peter furthered learning and scholarship and was one of the first to have an Arabic scholar among his monks.

He was admired and loved as a peacemaker, a deeply holy man, and a superb spiritual director. He died on Christmas Day, 1156, after preaching a sermon on the feast. His gentle spirit influenced his age and he was known as Venerable even in his lifetime.

Thought for the Day: Blessed Peter the Venerable tried to soften the militant spirit of his age and its love of war and conquest. He saw that mutual respect and dialogue were far better than conflict and confrontation. He was far ahead of his time and worked to bring about peace among kings, monks, and debating theologians. His is an example for our times.

From 'The Catholic One Year Bible': . . . The city has no need of sun or moon to light it, for the glory of God and of the Lamb illuminates it. Its light will light the nations of the earth, and the rulers of the world will come and bring their glory to it. — Revelation 21:23-24

St. Sylvester *(DECEMBER 31)*

"Sylvester Night" is the last night of the year and is celebrated in many countries as a New Year's celebration. Long before the custom of giving gifts at Christmas, gifts were exchanged on Sylvester Night and good wishes for the new year given. The night is named after St. Sylvester, the first pope to rule a free Church after the Peace of Constantine.

He was Roman by birth and was consecrated pope on January 31, 314, after the death of Pope Miltiades (Melchiades). It was he who welcomed Constantine to the city, when Constantine became emperor of the West, and it was he who directed the Church in the difficult days when Christianity became the official religion of the empire.

Sylvester was pope when the first ecumenical council was called at Nicaea by the emperor, and he saw the Church through the difficult days of the Arian heresy. It was during his pontificate that Constantine began a building program in Rome, constructing churches, basilicas, and shrines to the martyrs, fashioning Rome into a truly Christian city. There are many legends of his influence upon Constantine, but these were written in later centuries, and the relations between Sylvester and the emperor were few.

In 330, Constantine moved his capital from Rome to Constantinople, leaving behind great Christian buildings for his old capital, including the Lateran basilica, which became the titular church of the pontiff. The strong hand of the emperor in Church matters made for a difficult pontificate for Sylvester, but the new freedom of the Church brought about a huge expansion of Christianity. Besides the Arian heresy, Pope Sylvester had to face the growing Donatist Schism in North Africa, which would divide the Church for another century.

He died in Rome in the year 335 and was buried on December 31 of that year in the cemetery of St. Priscilla on the Via Salaria. For a number of centuries, his remains were enshrined in a basilica there, but in 762 Pope Paul I moved them to the church of St. Sylvester inside the city walls.

Thought for the Day: St. Sylvester faced a whole new world with the victory of Constantine and saw a greater expansion of Christianity than there had been for the previous three centuries. He was faced with something entirely new and had to adapt the Church to a totally new age. As we face the New Year, we should pray to St. Sylvester to help us make a new beginning.

From 'The Catholic One Year Bible': "I am the A and the Z, the Beginning and the End, the First and Last. . . . I am both David's Root and Descendant. I am the bright Morning Star. . . . He who has said all these things declares: Yes, I am coming soon!" Amen! Come, Lord Jesus! — Revelation 22:13, 16, 20

ALPHABETICAL INDEX OF NAMES

A

✠ B ✠

✠ C ✠

✠ *D* ✠

✠ *E* ✠

✠ F ✠

✠ G ✠

✠ H ✠

✠ I ✠

✠ J ✠

✠ *K* ✠

✠ *L* ✠

✠ *M* ✠

✠ *N* ✠

✠ O ✠

✠ P ✠

✠ R ✠

✠ S ✠

✠ T ✠

✠ V ✠

✠ W ✠

✠ Z ✠